THE EXPROPRIATION OF
ENVIRONMENTAL
GOVERNANCE

Recent years have seen an explosive increase in investor–state disputes resolved in international arbitration. This is significant not only in terms of the number of disputes that have arisen and the number of states that have been involved, but also in terms of the novel types of dispute that have emerged. Traditionally, investor–state disputes resulted from straightforward incidences of nationalization or breach of contract. In contrast, modern disputes frequently revolve around government measures taken to further public policy goals, such as the protection of the environment.

This book explores the outcomes of several investor–state disputes over environmental policy. In addition to examining the pleadings of parties and decisions of arbitral tribunals in disputes that have been resolved in arbitration, the influence that investment arbitration has had in negotiated outcomes to conflicts is also explored.

KYLA TIENHAARA is a postdoctoral fellow at the Regulatory Institutions Network (RegNet), Australian National University, and a research fellow with the Global Governance Project and the Earth Systems Governance project.

THE EXPROPRIATION OF ENVIRONMENTAL GOVERNANCE

Protecting foreign investors at the expense of public policy

KYLA TIENHAARA

Australian National University, Canberra

CAMBRIDGE
UNIVERSITY PRESS

CAMBRIDGE UNIVERSITY PRESS
Cambridge, New York, Melbourne, Madrid, Cape Town, Singapore,
São Paulo, Delhi, Dubai, Tokyo

Cambridge University Press
The Edinburgh Building, Cambridge CB2 8RU, UK

Published in the United States of America by Cambridge University Press, New York

www.cambridge.org
Information on this title: www.cambridge.org/9780521114875

First published 2009

Printed in the United Kingdom at the University Press, Cambridge

A catalogue record for this publication is available from the British Library

ISBN 978-0-521-11487-5 hardback

CONTENTS

Acknowledgements   vii
Acronyms and abbreviations   ix

Introduction   1

1   Concepts and methods   4
    1.1   Foreign investment and the global economy   4
    1.2   Conflicts between foreign investors and host states   8

2   Foreign investment and the environment   18
    2.1   Economic growth and environmental protection   19
    2.2   Capital mobility and environmental regulation   21
    2.3   Doing what is 'best'?   26

3   The institution of investment protection   38
    3.1   Emergence of the institution   39
    3.2   A public or private institution?   54
    3.3   Effectiveness of the institution   58

4   International investment agreements   63
    4.1   Key provisions   64
    4.2   Environmental impact assessments   85
    4.3   Potential implications for environmental governance   89

5   Foreign investment contracts   95
    5.1   Key provisions   96
    5.2   Contract negotiations and contract disclosure   113
    5.3   Potential implications for environmental governance   116

6   International investment arbitration   121
    6.1   Introducing ICSID and UNCITRAL   122
    6.2   Transparency and non-party participation   131
    6.3   Potential implications for environmental governance   142

7   Investor-state disputes   151
    7.1 Cases completing the jurisdictional phase   152
    7.2 Cases completing the merits phase   162
    7.3 Pending cases   198
    7.4 Analysis   204
    7.5 Implications for environmental governance   208

8   The threat of arbitration   217
    8.1 Conflicts over policy   217
    8.2 Conflicts over domestic court proceedings   249
    8.3 Implications for environmental governance   261

9   Conclusions   267
    9.1 The bigger picture   267
    9.2 Once BITten, twice shy?   278
    9.3 Moving forward   283

    References   294
    Index   319

ACKNOWLEDGEMENTS

In November 2004, I attended a conference on trade, environment and development at the Royal Netherlands Academy of Arts and Sciences in Amsterdam. In a conference that spanned a broad range of topics, the presentation of Konrad von Moltke clearly stood out. This was partially attributable to the charisma of the speaker and the fervour with which he addressed the audience. However, it is also a result of the fact that Konrad was discussing what was, for many in the room (myself included), uncharted territory. While 'trade and environment' was by that time a well-worn debate, 'investment and environment' did not appear to be on anyone's radar. I like to consider myself a relatively well-informed individual and yet I had never heard of a bilateral investment treaty, let alone considered how such a treaty might affect environmental governance. Konrad's presentation left me disturbed, inspired, and determined to find out more.

I did, in the end, find out a great deal. However, the journey was not an easy one. To begin with, I am not a lawyer by trade, and international investment law is not the easiest area for a novice. I am, therefore, greatly indebted to those experts who took the time to read my work and to provide me with their insight. In particular I would like to thank Frank Biermann, Jennifer Clapp, Joyeeta Gupta, David Hunter, Ans Kolk, Howard Mann, Andrew Newcombe, Luke Eric Peterson, Andrea Shemberg, M. Sornarajah, Gus Van Harten and Lyuba Zarsky. The next obstacle that I faced was in accessing information. Investment arbitration is an area sorely lacking in transparency. Luckily, I discovered that there are a number of dedicated individuals and organizations that have devoted considerable time and energy to posting arbitral documents on the Internet and reporting on cases. In this respect, I must highlight the following invaluable resources: www.naftaclaims.com (a project of Todd Weiler); http://ita.law.uvic.ca (a project of Andrew Newcombe); and the e-newsletters *Investment Treaty News* (published by the International Institute for Sustainable Development) and *Investment Arbitration Reporter* (edited by Luke Eric Peterson).

Although there were certainly difficulties in the course of my research, there were also very rewarding periods. The most memorable time is certainly that which I spent in Ghana and Indonesia. I owe a great debt of gratitude to all of the people in those countries that generously gave up their time to speak with me. I would also like to acknowledge the Netherlands Scientific Organisation which funded my trips as well as other research activities.

When I was not travelling, I was based at the Institute for Environmental Studies at the Vrije Universiteit Amsterdam. I would like to thank all of my colleagues and friends there, in particular: Sliman Abu Amara, Bram Büscher, Chris Evans, Maria Falaleeva, Constanze Haug, Sebastiaan Hess, Julia Martin-Ortega, Aysem Mert, Elissaios Papyrakis, Philipp Pattberg and Francesco Sindico. I would also like to thank everyone at the Peace Palace Library in The Hague, which is by far the best library in which I have had the pleasure to sit.

I left Amsterdam at the end of 2007. Much of the writing and editing of this book was completed in my new academic home at the Regulatory Institutions Network (RegNet) at the Australian National University in Canberra. My colleagues there have made the transition from Dutch rain to Australian sunshine even easier than it would have otherwise been. Special thanks to Valerie and John Braithwaite, Russell Brewer, Christian Downie, Jo Ford, Neil Gunningham, Jacqui Homel, Luigi Palombi, Paulina Piira, Petrina Schiavi and Sally Thompson.

While some of my research has been published in articles, and some parts of those articles are reproduced here, the whole story that unfolds in these pages would have never have reached the editorial desk at Cambridge University Press without the encouragement and support of my friend and colleague Thijs Etty. I am indebted to him and to the editorial team at Cambridge; in particular Finola O'Sullivan, Helen Francis, Dan Dunlavey and Richard Woodham. I also appreciate the comments of two anonymous reviewers.

Just as Konrad's presentation stood out in a conference full of interesting speakers, so do a few individuals stand out as being particularly important in helping me to finish this book. They may not have been able to contribute insight on the finer points of investment law, but their friendship has been invaluable. For that I thank Stefan Simis and Marianne Kettunen, Joanna Robinson and Dan Zuberi, Anne Campbell, Andrea Lanthier-Seymour and Harro van Asselt. I would also like to thank the Hanson family for their warmth and generosity. I cannot thank my parents, Nancy and Martti, enough for their unwavering support and enthusiasm for all of my endeavours. Last, but definitely not least, I would like to thank Kyle for making anywhere in the world feel like home.

ACRONYMS AND ABBREVIATIONS

AAA	American Arbitration Association
ADM	Archer Daniels Midland
ALBA	Alternativa Bolivariana para las Américas
ASEAN	Association of South-East Asian Nations
BIT	bilateral investment treaty
BTC	Baku-Tbilisi-Ceyhan (pipeline)
CAFTA-DR	Central America-Dominican Republic-United States Free Trade Agreement
CEO	Chief Executive Officer
CERDS	Charter of Economic Rights and Duties of States
CIEL	Center for International Environmental Law
CoW	contract of work
DCF	discounted cash flow
DPR	House of Representatives (Indonesia)
EIA	environmental impact assessment
EITI	Extractive Industries Transparency Initiative
EKC	Environmental Kuznets Curve
EPA	Environmental Protection Agency
EU	European Union
FAO	Food and Agriculture Organization
FCN	friendship, commerce and navigation treaty
FDI	foreign direct investment
FOE	Friends of the Earth
FTA	free trade agreement
FTAA	Free Trade Area of the Americas
FTC	Free Trade Commission (NAFTA)
GATT	General Agreement on Tariffs and Trade
GDP	gross domestic product
GRI	Global Reporting Initiative
HGA	host government agreement
ICC	International Chamber of Commerce

ICSID	International Centre for the Settlement of Investment Disputes
IFC	International Finance Corporation
IIA	international investment agreement
IISD	International Institute for Sustainable Development
ILA	International Law Association
ILM	International Legal Materials
IMF	International Monetary Fund
INE	National Ecology Institute (Mexico)
IPA	International Project Agreement
ISO	International Organization for Standardization
ITO	International Trade Organization
JATAM	Mining Advocacy Network (Indonesia)
JOA	joint operating agreement
MAI	Multilateral Agreement on Investment
MIGA	Multilateral Investment Guarantee Agency
MINAE	Ministry of Environment and Energy (Costa Rica)
MMT	methylcyclopentadienyl manganese tricarbonyl
MTBE	methyl tertiary butyl ether
NAAEC	North American Agreement on Environmental Cooperation
NAFTA	North American Free Trade Agreement
NBV	net book value
NGO	non-governmental organization
OECD	Organisation for Economic Cooperation and Development
OPIC	Overseas Private Investment Corporation
PCB	polychlorinated biphenyl
PROFEPA	Federal Attorney's Office for the Protection of the Environment (Mexico)
RECIEL	Review of European Community and International Environmental Law
SEC	Securities and Exchange Commission
SETENA	Environmental Agency (Costa Rica)
SOCAR	State Oil Company of the Azerbaijan Republic
TNC	transnational corporation
TPA	Trade Promotion Authority Act (US)
UK	United Kingdom
UN	United Nations

UNCED	United Nations Conference on Environment and Development
UNCITRAL	United Nations Commission on International Trade Law
UNCTAD	United Nations Conference on Trade and Development
UNCTC	United Nations Centre on Transnational Corporations
UNMIL	United Nations Mission in Liberia
UPS	United Parcel Service
US	United States
USTR	United States Trade Representative
WAGP	West African Gas Pipeline
WALHI	Friends of the Earth Indonesia
WSSD	World Summit on Sustainable Development
WTO	World Trade Organization

~

Introduction

What do a Canadian ban on the exportation of hazardous wastes, California's remediation requirements for open-pit mines and the Municipality of Lima's closure of a pasta factory have in common? They are all government measures that have been the subject of investor–state disputes resolved in international investment arbitration.

Over the last decade there has been an explosive increase of cases of investment arbitration. This is significant in terms of not only the *number* of disputes that have arisen and the number of states that have been involved, but also the novel *types* of dispute that have emerged. Rather than solely involving straightforward incidences of nationalization or breach of contract, modern disputes often revolve around public policy measures and implicate sensitive issues such as access to drinking water, development on sacred indigenous sites and the protection of biodiversity.

How did such matters become the purview of unelected *ad hoc* panels whose expertise lies in the realm of commercial law? The answer is not immediately evident. It could be argued that it is states themselves that are responsible. Governments have quietly been negotiating bilateral and regional investment agreements which provide foreign investors with considerable legal protection and access to international arbitration. They have also been signing contracts directly with foreign investors that contain such privileges. However, while governments may have opened the door to investor-state dispute resolution, they arguably did not anticipate that arbitral tribunals would reach so far into the public policy domain. Investment agreements were created to promote foreign investment in developing countries and designed to protect investors from discrimination and particularly egregious conduct on the part of the host state. While the success that states have had in attracting foreign investment through investment agreements is a subject of heated debate, the success that investors have had in stretching the traditional meaning of clauses on 'expropriation' and 'fair and equitable treatment' is unquestionable.

Is the manifold increase in disputes and the extension of arbitration into the public policy sphere just another example of the changing nature of governance in the age of globalization? Does it matter? Should policymakers and the public be concerned? This study aims to answer these questions by exploring the implications of investment agreements, foreign investment contracts and investment arbitration for one particularly topical area of public policy: the protection of the environment. Aside from the increasing public interest in environmental protection, the potential for foreign investment to have a substantial impact (whether positive or negative) on environmental conditions, particularly in developing countries, makes this an especially pertinent area for study.

To date, a number of conflicts between investors and states related to environmental policy have been resolved in arbitration. These disputes have concerned a wide range of regulatory actions and several different environmental issues (e.g., hazardous waste, biodiversity, air/water pollution). Disputes between investors and the governments of Canada, Costa Rica, Mexico, Peru and the United States are discussed in this study. While the cases are, in many respects, illuminating, they raise more questions than they answer. This is, in part, because the decisions made by the arbitral tribunals in these cases are inconsistent. However, despite this, several trends in arbitral practice are identifiable. Significantly, it is clear that tribunals are not likely to accept a state's purported reason for adopting an environmental measure on its face, but will instead assess the measure's *legitimacy*. There is a certain degree of irony in this, given that many scholars have described the system of investment arbitration as being in the midst of its own 'legitimacy crisis'. Another critical development is the growing acceptance of *positive obligations*; states are required not only to refrain from taking certain actions, but must also comply with various tenets of 'good governance'. Again, it is worth noting that such principles (e.g., transparency, predictability) are not uniformly applied in investment arbitration itself.

Arbitrators have made it clear that they can, and will, award compensation to investors that claim to have been harmed by environmental regulation. But is this the whole story? Are the pleadings of the parties and the decisions of the tribunals in a few environmentally relevant cases all that need be assessed? One of the core claims of this book is that there is, in fact, much more to be told. It is contended that although many investor-state conflicts will not reach the stage of a formal dispute, they will nevertheless be resolved *in the shadow* of arbitration. Arbitration is expensive for both investors and states, but the *threat* of arbitration is cheap and potentially very effective. This study highlights several conflicts between investors and states concerning both environmental policy (in Ghana, Indonesia and Costa Rica) and domestic court proceedings related to corporate liability for environmental damage (in Indonesia and Ecuador), where an investor threatened to initiate arbitral proceedings. Some of the cases suggest that the mere threat of arbitration is sufficient to *chill* environmental policy development. Equally concerning, is the possibility that a government may use the threat of arbitration as an excuse or *cover* for its failure to improve environmental regulation.

Individually, the cases illustrate that the outcome of a conflict resolved in, or in the shadow of, arbitration may be positive or negative from an environmental policy perspective. States do not always capitulate to threats and investors do not always prevail in arbitration. However, taken together, the cases paint a bleak picture. It is evident that arbitrators have *expropriated* certain fundamental aspects of environmental governance from states. As a result, environmental regulation has become riskier, more expensive and less democratic, especially in developing countries.

What can governments do to reclaim their policy space? This book does not offer a 'silver bullet' solution, although several practical suggestions for moderate reform of investment agreements, foreign investment contracts and investment arbitration are presented. Ultimately, governments in developing countries need to be much more careful about the commitments that they make to other states and to foreign investors. For their part, governments in developed countries need to reassess their priorities; if they are serious about their commitments to 'sustainable development' they should devote resources to helping, not handicapping, developing countries in their efforts to regulate foreign investors.

1

Concepts and methods

The existing literature on the relationship between investment protection and environmental protection is generally written either from the perspective of investment lawyers, who often neglect many issues that are critical to the effective regulation of the environment, or from the perspective of environmental lawyers, who are not always adequately versed in the highly specialized field of investment law. This study aims to provide a more comprehensive treatment of both investment law and environmental regulation. Furthermore, it adds a distinctly *political* dimension to a topic that often remains within the purview of legal studies.

In this chapter, the fundamental concepts of 'foreign direct investment', 'international investment agreements', 'foreign investment contracts', 'investor-state conflicts' and 'disputes', and 'environmental governance' are defined. The methodology employed in the empirical portion of the study is also explained. Finally, justification is provided for the especial attention that is given in this book to the interests and concerns of developing countries.

BOOK FOCUSES ON DIRECT INVESTMENT, NOT PORTFOLIO

1.1 Foreign investment and the global economy

Foreign investment can be defined as: 'The transfer of tangible or intangible assets from one country into another for the purpose of their use in that country to generate wealth under the total or partial control of the owner of the assets.'[1] This definition encompasses both foreign direct investment (FDI), the transfer of physical property, and 'portfolio investment', the movement of money through the purchase of shares in foreign corporations.[2]

---

[1] Sornarajah 2004a: 7.

[2] *Ibid.* Portfolio investment composes an increasingly large share of global flows of investment, but this study focuses on FDI which has a greater potential to contribute to development and also presents clearer environmental implications. For a brief overview of some of the key environmental issues related to portfolio investments, see Araya 2005: 48.

4

While historically, developing countries have often exhibited animosity towards foreign investors, since the late 1980s there has been a discernible shift in most parts of the world toward openness to, and indeed active courting of, FDI. There is a belief among many developing countries that FDI can play an important role in the development process and can help to fill resource, technology and foreign exchange gaps.[3] FDI is currently the most important source of external finance in most developing countries because it is more stable than portfolio investment and bank lending, and far more available than official development assistance.[4]

why FDI good

FDI is also increasingly considered a key ingredient for achieving *sustainable development*; 'development which meets the needs of the present without compromising the ability of future generations to meet their own needs'.[5] At the World Summit on Sustainable Development (WSSD) held in Johannesburg in 2002, a great deal of emphasis was put on the importance of investment.[6] In the Political Declaration that emanated from that meeting was the remark that 'significant increases in investment flows around the world have opened new challenges and opportunities for the pursuit of sustainable development'.[7] The Summit's Plan of Implementation noted the need for 'an enabling environment for investment' which was viewed, as a part of good governance, as 'the basis for sustainable development'.[8] Finally, the Plan of Implementation also called for the creation of:

> the necessary domestic and international conditions to facilitate significant increases in the flow of foreign direct investment to developing countries, in particular the least developed countries, *which is critical to sustainable development*, particularly foreign direct investment flows for infrastructure development and other priority areas in developing countries to supplement the domestic resources mobilized by them.[9]

FDI flows have rapidly increased in recent history and, while downturns have periodically occurred, on average FDI flows have multiplied more rapidly than trade flows.[10] Global FDI reached a new record high in 2007 with inflows of US$1,833 billion.[11] While largely concentrated in

---

[3] Mosoti 2005: 95.   [4] Morgera 2004: 215.
[5] World Commission on Environment and Development 1987: 43.
[6] Report of the World Summit on Sustainable Development (WSSD), Johannesburg, South Africa, 26 August–4 September 2002, UN Doc. A/CONF.199/20, www.un.org/esa/sustdev.
[7] Political Declaration (in Report of the WSSD): para. 14.
[8] Plan of Implementation (in Report of the WSSD): para. 4.
[9] *Ibid*: para. 84(a), emphasis added.   [10] Cohn 2004: 313.   [11] UNCTAD 2008: 3.

WHO INVESTS

the 'triad' of Western Europe, North America and Japan, the share of FDI flows directed to developing countries has increased in the last decade. However, this fact masks the reality that only a small group of developing countries – particularly China, Mexico, Singapore, Malaysia and Brazil – are really benefiting from these increased flows while other countries, especially those in sub-Saharan Africa, are increasingly marginalized.[12]

1.1.1   Competition for foreign investment

As there is not an unlimited supply of foreign investment that is equally distributed around the world, it is often argued that states must compete for FDI.[13] This notion of state competition for FDI has 'become deeply entrenched in the conventional policy rhetoric'.[14]

INCENTIVES

Governments compete for investment by providing incentives (such as tax holidays, loan guarantees and cash grants) and also by differentiating their legal jurisdictions from those of their competitors.[15] In this latter sense, legal reform has become an important asset for developing countries in their bid to attract FDI.[16] According to the 2005 World Investment Report, 2,156 measures related to foreign investment were adopted by 102 developing countries between 1991 and 2004, the vast majority of which (93 per cent) were aimed at creating a more favourable environment for investors.[17] Similarly, around 120 countries reformed their mineral regimes between 1985 and 2002.[18] These mineral reforms have generally aimed at liberalization as well as at establishing an investment climate based on stability and predictability.[19]

As Van Harten points out, when states compete for investment 'the bar rises as to what qualifies as a hospitable investment climate'.[20] Guzman describes this as a 'bidding up' of concessions to foreign investors.[21]

1.1.2   Protecting foreign investors

Developing countries can make numerous unilateral efforts to advertise themselves as desirable hosts for FDI, but such measures will be limited by the 'credible commitment' problem. That is to say, governments cannot signal to investors in a meaningful way that national laws providing them

---

[12] Cohn 2004: 325.   [13] Oman 2000: 15–16.
[14] Kozul-Wright and Rayment 2007: 160.   [15] Encarnation and Wells 1985: 48.
[16] Trubek *et al.* 1994: 477.   [17] UNCTAD 2005c: 26.   [18] Otto and Cordes 2002: III–3.
[19] Bastida 2002.   [20] Van Harten 2007a: 43.   [21] Guzman 1998: 671–2.

with protection will not simply be reversed once they have established themselves in the country. Consequently, even when developing countries make fervent overtures to the investment community, perceived political risk may continue to hinder FDI flows.

The purported solution to this problem has been the creation of agreements that govern the relationship between investors and governments and shift dispute resolution out of local courts and into international arbitration. Traditionally, investment was mainly protected through investor-state agreements, variously referred to in the literature as 'host government agreements', 'economic development agreements' or 'state contracts', and described herein as 'foreign investment contracts'. Foreign investment contracts are still used extensively in developing countries, especially in the natural resource sectors, and are given particular attention in this study. However, in addition to these contracts which cover only specific investments, protection can also be more generally provided through intergovernmental agreements.

In 1995, negotiations on one such intergovernmental agreement, the Multilateral Agreement on Investment (MAI), were commenced under the auspices of the Organisation for Economic Cooperation and Development (OECD). While the OECD is not a global forum, the MAI, once completed, would have been opened up for signature by any country. However, the negotiations were plagued by disagreements among OECD members as well as ardent opposition from civil society. In 1998 the MAI talks fell apart and the anti-globalization movement claimed this as its first major victory.[22] However, in 2003, the issue of a multilateral agreement on investment protection again came to the fore at the World Trade Organization (WTO) Ministerial Conference in Cancún. These talks were also a dramatic failure and, as a result, there is currently no prospect for a global treaty on investment (see further Section 3.1.3.2).

The main concern expressed by non-governmental organizations (NGOs) about the MAI and WTO negotiations on investment was that foreign investors would be given the right to sue states when public policy measures negatively affected their investments. However, little notice has been taken (by the media, the public, or most NGOs) of the fact that over the last two decades governments have quietly committed to equivalent levels of investment protection, including investor access to international

---

[22] Klein 2000: 443.

arbitration, in a massive number of regional, sectoral and bilateral agreements.[23] As of the end of 2008, there were 2,676 bilateral investment treaties (BITs) and 273 free trade agreements (FTAs) and economic cooperation agreements containing investment provisions.[24] These agreements are collectively referred to in this book as international investment agreements (IIAs).

Only one IIA, the North American Free Trade Agreement (NAFTA), which has a chapter on investment protection (see Section 3.1.3.1), has received significant scrutiny from scholars, although it remains poorly understood by the public. While NAFTA's Chapter 11 has been a focal point of debate, particularly in the wake of several controversial investor-state disputes, it is only one agreement among many. In fact, as a result of the proliferation of IIAs and the chameleon-like ability of transnational corporations (TNCs)[25] to change their nationality, investments all over the world receive legal protection similar to that provided by Chapter 11.

1.2   Conflicts between foreign investors and host states

There is an extensive literature on the impact of FDI on the environment, and this is briefly reviewed in Chapter 2. However, this book is primarily about the impact of foreign investors and the agreements that protect them on *environmental governance* in the host state.

Environmental governance can be defined as 'the resolution of environmental conflicts through the establishment, reaffirmation or change of institutional arrangements, which may either facilitate or limit the use of environmental resources'.[26] Significant developments in *global* environmental governance have occurred in recent years, but binding rules on

---

[23] Regional investment agreements cover many sectors and involve more than two states bound within a geographic area. Sectoral agreements cover only one sector of investment (e.g., energy) but involve more than two states. It should be noted that the Energy Charter Treaty, which contains a chapter on investment, is a significant sectoral investment agreement, but it is not addressed further in this study. For a discussion of the Energy Charter Treaty with specific reference to the relationship between investment protection and environmental protection see Wälde 1998b; Chalker 2006. Finally, bilateral agreements involve only two states. Investment agreements may be stand-alone agreements or only one part of a larger agreement which covers several issues (e.g., trade, economic cooperation).

[24] UNCTAD 2009b: 2, 8.

[25] Brewer and Young 1998: 11, define a TNC as 'an enterprise which owns (in whole or in part), controls, and manages value-adding activities in more than one country'. TNCs are also commonly referred to as multinational corporations or multinational enterprises.

[26] Adger *et al.*, qtd in Paterson *et al.* 2003: 3.

corporate conduct have not yet emerged (see Section 2.3.2). Host states, with varying capacities in monitoring and enforcement, are therefore responsible for regulating foreign investment to ensure that sustainable development goals are met and the environment is protected. However, when domestic regulation negatively impacts an investment, conflicts between a foreign investor and the host state may emerge.

Increasingly, domestic environmental policies and opposition to investment projects from communities and NGOs are seen as major risks for foreign investors.[27] For example, the imposition of a new environmental policy can be costly, and may be particularly onerous if it was not anticipated by the investor and therefore was not taken into account in the cost-profit analysis that informed the decision to invest in the first place.[28] In such a situation, there are three possible strategies for an investor to pursue: to accept the environmental policy and associated costs; to relocate to another jurisdiction; or to contest the policy through lobbying, litigation, etc.[29]

WHAT TO DO IF INCREASED ENV'L REGULATION

An investor may accept the new regulation for a variety of reasons: it may not significantly interfere with his investment; he may be concerned with damaging his relationship with the government by 'kicking up a fuss'; he may be aiming to improve his image as an environmental leader in the industry; or he may fear reprisals from domestic or international NGOs if he does not accept the policy. In any event, the investor's decision to *not act* presumably has no negative implications for environmental governance. However, the issue is far more complicated in cases where an investor *does act.*

FACTORS

WHY

In studies of the relationship between foreign investment and the environment, considerable focus has been given to the fact that *'states have roots while investors have wings'.*[30] While this is certainly an important observation, it is nevertheless the case that when investors have a choice between *fight* or *flight,* they often opt for the former. This is particularly the case in capital-intensive investments with large sunk costs, such as mining and oil operations.[31] Furthermore, investors may have several projects in a country (and only be in conflict in respect of one) or may have an interest in future investment opportunities which would be ruled out by a strategy of exit.

Investors faced with a conflict with the host state may, therefore, choose instead: to lobby or negotiate directly with the host government; to

---

[27] Wälde 1998b: 245; Bastida 2001: 42.   [28] Bekhechi 2001: 86.   [29] Murphy 2004: 87.
[30] Beck 2005: 72.   [31] Murphy 2004: 88; Newcombe 2007b: 439–40.

delegate resolution of the conflict to a third party; to utilize reputation and shame sanctions;[32] to enlist the assistance of its home state; and/or to *threaten* to exit or to utilize one or more of the measures listed above.

Within the category of delegation to a third party, the investor may have several choices. Depending on the circumstances, an investor could litigate (i.e., pursue a case in the local courts of the host state or in foreign courts), utilize conciliation or mediation mechanisms, or arbitrate (in international investment arbitration). It is the use of, or the threat to use, international investment arbitration to resolve investor-state conflicts that is the focus of this book.

1.2.1   Case studies of investor-state conflict

The empirical part of this study (Chapters 7 and 8) is concerned with the role that international arbitration plays in the outcome of conflicts between investors and states that are related to the environment. This issue is addressed through a number of case studies. The aim of the case studies is to assess how a conflict is interpreted by members of the community (investors, states, tribunal members, NGOs) as well as the communicative action that the conflict gives rise to, such as reproaches, excuses, justifications, etc.[33]

Identifying when a conflict between an investor and a state is related to the environment is a complicated matter. If one were to define conflict at a normative level, one would require precise definitions of the norms relevant to investment protection and to environmental protection in order to identify when these norms are in conflict. However, the norms of both investment protection and of environmental protection are notoriously vague and require case-by-case interpretation (see Chapter 4). As such, defining a conflict as environmentally relevant on a normative basis is problematic.

To simplify matters, in this study a conflict between an investor and a state is considered relevant when one or both of the actors subject to the conflict *individually or collectively identifies it as relating to both an environmental issue and to a foreign investment contract or an IIA*. To be clear, this definition does not require that both parties *agree* that the conflict is related to an environmental issue or to a foreign investment contract/IIA. For instance a government could argue that a measure was introduced

---

[32] Ginsberg 2005: 107.
[33] Kratochwil and Ruggie 1986: 768; Hasenclever *et al.* 1997: 16.

for the purpose of protecting the environment, whereas an investor might conversely claim that the government was only using environmental concern as a cover for protectionism. At the same time, a government might argue that a foreign investment contract or an IIA is not applicable to the investment in question, while the investor maintains that it is. The arguments of investors and governments will be considered in the analysis of the conflicts studied, but it simplifies matters to keep the definition rather broad at the outset.

Further differentiation is made in this study between conflicts that are resolved *directly* through international arbitration and those resolved *in the shadow* of international arbitration. In the case of the former, an arbitral tribunal is formed and is involved in the outcome of the conflict. In the case of the latter, there is a threat of arbitration, but the conflict is resolved without the input of arbitrators.

A conflict that enters into an arbitration process is typically referred to in the literature as an *investor-state dispute* (see Chapter 7). In these cases, the main methodology is content analysis of the legal materials of the arbitration proceedings (e.g., notices of arbitration, statements of claim and defence and tribunal decisions and awards) combined with a survey of the literature and supplemented by 'grey' material (newspaper articles, reports and websites of governments, international organizations and NGOs, etc.). The choice of cases was based on the following criteria:

(i) the conflict pertained to the environment (see explanation above);
(ii) arbitral awards were made on the jurisdiction and possibly on the merits of the case; and
(iii) arbitral awards were made publicly available.

A second set of cases is discussed in Chapter 8. These are cases where an investor *publicly invoked a claim of a breach of an investment agreement or contract,* or a government *made public that it had been threatened with arbitration,* but the conflict was not, in the end, resolved through arbitration.[34] The threat must have been publicized for the simple reason that, otherwise, it would not have been knowable at the stage of case selection. For this reason, no arguments are made about the number or frequency of cases in which investors make such a threat but subsequently resolve the conflict outside of arbitration; it is quite likely that there are far more than are assessed in this study. Furthermore, nothing can be

---

[34] The majority of the cases assessed were resolved through negotiation. In one case the matter was resolved in a foreign court.

stated about the importance of a purely *implicit* threat of arbitration. It is also acknowledged that by choosing only publicly known cases, the study is potentially biased toward an examination of conflicts involving large corporations which, in general, receive more attention in the press. It should also be noted that only those cases for which a reasonable amount of information, in English, could be collected (i.e., more than one or two reports identifying a conflict) were chosen.

While the investor-state disputes discussed in Chapter 7 only relate to conflicts over *policy*, two of the cases in Chapter 8 relate to conflicts over *domestic court proceedings*. Although, in the latter category, it is the actions of domestic courts rather than governments that are the source of conflict, it should be emphasized that only the national government can be held liable under IIAs and foreign investment contracts.

Finally, it should be noted that in Chapter 8 an exclusive focus is given to cases in developing countries (see explanation below). In summary, the criteria for the selection of these cases were:

  (i) the conflict was between a foreign investor and a developing country government;
 (ii) the conflict pertained to the environment (see explanation above);
(iii) no tribunal decision was made on the jurisdiction or the merits of the case; and
(iv) sufficient information on the case was publicly available.

The cases in Chapter 8 can be further divided into field-cases and desk-cases. In the two field-cases, in Indonesia and Ghana, a survey of the literature and grey material is complemented by stakeholder interviews. These interviews were conducted in May/June (Ghana) and July/August (Indonesia) of 2005. Interviewees in the government, academic, non-governmental and private sectors were contacted using the 'snowball' method.[35] First, relevant individuals were identified based on the survey of the literature and grey material. Second, each interviewee was asked to suggest further relevant individuals for interview. The interviews were semi-structured; questions were open-ended to encourage discussion and to avoid leading the interviewee.[36] The average interview lasted one hour and was conducted upon the condition of anonymity. All interviews referred to in the text, therefore, are accredited only to the 'type' of interviewee, with reference to the date and location of the interview.

---

[35] Minichiello *et al.* 1990.   [36] Yin 2003: 90.

Desk-cases are structured in the same manner as field-cases, but they rely only on literature and grey material, not interviews.

In order to minimize bias in the case studies, multiple sources are drawn upon and information is triangulated.[37] Furthermore, in an attempt to differentiate between the influence of the threat of arbitration and 'background noise of general political developments, ranging from the activities of other actors to more generic factors that influence behavioural changes, such as economic changes, elections, or some form of crisis',[38] counterfactual analysis is employed.

Finally, it should be emphasized that the focus in this book is on the *outcome* of conflicts between investors and states. The *impact* of these conflicts is a different matter. It is beyond the scope of this study to assess the long-term effect of a given outcome on the development of environmental policy, particularly given that the cases discussed have either been resolved very recently, or are in fact still awaiting resolution. Moreover, there are no claims as to the actual impact on the environment itself. It is a basic assumption made in this study that the progressive development of environmental policy is necessary to achieve environmental protection; however, it cannot be assumed that, in the absence of a conflict, a given policy would have resulted in the attainment of a specific environmental goal.

1.2.2   A focus on conflicts in developing countries

It has been pointed out by many observers that it no longer makes sense to lump together all of the countries of 'the South', as they are economically, culturally and politically diverse. There are also some countries that, as Kozul-Wright and Rayment put it, 'have *de facto* graduated to developed-country status' but are still formally classified as developing countries.[39]

However, while it is important to acknowledge the differences between countries, the use of some form of categorization in a work such as this appears inevitable. The term 'developing countries' will be employed in this book, following the definition provided the United Nations Conference on Trade and Development (UNCTAD).[40] However, it should be

---

[37] *Ibid*: 97.   [38] Biermann and Bauer 2004: 191.

[39] Kozul-Wright and Rayment 2007: 134.

[40] The country categorizations provided by UNCTAD identify 'developed' areas as Western Europe, North America and 'other' (Australia, Israel, Japan, Malta, New Zealand). Developing areas and territories, on the other hand, include Africa, East, South and South-East Asia (excluding Japan), West Asia (excluding Israel), Central Asia, Latin America

noted that it is capital-importing, weaker developing countries that this
study is primarily interested in. The conclusions may, therefore, be less
applicable to fast-growing and powerful developing economies such as
Brazil, India and China.

Why focus on developing countries at all? The bulk of research on the
relationship between investment protection and environmental protection
addresses investor-state disputes arising under Chapter 11 of NAFTA, and
much of the concern in both governmental and non-governmental circles
has been on the implications of this agreement for Canada and the US. This
is understandable, in some respects, because most of the investor-state
disputes relating to the environment have been brought under NAFTA
and because there is far more information available about these cases
as a result of a greater degree of transparency in NAFTA arbitrations
(see Section 6.2.1). However, there is an increasing number of disputes
in developing countries which have not been extensively researched and
there are quite a number of instances of threats of arbitration in these
countries that have been completely neglected in the academic literature.
This clear gap in research alone would be sufficient justification for a
special focus on developing countries in this study. However, there are
several further arguments worth mentioning.

To begin with, the vast majority of IIAs are signed by developing countries and yet these countries are often poorly prepared to negotiate international agreements. However difficult it is for developing countries to
negotiate fair deals in the multilateral sphere, it is arguably even harder
for them to negotiate fair deals on a bilateral basis. José E. Alvarez, a
professor at Columbia University and a former member of the American
State Department BIT negotiating team, claims that for many countries 'a
BIT relationship is hardly a voluntary, uncoerced transaction' and that 'to
date the American model BIT has been regarded as, generally-speaking,
a take it or leave it proposition, with the United States calling the shots
and the BIT partner as supplicant'.[41] Developing countries may also face
difficulties when negotiating with foreign investors that are represented
by sophisticated legal teams. As a result of this, and their desperation to
attract FDI, developing countries often agree to terms in their foreign
investment contracts that developed countries would never consider.

---

and the Caribbean and The Pacific (excluding Australia and New Zealand). The transition economies of Central and Eastern Europe are not included in either category. See
UNCTAD's website: www.unctad.org.
[41] Qtd in Garcia 2004: 316.

In addition to signing more agreements, developing countries are often the only parties with real obligations under IIAs, as these agreements outline requirements for the state that is *hosting* investment. While IIAs are reciprocal (with each state able to act as a 'home' and 'host' to investors), the asymmetry of investment flows that often exists between parties to an IIA means that, in practice, only one state has real obligations under the agreement. For example, imagine that an agreement is signed between State A and State B: on the one hand, State A is an exporter of capital, with investors operating in State B; on the other hand, State B is primarily an importer of capital, and has no investors operating in State A. In this scenario, only State B has categorical obligations. Developing countries, with a few notable exceptions (i.e., Brazil, China, India and Malaysia) are, at present, primarily importers and not significant exporters of capital.[42] Instances of agreements between capital-exporting states are rare and developed countries are not frequently exposed to investor claims.[43] Given the broad range of variation in economic power amongst developing economies, it is not surprising that there is also inequality in so-called South-South agreements.[44]

The asymmetry between states is reflected in an evaluation of the claimants and respondents in the investment arbitration cases initiated to date. As of 2005, there were only eleven known instances where developing-nation firms had filed investment treaty claims.[45] Of the 27 claims filed under Chapter 11 of NAFTA as of the start of 2007, none had been filed by an investor from NAFTA's one developing country member, Mexico.[46] As of early 2007, 74 per cent of the concluded and pending cases filed under one set of arbitral rules were against 'middle-income developing countries', and another 19 per cent against 'low-income developing countries'.[47] A mere 1.4 per cent of cases had been filed against G8 countries.[48] Van Harten suggests that middle-income states are particularly susceptible to claims because they are big enough to host substantial investments but not powerful enough to refuse to conclude investment treaties in the first place.[49] However, it is important to consider that low-income countries may have faced many threats of arbitration that are not captured by these statistics because the governments chose to settle rather than risk losing in arbitration. In any event, it is clear that

---

[42] Mosoti 2005: 97. [43] Van Harten 2007a: 40. [44] Bubb and Rose-Ackerman 2007: 300.
[45] See UNCTAD 2005b: 4. [46] Chung 2007: 956. [47] Anderson and Grusky 2007: ix.
[48] All of which were filed against the US under NAFTA. Cases against Canada under NAFTA have been filed under another set of arbitral rules.
[49] Van Harten 2007a: 33–4.

developing countries face the vast majority of claims. UNCTAD predicts that in the near future the number of disputes will continue to rise and that developing countries 'are likely to bear the brunt' of this increase.[50]

The system of international investment arbitration may also be structured in such a way that developing countries are more likely to be penalized.[51] It is often argued that weak states will support legalism over power politics, but as Hurrell suggests: 'While it is certainly true that the international legal order provides many power-leveling possibilities for weaker states, it is also true that power influences the character of that legal order.'[52] Additionally, capacity is recognized as a central factor in the implementation of international commitments.[53] Kahler notes that '[d]eveloping countries often lack highly developed legal systems and the resources that accrue to such systems' which in turn affects their approach to legalized systems of dispute settlement such as investment arbitration.[54]

Finally, because of economic and political factors, the experiences of developing countries in dealing with investment protection will be very different from those of their more developed counterparts. Phillips argues that:

> The implications of globalization look very different in regions such as sub-Saharan Africa, the Caribbean, or Eastern and Central Europe, among many others, where foreign capital occupies a very different place in economic development processes, issues of credibility and competitiveness present much greater challenges, and other constraining conditions are put in place by the much greater prominence of multilateral agents such as the IMF and World Bank.[55]

Developing countries are more desperate to attract FDI and are dependent on aid and trade relationships with the home states of investors.[56] These factors influence how developing countries will perceive their options when faced with a conflict with a foreign investor.

In sum, developing countries are in a weaker negotiating position than developed countries, they have made more commitments to protect investors (and these commitments *mean* more), they have less capacity to deal with investment arbitration, and they have different perceptions about the world order based on economic and political realities. As such, it is not possible to simply transfer the experiences of developed countries, or the theories which emanate from those experiences, to the context of the

---

[50] UNCTAD 2005b: 9.   [51] For an extensive discussion of this issue see Shalakany 2006.
[52] Hurrell 2005: 41.   [53] VanDeveer 2005: 95.   [54] Kahler 2000: 666.
[55] Phillips 2005: 107–8.   [56] Stiglitz 2008: 477.

developing world. Nor is it acceptable to ignore the particular experiences of these countries. If any further justification were needed, this special focus is also warranted by the importance of protecting the environment in developing countries and the significant role that FDI could potentially play in sustainable development.

2

Foreign investment and the environment

Policy-makers, international development organizations and scholars have emphasized the importance of FDI in reducing the global gap between wealthy and poor nations.[1] In addition to providing capital, FDI brings new technologies and knowledge to the host country and at least some 'spillovers' to the domestic sector are expected to ensue. There has also been an increasing amount of discussion about the importance of foreign investment for *sustainable* development.

Implicit, and often explicit, in the suggestion that foreign investment is necessary for sustainable development is the notion that FDI can be beneficial for the environment. However, the policy rhetoric tends to mask the fact that there is no consensus in academia about the relationship between foreign investment and economic development, let alone between foreign investment and the protection of the environment.

This chapter provides an overview of the debates on the relationship between foreign investment and the environment, divided here into three interrelated categories. First is the broadest debate about the relationship of economic growth to environmental protection, which is relevant because FDI, in theory, contributes to the economic growth of a country. Therefore, depending on whether economic growth is good or bad for the environment, one can draw conclusions about the potential benefits or harms of FDI. Second is the issue of whether the variable stringency of environmental regulation across states affects investment decisions, commonly known as the 'pollution havens debate'. Finally, there is the issue of whether, instead of creating pollution havens, foreign investors apply 'best international practices' and 'best available technologies' leading to improved environmental performance and possibly a ratcheting up of environmental standards in host states. What the chapter does not cover,

---

[1] For example, see the Monterrey Consensus of the International Conference on Financing for Development, 18–22 March 2002, Monterrey, Mexico, www.un.org/esa. See also the series of World Investment Reports produced annually by UNCTAD, www.unctad.org.

for the sake of brevity, is the issue of the influence that foreign investors may have on environmental policy in host states as a result of lobbying and/or corrupt activities.

While both optimists and pessimists about the impacts of foreign investment on the environment exist, this chapter will show that empirical evidence to support either position remains thin. It appears that the only overarching conclusion that can be drawn is that *context* is important, particularly the *regulatory* context in the host state.[2] It is therefore sensible to conclude that it is crucial that states have sufficient 'room to regulate' if FDI is to be compatible with environmental protection.

2.1   Economic growth and environmental protection

According to Kozul-Wright and Rayment, it is questionable whether FDI is an independent accelerator of economic growth.[3] However, for the purpose of this chapter, this issue will be left to one side and it will be assumed that FDI does contribute to economic growth in some cases. The question addressed in this section is what the environmental impact of such growth is likely to be.

In the early 1990s, economists Grossman and Krueger posited that there exists an inverted-U relationship between pollution and economic growth.[4] This was dubbed the Environmental Kuznets Curve (EKC). The typical explanation for the occurrence of the EKC is that in early stages of development people are occupied with basic concerns such as employment and income; environmental protection is therefore not a priority. However, as per capita income rises, people come to value the environment more and therefore demand stricter regulation, and companies may also voluntarily improve performance through investment in cleaner technologies when they have the resources to do so. It is postulated that, as a result of these factors, at a certain level of per capita income, the amount of pollution begins to stabilize and eventually tapers off, theoretically falling to pre-industrial levels in wealthy societies. It has also been suggested that the EKC could be explained by the fact that, at a certain point in the development of an economy, there is likely to be a compositional shift,

---

[2] Subedi 1998: 415; Clémençon 2000: 219; Mann and Araya 2002: 164; Brooks *et al.* 2004: 8; Peterson 2004b: 7–8; Gallagher and Zarsky 2007: 188.

[3] Kozul-Wright and Rayment 2007: 144.

[4] Grossman and Krueger 1993; Grossman and Krueger 1995.

for example from an economy dominated by manufacturing to a service-oriented economy (the former is associated with more pollution than the latter).[5]

Given the concordance that this theory has with neo-liberal ideas of economic progress, it is perhaps unsurprising that the EKC has been enthusiastically embraced by many authors both in and outside of economics.[6] However, others have argued that 'EKC results have a very flimsy statistical foundation' and that policies based on these results will be misguided.[7] Nevertheless, according to Dasgupta *et al.*, some policy-makers in developing countries have interpreted the EKC research as conveying the message that they should '[g]row first, then clean up'.[8] A major concern with this type of policy prescription is that environmental degradation that can occur during the initial economic growth period can result in irreversible losses of biodiversity, of clean water and even of human lives.[9]

Several important critiques of EKC research that are not based on the issue of statistical validity should also be considered. First, there is the fact that the early EKC studies were focused on a small number of pollutants (e.g., sulfur oxides, particulate matter) that had visible effects on the local environment.[10] There is no evidence to suggest that the EKC holds for all pollutants, nor for all other types of environmental degradation. There are untold numbers of new, unregulated and potentially toxic pollutants that are continually created through industrial activity.[11] Furthermore, while the EKC may hold for some pollutants arising from production, it does not appear to hold for those arising from consumption.[12] For example, both carbon dioxide (a greenhouse gas) and municipal solid waste commonly rise rather than decline with per capita income.[13] Nahman and Antrobus suggest that the reason why pollutants related with consumption do not fit the EKC is that they are easily externalized and therefore more difficult to regulate.[14] The fact that a U-shaped curve does not occur in these cases is particularly significant given that it is increasingly accepted in the environmental policy field that consumption is the principal driving force behind environmental degradation.[15]

The second major critique is that proponents of the EKC do not account for trade and investment patterns which may result in polluting

---

[5] Dasgupta *et al.* 2002: 147.   [6] See, e.g., Lomborg 2001.   [7] Stern 2004: 1419.
[8] Dasgupta *et al.* 2002: 147.   [9] Gallagher and Zarsky 2005: 30.   [10] Jenkins 2002c: 10.
[11] Dasgupta *et al.* 2002: 148.   [12] Nahman and Antrobus 2005a: 114.   [13] *Ibid*: 111.
[14] *Ibid*: 114.
[15] Clapp and Dauvergne 2005: 110–15. See also Paterson 2000 and Dauvergne 2008.

activities moving from developed to developing countries.[16] Even if there is no evidence to support the pollution havens hypothesis (which suggests that foreign investors are attracted to states with lax environmental standards; see Section 2.2.1), this does not mean that trade and investment patterns have no impact on the shape of the EKC.[17] Polluting industries may relocate to developing countries for reasons other than the level of environmental regulation, but this movement of industry will nevertheless decrease the amount of pollution that developed countries experience. As such, some critics have argued that the EKC may be a 'historical artefact' and, in the absence of less-developed countries to which current developing countries can export environmentally damaging industries, represents a development path that is no longer available.[18] Furthermore, given that residents of developed countries continue to consume the same products as they did before (they are just manufactured elsewhere) then, as Rothman has argued, 'what appear to be improvements in environmental quality [in developed countries] may in reality be indicators of increased ability of consumers in wealthy nations to distance themselves from the environmental degradation associated with their consumption'.[19]

While these criticisms of the EKC are important, the most relevant conclusion of work in this area is the fact that, as Dasgupta *et al.* point out, 'the available evidence suggests that regulation is the dominant factor in explaining the decline in pollution as countries grow beyond middle-income status'.[20] Even Grossman and Krueger have suggested that there is 'nothing automatic about the relationship between economic growth and the environment' and that 'growth and development cannot be a substitute for environmental policy'.[21] If this is the case, then the take-home message for a developing country should not be to 'grow first, then clean up', but rather to increase capacity and maintain flexibility to regulate. As such, its approach to FDI must also not be unmitigated enthusiasm, but rather a careful consideration of the potential environmental costs of a project and how they can best be minimized through appropriate regulation.

2.2 Capital mobility and environmental regulation

With globalization, capital has become more mobile.[22] Concurrently, the interest amongst developing and developed countries in attracting FDI

[16] Cole 2004: 71.   [17] Nahman and Antrobus 2005a: 107.
[18] Cole 2004: 79; Nahman and Antrobus 2005b: 804.   [19] Rothman 1998: 177.
[20] Dasgupta *et al.* 2002: 152. See also Copeland and Taylor 2004: 8.
[21] Grossman and Krueger 1996: 120.   [22] Strange 1996: 110.

has increased. This has been said to have resulted in *competition* between states to attract investment.[23]

Foreign investors are generally motivated by the availability of natural resources (resource-seeking FDI), access to new markets for goods and services (market-seeking FDI) and/or cost minimization (efficiency-seeking FDI).[24] Investors may, therefore, exit a jurisdiction when resources are exhausted or when a market is too small to support production. However, it is the notion that investors will exit a jurisdiction for reasons of cost, more commonly referred to as 'industrial flight', that has been the subject of significant scholarly attention.

The reason for this attention is the link between cost minimization and regulation. For example, labour laws, health and safety standards and environmental regulation all impose costs on investors. These standards are not harmonized across states, or even in some cases across sub-state jurisdictions (e.g., provinces), and major differences exist between environmental regulations in developed and developing countries.[25] Most developing countries did not establish systems of environmental regulation until the 1990s, twenty years after OECD countries.[26] Even where regulations appear strong on the books, enforcement is often lacking.[27] Given these disparities, it has been hypothesized that investors will leave jurisdictions with stringent regulation in favour of those with more lenient rules, for efficiency reasons. This sparked concern within highly regulated jurisdictions (mainly developed countries) over potential job losses. It also led some observers to postulate that, in an attempt to keep or regain investment, countries would lower their labour, health and environmental standards, leading to a 'race to the bottom'.[28]

2.2.1   Pollution havens

Research that has specifically addressed the relationship between the locational decisions of foreign investors and environmental regulation comprises the 'pollution havens' debate.[29] The debate is over whether or not

---

[23] Oman 2000: 15–16.   [24] Dunning 1993, cited in Caspary and Berghaus 2004: 684.
[25] Jenkins 2002c: 4.   [26] Zarsky 2002: 35.   [27] *Ibid.*
[28] As Porter 1999: 136, indicates, the term 'race to the bottom' does not imply that standards literally fall to the bottom, but only that standards are reduced to a suboptimal level and are therefore 'inefficient for the entire system of jurisdictions in the sense of causing distortion in the allocation of resources'.
[29] For an overview of pollution havens literature see OECD 1997 and the special issue of *Global Environmental Politics* (vol. 2, issue 2) devoted to this topic.

investors will migrate to jurisdictions (e.g., developing countries) with lax environmental standards. According to Neumayer, there is a popular misconception that 'any country with less strict environmental standards than one's own country is guilty of providing a pollution haven'.[30] Neumayer argues that such a definition is inappropriate because countries cannot be expected to have the same levels of environmental regulation, particularly given the wide disparities in wealth and resources between developing and developed states. He therefore provides the following definition of a pollution haven:

> A country provides a pollution haven if it sets its environmental standards below the socially efficient level or fails to enforce its standards in order to attract foreign investment from countries with higher standards or countries that better enforce their standards.[31]

Similarly, according to Wheeler: 'What really counts for the pollution havens debate is neither market ownership nor market location, but the willingness of the host government to "play the environment card" to promote growth'.[32]

By the mid-1980s, researchers had concluded that the new strict environmental regulations in developed countries had not resulted in industrial flight, and thus rejected the validity of the pollution haven hypothesis as a whole.[33] By way of explanation, it was argued that environmental costs make up only a small proportion of a company's total costs, and therefore they have little impact on a firm's locational decisions, particularly in comparison to other factors such as the size of the domestic market or the level of infrastructure in a country.[34] Furthermore, it was suggested that governments in developed countries respond to high levels of public demand for environmental protection, and this counteracts any inclination to lower standards to keep or attract investment, thus precluding a race to the bottom.

Despite the initial lack of empirical evidence, research in the area continued and recently several studies, using more sophisticated techniques, have found 'statistically significant pollution haven effects of reasonable magnitude'.[35] One possible reason, aside from methodological issues, why researchers are now finding evidence of pollution havens is that the environmental costs for foreign investors in the most hazardous industries have increased significantly in the last two decades.[36]

---

[30] Neumayer 2001b: 147.   [31] *Ibid*: 148.   [32] Wheeler 2002: 1. See also Jenkins 2002b: 294.
[33] Strohm 2002: 31.   [34] Kelemen 2004: 289.   [35] Brunnermeier and Levinson 2004: 38.
[36] Jenkins 2002a: 31.

Many scholars have also critiqued early pollution havens research. Jenkins suggests that studies which are based on foreign investment flow data are at much too high a level of aggregation, both in terms of the sectors analysed and in terms of the countries considered, while surveys of firm managers about their investment decisions may be hindered by unwillingness to disclose a preference for lax environmental regulation.[37] He argues that outcomes are likely to be highly context specific, which suggests that generalized statistical research will be unlikely to locate pollution havens.[38] One important aspect of the 'context' that has been identified by Cole *et al.* is corruption. Their research indicates that in countries where corruption is high, pollution havens are more likely to emerge as a result of officials selling policy favours to polluting foreign investors.[39]

Another criticism of the pollution havens debate is that it has been narrowly confined by the definition of 'dirty industry' adopted by most researchers. The data used to determine which sectors are highly polluting largely consists of emissions data or information on expenditures related to emission controls.[40] Habitat destruction, biodiversity loss and numerous other environmental impacts are not captured by this limited scope. The primary focus has been on the manufacturing sector, rather than the extractive industries that make up the bulk of investment flowing to many low-income countries.[41] Neumayer notes that:

> Especially in the mining and other resource extraction sectors, multinational corporations also at times do take advantage of low environmental standards in the host country – an impact on the environment that is outside the pollution haven hypothesis proper.[42]

In one study that has looked at mining as well as the chemical industry, Xing and Kolstad found that the strictness of environmental regulation had a significant effect on FDI flows.[43] They did not find the same result for the less polluting industries that they studied.

The focus of the majority of pollution havens research has been restricted even further by a preoccupation with industrial flight and the fears within developed countries about potential job losses.[44] This bias toward concern for the impact on developed countries has skewed the findings. Even if existing evidence does not support the industrial flight

---

[37] *Ibid*: 34.   [38] Jenkins 2002b: 312.   [39] Cole *et al.* 2006: 160.   [40] Clapp 2002: 12.
[41] *Ibid*: 12; Mabey and McNally 1998: 11.   [42] Neumayer 2001b: 173.
[43] Xing and Kolstad 2002: 3.
[44] Mabey and McNally 1998: 30; Clapp 2002: 11; Strohm 2002: 29.

hypothesis, some authors argue that research indicates that environmental regulation does in fact influence some firms' locational decisions, particularly in resource- and pollution-intensive sectors.[45] Moreover, while competitive pressure to attract FDI may be counteracted in developed countries where governments are responsive to high levels of demand for environmental quality, the situation may be considerably different in developing countries.[46]

2.2.2   Regulatory chill

Many authors who are disparaging of the pollution havens debate have suggested that the regulatory chill hypothesis offers a new avenue of research. This hypothesis suggests that countries fear raising environmental standards because they *believe* that it may deter new investment or lead to industrial flight. Porter notes that:

> Regardless of the empirical evidence of the impact of standards on trade competitiveness and firm location ... many officials of industrial firms as well as government officials clearly *believe* differences in environmental costs affect competitiveness and investment decisions and tend to act accordingly.[47]

Similarly, Neumayer argues that 'what really matters is what policymakers believe, not what economic theory and evidence says, and there can be no doubt that they actually do believe that countries compete with each other'.[48]

However, empirically, the regulatory chill hypothesis is very difficult to prove because as Mabey and McNally cogently remark, 'evidence is needed of *what has not happened*'.[49] The result of regulatory chill is also not necessarily a race to the bottom in standards, but rather the maintenance of the status quo. As Clapp rightly notes:

> If the status quo is as stringent as environmental regulations are going to get, then the effect will be an entrenchment of poor quality regulations, and the entrenchment of differences in the stringency of those regulations between rich and poor countries.[50]

This entrenchment has alternatively been referred to as the 'stuck at the bottom' effect,[51] or the 'stuck in the mud' phenomenon.[52]

---

[45] *Ibid.*   [46] Porter 1999: 134.   [47] *Ibid*: 136.   [48] Neumayer 2001a: 20–1.
[49] Mabey and McNally 1998: 40, emphasis added.   [50] Clapp 2002: 17.
[51] Porter 1999: 134   [52] Zarsky 1997.

2.3   Doing what is 'best'?

There are quite a number of scholars who contend that foreign investors, contrary to the pollution havens hypothesis, are not only generally cleaner than their domestic counterparts, but also may help to ratchet up environmental standards in developing countries, creating 'pollution halos' and a race to the top.[53]

When it comes to environmental performance in the host state, there are two critical management decisions that foreign investors make; the choice of what technologies to employ and the choice of what standards to apply in their operations.[54] This section looks at both of these issues.

2.3.1   Best available technology

When an investor arrives in a country that does not have stringent environmental regulations that would dictate what type of technologies can be applied in its operations, it has the choice of whether to bring in the 'best available' technology, or instead to 'dump' older, dirtier technologies that may have been regulated out of use in the investor's home state.[55] If foreign investors employ better techniques or cleaner technologies then, in theory, this may minimize and even offset the scale effects of increased industrial activity in the host country.[56] However, empirical evidence about the extent to which companies employ better or best technologies appears to be mixed.[57] The degree of adoption of clean technologies varies by sector, and both host and home country regulations are also likely to be determining factors.[58]

While the use of the best available technology can mitigate the environmental damage caused by an individual investment project, the diffusion or transfer of such technology to domestic investors can have a much more extensive and long-term impact on environmental management in a host country. It has been suggested that developing countries could even 'leapfrog' past some of the environmental consequences of industrialization through the wide-scale adoption of clean technologies.[59] However, as with the employment of best technologies, empirical evidence about the diffusion of such technologies appears to be mixed and there are reasons to be sceptical about the potential for FDI to bring about leapfrogging.[60]

---

[53] Dean *et al.* 2005; Dasgupta *et al.* 2002.   [54] Gallagher and Zarsky 2005: 27.
[55] *Ibid.*   [56] Araya 2005: 53.   [57] *Ibid*: 54–8; Chudnovsky and Lopez 1999: 2.
[58] *Ibid*: 4; Jenkins 2002a: 24.   [59] Perkins 2003.
[60] Gallagher 2004, qtd in Gallagher and Zarsky 2007: 34.

Critically, there are important limitations in terms of the willingness of companies to transfer technology and knowledge, as well as the capacity of domestic companies to absorb such transfers.[61] There is also a concern, raised by Clapp, that in many cases the technologies being transferred to developing countries, particularly in the most hazardous industries (e.g., chemicals), are 'not so much "clean production" technologies, as they are "clean-up" technologies'.[62] She argues that companies have a greater motivation to transfer such technologies because then they can set up subsidiaries that specialize in environmental clean-up and generate additional profits.

The mixed performance of foreign investors in employing and transferring best available technologies has led to the inclusion of provisions on the issue in several international codes of corporate conduct that have been developed in recent years. The efficacy of such codes is discussed further in the next section.

2.3.2   Best international practice

As Gallagher and Zarsky note, in many developing countries where environmental standards are low and/or monitoring and enforcement capacity is weak, foreign investors have one of four choices: follow local practice (e.g., do what domestic companies do); comply with national regulation; adopt home country standards; or adopt best international practice.[63]

Investors are left to make this choice because, to date, very little has been accomplished at the international level in terms of binding environmental standards for non-state actors. In fact, as is noted in a textbook on global business law, when it comes to the regulation of foreign investors 'it is probably accurate to say that multilateral rules that are of a directly binding character are virtually nonexistent'.[64] There was a concerted effort in the 1970s and 1980s by the UN Centre on Transnational Corporations (UNCTC) to codify the duties of investors, including their environmental responsibilities.[65] However, due to opposition from developed countries, an economic recession and the debt crisis, the drive to adopt the UNCTC Code faded in the 1980s.[66] Despite an attempt to revive it in 1990, the UNCTC was officially dismantled in 1992. Some of its work was carried on by UNCTAD, which remains an important forum for discussion on the

---

[61] Saggi 2002: 229.   [62] Clapp 1998: 105.
[63] Gallagher and Zarsky 2005: 28.   [64] Head 2007: 500.
[65] Correa and Kumar 2003: 32; Hansen 2002: 162.   [66] Ibid.

regulation of investors (as well as investment protection), but the UNCTC Code was abandoned altogether.

With the demise of the UNCTC, and the dramatic shift of developing countries toward actively seeking FDI, the notion of corporate account-ability has been put on the back-burner of international politics. In its place, the notion of 'corporate social responsibility' (CSR), the process whereby companies 'integrate social and environmental concerns in their business operations and in their interaction with their stakeholders on a voluntary basis', has gained prominence.[67] As Utting explains:

> The confrontational politics of earlier decades, which had pitted a pro-regulation and redistributive lobby against TNCs, lost momentum as governments, business and multilateral organizations alike, as well as an increasing number of NGOs, embraced ideas of 'partnership' and 'co-regulation' in which different actors or 'stakeholders' would work together to find ways of minimizing the environmental cost of economic growth and modernization. The hands-on regulatory role of the state ceded ground to 'corporate self-regulation' and 'voluntary initiatives' as the best approach for promoting the adoption of instruments and processes associated with corporate environmental responsibility.[68]

Supporters of CSR argue that it is logical for foreign investors, partic-ularly large TNCs, to voluntarily apply the same standards across juris-dictions or to adopt international standards for the sake of efficiency, risk reduction and/or reputation.[69] However, others are sceptical of the prospects for CSR, particularly in industries where brand-image and rep-utation with consumers is not a significant determinant of profits.[70] It has also been argued that, in order to be effective, self-regulatory regimes require specific conditions to be present in the host state, including trans-parency (access to information) and monitoring capacity.[71] Such condi-tions are often not present in developing countries. As Lock notes:

> Even the literature supporting CSR assumes that this institutional setting includes the existence of efficient and effective government regulation and enforcement of existing laws. This may be achievable in many of the industrialized countries. However, the assumption is problematic for many Southern countries, and corporate double standards in the North and South are not uncommon.[72]

Some voluntary initiatives have even been labelled as 'greenwash' because they permit companies to sell a positive image without actually making significant improvements in their environmental performance.[73]

[67] European Commission 2001: 8.   [68] Utting 2002: 1.
[69] Christmann and Taylor 2004: 138; Lundan 2004: 14.   [70] Sayer 2006: 17.
[71] Utting 2000: ix; Graham and Woods 2006: 870.   [72] Lock 2006: 128.
[73] Utting 2006: 66.

Between the proponents and sceptics, there is perhaps the most pragmatic position which highlights that voluntary codes of conduct and mechanisms of self-regulation do not 'amount to an adequate or appropriate replacement for regulation at the state or international level'[74] and therefore must supplement rather than supplant binding rules.[75] While recognizing their limitations, it is worth briefly overviewing some of the main codes of conduct and other initiatives for ensuring best practices that have been developed to date.

2.3.2.1 The Global Compact

The shift away from the corporate *accountability* approach toward the softer corporate *responsibility* approach is perhaps best exemplified by the Global Compact. This initiative was launched at the World Economic Forum in Davos, Switzerland, in 1999, by then UN Secretary-General Kofi Annan. The Compact is aimed at bringing together large TNCs and the UN to make globalization more equitable and sustainable.[76] The original Compact was based on nine principles, drawn from the Universal Declaration of Human Rights, the International Labour Organization's Fundamental Principles and Rights at Work and the Rio Declaration on Environment and Development. In 2004, a tenth principle, dealing with anti-corruption, was added to the list. The three environmental principles cover general environmental responsibility, the precautionary principle[77] and the development and dissemination of environmentally friendly technologies.

While many welcomed the initiative as a creative step, NGOs generally viewed the Compact as not only ineffective, but also potentially dangerous as it could act as a 'bluewash' for companies with poor social and environmental records. It has been pointed out that many corporations that have signed up to the Global Compact, far from exhibiting 'best practices', are instead considered by NGOs to be 'bad practitioners'.[78] For example, the mining company Rio Tinto is a participant in the Compact, and is also

---

[74] Newell 2001: 913. See also Hansen 2002: 177, who states: 'it would be naive to believe that business self-regulation is an alternative to government action'.

[75] Sayer 2006: 23. See also Christmann and Taylor 2004: 140.

[76] 'Blue Washed and Boilerplated', *The Economist* 2004 (371): 61–2.

[77] The 'precautionary principle' (or approach) is defined in the Rio Declaration as follows: 'Where there are threats of serious or irreversible damage, lack of full scientific certainty shall not be used as a reason for postponing cost-effective measures to prevent environmental degradation.' Principle 15, Rio Declaration on Environment and Development, 14 June 1992, Rio de Janeiro, www.unep.org. Reproduced in 31 ILM (1992): 874.

[78] Lock 2006: 125.

accused of numerous human rights and environmental abuses related to its operations in Indonesia.[79]

On the other hand, John Ruggie, who acted as Assistant Secretary-General and Chief Adviser for Strategic Planning to Kofi Annan from 1997 to 2001, argues that the critics are seriously underestimating the Compact's potential, although he also acknowledges that its supporters may be holding excessive expectations for what the initiative can achieve.[80] Ruggie claims that the principal role of the Compact is to act as a learning forum for corporations. He suggests that the UN launched the Global Compact, rather than attempting to initiate negotiations on a binding set of rules of corporate conduct, for several reasons:

(i) countries were not interested in adopting a meaningful code of conduct at the time;
(ii) the logistical and financial requirements to monitor global companies and their supply chains far exceeded the capacity of the UN;
(iii) the business community would have opposed the imposition of a code of conduct and even progressive business leaders would have been drawn into an anti-code coalition;
(iv) many principles of human rights, labour rights and environmental stewardship could not be precisely defined at the time; and
(v) the pace of change in corporate strategies, structures and production processes made it exceedingly difficult to specify what desired/prohibited practices a code should have included.[81]

2.3.2.2   The revised OECD Guidelines for Multinational Enterprises

The OECD Guidelines for Multinational Enterprises are part of the 1976 Declaration on International Investment and Multinational Enterprises and associated Decisions of the OECD Council.[82] The Guidelines consist of voluntary principles and standards relating to employment and industrial relations, human rights, environment, information disclosure, combating bribery, consumer interests, science and technology, competition and taxation. The Guidelines are addressed to TNCs operating in, or from, countries that have adopted them.[83] The Guidelines were reviewed

---

[79] Bruno and Karlinger 2002: 35.   [80] Ruggie 2001: 371.   [81] *Ibid*: 373.
[82] The OECD Declaration and Decisions on International Investment and Multinational Enterprises: Basic Texts, DAFFE/IME(2000)20, www.oecd.org.
[83] All of the OECD countries and ten non-OECD countries are signatories.

in 2000 and updated to reflect the shift in the international community to a sustainable development agenda.

Section V on the environment states that enterprises should 'take due account of the need to protect the environment' and 'generally conduct their activities in a manner contributing to the wider goal of sustainable development'. To achieve this they should take heed of domestic laws and regulations as well as international agreements, principles, objectives and standards. More specifically they should:

  (i) establish and maintain a system of environmental management;
 (ii) provide timely information on environmental impacts of their activities and communicate and consult with communities that are directly affected by these activities;
(iii) address environmental impacts in decision-making and prepare environmental impact assessments;
 (iv) not use the lack of scientific certainty as a reason for postponing cost-effective measures to prevent or minimize environmental damage (precautionary principle);
  (v) plan for environmental accidents and emergencies;
 (vi) improve environmental performance through improved technologies, research, development of environmentally friendly products and the promotion of consumer awareness;
(vii) educate and train employees in environmental health and safety matters; and
(viii) contribute to the development of environmentally meaningful and economically efficient public policy (e.g., partnerships, awareness-raising initiatives, etc.).[84]

The Guidelines contain a mechanism of implementation: National Contact Points are set up in each country that endorses the Guidelines to receive complaints about companies. However, this mechanism is considered largely ineffective.[85] According to Jenkins, 'the OECD Guidelines did not represent a genuine attempt to control transnationals, but was rather designed to deflect criticism of their activities'.[86]

---

[84] OECD Guidelines: paras. V.1–8.
[85] In 2002, the UN Expert Panel on Illegal Exploitation of the Natural Resources of the Democratic Republic of the Congo named 85 companies in breach of the OECD Guidelines, but no significant action was taken by governments to respond. See 'Illegal Exploitation of Natural Resources in the Democratic Republic of Congo', Public Statement by the OECD Committee on International Investment and Multinational Enterprises, 12 February 2004, www.oecd.org.
[86] Jenkins 2001: 4.

2.3.2.3   The UN Norms on the Responsibilities of Transnational Corporations and other Business Enterprises with regard to Human Rights

The UN Norms on the Responsibilities of Transnational Corporations and other Business Enterprises with regard to Human Rights (UN Norms) were adopted by the UN Sub-Commission on the Promotion and Protection of Human Rights in August 2003.[87]

The UN Norms are focused on human rights, but they also relate to environmental protection:

> Transnational corporations and other business enterprises shall carry out their activities in accordance with national laws, regulations, administrative practices and policies relating to the *preservation of the environment* of the countries in which they operate, as well as in accordance with relevant international agreements, principles, objectives, responsibilities and standards with regard to the environment as well as human rights, public health and safety, bioethics and the *precautionary principle*, and shall generally conduct their activities in a manner contributing to the wider goal of *sustainable development*.[88]

The Commentary on the UN Norms, provided in a separate report, lays out in further detail what this paragraph is meant to entail.[89] According to the Commentary, TNCs and other businesses are expected to:

(i) respect the right to a clean and healthy environment, concerns for intergenerational equity, internationally recognized environmental standards and the wider goal of sustainable development;

(ii) be responsible for the environmental and human health impact of all of their activities;

(iii) assess the impact of their activities on the environment and human health and in these assessments address the impact of proposed activities on certain groups, such as children, older persons, indigenous peoples and communities (particularly in regard to their land and natural resources) and/or women;

---

[87] Norms on the Responsibilities of Transnational Corporations and Other Business Enterprises with Regard to Human Rights, UN Doc. E/CN.4/Sub.2/2003/12/Rev.2 (2003), www1.umn.edu/humanrts/links/norms-Aug2003.html.

[88] *Ibid*: para. 14, emphasis added.

[89] Commentary on the Norms on the Responsibilities of Transnational Corporations and Other Business Enterprises with Regard to Human Rights, UN Doc. E/CN.4/Sub.2/2003/38/Rev.2 (2003), www1.umn.edu/humanrts/links/commentary-Aug2003.html.

(iv) distribute assessment reports in a timely manner and in a manner that is accessible to the UN Environment Programme and other international bodies, governments and the public;

(v) respect the prevention principle and the precautionary principle, and not use the lack of full scientific certainty as a reason to delay the introduction of cost-effective measures intended to prevent environmental damage;

(vi) ensure effective means of collecting or arranging for the collection of products that have reached the end of their life-cycle for recycling, reuse and/or environmentally responsible disposal; and

(vii) take appropriate measures in their activities to reduce the risk of accidents and damage to the environment by adopting best management practices and technologies.[90]

Weissbrodt and Kruger suggest that the UN Norms represent:

> a landmark step in holding businesses accountable for their human rights abuses and constitute a succinct, but comprehensive, restatement of the international legal principles applicable to businesses with regard to human rights, humanitarian law, international labour law, environmental law, consumer law, anti-corruption law and so forth.[91]

However, while the text details how the UN Norms are to be implemented and provides for independent and transparent monitoring, the Norms do not represent legally binding obligations.

2.3.2.4 Private and public-private initiatives

In addition to the intergovernmental initiatives on corporate conduct mentioned above, there are an increasing number of private and public-private regulatory efforts that are voluntary and often market-based.[92] One of the best-known initiatives with respect to foreign investment is the development of International Organization for Standardization (ISO) environmental management standards.[93]

The ISO 14000 family of standards on environmental management is primarily concerned with what an organization does to 'minimize harmful

---

[90] *Ibid*: para. G.14.   [91] Weissbrodt and Kruger 2003: 901.

[92] Examples of such regulation include certification and labelling schemes such as those developed by the Forest Stewardship Council. See Pattberg 2007.

[93] The International Organization for Standardization (ISO), established in 1946, is a network of the national standards institutes of 157 countries and the world's largest developer of standards. In the run-up to the UNCED, the ISO set up a Strategic Advisory Group on Environment to look into the possibility of creating environmental management standards. In 1993 the ISO created a new committee on environmental management (TC 207).

effects on the environment caused by its activities', and to 'achieve continual improvement of its environmental performance'.[94] While the majority
of ISO standards are highly specific to a particular product, material or
process, ISO 14000 standards are 'generic management system standards',
meaning that they can apply to any product or process in any sector.
The 14001 standard is the best known in the 14000 series. It basically
requires that firms comply with domestic environmental regulation, that
they commit to continual improvement and prevention of pollution, and
that they set up an environmental management system and have that system audited.[95] By the end of 1999, over 13,000 firms in 75 countries had
obtained ISO 14001 certification.[96]

While it is certainly not the only set of international environmental
guidelines aimed at corporations,[97] ISO 14001 has gained wide recognition, and according to Clapp, it has eclipsed other voluntary initiatives,
becoming a 'condition for firms that wish to compete in the global marketplace'.[98] However, there are debates about the legitimacy of the ISO (and
other such schemes), as it is an industry-dominated body and is lacking
transparent and participatory procedures.[99] There are also questions as
to the actual value that ISO standards play in improving environmental
conditions. For example, Clémençon points out that:

> ISO 14001 certification of a company does not require the company to
> set verifiable environmental quality targets and does not require standard-
> ized reporting or provide for outside environmental performance reviews.
> Environmental groups have therefore criticized the voluntary ISO 14001
> standardization as little more than a labeling ploy of many companies to
> gain access to Northern markets.[100]

ISO 14001 has also been said to provide little incentive for firms to
go beyond the minimum requirement of meeting domestic laws and regulations, which in many developing countries is insufficient to ensure
environmental protection.[101]

Another notable development is the emergence of the Global Reporting
Initiative (GRI) which sets out guidelines for companies to report their
environmental and social performance.[102] While environmental reporting in and of itself does not ensure that companies will behave in the

---

[94] 'ISO 9000 and ISO 14000', ISO website, www.iso.org, accessed 5 January 2009.
[95] Clapp 2005: 230.   [96] Morrison *et al.* 2000, cited in Clapp 2005: 223.
[97] Other examples include the CERES Principles, www.ceres.org, and the ICC Business
Charter for Sustainable Development, www.iccwbo.org/home/environment/charter.asp.
[98] Clapp 2005: 229–30.   [99] *Ibid*: 224.   [100] Clémençon 2000: 217.
[101] Gulbrandsen 2004: 84 and 86.
[102] See the website of the GRI at www.globalreporting.org.

manner that they claim to on paper, the information in reports can be checked and may even be verified by third parties.[103] According to Graham and Woods, the GRI indicators 'offer a strong prospect of escaping the problems of anecdote and incomparability that have dogged reporting of environmental and social impacts'.[104]

It is difficult to assess the importance of ISO 14001, the GRI and other private and public-private initiatives intended to 'green' business in the South, because research on their impact in developing countries has been limited.[105]

2.3.2.5 Conditions tied to investment risk insurance and project financing

In addition to purely voluntary initiatives, TNCs may also be required to follow better or best practices by the agencies that finance and insure their projects. According to Sornarajah, '[o]fficial insurance companies and banks ... are increasingly wary of assisting multinational corporations that cause massive pollution' and there is 'recognition of the duty not to assist corporations which pollute in other states and the possibility of legal responsibility for complicity of those who assist such companies which pollute'.[106]

In the realm of project financing, the Equator Principles, launched by the International Finance Corporation (IFC) and a number of private banks in 2003, are noteworthy.[107] The Equator Principles apply to all new projects with total project capital costs of US$10 million or more that are financed by signatory organizations. The Equator Principles relate to: social and environmental assessment; social and environmental standards; action plans and management systems; consultation and disclosure; grievance mechanisms; independent review; covenants (on compliance with host country laws and certain other conditions); and reporting (by financial institutions on implementation of the Principles). The Principles appear to have attracted broad participation, but it is perhaps too soon to be able to assess their impact on the ground.

International insurers such as the Multilateral Investment Guarantee Agency (MIGA) (part of the World Bank Group) and various national

[103] Kolk and von Tulder 2004: 112.   [104] Graham and Woods 2006: 874–5.
[105] Utting 2002: 10.   [106] Sornarajah 2000: 364.
[107] 'The Equator Principles: A Financial Industry Benchmark for Determining, Assessing and Managing Social and Environmental Risk in Project Financing', July 2006, www.equator-principles.com.

export credit guarantee agencies[108] also have conditions attached to their policies. For example, according to the MIGA Policy on Social and Environmental Sustainability, the Agency:

> strives for positive development outcomes in the private sector projects for which it provides guarantee support. An important component of positive development outcomes is the social and environmental sustainability of projects, which MIGA expects to achieve by applying a comprehensive set of social and environmental performance standards.[109]

Insurers increasingly require foreign investors to complete environmental impact assessments (EIAs) of their proposed projects.

2.3.2.6   Home state measures and foreign direct liability

While it has been suggested that foreign investors may automatically adopt home country standards for reasons of efficiency or reputation, such behaviour may also be encouraged or required by the home state government. As mentioned above, this can be achieved through the policies of a national export credit guarantee agency. Some countries, such as Australia, have also considered legislation that would impose standards on nationally domiciled corporations when they operate abroad.

Home states may also facilitate 'foreign direct liability', that is, liability for companies in home states for their (or their subsidiaries') actions in other countries. The most famous example of legislation permitting such liability claims is the Alien Tort Claims Act in the US.

There are several reasons why it may be advantageous to bring a claim against a parent company in the home state rather than against a local subsidiary in the host state: corporations can organize themselves so that the subsidiary is insolvent, not worth suing, or uninsured; there may be limited access to justice in host country courts; and workers' compensation schemes may preclude claims by victims against an employer.[110] Bringing a claim in a foreign court is the only option other than a domestic claim as TNCs do not have formal international legal personality and, therefore, do not have standing before any international court.[111]

Sornarajah argues that there may be a basis in international law for duty on the part of states to entertain litigation of TNCs based on their activities in foreign states.[112] Because the home state permits hazardous technology or investment to be taken out of its territory, it is partially responsible

[108] E.g., the US Overseas Private Investment Corporation (OPIC), the UK Export Credits Guarantee Department, and Export Development Canada.

[109] 'Policy on Social and Environmental Sustainability', 1 October 2007, www.miga.org.

[110] Cordonier Segger 2003: 300.   [111] Sornarajah 2000: 361.   [112] Ibid: 363–4.

for any harm that may ensue as a result and, therefore, should permit litigation before its courts to reduce or redress the harm. It can also be argued that certain norms of international environmental law have such overwhelming support that domestic courts should provide sanctions for violations of these norms.

Newell suggests that foreign direct liability 'provides a potentially vital channel for ensuring that TNCs do not exploit lower environmental standards and poor enforcement regimes at the expense of workers and their environment', but he also recognizes the limitations of this mechanism.[113] The main barrier to foreign direct liability suits is the principle of *forum non conveniens.* Investors can rely on this principle to argue that a court in the host state is a more appropriate venue for the resolution of a dispute than a court in the home state. This barrier proved significant in the Bhopal case, which was the first time that foreign direct liability was used in response to an environmental disaster. The Indian government tried to bring a claim against Union Carbide in the US but it was unsuccessful; the court declined jurisdiction on the basis that the courts in India were a more convenient forum. However, according to Sornarajah, since the delivery of this much-criticized judgment there has been a greater willingness of courts to extend jurisdiction in similar cases.[114]

Other problems with using litigation to hold investors accountable relate to: the difficulty of establishing cause-effect relationships in cases of environmental damage; the need to 'pierce the corporate veil' to establish connections between subsidiaries and parent TNCs; the length of time that the process requires; and the limited capacity of many potential claimants to bring cases.[115] Furthermore, as Newell remarks, litigation 'reduces complex social problems to questions of monetary compensation'.[116] Thus, despite the potential for foreign direct liability to act as an important tool, particularly in the case of disasters like Bhopal or situations of especially grave abuses of human rights, as Cordonier Segger argues, 'it would be unrealistic and undesirable' to attempt to resolve all cases of TNC misconduct in this manner.[117]

Overall, measures within home states to regulate the activities of corporations when they invest abroad remain limited. This may change in the future, but for the moment it is the domestic arena within host states, regardless of their development status or capacity to regulate, that is the primary site for environmental governance of foreign investment projects.

---

[113] Newell 2001: 914.   [114] Sornarajah 2000: 361.
[115] Newell 2001: 915–16; Ayine and Werksman 1999.   [116] Newell 2001: 915.
[117] Cordonier Segger 2003: 302.

The institution of investment protection

International investment law has often been likened to a 'spaghetti bowl'. This metaphor is generally used to illustrate why a multilateral treaty is needed to replace the complex and messy web of overlapping agreements that are currently in place. However, it is argued here that while investment protection has been regionalized, bilateralized and even contractualized, there is an emerging set of common norms and rules that could be thought of as composing an *institution* of investment protection.[1]

As Duffield notes, the term institution 'is frequently used to refer to distinctly different empirical phenomena, such as intergovernmental organizations . . . international regimes, and sets of norms'.[2] In this study, the concept of an institution is used to group together a variety of norms and rules that interact to provide protection to foreign investors. While each IIA, foreign investment contract, or set of arbitral rules could individually be classified as an institution, it is the collection of norms and rules that constitute these agreements that is of interest here. Although treating these norms and rules collectively risks ignoring potentially significant discrepancies between various agreements, this approach allows for cross-case comparison and a more comprehensive treatment of issues that transcend one individual agreement.

This study adopts Duffield's conceptualization of international institutions as 'relatively stable sets of related constitutive, regulative, and procedural norms and rules that pertain to the international system, the actors in the system (including states as well as non-state entities), and their activities'.[3] However, as this is a definition of international institutions, it focuses explicitly on norms and rules that pertain to the *international system*. As such, it reifies an international-domestic divide and this, it is argued here, is inappropriate in a study of investor-state interaction. Instead, it is suggested that the institution of investment protection is

---

[1] For a similar argument see Schneiderman 2008: 26.
[2] Duffield 2007: 1.   [3] *Ibid*: 2.

transnational in nature. Processes within this institution transcend territorial boundaries, but foreign investors operate within the bounds of the state. It then follows that the transnational institution of investment protection *operates simultaneously at the international, national and subnational levels, and is composed of a relatively stable set of related constitutive, regulative and procedural norms and rules that pertain to the protection of foreign investors and their investments within host states.*

There are three main sources of norms and rules of investment protection that are discussed in this book: IIAs; foreign investment contracts; and arbitral rules. A fourth source that could be considered is customary international law. Customary international law consists of norms and rules that are deduced from the behaviour of states. In order for law to be customary, a substantial number of states must have acted consistently as if they believed that they were required by law to behave in a given way (*opinio juris*). The content of customary international law in the area of investment protection is highly contested. While this topic will not be extensively dealt with here, reference will be made at times to how customary international law has influenced the interpretation of particular norms and rules that originate from the other three sources.

Before delving into the details of the norms and rules of investment protection, which will be examined in the three chapters that follow, this chapter briefly overviews the emergence of the institution over the course of the twentieth century, discusses the public-private nature of the institution, and examines the effectiveness of the institution with respect to one of its goals: the promotion of FDI flows.

3.1 Emergence of the institution

Although BITs and investor-state disputes have only really begun to proliferate in the last ten to fifteen years, the norms and rules of investment protection have a much longer history and have been evolving, in particular over the last century. This section provides a brief history of investment protection in order to place the modern institution in context.

3.1.1 The colonial period: pre-1945

With the exception of the Dutch, who directly invested in various commercial projects throughout Europe as early as the seventeenth century, prior to the 1800s most countries were deterred from participating in FDI by limitations of travel and communication.[4] However, during the Industrial Revolution significant capital surpluses were produced which fuelled demand for the development of large manufacturing and transportation enterprises, thus requiring and facilitating more investment. The majority of this early investment was portfolio and not direct investment, and was confined mainly within Europe and North America.[5] This changed in the colonial period when the colonies became a major source of the raw materials required to propel Western industrialization.

In the colonial period, there was little need for the development of an international law for the protection of foreign investment, as in many developing countries the colonial legal systems were integrated into those of the imperial powers, and in areas that remained uncolonized the use of 'gunboat diplomacy' was considered an acceptable means of protecting foreign interests abroad.[6] However, that is not to say that no concepts of appropriate treatment of foreign investors had emerged prior to decolonization. The first friendship commerce and navigation (FCN) treaty[7] (a precursor to IIAs) was signed between the US and France in 1778.[8] Numerous attempts to formulate a broader investment protection regime were also made in the first half of the twentieth century.[9] Furthermore, there were several critical developments which occurred in the specific context of relations between the US and several Latin American countries that had already gained independence.

3.1.1.1   The Calvo doctrine and the Hull formula

Historically, the direct taking of foreign property was one of the most significant risks to foreign investment and usually came in the form of

---

[4] Vandevelde 1998: 376.   [5] *Ibid*: 376–7.

[6] Lipson 1985: 12; Sornarajah 2004a: 19–20.

[7] The American FCN treaties were primarily aimed at promoting trade, but often included investor protections such as prohibitions on expropriation without compensation. The FCN programme wound down in the 1960s with the emergence of the General Agreement on Tariffs and Trade (GATT). See further Guzman 1998: 653.

[8] Mosoti 2005: 108.

[9] Muchlinski 1999, notes the following examples: in 1929, the League of Nations held a conference with the aim of developing an international convention on the treatment of foreigners and foreign enterprises; in 1930, the Hague Conference on the Codification of International Law covered the topic of state responsibility for damages caused to foreigners and their property; and in 1931 the International Chamber of Commerce (ICC) launched a campaign to develop a convention on the topic, and followed up with a draft code for the Fair Treatment of Foreign Investments in 1949. All of these initiatives failed as a result of a lack of consensus among states. See also Van Harten 2007, ch. 2.

what is termed 'nationalization'. Nationalization involves the host government performing an outright taking of property in all economic sectors
or on an industry-specific basis. In contrast to nationalization, 'expropriation' involves takings targeted at specific properties and enterprises.
Capital-exporting states have long supported the notion that there is a
requirement under customary international law that a state compensate
a foreign investor whose property is expropriated or nationalized. They
have further argued that there is an international minimum standard of
treatment that should be applied to aliens even when the treatment of
nationals falls below this standard.

One of the first major nationalizations in the twentieth century occurred
in the Soviet Union following the Communist Revolution. Contrary to
the Western view, the Bolshevik government took the position that international law can impose no requirement on the host state to compensate
a foreign investor for expropriation and that only the national law of the
host state is relevant.[10]

However, it was not only socialism which challenged the dominant view
on the international minimum standard and compensation for expropriation.[11] Economic nationalism was the ideological underpinning of one of
the most famous dissents from these norms, formulated by Carlos Calvo,
a distinguished jurist from Argentina, who declared in 1896: 'The responsibility of Governments towards foreigners cannot be greater than that
which these Governments have towards their own citizens.'[12] The Calvo
doctrine thus rejected the notion that special international law norms
apply to the treatment of foreign nationals by a host state. It furthermore
rejected the right of home states to exercise diplomatic protection of their
nationals abroad and challenged the very basis of international tribunals.[13]

Calvo clauses appeared in a number of constitutions in newly independent Latin American states. Lipson points out that the Mexican Constitution (1917), for example, 'contained strict, and unprecedented, restraints
on foreign corporations . . . guaranteed free land to every landless peasant
and allowed the government to carry out expropriation at any time for the
nation's welfare'.[14] It was not until 1938 that the provisions of the Constitution were applied in practice when the Mexican government announced
that it would expropriate the property of several American and British oil
companies operating in Mexico (as well as several agrarian properties).

---

[10] Vandevelde 1998: 380–1.   [11] Muchlinski 2001: 117; 1999: 48–9.
[12] Qtd in Center for International Environmental Law (CIEL) 2003b: 1.
[13] Lipson 1985: 18–19; Vandevelde 1998: 380.   [14] Lipson 1985: 18–19.

Both the US and the United Kingdom (UK) protested this action, and the British went so far as to suspend diplomatic relations with Mexico. The Americans recognized the right of the Mexican government to expropriate property within its territory, but demanded that the companies be compensated for their lost investment. A famous exchange of notes occurred between the the American Secretary of State Cordell Hull and his Mexican counterpart, the Minister of Foreign Affairs Eduardo Hay, and the Mexican Ambassador in Washington. These notes were illustrative of the divide between the two countries, and more broadly between capital-exporting and capital-importing states, on the issue of appropriate treatment of foreign investors. In a note of 3 April 1940 to the Mexican Ambassador in Washington, Hull articulated what would become known as the Hull formula for compensation:

> The Government of the US readily recognizes the right of a sovereign state to expropriate property for public purposes. This view has been stated in a number of communications addressed to your government during the past two years ... On each occasion, however, it has been stated with equal emphasis that the right to expropriate property is coupled with and conditioned on the obligation to make *adequate, effective, and prompt compensation.* The legality of an expropriation is in fact dependent upon the observation of this requirement.[15]

In summary, by the end of the colonial period there were three main views expressed by states concerning the protection of foreign investors. First, capital-exporting states (whether following a liberal or economic nationalist policy) supported the notion of an international minimum standard of treatment, and the requirement for prompt, adequate and effective compensation (Hull formula) when an investment was expropriated. Secondly, the 'Calvo states' (developing countries not under colonial rule, largely Latin American, and following economic nationalism) argued that foreign investors were only entitled to the same treatment as nationals. Thirdly, socialist states, following Marxism, rejected the entire notion that international law protected foreign investment. These three views would spread throughout the rest of the world following the dissolution of the colonial empires.

3.1.2   The post-colonial period: 1945–1980

A decade of expropriation in the newly socialist countries of Eastern Europe and China followed the end of World War II. As Vagts points out:

---

[15] Qtd in Einhorn 1974: 21, emphasis added.

'In the meantime, the rest of the world remained fairly quiet.'[16] The focus would shift to developing countries from 1950 onward as improvements in communication and transportation facilitated FDI flows around the world. Although notable expropriations were occurring in Guatemala, Iran, Algeria and Cuba, many developing states actively sought FDI in this period under a strategy known as import substitution industrialization, whereby they aimed to develop industries to manufacture goods to displace imports.[17]

While in the 1950s many developing countries encouraged investment and enacted investment codes, by the late 1960s many countries had become, as Akinsanya puts it, 'more circumspect' about the value of FDI for development, leading to further expropriations.[18] The mean number of expropriations annually peaked at fifty-one in the early 1970s.[19] Gun-boat diplomacy was no longer a viable option for capital-exporting states to protect property abroad. The focus then turned to alternatives, mainly in the form of economic sanctions and the development of international law. Developing countries also turned to international law to strengthen their own position, largely in the UN General Assembly.

3.1.2.1   The Havana Charter

The Havana Charter, which laid the framework for the International Trade Organization (ITO) (intended to be the 'third pillar' of the Bretton Woods system), included a provision on investment.[20] The debates over the provision were heated, and Lipson argues that they 'clearly demonstrated the lack of broad international approval for traditional investment laws'.[21] The final formulation of the article allowed host countries significant leeway to determine investment policy, although developing countries continued to view the provision as too lenient with respect to investors.[22] In any case, the Havana Charter never came into force as it was repeatedly rejected by the US Congress, in part because the investment provisions, if not the agreement as a whole, were viewed as a threat to the interests of American corporations.[23] Muchlinski suggests that:

---

[16] Vagts 1987: 4.   [17] Vandevelde 1998: 381–2.   [18] Akinsanya 1980: 2.
[19] Brewer and Young 1998: 53.
[20] Havana Charter for an International Trade Organization, Final Act and Related Documents of the United Nations Conference on Trade and Employment, 21 November 1947–24 March 1948, Havana, Cuba, UN Doc E/Conf. 2/78: Art. 12.
[21] Lipson 1985: 87.   [22] Dattu 2000: 288.   [23] Brewer and Young 1998: 68.

The inclusion of a right of capital importing states to control the conditions of foreign investment, and the absence of any unequivocal provision for compensation in the case of expropriation, caused widespread opposition to the Havana Charter among business interests and contributed to its demise.[24]

The General Agreement on Tariffs and Trade (GATT), which became the *de facto* basis of international trade law, did not cover investment. Brewer and Young argue that the debate over investment in the ITO was significant for drawing the lines of conflict between developed and developing countries over a series of issues and for (temporarily) resolving the issue of whether international cooperation on investment should be sought on a multilateral or bilateral basis, with the US showing a clear preference for the latter.[25]

3.1.2.2   Permanent sovereignty over natural resources

The notion of permanent sovereignty over natural resources first emerged in the 1950s, and has since been 'one of the most frequently employed legal precepts in the debate on the relations between host States and transnational companies'.[26] The concept was first elucidated in UN Resolution 626 (VII) of 21 December 1952 on the Right to Exploit Freely Natural Wealth and Resources. The US voted against this Resolution because it failed to indicate that states expropriating private property should recognize rights of foreign investors under international law.[27] Nevertheless the Resolution passed and was later invoked by Guatemala when the country expropriated the assets of Compania Agricola de Guatemala (a subsidiary of the United Fruit Company).[28]

From the early 1960s to the mid-1970s, developing countries pushed through a series of resolutions in the UN General Assembly in an effort to universalize the Calvo doctrine and to affirm a position of sovereignty of nations with respect to foreign investment and the exploitation of natural resources.[29] This included the 1962 and 1973 Resolutions on Permanent Sovereignty over Natural Resources,[30] the 1974 Resolution on a New International Economic Order,[31] and the 1974 Resolution on the Charter of Economic Rights and Duties of States (CERDS).[32] These Resolutions all focused on the rights of states to regulate investment in the manner

---

[24] Muchlinski 1999: 53.   [25] Brewer and Young 1998: 68.   [26] Paasivirta 1989: 339.
[27] Akinsanya 1980: 49.   [28] *Ibid*: 50.   [29] Guzman 1998: 648.
[30] Res. 1803 and 3171.   [31] Res. 3201.   [32] Res. 3281.

that they chose, to nationalize and expropriate foreign property, and to pay 'appropriate' compensation to investors.[33]

3.1.2.3   The responses of capital-exporting states

There was a variety of responses from capital-exporting states to the sweeping nationalization programmes in many developing countries and to the General Assembly Resolutions. In particular, economic sanctions were employed on several occasions to pressure governments to provide compensation to affected companies. Sanctions were made in the areas of finance (e.g., suspension of bilateral foreign aid programmes, voting against loan applications in international financial institutions, blocking/freezing of assets) and trade (e.g., denial of preferential treatment).[34] However, as Akinsanya points out, the response was not uniform:

> while expropriations of alien-owned investments in the banking, insurance, and agricultural sectors do not generate much acrimony between the host and aliens' home governments, expropriations of mining and petroleum corporations as well as telecommunications corporations generate heated controversies that more often than not bring the aliens' home governments to the rescue of their nationals.[35]

Sanctions were particularly important in American policy, and the US was also, of course, the preeminent economy at the time.[36] In 1962, the US Congress passed an amendment to the Foreign Assistance Act, known as the Hickenlooper Amendment (named after a Senator from Iowa). The Amendment stipulated that in the event of an expropriation of an American investment, if the host state did not take 'appropriate steps' to compensate the investor within six months, the US President was required to cut off aid to that country.[37] In 1963, the Amendment was invoked against Sri Lanka (then Ceylon).[38]

This strategy was extended in 1965 in an amendment to the Act which authorized the US government to make contributions to the Inter-American Development Bank Fund for Special Operations. The amendment required that the US government vote against any loan to a country to which American assistance had been suspended under the Hickenlooper

---

[33] For a comprehensive discussion of these resolutions see Schrijver 1997.
[34] Akinsanya 1980: 284.   [35] *Ibid*: 176.
[36] The US accounted for more than half of the world stock of FDI by the late 1960s. See Brewer and Young 1998: 87.
[37] Einhorn 1974: 23.   [38] Brookens 1978: 51.

Amendment. The Overseas Private Investment Corporation (OPIC)[39] was also prohibited from insuring contracts in countries that were not in compliance with the Amendment, and similar steps were taken to suspend import quotas under the Sugar Act to any country that expropriated property without providing compensation.[40] Finally, the US also utilized its power within the World Bank to withhold loans. For example, it abstained from voting on a loan to upgrade Guyana's sea defences because compensation talks between the government of Guyana and an American mining company whose assets in the country had been expropriated had not 'proceeded sufficiently'.[41] Similar arguments were made when the US failed to support loans to Bolivia, Iraq and Peru in the early 1970s.[42]

Economic sanctions were not always successful and capital-exporting states also sought to improve the protection of foreign investors through international law. In the period when developing countries were collectively arguing for permanent sovereignty over natural resources, they were simultaneously agreeing under bilateral terms to more traditional/Western concepts of foreign investment protection. These bilateral agreements are discussed in Section 3.1.3.3.

Developed countries also pushed the theory of the 'internationalization' of foreign investment contracts. This theory was centred around two main issues:

(i) what law should govern contracts; and
(ii) in what forum should disputes be settled.

In terms of the first issue – 'choice of law' – it was argued by proponents of internationalization that contracts should be governed by 'general principles of law'[43] rather than the domestic law of the host state. In terms of the second issue, proponents of internationalization argued that disputes should be convened in international arbitration rather than in local courts. Arbitration between investors and states became much more feasible in 1966, when the Convention on the Settlement of Investment Disputes between States and Nationals of Other States (ICSID Convention) came into force (see further Section 6.1).

Private sector interests in the US, the UK and West Germany also initiated their own efforts to push for a broad agreement on investment

---

[39] OPIC is a US government agency that provides financing and political risk insurance for US businesses investing abroad. See www.opic.gov.
[40] Einhorn 1974: 24; Brookens 1978: 52.   [41] Einhorn 1974: 86.   [42] Brookens 1978: 51.
[43] UNCTAD 2004b: 6. Also referred to as 'principles of law recognized by civilized nations', 'transnational law of business', '*lex mercatoria*', or simply 'international law.'

protection. In 1959, investor organizations completed the Abs-Shawcross Draft Convention on Investment Abroad.[44] The Draft Convention, which has been described as the 'Magna Carta' of private investors, introduced the idea of investors *directly* pursuing claims against states in international arbitration.[45] The Convention was evaluated by the Organisation for European Economic Cooperation, now known as the OECD, and this led to the OECD Draft Convention on the Protection of Foreign Property of 1962.[46] While the OECD Draft Convention was never adopted due to opposition from some countries, it was revised in 1967 and approved by the Council of the OECD (with Turkey and Spain abstaining) as a model for bilateral agreements adopted by Member States.[47] An UNCTAD report remarks that the importance of the OECD Draft Convention 'rests mainly in the fact that, at a time when most developing countries – and some developed countries too – were very supportive of national controls over foreign direct investment, it placed emphasis on the protection of foreign investments'.[48]

Finally, capital-exporting countries also made efforts to diminish the standing of the UN General Assembly Resolutions. In this respect CERDS was the main target. The US Council of the International Chamber of Commerce (ICC) described the Charter as 'the cutting edge of a threat to the well-being – and even the existence – of foreign-owned private enterprise and to the security of foreign investment in many countries'.[49] The Charter was denied legal authority and status as customary international law by many capital-exporting countries.[50] While it was supported by a majority of states, it was not endorsed by any of the most important economies, which represent the bulk of outward international investment flows.

3.1.3 The modern period: 1980–present

The modern period marks a paradigm shift in attitudes and policies in developing countries in terms of foreign investment. As Vandevelde remarks, '[n]o single event accounts for the sudden reversal in investment policy and the emergence of the contemporary consensus' on the benefits of FDI.[51] However, many observers suggest that the most significant factor

---

[44] Reproduced in UNCTAD 2000a: 301.   [45] Van Harten 2007a: 20.
[46] OECD Doc. C(67)102, www.oecd.org. Reproduced in 7 ILM (1968): 117.
[47] Muchlinski 2001: 117–18.   [48] UNCTAD 1999a: 8.   [49] Qtd in Akinsanya 1980: 66.
[50] Mosoti 2005: 112.   [51] Vandevelde 1998: 386.

was the debt crisis that erupted in 1982.[52] As a result of the crisis, developing countries were desperate for foreign capital and were finding financial aid and preferential loans increasingly scarce. Furthermore, their experience suggested that perhaps foreign investors were less likely to interfere in their economies than were international and foreign lending organizations.[53] In addition, some of these organizations, such as the World Bank and International Monetary Fund (IMF), placed pressure on developing countries to open their doors to investors, as did capital-exporting states.[54]

As a result of the shift in attitude and approach to investment in developing countries, there have been extensive changes in the national laws of host states, both in terms of the development of general investment codes and in terms of the policies adopted in specific sectors. However, investment protection is limited when it is only enshrined in national laws which can be modified at will. Furthermore, due to the perceived or real corruption of local courts in many countries, investors do not feel that they are a neutral or fair forum for the resolution of disputes.[55] In this view, therefore, international agreements and access to international arbitration are required to ensure the protection of foreign investors, and thereby to facilitate flows of investment to developing countries. This is the reasoning behind the push in the modern period for the development of IIAs.

3.1.3.1   Free trade agreements

While von Moltke argues that it is 'a mistake to view foreign direct investment simply as an adjunct to trade', there are clear links between trade and investment which some have used as justification for negotiating a multilateral agreement on investment within the WTO (see below).[56] The inclusion of investment provisions within free trade agreements (FTAs) is also becoming increasingly common. The first FTA to contain significant protections for foreign investors, including access to international arbitration, was NAFTA involving Canada, Mexico and the US.[57]

---

[52] Moran and Pearson 1990: 29; Balasubramanyam 1999: 36; Brooks *et al.* 2004: 1; Sornarajah 2004b: 210; Van Harten 2007a: 42.

[53] Vandevelde 1998: 389.   [54] Subedi 2008: 86; Van Harten 2007a: 42.

[55] Peter 1995: 328.   [56] von Moltke 2002: 347.

[57] North American Free Trade Agreement, 17 December 1992, Ottawa, Mexico City, Washington. While it is not directly relevant to this study, it is worth briefly mentioning the North American Agreement on Environmental Cooperation (NAAEC), a side agreement to NAFTA enacted in 1993. The aim of the agreement is to ensure that states effectively enforce their environmental laws and regulations (essentially it is based on concerns about pollution havens – see Section 2.2). The Commission on Environmental Cooperation was

NAFTA's Chapter 11 on investment marks a significant milestone in investment law, despite the fact that the language of many of the provisions in the agreement is essentially drawn, with relatively minor modifications, from BITs that the US had concluded prior to 1993.[58] It is nonetheless noteworthy, first, because it marks what was and remains a rather rare occurrence – an investment agreement involving more than one developed state. Secondly, investor-state dispute settlement under Chapter 11 has been extensively employed by investors, marking a new era of investment arbitration and arguably triggering the current surge in disputes brought under other agreements.[59] Despite the fact that the investment chapter was largely aimed at constraining Mexico,[60] suits have been brought by investors against all three signatory countries. Thirdly, the pleadings in these suits were argued in ways not previously contemplated by governments, and through NAFTA tribunal decisions the substantive content of investor rights has arguably evolved and expanded. The public policy implications of investment agreements first became apparent in NAFTA disputes (see Chapter 7) and the agreement has also become a focal point for debate on the 'right to regulate'.

In recent years, several similar treaties have been negotiated which expand NAFTA-style investment protection to the south. The Central American Free Trade Agreement (CAFTA) was signed in 2004 by the US, Costa Rica, El Salvador, Guatemala, Honduras and Nicaragua. When the Dominican Republic joined the group later in the year, the acronym was modified to CAFTA-DR.[61] In 2007, the first two investor-state disputes under the agreement were initiated.[62] While the CAFTA-DR is viewed as an important agreement, many see it as merely a stepping-stone for the Free Trade Area of the Americas (FTAA), an agreement that would cover North, Central and South America, and the Caribbean (excluding only Cuba). The agreement was originally proposed at the 1994 Summit of the Americas. The 1998 Declaration of the

established by the NAAEC to adjudicate environmental claims. Non-enforcement of existing environmental laws can be challenged, but laws on the exploitation of natural resources are excluded.

[58] Gantz 2001: 671.

[59] Weiler 2003: 67, remarks that Chapter 11 'acted as the catalyst for an explosion of investment claims'.

[60] Brower 2001b: 51.

[61] Central America-Dominican Republic-United States Free Trade Agreement, 5 August 2004, Washington, DC.

[62] UNCTAD 2008: 16.

Second Summit of the Americas in San José called on the negotiators to:

> establish a fair and transparent legal framework to promote investment through the creation of a stable and predictable environment that protects the investor, his investment and related flows, without creating obstacles to investment from outside the hemisphere.[63]

As with the CAFTA-DR, the draft FTAA followed the NAFTA model with some modification. In the most recent publicly available draft of the proposed text, it is clear that consensus has not been reached on many investment issues; even the definition of the pivotal and basic concepts of 'investor' and 'investment' is disputed.[64]

If successfully concluded, the FTAA would be the most far-reaching trade agreement in history, as well as the most significant IIA. However, the initial deadline of January 2005 for the signing of the agreement was not met, and negotiations have remained deadlocked since February 2004, primarily due to ongoing disagreements between the delegates on farm subsidies and intellectual property rights.[65]

3.1.3.2   The fall of the multilateral agreement on investment

Despite the strong desire amongst most countries in the world to promote and to attract FDI, a truly multilateral agreement on investment has not emerged. However, there have been several attempts to develop such an agreement, the most significant being the negotiation of the Multilateral Agreement on Investment (MAI) in the mid-1990s. It is worthwhile to briefly review the MAI negotiations, as they brought environmental issues to the forefront of discussions on investment protection for the first time.

The MAI negotiations took place within the OECD commencing in 1995. The OECD was viewed by the US government as a 'friendly forum' where a 'high standards' regime could be negotiated, which could subsequently be opened for ratification by non-OECD states.[66] Despite the advantages of a friendly forum, European governments and business lobbies were not convinced that the OECD was an appropriate locus for

---

[63] Qtd in Mann and Araya 2002: 172.
[64] Third Draft FTAA Agreement, 21 November 2003, www.ftaa-alca.org.
[65] 'Summit of the Americas Fails to Resurrect FTAA', *Bridges Weekly Trade News Digest* 9(38), 9 November 2005.
[66] Crane 1998: 431; Mabey 1999: 63; Dattu 2000: 276.

discussions and continued to favour the WTO instead.[67] However, given the opposition of developing countries to opening negotiations in the WTO, the American position eventually prevailed. Five non-OECD countries (Argentina, Brazil, Chile, Hong Kong and the Slovak Republic) were granted observer status in the negotiations. The initial deadline for an agreement to be reached was 1997, which was subsequently pushed back to 1998. Negotiations were effectively abandoned in October of 1998 when France withdrew its delegation.

Various factors contributed to the breakdown of the MAI negotiations. According to an article in *The Economist*, the problems began with the choice of the OECD as the forum.[68] The OECD has a membership of only thirty countries. OECD countries act both as the primary source and as the main destination for FDI, but it was widely acknowledged that an agreement on investment between only these countries would be largely irrelevant, given that they already have strong domestic protections for foreign investors. The strategy of drafting an agreement among countries where it was relatively unnecessary and later expanding it to the rest of the world was problematic given the likely reluctance of non-OECD countries to sign an agreement that they had not been involved in drafting.[69] However, opponents of the MAI argued that developing countries would feel compelled to ratify the agreement for fear of losing foreign investments from signatory nations.[70] Some countries were concerned that signing the MAI could even become a requirement for receiving financial assistance from organizations such as the World Bank and IMF (which are effectively controlled by OECD countries).[71]

The collapse of the MAI negotiations could also be attributed, at least in part, to a concerted effort on the part of environmental and labour groups to stop, or at least influence the outcome of, the negotiations.[72] Environmental and social issues barely featured at the start of MAI talks but became key points of contention in the end.[73] Following the leak of a confidential draft of the agreement on the Internet, a broad coalition was formed between environmental NGOs, human rights and consumer advocate groups, trade unions, indigenous peoples' organizations, local

---

[67] Walter 2001: 60. According to Muchlinski 2001: 121, the WTO was also preferred by the European Community because in that forum it had direct negotiating rights on behalf of its Member States.
[68] 'The Sinking of the MAI', *The Economist*, 2004 (346): 81–2.
[69] *Ibid.*   [70] Crane 1998: 436.   [71] *Ibid*: 437.   [72] Mabey 1999: 61; Muchlinski 2001: 132.
[73] 'The Sinking of the MAI', *The Economist*, 2004 (346): 81–2.

governments and communities opposed to the MAI.[74] The coalition campaigned for the inclusion of environmental and labour standards in the agreement and also argued that the MAI conflicted with many international commitments that OECD countries had made, including those found in the Rio Declaration on Environment and Development and Agenda 21.[75] NGO activities also sparked the interest of the social and environmental ministries of OECD governments that had been excluded from, and often unaware of, the negotiations and the implications of the MAI for their policy areas.[76] However, even at the height of the discussions on environmental issues in the MAI, only two countries sent delegates from their environmental ministries to the negotiations.[77]

NGOs were particularly concerned that provisions on expropriation and investor-state dispute settlement would allow corporations to challenge domestic laws and standards that could be shown to have the equivalent effect of expropriation. Given their experience with Chapter 11 of NAFTA, it was American and Canadian NGOs that provided the strongest opposition to the MAI.[78] In fact, the settlement of a particular investor-state dispute (*Ethyl* v. *Canada*, see Section 7.1.1), which seemed to indicate that certain provisions included in the MAI could be interpreted in unexpected ways, lent support to the NGO position and may have influenced the MAI drafters.[79]

Walter argues that the push from NGOs for labour and environmental standards to be included in the MAI led to a weakening support for the agreement from business lobbies, which in turn eventually led to the demise of the entire process.[80] However, there were also other complicating factors: business lobbies were pushing for provisions related to taxation, which governments strongly opposed; and the French and Canadian governments wanted 'cultural industries' to be exempted from the agreement, which was unpopular with the American business lobby in particular.[81] Other 'deal-breakers' concerned the US desire to introduce provisions on the rights of owners of illegally expropriated property to pursue claims against the current owners of that property, and the EU position on the need for an exemption for 'regional economic integration organizations'

---

[74] Henderson 1999: 27.   [75] Crane 1998: 439.   [76] Mabey 1999: 64.   [77] *Ibid.*
[78] Walter 2001: 62.
[79] Muchlinski 2001: 128; Sornarajah 2004a: 293; Newcombe 2007b: 392; Schneiderman 2008: 202.
[80] Walter 2001. See also Sikkel 2001.
[81] UNCTAD 1999b: 24; Malanczuk 2000: 418; Muchlinski 2001: 130; Walter 2001: 62.

from certain provisions.[82] In contrast to the general feeling in 1995 that negotiating an agreement among such 'like-minded' countries should be relatively easy, over the three years of negotiations it became quite evident that there were substantial differences between OECD countries with regard to their views on investment protection.

Since that time, efforts to negotiate a multilateral agreement on investment within the WTO have also failed rather spectacularly. Most recently, efforts to launch negotiations at the 2003 WTO Ministerial Conference in Cancún were blocked by developing countries who argued that investment protection should only be considered if there was also agreement to expand the discussions to corporate conduct and liability.[83] Following Cancún, the EU continued to push for optional investment negotiations on a plurilateral basis, despite diverging views on this position amongst EU member countries.[84] On 1 August 2004, the General Council of the WTO adopted a Decision on the so-called July Package, which broke the Cancún deadlock.[85] This Decision makes it clear that investment will not be an issue for negotiation within the WTO in the Doha Round.[86]

3.1.3.3   The rise of the bilateral investment treaty

Although it is widely reported that the first BIT was signed between Germany and Pakistan in 1959, Yackee points out that this agreement had no investor-state dispute settlement provision and actually more closely resembled a FCN treaty.[87] It is, therefore, more appropriate to consider an agreement signed in 1969 between Italy and Chad as the first true BIT. While the pace of BIT signing was initially slow, this changed in the 1990s. There are now more than 2,600 BITs worldwide.[88]

---

[82] Muchlinski 2001: 129–30.

[83] Kerremans 2004: 363; Sornarajah 2004a: 28.

[84] The UK has argued that it would be better to remove investment from the WTO agenda altogether. See Peterson 2004b: 1.

[85] 'The July 2004 Package', WTO website, www.wto.org.

[86] Specifically, it includes a paragraph on the Relationship between Trade and Investment, Interaction between Trade and Competition Policy and Transparency in Government Procurement stating that 'the Council agrees that these issues, mentioned in the Doha Ministerial Declaration in paragraphs 20–2, 23–5 and 26 respectively, will not form part of the Work Programme set out in that Declaration and therefore no work towards negotiations on any of these issues will take place within the WTO during the Doha Round'.

[87] Yackee 2008a: 430.

[88] UNCTAD 2009b: 2. Not all BITs have entered into force. UNCTAD 2006b estimates that of the 2,495 BITs concluded prior to 2006, 1,891 (i.e., 75.8 per cent) had entered into force.

The early BITs were created to deal with the period of uncertainty following decolonization, and the main purpose of BITs today is still to protect foreign investors in the developing world. OECD countries participate in BITs almost exclusively with developing countries; while there is an increasing number of South-South BITs, there is a dearth of agreements between industrialized nations.[89]

BITs typically last for ten years, with an automatic extension of this term unless a party files notice to terminate the treaty. It is also typical for there to be a period following the termination of an agreement in which the provisions continue to apply to existing investments.[90] As most BITs are of a relatively recent vintage, there is little experience with their expiry or termination.[91]

Despite the large number of BITs, these agreements have enjoyed a relatively low profile in comparison with regional trade and investment agreements such as NAFTA, and the controversial and well-publicized attempts of states to develop a multilateral agreement on investment. This is now beginning to change, as Spiermann notes:

> The times are gone when bilateral investment treaties could be treated as 'mainly bureaucrats' treaties' tucked away from the hustle and bustle of the financial world.[92]

Part of the reason for the increased interest in BITs is the sudden and dramatic rise in investor-state disputes, many of which have concerned issues of great public import.

3.2   A public or private institution?

Weintraub points out that the concepts of 'public' and 'private' mean very different things to different people, and therefore 'any discussion of public and private should begin by recognizing, and trying to clarify, the multiple and ambiguous character of its subject matter'.[93] In this study, the distinction between private and public is meant in the sense of the individual versus the collective.[94] This distinction is used to differentiate between *state* and *non-state* actors, but also between the *public* and *private* acts of a state (i.e., acts that affect or do not affect the *public* interest).

Scholars have observed that non-state actors are increasingly taking on new and significant roles in the development, implementation and

---

[89] Garcia 2004: 315; Hallward-Driemeier 2003: 8.
[90] Reed *et al.* 2004: 61.   [91] *Ibid*: 62.   [92] Spiermann 2004: 179.
[93] Weintraub 1997: 3.   [94] *Ibid*: 5.

enforcement of international rules. New forms of private and hybrid (public-private) governance are emerging in a multitude of issue areas.[95] Examples include reporting schemes (e.g., the GRI), certification and labelling schemes (e.g., the Forest Stewardship Council), sets of voluntary principles (e.g., the ICC Business Charter for Sustainable Development) and standards regimes (e.g., the ISO).[96]

Cutler *et al.* define a 'private regime' as 'an integrated complex of formal and informal institutions that is a source of governance for an economic issue area as a whole'.[97] Falkner presents a broader notion of 'private governance':

> 'Private governance' emerges at the global level where the interactions among private actors, or between private actors on the one hand and civil society and state actors on the other, give rise to institutional arrangements that structure and direct actors' behavior in an issue-specific area. These structuring effects resemble the 'public' governing functions of states and intergovernmental institutions, and for this reason the notion of governance, and indeed authority, has been applied to private actors.[98]

It may not be immediately apparent how the institution of investment protection fits in to this debate, given that IIAs are intergovernmental (i.e. public) agreements. However, it is evident from the historical discussion above that private actors have played an important role in the development of the institution of investment protection. The Abs-Shawcross Draft Convention, drawn up by investors, had a substantial influence on the OECD work in the area of foreign investment, which in turn has been the model for individual OECD countries in the drafting of bilateral agreements. Clearly the business lobby was also an important factor in the push for a multilateral agreement on investment. Furthermore, when one looks at the broader architecture of investment protection, which includes foreign investment contracts negotiated directly between an investor and a state, and arbitral rules that have been developed by non-state organizations (e.g., the ICC) with the original intention of governing purely private disputes, it is clear that the line between public and private has been blurred. The arbitration process is a particularly grey area. It brings together public and private rules, state and non-state actors, and vests authority in private actors (arbitrators) in a selection process that is not controlled by states.[99]

---

[95] Hall and Biersteker 2002; Cutler *et al.* 1999.

[96] Pattberg 2007; Clapp 2005; Hall and Biersteker 2002; Cutler *et al.* 1999.

[97] Cutler *et al.* 1999: 13.   [98] Falkner 2003: 72–3.

[99] The state chooses one arbitrator, the investor a second, and they collectively agree on a third. See further Section 6.1.1.2.

The legal literature emphasizes that arbitrators only 'interpret' the rules that have been laid out by states. However, Stone Sweet suggests that arbitration is more accurately described as a form of *governance*.[100] First, by resolving a dispute, the arbitrator 'makes rules that are concrete, particular, and retrospective'.[101] Second, in providing a justification for the decision, the arbitrator 'makes rules of an abstract, general, and prospective nature'.[102] In the first instance the decisions reflect the particular circumstances of the dispute at hand and determine the resolution of that dispute. In the second instance, the decisions affect the very relationship between the parties to the dispute, causing them to reflect on their own interpretations of what that relationship entailed, and likely affecting the future of the relationship and the occurrence and/or outcome of any future disputes.

In addition to conferring the authority to govern to arbitrators, investor-state dispute settlement, by its very nature, elevates foreign investors to a level of recognition in international law and politics not usually afforded to non-state actors. Foreign investors, like all non-state actors, are considered 'objects' rather than 'subjects' of public international law.[103] According to the International Law Association (ILA) International Law on Foreign Investment Committee, investors are not acquiring international legal personality through investment law *per se*, but they 'enjoy a measure of international *locus standi*'.[104] However, as Cutler argues, no matter what terminology is used, 'today transnational corporations are significant *de facto* subjects of law'.[105] The analytical distinction only serves to make corporations 'invisible' under international law when it comes to issues of corporate conduct.[106] Sornarajah points out that, ironically, while IIAs and contracts give investors standing in international law, efforts to create responsibilities on the part of investors have been resisted on the grounds of the absence of international legal personality:

> The classic ploy has been to recognise that there is a problem as far as accountability is concerned but that the only method by which the matter can be dealt with is through the formulation of non-binding codes containing exhortations to multinational corporations to conform to its prescriptions. The emergence of strong norms has been stunted through countermanding of such efforts by the home states of multinational corporations. The phenomenon that results is that while treaties protecting

---

[100] Stone Sweet 1999: 147.   [101] *Ibid*: 156.   [102] *Ibid*: 157.   [103] Horn 2004: 9.
[104] ILA International Law on Foreign Investment Committee 2006: 5.
[105] Cutler 2003: 21.   [106] *Ibid*.

multinational corporations are increasing, the rules that seek to impose duties on these corporations are aborted.[107]

Elevating private actors to a level playing field with states is generally considered acceptable when states are acting in a *private* capacity. Van Harten explains how states can act as private parties under contracts:

> When a legislature expropriates property, leading to a dispute with its private owner, the passage of the legislation is quintessentially a sovereign act and the resulting dispute quite clearly a matter of public law. Alternatively, when the Government contracts with a company to tend the lawn in front of Parliament, the Government's conclusion of the contract is a commercial act of the State, one that a private party could carry out, and its resolution by arbitration can credibly be positioned within the private domain.[108]

Van Harten admits that in practice it may be difficult to separate the private and public acts of states, but he argues that in two particular situations the distinction is clear. In IIAs the relationship between the state and an investor is one of *regulator* and *regulated*, and therefore any government acts that are challenged in arbitration will be of a public nature. In contrast, foreign investment contracts generally reduce states to private actors participating in commercial relationships and do not cover regulatory acts, and as such 'arbitration does not usually determine core questions of public law'.[109] However, if a contract contains certain types of clauses (e.g., stabilization clauses) it will cover regulation, and the relationship ceases to be private (see Chapter 5).

In summary, the institution of investment protection is a hybrid of public and private authority. States make some of the rules, often influenced by the work of international organizations and private actors, while other rules are developed by private organizations. Private actors are delegated the authority to 'interpret' and apply these rules to specific disputes. This constitutive aspect of the institution is particularly significant in light of the broad and vague nature of the regulative rules and norms of investment protection (see Chapter 4). The elevation of foreign investors to *de facto* subjects of international law is also an important constitutive aspect of the institution. Finally, this hybrid institution has implications for *public policy* when it determines the outcome of regulatory disputes that arise under an IIA or a foreign investment contract.

[107] Sornarajah 2006b: 32. [108] Van Harten 2007b: 373. [109] Van Harten 2007a: 25.

Scholarly inquiry on the issue of private authority in international affairs has focused on two main questions:

(i) what does increasing transnational private authority mean for the continuing existence/relevance of public authority (i.e., the state)?; and

(ii) what does increasing transnational private authority mean in terms of democratic accountability and legitimacy at all levels of governance?[110]

Both of these issues are addressed in this study with specific reference to environmental governance.

3.3   Effectiveness of the institution

Institutional analysis in international relations has in the past been dominated by the question of *whether* international institutions matter, rather than *how they matter*. As Martin and Simmons point out: 'Too often over the last decade and a half the focal point of debate has been crudely dichotomous: institutions matter, or they do not.'[111] However, more recent scholarship, particularly in the study of global environmental governance, has concentrated specifically on examining institutional *effectiveness*; that is the impact of institutions on state behaviour.[112] The focus of this line of research has been overwhelmingly on effectiveness as *problem solving* or *goal attainment*; an institution is considered effective to the extent that its members abide by its norms and rules and to the extent that it achieves certain objectives.[113]

Determining the effectiveness of institutions is a complicated matter. First of all, there may be more than one implicit or explicit goal of the institution against which its success should be evaluated. Second of all, there are questions in terms of how success should be measured. To avoid some of these problems, this section takes a very narrow approach to the question of effectiveness by examining the success that the institution of investment protection has had in achieving only one of its explicit goals (the promotion of FDI flows) through a survey of the current literature on the topic. It then shifts gears to examine the question of the so-called side effects of the institution, which are the focus of the remainder of the book.

[110] Hall and Biersteker 2002: 7; Cutler 2003: 28.
[111] Martin and Simmons 1998: 730.   [112] See, e.g., Biermann and Bauer 2004.
[113] Young 1994: 143–5; Hasenclever *et al.* 1997: 2.

3.3.1 Promoting investment

From the perspective of capital-importing states, the institution of investment protection would be considered effective if it were successful in promoting FDI flows. The ultimate goal is, of course, for these flows to be translated into economic development. If this is a primary goal of the institution, one might question why it has not been referred to as the institution of investment *promotion* and protection in this book. This is not accidental. As Newcombe remarks, in IIAs 'promotion is largely the assumed byproduct of protection',[114] and as an UNCTAD report also notes: 'Only a small minority of existing IIAs actually include *specific* provisions on investment promotion'.[115] Ultimately, as will be explained below, there is no convincing evidence that the institution is actually effective in promoting investment flows.

Empirically, there are examples that raise doubts about the relationship between IIAs and FDI flows. For example, Brazil is a recipient of a large amount of FDI and yet has not ratified any BIT.[116] Conversely, many African countries that have ratified numerous BITs have remained marginalized in terms of global investment flows. This is consistent with the mixed anecdotal evidence of investor awareness of, and interest in, IIAs.[117]

In recent years, several studies have attempted to prove statistical correlation, or lack thereof, between BITs and investment flows. Franck divides the studies into those which represent a 'market protagonist' view (BITs have a minor impact on FDI and market forces are far more critical determinants of flows), and those that take a 'treaty protagonist' stance (BITs play an important role in attracting FDI).[118]

One study, conducted by a World Bank economist, falls into the former category.[119] Hallward-Driemeier assessed twenty years of FDI flows from OECD countries to developing countries and found that there is little evidence that BITs have stimulated additional investment.[120] Tobin and Rose-Ackerman, in a 2005 study, also found the relationship between BITs and FDI to be weak.[121] However, in 2006 the same authors reported that they had developed a more sophisticated model and concluded, in contradiction with their previous results, that BITs do have a positive impact on FDI flows to developing countries.[122] Nevertheless, Tobin and

[114] Newcombe 2007a: 373.   [115] UNCTAD 2008: 17.   [116] Newcombe 2007a: 372.
[117] Franck 2007: 347–8.   [118] *Ibid*: 349.   [119] Hallward-Driemeier 2003.
[120] For another study reaching similar conclusions, see UNCTAD 1998.
[121] Tobin and Rose-Ackerman 2005.   [122] Tobin and Rose-Ackerman 2006.

Rose-Ackerman qualified this finding by noting that the impact of BITs is highly dependent on the political and economic environment in the host country.[123] Furthermore, they suggested that as the global coverage of BITs increases, the marginal effect of one country's BITs on its FDI inflows will decline.[124]

In a more overtly treaty protagonist study, Neumayer and Spess critiqued Hallward-Driemeier's study (as well as others) and argued that BITs do live up to their purported purpose of fostering FDI flows.[125] Others have also come to this conclusion, although research has at times produced conflicting results. For example, Salacuse and Sullivan found that if a country signed a BIT with the US it would receive more FDI from that country, whereas Gallagher and Birch found that the total number of BITs signed by a country can be positively correlated to greater FDI flows, but that specifically signing a US BIT had no impact on inflows of US FDI.[126]

In one of the most comprehensive studies, which also specifically evaluated the results attained by Neumayer and Spess, Yackee found 'only inconsistent evidence that BITs might, on average, succeed in inducing additional FDI'.[127] He suggested that while BITs with strong dispute settlement mechanisms might increase what he calls FDI 'penetration' (FDI inflows as a percentage of gross domestic product), they do not seem to help states in the *competition* for FDI flows.[128] He also concluded, similarly to Tobin and Rose-Ackerman, that BITs become less effective as more and more of them are signed.

Yackee is critical of most empirical BIT studies, arguing that they should be approached 'with a substantial grain of salt'.[129] He suggests that the focus on BITs itself is inappropriate as there are comparable substitutes for BITs such as foreign investment contracts and also other sources of investment protection such as insurance that could affect FDI flows.[130] Yackee also argues that the potential *costs* of signing a BIT (in terms of the cost of arbitration as well as the cost of reduced regulatory flexibility) is likely to outweigh any benefits.[131] This is an argument extended by Stiglitz, who suggests that:

> Even if it could be established that BITs lead to increased investment, and even if that investment could be shown to lead to higher growth, as measured by increased gross domestic product ("GDP"), it does not mean

---

[123] *Ibid*: 4.   [124] *Ibid*.   [125] Neumayer and Spess 2005.
[126] Salacuse and Sullivan 2005; Gallagher and Birch 2006.   [127] Yackee 2006: 8.
[128] *Ibid*.   [129] Yackee 2008a: 410.   [130] Yackee 2006: 7; 2008a: 410.
[131] Yackee 2006: 31.

that societal welfare will increase, especially once resource depletion and environmental degradation are taken into account.[132]

3.3.2   Side effects

While it is important to consider the effectiveness of an institution with regard to its stated or implicit goals, it is also critical to recognize the potential *unintended* effects of institutions, which Young refers to as 'side effects'. Young notes that:

> In individual cases, the impact of the relevant side effects may equal or even exceed the magnitude of the intended effect attributable to the operation of international regimes, a fact that should give pause to regime enthusiasts who advocate the creation of new institutions as a solution to every problem.[133]

Side effects are possibly not even *anticipated* by a government when it negotiates a contract or an IIA. Martin and Simmons argue that it is important to differentiate between unintended and unanticipated effects:

> Effects may be anticipated but unintended. For example, it is generally expected that arrangements to lower the rate of inflation will lead to somewhat higher levels of unemployment. Thus, higher unemployment is an anticipated, although unintended, consequence of stringent monetary policies. It is best understood as a price actors are sometimes willing to bear to gain the benefits of low inflation. Such unintended but anticipated consequences of institutions present little challenge to a rationalist approach, since they fit neatly into a typical cost-benefit analysis. Genuinely unanticipated effects, however, present a larger challenge.[134]

According to Martin and Simmons, unanticipated effects are more likely 'in situations that have relatively complex and permutable secondary rules, such as legalized institutions'[135] and Abbott and Snidal suggest that delegation (e.g., to an arbitral tribunal) 'provides the greatest source of unanticipated sovereignty costs'.[136]

In the specific case of NAFTA, Abbott suggests that Chapter 11 'has been invoked by private investors in circumstances that were not contemplated by NAFTA negotiators' and that disputes have 'yielded certain unanticipated results'.[137] Dhooge similarly argues that NAFTA's

---

[132] Stiglitz 2008: 455.   [133] Young 1994: 151–2.
[134] Martin and Simmons 1998: 750, emphasis added.   [135] *Ibid.*
[136] Abbott and Snidal 2000: 438.   [137] Abbott 2000: 522 and 547.

Chapter 11 has 'opened a proverbial Pandora's Box of unintended and unanticipated consequences for future environmental regulation'.[138] Comments made by US Senator Kerry in 2002 further support the claim that the legislators who passed NAFTA did not anticipate the investor-state arbitrations that resulted:

> When we passed NAFTA, there wasn't one word of debate on the subject of the Chapter 11 resolution – not one word. Nobody knew what was going to happen. Nobody knew what the impacts might be.[139]

Abner Mika, President Clinton's General Counsel, has also been quoted as stating (with reference to the expropriation provisions in Chapter 11): 'If Congress had known that there was anything like this in NAFTA, they would never have voted for it.'[140] Additionally, Stiglitz claims that President Clinton himself was unaware of the potential of Chapter 11 to be used to challenge government regulation, and goes on to point out that: 'If the United States, a country with a great deal of experience adopting such agreements, was not fully aware of NAFTA's import, developing countries are even less likely to understand the complexities of such agreements.'[141] A statement from the Attorney General of Pakistan, Makhdoom Ali Khan, supports this concern; he claims that BITs 'are signed without any knowledge of their implications' and that it is not until 'you are hit by the first investor-state arbitration [that] you realize what these words mean'.[142]

---

[138] Dhooge 2001: 274.   [139] Qtd in Kinnear and Hansen 2005: 104.
[140] '11 Feet Under', *Globe and Mail*, 26 November 2004: 58.
[141] Stiglitz 2008: 460–1.
[142] 'Pakistan Attorney General Advises States to Scrutinize Investment Treaties Carefully', *Investment Treaty News*, 1 December 2006, www.iisd.org/investment/itn.

4

International investment agreements

As of the end of 2008, there were 2,676 BITs, 273 free trade and economic cooperation agreements containing investment provisions[1] and five WTO agreements covering foreign investment-related issues.[2] This study does not explore the provisions of the WTO agreements in any detail but rather focuses on the remainder of the agreements, collectively referred to herein as international investment agreements (IIAs).

IIAs vary based on the relative bargaining strengths of the countries involved and the time at which a treaty was negotiated.[3] Many developed countries have taken up the practice of producing what is called a 'model' or 'prototype' BIT, a template used in negotiations for BITs and for investment chapters of trade agreements. While each country develops its own model they generally fit into two broad categories: North American and European.[4] The main differences between the two types are that North American IIAs cover the pre-establishment phase of investment in addition to the post-establishment phase and include provisions on performance requirements (see Section 4.1.6), whereas European IIAs generally do not.[5]

This chapter provides an overview of the key provisions (other than those on dispute resolution which are covered in Chapter 6) that are found in most IIAs and that are relevant to environmental governance. Generalizations about these key provisions are made, but where significant discrepancies between agreements occur they are highlighted. In particular, reference will be made to several very recent agreements that include

---

[1] UNCTAD 2009b: 2, 8.
[2] The Agreement on Trade Related Investment Measures; the Agreement on Trade Related Intellectual Property Rights; the General Agreement on Trade in Services; the Agreement on Subsidies and Countervailing Measures; and the Agreement on Government Procurement.
[3] Sornarajah 2003: 181.
[4] Houde and Yannaca-Small 2004: 3; Brewer and Young 1998: 76.   [5] *Ibid.*

substantial modifications to the typical wording of common provisions. In these cases it will be emphasized that, at present, such novel developments do not represent widespread practice. Following the overview of key provisions, a brief analysis of the recent trend of conducting environmental impact assessments of IIAs is provided. The chapter concludes with a discussion of the potential implications of IIAs for environmental governance, particularly in developing countries.

4.1   Key provisions

This section analyses the key investment protection standards of IIAs relevant to the protection of the environment, namely those on: definitions of an investor and an investment; national treatment; most-favoured-nation treatment; the international minimum standard of treatment, fair and equitable treatment and full protection and security; expropriation; performance requirements; observance of obligations (umbrella clauses); and environmental issues.

4.1.1   Definitions of investor and investment

The definition of 'investment' has evolved over time; while it was traditionally confined to the tangible or physical assets of an investor, it has broadened in both academic discourse and international agreements not only to include intangible assets but also to expand their scope. Shares in corporations established by the foreign investor, intellectual property rights, contractual rights and administrative rights are now among the intangible assets that are included in many IIAs. While some IIAs limit the scope of protection (e.g., to investments that have been approved by the government), other agreements focus on measures (laws and regulations) 'relating to' investments. In this latter form, 'a broad range of regulations in the host country could potentially fall under the scope of application of the [agreement]'.[6]

   In terms of the definition of 'investor', most IIAs cover both natural persons and legal entities such as corporations. There are several criteria commonly used (separately or in combination) to determine whether a legal entity qualifies under the *ratione personae* requirement of an agreement such as: place of incorporation; location of seat (i.e., where effective management takes place); and nationality of control or ownership.[7] Some

---

[6] UNCTAD 2007: 7.   [7] UNCTAD 2004a: 111.

agreements extend the meaning of the term 'investor' to include entities established in third countries if nationals of a party have a controlling interest in the entity, while other agreements specifically preclude this through a 'denial of benefits' clause. Broad and open-ended definitions of 'investor' leave open the opportunity for companies to structure investments through a chain of holding companies located in different jurisdictions, and this provides them with the option of 'forum shopping' or pursuing multiple claims through different IIAs.[8] As Subedi notes: 'This state of affairs has the potential to make the dispute settlement mechanism of a given BIT available to all foreign investors, which perhaps is not what a host state may have contemplated at the time of concluding the BIT concerned.'[9]

4.1.2 National treatment

National treatment is one of the core provisions of investment protection.[10] Essentially, it requires that countries not discriminate against foreign investors in favour of domestic ones. The standard of treatment can be defined in two ways: 'same' or 'as favourable as' treatment; or 'no less favourable' treatment. The difference is subtle, but the 'no less favourable' formulation, which is the most common in IIAs, leaves open the possibility that investors may be entitled to treatment that is more favourable than that granted to domestic investors, in accordance with international standards.[11]

National treatment provisions may refer to the treatment of only investors, only investments or, as is the case in an increasing number of IIAs, to both investments and investors in order to avoid ambiguity on this issue. For example, the Japan-Sri Lanka BIT states first that:

---

[8] Houde and Yannaca Small 2004: 4. For an example of forum shopping see *Aguas del Tunari, S.A.* v. *Republic of Bolivia*, ICSID Case No. ARB/02/3, where the claimant, an American company, set up a shell company in the Netherlands to benefit from the Netherlands-Bolivia BIT. For an example of multiple claims/awards, see *CME Czech Republic B.V.* v. *Czech Republic*, Final Award and Separate Opinion, 14 March 2003, and *Lauder* v. *Czech Republic*, Final Award, 3 September 2001.

[9] Subedi 2008: 60.

[10] Although it is unusual, some IIAs, such as the Association of South-East Asian Nations (ASEAN) Agreement for the Protection and Promotion of Investments and the early BITs signed by China, Norway and Sweden, do not grant national treatment. See UNCTAD 1999c: 16.

[11] *Ibid*: 37.

> Neither Contracting Party shall within its territory subject *investments* and returns of nationals and companies of the other Contracting Party to treatment *less favourable* than that accorded to investments and returns of nationals and companies of the former Contracting Party or of nationals and companies of any third country.[12]

It then goes on to state that:

> *Nationals and companies* of either Contracting Party shall within the territory of the other Contracting Party be accorded treatment *no less favourable* than that accorded to nationals and companies of such other Contracting Party or to nationals and companies of any third country in all matters relating to their business activities in connection with their investment.[13]

National treatment can be read narrowly to cover only *de jure* discrimination or broadly to cover also *de facto* discrimination. *De facto* discrimination occurs when a measure not specifically aimed at a foreign investor has the practical effect of less favourable treatment.[14] *De facto* discrimination focuses on the result of the treatment, and therefore evidence of intent to discriminate on the part of the host state is not necessary.[15]

Some IIAs, particularly those signed by Canada and the US, qualify the definition of national treatment by including the provision that it only applies in 'like circumstances' or 'similar circumstances'. While, in theory, this approach offers a narrower scope for comparison than IIAs with no qualifying language, in practice a large ambit for interpretation remains.[16] The issue of 'likeness' has been controversial in the context of international trade, where the 'likeness' of products is often compared. In the WTO jurisprudence, likeness has been assessed largely on the basis of whether the products can be considered to be substitutes in the marketplace, leaving aside the environmentally relevant issue of the processes and production methods utilized in their creation.[17] While regulating 'like products' and regulating investments or investors in 'like circumstances' are quite different undertakings (in the case of the latter the production facilities will be within the jurisdiction of the regulating state), claimants and arbitrators in investor-state disputes often draw on WTO jurisprudence to support their arguments and decisions.[18]

---

[12] Japan and Sri Lanka Agreement Concerning the Promotion and Protection of Investments, 1 March 1982, Colombo: Art. 3.1, emphasis added.

[13] *Ibid*: Art. 3.2, emphasis added.   [14] Van Harten 2007a: 85; UNCTAD 1999c: 12.

[15] Weiler 2004: 171.   [16] Gantz 2001: 677; UNCTAD 1999c: 34.   [17] UNCTAD 2007: 37.

[18] Kurtz 2007: 311.

A further question that has been raised with respect to national treatment is the extent to which the standard applies to subnational authorities.[19] For example, in a federalist country composed of provinces, would national treatment require that foreign investors be given no less favourable treatment than that accorded to nationals or enterprises from within the province? Or would it only require that they be treated as all other out-of-province nationals are treated? Some IIAs now explicitly refer to such situations; for example, the CAFTA-DR states:

> The treatment to be accorded by a Party under paragraphs 1 and 2 means, with respect to a regional level of government, treatment no less favorable than the most favorable treatment accorded, in like circumstances, by that regional level of government to investors, and to investments of investors, of the Party of which it forms a part.[20]

This formulation suggests that national treatment in the CAFTA-DR requires only out-of-province treatment.

Finally, IIAs differ on whether national treatment applies only to existing investments and investors or also to the prospective ones (i.e., whether the treaty provides a right of establishment). The latter type of treatment is found mainly in agreements negotiated by Canada, the US and, more recently, Japan. For example, the Canada-Costa Rica BIT states that:

> Each Contracting Party shall permit establishment of a new business enterprise or acquisition of an existing business enterprise or a share of such enterprise by investors or prospective investors of the other Contracting Party on a basis no less favourable than that which, in like circumstances, it permits such acquisition or establishment by ... its own investors or prospective investors.[21]

National treatment provisions may be subject to general, subject-specific and industry-specific exceptions.[22]

4.1.3 Most-favoured-nation treatment

Most-favoured-nation treatment requires that a government not discriminate between foreign investors and/or investments from different countries. As with national treatment, the standard can be defined as 'same',

[19] UNCTAD 1999c: 25.   [20] CAFTA-DR: Art. 1003.3.
[21] Agreement between the Government of Canada and the Government of the Republic of Costa Rica for the Promotion and Protection of Investments, 18 March 1998, San José: Art. 3.
[22] UNCTAD 1999c: 43–6. For examples of exceptions see UNCTAD 2007.

'as favourable as' or 'no less favourable', with the latter choice being the most common. For example, the Sweden-Argentina BIT states that: 'Each Contracting Party shall apply to investments in its territory by investors of the other Contracting Party a treatment which is *no less favourable* than that accorded to investments by investors of third States.'[23]

As with national treatment, some IIAs qualify most-favoured-nation treatment so that it does not require the host country to treat enterprises in different sectors or in different 'situations' or 'circumstances' the same, and refer to the treatment of both investments and investors. For example, NAFTA Article 1103 states in the first paragraph that:

> Each Party shall accord to investors of another Party treatment *no less favorable* than that it accords, *in like circumstances,* to investors of any other Party or of a non-Party with respect to the *establishment,* acquisition, expansion, management, conduct, operation, and sale or other disposition of investments.

It repeats this formulation for 'investments of investors of another Party' in the second paragraph. While NAFTA and BITs involving Canada or the US extend most-favoured-nation treatment to the pre-establishment phase of investment, the provisions in most other agreements only apply to established investments.

There has been some controversy over whether most-favoured-nation treatment allows investors to 'import' more favourable provisions from other investment agreements signed by the host country ('treaty piggy-backing'). In *Maffezini* v. *Spain,* the tribunal decided that the most-favoured-nation clause in the Spain-Argentina BIT could be applied to allow the claimant to have access to dispute resolution provisions in a BIT between Spain and Chile.[24] The *Maffezini* decision prompted the parties to the CAFTA-DR to include a footnote in the 2004 draft text of the agreement, referred to as the 'Maffezini exclusion', stating that the Parties did not agree with this interpretation of most-favoured-nation treatment.

---

[23] Agreement between the Government of the Kingdom of Sweden and the Government of the Republic of Argentina on the Promotion and Reciprocal Protection of Investments, 22 November 1991, Stockholm: Art. 3.1, emphasis added.

[24] *Emilio Agustín Maffezini* v. *Kingdom of Spain,* ICSID Case No. ARB/97/7, Decision on Objections to Jurisdiction, 25 January 2000, 16 *ICSID Review* (2001): 212, http://icsid.worldbank.org. Under the Argentina-Spain BIT the investor was required to employ domestic remedies before submitting the dispute to international arbitration. This requirement was not present in the Chile-Spain BIT. For further discussion see Singh 2004. See also Vesel 2007, and Egli 2007, who discuss *Maffezini* as well as several other disputes where tribunals have either accepted or rejected the use of most-favoured-nation clauses to import dispute settlement provisions from other treaties.

Another possible issue is the importation of pre-establishment rights into IIAs that only cover post-establishment rights.[25]

There are some common exceptions to most-favoured-nation treatment that can be found in IIAs: to exclude treatment provided under a customs union, common market or free trade area; and also, in some cases, to exclude matters of taxation, government procurement and subsidies.[26] For example, the Australia-Philippines BIT states that:

> The provisions of this Agreement relative to the grant of treatment not less favourable than that accorded to the investors of any third State shall not be construed as to oblige one Party to extend to investors of the other Party the benefit of any treatment, preference or privilege resulting from:
>
> (a) any existing or future customs union, common market, free trade area, regional economic organisation, interim agreement or arrangement leading to the formation of a customs union, common market, free trade area or regional economic organisation to which either Party is or may become a member or other arrangement for the facilitation of frontier trade; or
> (b) the provisions of a double taxation agreement with a third country.[27]

Agreements may also include specific exceptions to most-favoured-nation treatment.[28]

4.1.4 The minimum standard of treatment, fair and equitable treatment and full protection and security

The international minimum standard of treatment can essentially be thought of as a 'floor', below which the treatment of foreign investors should not fall. In other words, the standard protects investors from unjust treatment without reference to how domestic investors or other foreign investors are treated.

As noted in Section 3.1.1, it has long been debated whether or not such a minimum standard exists in customary international law. Defining the precise nature and content of the standard remains quite problematic, as it is rarely laid out explicitly in the texts of agreements. Referring to cases on state responsibility, one could conclude, as Sornarajah does, that the standard potentially relates to three areas: compensation for expropriation;

---

[25] UNCTAD 2007: 25.   [26] OECD 2004: 5.

[27] Agreement between the Government of Australia and the Government of the Republic of the Philippines on the Promotion and Protection of Investments, 25 January 1995, Manila: Art. 4.3.

[28] For examples of exceptions see UNCTAD 2007.

responsibility for destruction or violence by non-state actors; and denial of justice.[29] However, as expropriation is dealt with separately in IIAs, and responsibility for destruction or violence is usually covered by reference to 'full protection and security' (see below), the only content unique to the minimum standard would be 'denial of justice'. The principle of denial of justice derives from customary international law and relates to the conduct of national courts. As Paulsson notes: 'Some denials of justice may be readily recognised: refusal of access to court to defend legal rights, refusal to decide, unconscionable delay, manifest discrimination, corruption, or subservience to executive pressure.'[30] However, Paulsson goes on to argue that other cases are less clear-cut, and that there is no 'definitive list' of acts or omissions that constitute denials of justice.[31]

Attempts to delineate the boundaries of the minimum standard are further hindered by its ambiguous relationship with two other standards: fair and equitable treatment and full protection and security. In one set of agreements, including those negotiated by the US, UK, France, Japan and Canada, reference to fair and equitable treatment and full protection and security is found in the same article or paragraph as the minimum standard.[32] In a second set of agreements, including those negotiated by Germany, Switzerland and Sweden, fair and equitable treatment and full protection and security are autonomous standards.[33]

For example, NAFTA Article 1105.1 reads: 'Each Party shall accord to investments of investors of another Party treatment in accordance with international law, including fair and equitable treatment and full protection and security.' On the other hand, the Netherlands-Chile BIT states:

> Each Contracting Party shall ensure fair and equitable treatment to the investments of nationals of the other Contracting Party and shall not impair, by unreasonable or discriminatory measures, the operation, management, maintenance, use, enjoyment or disposal thereof by those nationals. Each Contracting Party shall accord to such investments full security and protection.

The Germany-India BIT simply states: 'Each Contracting Party shall accord to investments as well as investors in respect of such investments at all times fair and equitable treatment and full protection and security in its territory.'[34]

---

[29] Sornarajah 2004a: 330.   [30] Paulsson 2005: 204–5.   [31] *Ibid*: 205.
[32] Dolzer 2005: 961; Yannaca-Small 2004: 10.   [33] *Ibid*.
[34] Agreement between the Federal Republic of Germany and the Republic of India for the Promotion and Protection of Investments, 10 July 1995, Bonn: Art. 3.2.

Many BITs that fall into the second category combine fair and equitable treatment with national and most-favoured-nation treatment. For
example, the Denmark-Ethiopia BIT states that:

> Each Contracting Party shall in its territory accord to investments made by
> investors of the other Contracting Party fair and equitable treatment which
> in no case shall be less favourable than that accorded to its own investors
> or to investors of any third state, whichever is the more favourable from
> the point of view of the investor.[35]

Full protection and security is generally accepted to mean that failure
to provide protection to an alien threatened with violence creates state
responsibility.[36] Tribunals that have considered claims of violation of full
protection and security have generally interpreted the standard as requiring the host state to employ 'due diligence' in actively protecting foreign
investors from harm.[37]

It is far more difficult to pin down a universal definition of fair and
equitable treatment. If one interprets fair and equitable treatment as
synonymous with the international minimum standard, then the test
to determine whether it has been violated would be based on the existing
customary international law on state responsibility for injury to aliens.
This is considered an objective method, although debates continue to
rage on the content of customary law in this area and its evolution
over time (see further Section 7.5.2). If, on the other hand, one seeks
to use a case-by-case test based on the 'plain meaning' of the standard,
the evaluation is far less objective. An UNCTAD report suggests: 'the
concepts "fair" and "equitable" are by themselves inherently subject-
ive, and therefore lacking in precision'.[38] It is further noted in another
report by the same organization that the fair and equitable treatment
standard is 'less amenable to a technical specification than rules requiring national treatment and [most-favoured-nation] treatment of foreign
investors' and that an established body of law or existing legal precedents
to assist in the evaluation is lacking.[39] Nevertheless, there appears to be
broad support for the plain meaning approach in the investment law
literature.[40]

---

[35] Agreement between the Federal Democratic Republic of Ethiopia and the Kingdom of
Denmark Concerning the Promotion and Reciprocal Protection of Investments, 24 April
2001, Addis Ababa: Art. 3.1.
[36] Sornarajah 2004a: 342.   [37] Robbins 2006: 427.   [38] UNCTAD 1999a: 10.
[39] UNCTAD 2007: 29; UNCTAD 2004a: 80.   [40] Subedi 2008: 65.

Following a review of recent arbitral awards, Westcott concluded that 'ensuring stability of the business and legal framework is now an established element of fair and equitable treatment'.[41] The ILA International Law on Foreign Investment Committee extends this even further suggesting that 'certain elements of an emergent standard of review of administrative action appear to be taking shape' which reflect 'contemporary approaches to good governance'.[42] In the view of the ILA International Law on Foreign Investment Committee, fair and equitable treatment requires quite significant obligations on the part of the host state:

> it is now reasonably well settled that the standard requires a particular approach to governance, on the part of the host country, that is encapsulated in the obligations to act in a consistent manner, free from ambiguity and in total transparency, without arbitrariness and in accordance with the principle of good faith. In addition, investors can expect due process in the handling of their claims and to have the authorities act in a manner that is non-discriminatory and proportionate to the policy aims involved. These will include the need to observe the goal of creating favourable investment conditions and the observance of the legitimate commercial expectations of the investor.[43]

With regard to the last point, about the observance of an investor's legitimate commercial expectations,[44] this is an issue that has also emerged in discussions of expropriation (see Section 4.1.5.2). As Coe and Rubins explain:

---

[41] Westcott 2007: 425.

[42] ILA International Law on Foreign Investment Committee 2006: 16. For examples of common definitions of good governance see those developed by: the OECD, www.oecd.org; the United Nations Development Programme, www.undp.org; the UN Office of the High Commissioner for Human Rights, www.unhchr.ch; the Asian Development Bank, www.adb.org; the Australian Parliament, www.aph.gov.au; and the Canadian International Development Agency, www.acdi-cida.gc.ca. See also the Convention on Access to Information, Public Participation in Decision-Making and Access to Justice in Environmental Matters, 25 June 1998, Aarhus, www.unece.org, reproduced in 38 ILM (1999): 517.

[43] ILA International Law on Foreign Investment Committee 2006: 16. Yannaca-Small 2004: 26, identifies similar categories of obligation falling under the fair and equitable treatment standard including: the obligation of vigilance and protection; due process including non-denial of justice and lack of arbitrariness; transparency; and good faith (which could cover transparency and lack of arbitrariness). See also Behrens 2007: 175, who lists good faith, non-discrimination, lack of arbitrariness, due process, transparency, consistency and proportionality as the key requirements of fair and equitable treatment.

[44] Also commonly referred to as simply 'legitimate' or 'reasonable' expectations, or 'reasonable investment-backed' expectations.

Under a common view of international investment law, the foreign investor
and host State are entitled to have the governmental interference with
the investor's enterprise considered in light of the investor's chosen business model, the nature of its enterprise, the regulatory regime in place at
the time of investment, and associated expectations. In recent practice,
this has sometimes been expressed in terms of the investor's reasonable
'investment-backed expectations' a formula invoked by disputants and
now found within certain investment treaties.[45]

An investor's expectations may be based on treaties signed by the host
state, national law, administrative licences or permits and even brochures
and other materials designed to entice foreigners to invest in the state.[46]
Additionally, as noted in Section 5.1.1.4, stabilization clauses in foreign
investment contracts are viewed by some as creating legitimate expectations amongst investors that certain regulations will not change over a
given period of time.

A final issue of contention concerns whether the failure to provide
other standards of treatment, such as national or most-favoured-nation
treatment, constitutes a breach of fair and equitable treatment as well.[47]
An UNCTAD report suggests that 'although some instances of practice
support the notion that the fair and equitable treatment encompasses
the other treatment standards in most investment instruments, this is the
minority position'.[48]

Some governments, particularly in the NAFTA context, appear to have
realized that the ambiguity of the fair and equitable treatment standard
may give arbitrators too much discretion. In the early cases under NAFTA,
tribunals had a propensity toward an expansive view of the standard,
which greatly increased arbitral power to determine whether state acts
were in compliance with the agreement.[49] In 2001, the NAFTA Free Trade
Commission (FTC) issued Notes of Interpretation of Certain Chapter 11
Provisions, rejecting the interpretation of the standard that some tribunals
had proffered by clarifying that fair and equitable treatment and full protection and security do not require treatment in addition to or beyond that
which is required by the customary international law minimum standard
of treatment.[50]

The standard has also been more explicitly defined in recent Canadian
and American IIAs. The 2004 US Model BIT clarifies that the minimum

---

[45] Coe and Rubins 2005: 624.   [46] Madalena 2003: 77.   [47] UNCTAD 1999a: 35.
[48] *Ibid*: 37.   [49] CIEL 2003b: 5.
[50] Notes of Interpretation of Certain Chapter 11 Provisions, NAFTA Free Trade Commission
(FTC), 31 July 2001, www.state.gov/documents/organization/38790.pdf.

standard of treatment does not entail anything beyond that provided in customary international law.[51] An accompanying annex defines customary international law as resulting 'from a general and consistent practice of States that they follow from a sense of legal obligation' and specifies that the minimum standard refers 'to all customary international law principles that protect the economic rights and interests of aliens'. The Model also explicitly spells out that a 'determination that there has been a breach of another provision of this Treaty, or of a separate international agreement, does not establish that there has been a breach of this Article'.[52] The 2003 Canadian Model Foreign Investment Promotion and Protection Agreement also stipulates that the minimum standard only requires treatment in line with customary international law, and that a breach of another provision or agreement does not establish a breach of the standard.[53]

4.1.5   Expropriation

As noted in Chapter 3, the direct taking of foreign property has historically been one of the most significant risks to foreign investment. Outright takings are now considered rare in most parts of the world, although recent events in Latin America are a reminder that direct expropriations are not completely a thing of the past.[54] However, with time, the meaning of expropriation has changed. As Lipson points out: 'It is important to remember that the social meaning of expropriation is neither intrinsic nor immutable. Its meaning, and that of investment protection, must be continually reestablished.'[55]

At the moment, the debate over expropriation primarily concerns the way it has been expanded to cover so-called *indirect* expropriation. Indirect expropriation falls short of actual physical taking of property but results in 'the effective loss of management, use or control, or a significant depreciation of the value of the assets of a foreign investor'.[56] Soloway suggests that 'an indirect expropriation can take an infinite number of forms; it can be

---

[51] Treaty between the Government of the United States of America and the Government of [Country] Concerning the Encouragement and Reciprocal Protection of Investment (US Model BIT), 2004: Art. 5, www.state.gov.

[52] *Ibid.*

[53] Agreement between Canada and .... for the Promotion and Protection of Investments (Canadian Model BIT), 2003: Art. 5, www.international.gc.ca.

[54] In 2006, Bolivia, Ecuador and Venezuela made moves to nationalize oil and gas reserves. See Jacobs and Paulson 2008.

[55] Lipson 1985: 31–2.   [56] UNCTAD 2000b: 4.

essentially *any action, omission, or measure* attributable to a government that interferes with the rights flowing from the foreign-owned property to an extent that the property has been functionally expropriated'.[57]

Indirect expropriations have variously been referred to in IIAs by language such as measures having a 'similar' or 'equivalent' effect to expropriation. For example, the Finland-Brazil BIT states that:

> Investments of investors of each Contracting Party shall not be nationalized, expropriated or subjected to *measures having a similar effect* (hereinafter referred to as 'expropriation') in the territory of the other Contracting Party . . .[58]

In the case of some IIAs, such as NAFTA, reference is made to measures 'tantamount' to expropriation; this language has been particularly contentious in investment arbitration (see Sections 7.2.2, 7.2.4 and 7.3.1).

For further clarity, a distinction can be made between 'creeping expropriations' and 'regulatory takings'. Creeping expropriations involve the slow and incremental encroachment on the ownership rights of a foreign investor, leading to the devaluation of the investment.[59] Regulatory takings, are defined by UNCTAD as 'those takings of property that fall within the police powers of a State, or otherwise arise from State measures like those pertaining to the regulation of the environment, health, morals, culture or economy of a host country'.[60] The latter form of indirect expropriation is of particular importance in this study.

4.1.5.1 Regulatory takings

It is not a simple matter to determine when regulation crosses the invisible line of what is acceptable and what is not. Soloway explains the difficulty in demarcating the boundaries of regulatory takings:

> If the definition is too expansive, the argument goes, it could impose potentially huge financial obligations on governments, create disincentives to enact health and safety regulations and introduce multiple distortions and social inefficiencies. On the other hand, a definition that is too restrictive would obliterate a key investment guarantee that protects foreign investors.[61]

---

[57] Soloway 2002: 133, emphasis added.
[58] Agreement between the Government of the Republic of Finland and the Government of the Federative Republic of Brazil on the Promotion and Protection of Investments, 28 March 1995, Brasilia: Art. 5.1, emphasis added.
[59] UNCTAD 2000b: 11.   [60] *Ibid*: 12.   [61] Soloway 2002: 31.

The issue of regulatory takings is also not confined purely to inter-national investment law. Some countries, notably the US, have strong domestic protections against regulatory takings,[62] and furthermore both the European Court of Human Rights and the European Court of Justice have issued significant decisions on indirect expropriation under Article 1, Protocol 1 of the European Convention for the Protection of Human Rights and Fundamental Freedoms (European Convention).[63] However, given the significance of this issue, and the potential implications for states, Byrne argues that the characterization of regulatory takings should be a matter of international consensus and: 'Consequently, it should not be assumed that the principles developed by any particular municipal or regional legal systems, for example, the US and the EU, can be automat-ically applied on a global basis.'[64] Furthermore, while the jurisprudence in these arenas may have some relevance to an understanding of the interna-tional law on expropriation, the standard set in the US Constitution and the European Convention differs significantly from that found in most IIAs.[65]

Another source of potential 'precedent' on indirect expropriation is the decisions of the Iran-United States Claims Tribunal. However, as Been and Beauvais point out, these dealt 'primarily with postrevolutionary actions such as governmental appointment of managers or supervisors of foreign companies, *de facto* nationalization, and failure to permit the exportation of foreign-owned equipment'.[66] In other words, the cases addressed government actions that are radically different from the type of regulatory takings that may arise in the environmental context.

4.1.5.2   The effects test and police powers

In establishing whether or not a regulatory taking has occurred, tri-bunals have tended to adopt one of two basic approaches. Under the first approach, the tribunal focuses solely on the *effect* of the regulation on the investor.[67] Those subscribing to the second approach will also examine the effect of a measure on an investor, but will additionally address the *purpose* of the regulation and assess whether it falls under the state's police powers.[68]

---

[62] The US Constitution contains specific protections against uncompensated takings in the Fifth and Fourteenth Amendments. See Been and Beauvais 2003.
[63] Been and Beauvais 2003: 56.   [64] Byrne 2000: 118.   [65] Been and Beauvais 2003: 56.
[66] *Ibid*: 58.   [67] Fortier and Drymer 2004: 300.
[68] Newcombe 2007b: 417; Mann and Soloway 2002.

As Gudofsky explains, the 'sole effect' or 'effects' test requires a tribunal to 'establish a line between when a government's measure goes "too far" and imposes too great an interference with the use and enjoyment of property'.[69] In evaluating the effect of a measure, tribunals will likely examine both the economic impact and the duration of the measure. While outside of IIA arbitration (e.g., in the European Court of Human Rights) there is indication that the investment must be rendered valueless or that the economic impact be at least 'severe' or 'substantial' for a measure to qualify as an expropriation, IIA tribunals place a stronger emphasis on the legitimate expectations of the investor.[70]

Muse-Fisher suggests that, in the context of regulatory takings, there is a two-part test to determine the reasonable investment-backed expectations of an investor:

(i) the tribunal must determine whether the investor had an actual expectation that his property would not be affected by a given regulation when he purchased it; and
(ii) if he did have such an expectation, the tribunal must evaluate whether this expectation was reasonable.[71]

The US courts have been hesitant to find an investor's expectations reasonable when he is entering a heavily regulated jurisdiction, particularly if newly enacted legislation only builds on the existing framework.[72] International investment tribunals have been less consistent in this respect (see Section 7.5.1). In addition to the severity of the economic impact of a measure, tribunals are also likely to consider its temporal aspect. A measure that is permanent, or of long duration, is more likely to be considered an expropriation than one that is temporary in nature.[73]

The task is even more complicated for a tribunal that chooses to examine the purpose of a measure in addition to its effect. The definition and scope of a state's 'police powers' are not agreed upon and it is debated whether they are quite strictly circumscribed to cover only measures necessary for the maintenance of public order and safety, or are broad enough to cover environmental regulation more generally.[74] Given the difficulty of drawing a 'bright line' between *bona fide* non-compensable regulation

---

[69] Gudofsky 2000: 259–60.
[70] Gutbrod and Hindelang 2006: 65; Fortier and Drymer 2004: 307. It can be recalled from the discussion above that investor expectations may also be factored into an evaluation of whether treatment has been fair and equitable.
[71] Muse-Fisher 2007: 518–19.   [72] *Ibid.*   [73] Coe and Rubins 2005: 620.
[74] See Muse-Fisher 2007; Baughen 2006; Turk 2005.

and a taking, many commentators and arbitral tribunals suggest that such a determination can only be achieved on a case-by-case basis.[75]

In order to deal with some of the difficulties in defining a regulatory taking, the 2004 US Model BIT and the 2003 Canadian Model BIT have both included an annex that lays out a three-part test, drawn from American jurisprudence, for the determination of whether a regulatory taking has occurred.[76] The factors to be considered are: the economic impact of the government action; the extent to which the government action interferes with distinct, reasonable investment-backed expectations; and the character of the government action.[77] The US Model BIT Annex also has a provision which states that:

> Except in rare circumstances, nondiscriminatory regulatory actions by a Party that are designed and applied to achieve legitimate public welfare objectives, such as the protection of public health, safety, and the environment, do not constitute indirect expropriations.[78]

The Canadian Model BIT contains a similar statement.[79]

4.1.5.3   The legality of expropriation

A regulatory measure which has been determined to constitute a taking can be assessed for legality in the same way as a direct expropriation.[80] According to customary international law and most IIAs, there are three conditions that must be satisfied for a taking to be lawful: it must be for a public purpose, it must be non-discriminatory and compensation must be paid to the affected investor. Some BITs and regional agreements also include a fourth condition, referred to as 'due process'. For example, the Japan-Sri Lanka BIT states that:

> Investments and returns of nationals and companies of either Contracting Party shall not be subjected to expropriation, nationalization, restriction or any other measure the effects of which would be tantamount to expropriation or nationalization, within the territory of the other Contracting Party unless such measures are taken for a public purpose and under due process of law; are not discriminatory; and, are taken against prompt, adequate and effective compensation.[81]

---

[75] Fortier and Drymer 2004: 314.
[76] Parisi 2005: 417; Muse-Fisher 2007: 509.
[77] US Model BIT: Annex B.4(a); Canadian Model BIT: Annex B.13(1).
[78] US Model BIT: Annex B.4(b).   [79] Canadian Model BIT: Annex B.13(1)(c).
[80] Reisman and Sloane 2003: 121.
[81] Japan and Sri Lanka Agreement Concerning the Promotion and Protection of Investments, 1 March 1982, Colombo: Art. 5.2.

Public purpose is fairly straightforward and certainly includes the protection of the environment.[82] However, it is important to stress that if a regulatory measure *is found to be a taking*, fulfilment of the public purpose requirement does not lead to a determination that compensation is not required. All three (or four) conditions must be fulfilled for an expropriation to be legal.[83]

Traditionally, non-discrimination required that any taking should not unreasonably single out a particular person or group of people, such as measures of retaliation or reprisal against another state or a particular racial group.[84] However, increasingly the scope of this requirement has expanded to cover any discriminatory or arbitrary action, or any action that is without legitimate justification, even if specific nationals are not targeted.[85]

Due process, a concept borrowed from the American legal system, generally requires that the regulation is made in accordance with host state law and that affected parties are given access to municipal courts if they choose to challenge the government measure.[86]

Akinsanya's statement in 1980 that the requirement for, and measurement of, compensation was 'the most important, and most controversial, issue of all rules governing expropriation of foreign property' remains accurate today.[87] There is a long-standing international debate over compensation that generally falls on a North-South divide. As mentioned in Section 3.1.1.1, capital-exporting states have long advocated the Hull formula as a means to calculate compensation. It dictates that compensation should be prompt, adequate and effective. In contrast to this, the 'appropriate compensation' doctrine often favoured by developing countries suggests a more complex calculation which factors in other considerations, such as the past practices of the investor, the depletion of natural resources or environmental damage that has occurred as a result of the investment, and the economic situation of the country.[88] Despite the fact that developing countries have historically objected to the Hull formula and have vehemently denied that it represents customary international

---

[82] It is important to emphasize that 'police powers' and 'public purpose' are different in both scope and form. The former is narrow and acts as an exception to the requirement for compensation, while the latter is broad and acts as a condition for an expropriation to be defined as legal under international law.

[83] Turk 2005: 69.   [84] UNCTAD 2000b: 13.   [85] *Ibid.*   [86] Madalena 2003: 77.
[87] Akinsanya 1980: 25.   [88] UNCTAD 2000b: 14.

law, they have signed numerous IIAs that contain obligations that are equally or even more demanding than this formula.[89]

Guidance for tribunals on how the specific amount of compensation in a given case should be determined is typically limited. Vague terms such as 'fair market value' or 'genuine value' are often used. For example, a BIT between the US and Bolivia states that:

> Compensation shall be paid without delay; be equivalent to the fair mar-ket value of the investment immediately before the expropriatory action was taken ('the date of expropriation'); and be fully realizable and freely transferable. The fair market value shall not reflect any change in value occurring because the expropriatory action had become known before the date of expropriation.[90]

There is no single valuation method that binds tribunals, and while investment agreements may provide some general indicators as to what should be considered in a calculation of the value of an expropriated prop-erty, relatively few provide for specific methods.[91] The two most common methods used by tribunals are net book value (NBV) and discounted cash flow (DCF).[92]

4.1.6   *Performance requirements*

Performance requirements are stipulations imposed by governments on investors requiring them to meet certain criteria, such as the exporta-tion of a certain percentage of production, the purchase of local products and services, or the employment of local labour. The aim of a perfor-mance requirement is to protect local entrepreneurs, to some extent, and to enhance the overall contribution of foreign investment to local

---

[89] See Guzman 1998, who uses a prisoner's dilemma game to explain why developing countries have accepted the Hull formula for compensation in BITs when they have traditionally rejected it in favour of an appropriate compensation doctrine. See also Bubb and Rose-Ackerman 2007, who offer an alternative explanation.

[90] Treaty between the Government of the United States of America and the Government of the Republic of Bolivia Concerning the Encouragement and Reciprocal Protection of Investment, 17 April 1998, Santiago: Art. III.2.

[91] Coe and Rubins 2005: 629; UNCTAD 2004a: 73.

[92] NBV is calculated based on the difference between a company's recorded assets and liabil-ities. DCF is calculated by discounting (based on inflation, etc.) the net cash flow (based on the anticipated future income and expenditures) of an investment over its potential lifespan. On the one hand, NBV has been criticized for not reflecting the cash-generating ability of a company, while on the other hand, it has been suggested that DCF is purely speculative and often generates an inflated value. For further discussion see Sabahi 2007: 564–7.

development.[93] However, there are divergent views as to the efficacy of performance requirements in these respects.[94]

Developed capital-exporting countries tend to view performance requirements as trade-distorting (and they have been addressed to some extent in the WTO), and certain countries, particularly Canada and the US, include provisions on the elimination of performance requirements in their IIAs. However, articles on performance requirements often contain an exception clause modelled on Article XX of the GATT. For example, NAFTA's provision on performance requirements is accompanied by the following text:

> Provided that such measures are not applied in an arbitrary or unjustifiable manner, or do not constitute a disguised restriction on international trade or investment, nothing in paragraph 1(b) or (c) or 3(a) or (b) shall be construed to prevent any Party from adopting or maintaining measures, including environmental measures:
>
> (a) necessary to secure compliance with laws and regulations that are not inconsistent with the provisions of this Agreement;
> (b) *necessary to protect human, animal or plant life or health*; or
> (c) *necessary for the conservation of living or non-living exhaustible natural resources.*[95]

4.1.7   Observance of obligations

Foreign investment contracts and their implications for environmental governance are discussed in the next chapter. However, it is worth noting here that there is considerable debate and divergent opinion, not only in academia but also seemingly amongst arbitrators, about the relationship between breach of contract and breach of treaty. As an UNCTAD report reflects, 'it is generally accepted that not every breach of State contract on the part of the State automatically entails a violation of international law, or a breach of an applicable IIA'.[96] There are thus independent standards for determining breach of contract and breach of treaty. However, it is possible for government action in relation to an investment protected under contract to amount to a breach of treaty, such as in the case of an expropriation or when a state's actions or omissions amount to a denial of justice.[97]

---

[93] Sornarajah 2004a: 237.   [94] UNCTAD 2003: 2.
[95] NAFTA: Art. 1106.6, emphasis added.   [96] UNCTAD 2004b: 9.
[97] *Ibid*: 10; Foy 2003: 75–6; Schreuer 2005: 298.

The debate chiefly rests on the effect of so-called umbrella clauses. Some IIAs, in fact approximately 40 per cent of existing BITs,[98] contain such provisions, which refer to the 'observance of obligations' undertaken by host states with respect to foreign investors.[99] For example, the UK-Jamaica BIT states that 'each Contracting Party shall observe any obligations it may have entered into with regard to investments of nationals or companies of the other Contracting Party'.[100]

Dolzer and Stevens have asserted that umbrella clauses protect an investor's contractual rights against 'any interference which might be caused by either a simple breach of contract or by administrative or legislative acts'.[101] Schreuer similarly argues that the purpose of the umbrella clause is to 'add extra protection' and to dispense 'with the often difficult proof that there has been an indirect expropriation or a violation of the fair and equitable standard under the treaty'.[102] In this view, a violation of a foreign investment contract automatically translates into a violation of an applicable IIA.[103] If this is the case, arguably an investor could get around a contractual provision that expressly placed disputes within the purview of the domestic courts of the host state.[104] However, this view falls into only one of several schools of thought on the nature of umbrella clauses.[105] As Cheng notes, the decisions of ten tribunals that have considered umbrella clauses are inconsistent, with five tribunals taking the view that the umbrella clauses in the respective BITs did not transform the purported contractual breaches of the host state into treaty breaches, and five tribunals finding that the umbrella clause could or did transform at least some contractual obligations into treaty obligations (though they differed on the precise scope of this transformation).[106]

While an investor faced with a choice of treaty rights and contract rights will normally choose to enforce the former,[107] it may be possible for an investor to pursue both types of claim. If the contract provides for international arbitration, this can lead to duplicative and potentially inconsistent tribunal awards.

---

[98] Figure cited in UNCTAD 2007: 73.   [99] UNCTAD 2004b: 19.
[100] Agreement between the Government of the United Kingdom of Great Britain and Northern Ireland and the Government of Jamaica for the Promotion and Protection of Investments, 20 January 1987, Kingston: Art. 8.
[101] Dolzer and Stevens 1995: 82.   [102] Schreuer 2005: 301.   [103] UNCTAD 2004b: 10.
[104] Subedi 2008: 96.   [105] Maniruzzaman 2008: 153.   [106] Cheng 2007: 1139.
[107] Cremades and Cairns 2004: 332.

4.1.8   *Environmental issues*

There are several ways in which concerns about the protection of the environment have been incorporated into IIAs. Preambular statements are one way; for example, the 2004 US Model BIT states in the preamble that the Parties are: 'Desiring to achieve these objectives in a manner consistent with the protection of health, safety, and the environment.'

However, this practice is not widespread, even in recent treaties. Newcombe reviewed seventy-one BITs dated between 2001 and 2005 and found very limited reference to sustainable development or the environment in the preambles of these agreements.[108] However, he notes that trade agreements (which may contain chapters on investment) are more likely to have such preambular statements.[109]

4.1.8.1   Consistency and pollution havens provisions

Another way in which IIAs may address environmental concerns is through general statements on the adoption and/or enforcement of environmental laws. These types of clauses come in two forms, which are referred to here as 'consistency provisions' and 'pollution havens provisions'.

Consistency provisions are statements that reiterate that governments are not prevented from adopting or enforcing environmental regulations which are *otherwise consistent* with the rest of the agreement. For example, the 2004 US Model BIT states that:

> Nothing in this Chapter shall be construed to prevent a Party from adopting, maintaining, or enforcing any measure otherwise consistent with this Chapter that it considers appropriate to ensure that investment activity in its territory is undertaken in a manner sensitive to environmental concerns.[110]

This provision is not novel; it copies Article 1114.1 of NAFTA.

Pollution havens provisions are statements discouraging countries from lowering environmental standards to attract investment. For example, the 2003 Canadian Model BIT states that:

> The Parties recognize that it is inappropriate to encourage investment by relaxing domestic health, safety or environmental measures. Accordingly, a Party should not waive or otherwise derogate from, or offer to waive

---

[108] Newcombe 2007a: 399.   [109] *Ibid.*
[110] US Model BIT: Art. 12.2. This provision has been incorporated into all new US BITs and FTAs, including the CAFTA-DR (Art. 10.11).

or otherwise derogate from, such measures as an encouragement for the establishment, acquisition, expansion or retention in its territory of an investment of an investor. If a Party considers that the other Party has offered such an encouragement, it may request consultations with the other Party and the two Parties shall consult with a view to avoiding any such encouragement.[111]

Again, this text has been drawn from NAFTA (Article 1114.2). The CAFTA-DR has slightly stronger wording:

(a) A Party shall not fail to effectively enforce its environmental laws, through a sustained or recurring course of action or inaction, in a manner affecting trade between the Parties, after the date of entry into force of this Agreement.

(b) The Parties recognize that each Party retains the right to exercise discretion with respect to investigatory, prosecutorial, regulatory, and compliance matters and to make decisions regarding the allocation of resources to enforcement with respect to other environmental matters determined to have higher priorities. Accordingly, the Parties understand that a Party is in compliance with subparagraph (a) where a course of action or inaction reflects a reasonable exercise of such discretion, or results from a bona fide decision regarding the allocation of resources.[112]

It is further stated in the CAFTA-DR that:

The Parties recognize that it is inappropriate to encourage trade or investment by weakening or reducing the protections afforded in domestic environmental laws. Accordingly, each Party shall strive to ensure that it does not waive or otherwise derogate from, or offer to waive or otherwise derogate from, such laws in a manner that weakens or reduces the protections afforded in those laws as an encouragement for trade with another Party, or as an encouragement for the establishment, acquisition, expansion, or retention of an investment in its territory.[113]

The 2004 US Model BIT contains the same wording.[114] Interestingly, the proposed FTAA additionally provides that:

[For smaller economies, a commitment not to relax domestic environmental laws should be allied with compensating access to the Hemispheric Cooperation Program for the purpose of introducing more modern machinery and industrial practices that would better protect the environment.][115]

---

[111] Canadian Model BIT: Art. 11.   [112] CAFTA-DR: Art. 1017.1.
[113] *Ibid*: Art. 1017.2.   [114] US model BIT: Art. 12.1.   [115] Draft FTAA: Art. 1719.2.

4.1.8.2 Chapters on the environment

The US has recently negotiated several FTAs which, in addition to containing chapters on investment, also contain chapters on the environment. In relation to investment, these environment chapters generally contain pollution havens type provisions, but unlike those found in standard BITs, these provisions are backed up by an enforcement mechanism. Parties may request the establishment of an arbitration panel to consider instances of a breach of the obligation to enforce environmental laws, which can impose an annual monetary fee of up to US$15 million per year, payable into a bilateral fund for environmental initiatives.[116] The FTAs also provide that in the event of inconsistency between the investment chapter of the agreement and the environment chapter, the latter shall prevail.[117] However, as Gagné and Morin are quick to point out:

> It is still unclear when an inconsistency between the two chapters can occur because a state can be forced under the labour and environment chapters to enforce a law discriminating against foreign investments and, at the same time, be forced under the investment chapter to offer monetary damages to foreign investors.[118]

COASE THEOREM

The authors hypothesize that the environment chapter may at least influence negotiations between an investor and a host state, because states will not want to risk an international dispute with another state over the non-enforcement of an environmental law. However, this claim seems somewhat dubious. One can question whether states will be willing to bring other states before arbitration for non-enforcement of environmental law, when they risk the mechanism being used against them in turn.

4.2 Environmental impact assessments

The newest generation of IIAs have been negotiated under increased scrutiny. In the US and Canada, this scrutiny has included formal assessments of the environmental impacts of the agreements.

---

[116] CAFTA-DR: Art. 20.17; US–Singapore FTA, 6 May 2003, Washington, DC: Art. 20.7; US–Chile FTA, 6 June 2003, Miami: Art. 22.16; US-Australia FTA, 18 May 2004, Washington, DC: Art. 21.12; US–Morocco FTA, 15 June 2004, Washington, DC: Art. 20.12.

[117] US-Singapore FTA: Art. 15.2; US-Chile FTA: Art. 10.2; US-Australia FTA: Art. 11.2; CAFTA-DR: Art. 10.2; US-Morocco FTA: Art. 10.2.

[118] Gagné and Morin 2006: 379–81.

4.2.1   United States

The development of the 2004 US Model BIT, and the subsequent negotiation of BITs and FTAs following this model, was within the broader
framework of the Bipartisan Trade Promotion Authority Act of 2002
(TPA). The TPA was developed, in part, to address concerns relating
to the investor-state dispute settlement process in trade agreements like
NAFTA. Investment provisions, and the question of the appropriate balance between investment protection and the ability of government to
regulate, were reportedly 'a matter of intense debate' during Congress's
consideration of the TPA.[119]

The TPA established a number of negotiating objectives and other priorities relating to the environment. Under the TPA and following a framework outlined in Executive Order 13141, all new investment and trade
agreements are to undergo an environmental impact assessment (EIA).[120]
It is stipulated that 'as a general matter, the focus of environmental reviews
will be impacts in the United States, [but] [a]s appropriate and prudent,
reviews may also examine global and transboundary impacts'.[121] Generally, the EIAs address two types of questions:

(i) the extent to which positive and negative environmental impacts may
    flow from economic changes estimated to result from the prospective
    agreement; and
(ii) the extent to which proposed agreement provisions may affect US
    environmental laws and regulations (including, as appropriate, the
    ability of state, local and tribal authorities to regulate with respect to
    environmental matters).

The Office of the US Trade Representative (USTR) conducted a number
of these EIAs in 2004. All of the reports emanating from the assessments
concluded that there would be no significant impact of the investment provisions of the agreements on the environment. For example, the authors
of the review of the CAFTA-DR claim that they 'were unable to identify any concrete instances of US environmental measures that would be
inconsistent with the Agreement's substantive investment obligations'.[122]
Furthermore, the report notes that the innovations in the agreement's
substantive obligations and investor-state dispute settlement procedures

---

[119] Final Environmental Review of the CAFTA-DR, 22 February 2005: 29, www.ustr.gov.
[120] Environmental Review of Trade Agreements, 64 Fed. Reg. 63169, and the Associated
Guidelines, 65 Fed. Reg. 79442, www.ustr.gov.
[121] Executive Order 13141: Section 5(b).   [122] CAFTA-DR Final Environmental Review: 2.

'should provide coherence to the interpretation of the FTA's investment provisions'.[123] The reviewers do acknowledge that the CAFTA-DR might have a greater impact on the *other states* party to the agreement, but suggest that the specific environmental implications cannot currently be predicted. Similarly, the review of the US-Chile FTA concluded that the agreement 'would not significantly affect the ability of U.S. governmental entities to regulate in order to meet domestic health, safety, and environmental policy objectives', and noted that the revisions of the investment provisions:

> provide greater clarity to the substantive investment obligations, significantly increase the transparency of the procedures for arbitrating investor claims, and help ensure that arbitral tribunals will interpret the investment provisions in accordance with the Parties' intent.[124]

The same conclusions are reached in the EIA of the US-Singapore FTA and the US-Morocco FTA.[125]

4.2.2 Canada

In 1999, a Cabinet Directive on Environmental Assessment of Policy, Plan and Program Proposals was promulgated, leading to the development of the 2001 Framework for the Environmental Assessment of Trade Negotiations. This framework covers Canada's BIT programme. According to the government website:

> The Government of Canada is committed to sustainable development. Mutually supportive trade, investment and environmental policies can contribute to this objective. To this end, the Minister of International Trade, with the support of his Cabinet colleagues, has directed trade officials to improve their understanding of, and information based on, the relationship between trade, investment and environmental issues at the earliest stages of decision making, and to do this through an open and inclusive process. Environmental assessments of trade and investment negotiations are critical to this work.[126]

---

[123] *Ibid.*
[124] Final Environmental Review of the U.S.-Chile Free Trade Agreement, June 2003: 5, www.ustr.gov.
[125] Final Environmental Review of the U.S.-Singapore Free Trade Agreement, 2003; Final Environmental Review of the United States-Morocco Free Trade Agreement, July 2004, www.ustr.gov.
[126] 'Regional and Bilateral Initiatives', Foreign Affairs and International Trade Canada website, www.international.gc.ca, accessed 17 December 2008.

The BIT with Peru was the first to be evaluated under the programme. Negotiations on the agreement recommenced in December 2003, following a hiatus of several years, and were based on the new Model BIT. An initial EIA was released for public comment in 2005.[127] The methodology of the assessment was to identify 'the likely economic effects of the [BIT] and, on this basis, [draw] conclusions about the potential environmental impacts *in Canada*'.[128] The report notes that Peru's total investment in Canada is small, at only CAD$1 million in 2003, and suggests that the BIT is not likely to change this situation significantly. On the other hand, the stock of Canadian foreign investment in Peru is significant, totalling CAD$1,790 million in 2003. The majority of this investment was in the mineral sector, an industry well known for its environmental impact. While the assessment does not rule out the possibility that Canadian investment in Peru may increase, it suggests that the protection of *existing* Canadian investment in the country is likely to be the main effect of the BIT.

As noted in the report, 'it is outside of the scope' of the study 'to assess the potential for positive or negative environmental impacts that could occur in Peru because of these negotiations, or to judge the measures in place within Peru to enhance or mitigate such impacts'. The Initial Environmental Assessment concludes that 'significant changes to investment flows into Canada are not expected as a result of these negotiations' and therefore 'the economic effects and resulting environmental impact in Canada are expected to be minimal to non-existent'. The assessment also concludes that the BIT 'will not have a negative effect on Canada's ability to develop and implement environmental policies and regulations'. The reasoning on this issue is based partly on the belief that the adjustments to the Model BIT (used as a template for the Peru agreement) deal effectively with this issue, as well as the fact that it is not anticipated that the BIT will result in significant inflows of investment into Canada from Peru (i.e., there will be no Peruvian investors to challenge Canada's laws under the agreement).

Despite the fact that it is repeatedly emphasized throughout the Peru assessment that the only aim of the EIA is to consider environmental impacts occurring within Canada, or transboundary impacts that can be shown to impact Canada's environment, the majority of public comments

---

[127] Initial Environmental Assessment of the Canada-Peru Foreign Investment Protection Agreement, 2005, www.international.gc.ca.

[128] *Ibid.*, emphasis added.

received by the committee responsible for the EIA pertained to the environmental impact of Canadian investment in Peru. While these comments were acknowledged, the negotiations for the Canada-Peru BIT were concluded successfully on 14 November 2006, with no modification to the environment-related provisions of the BIT model.

NGOs have expressed concern that the EIA process is ignoring the fundamental issue of the impacts of Canadian investors abroad, but there has been no change as of yet in the protocol. In the case of the most recent BIT (with Madagascar) to be evaluated, the assessors came to largely the same conclusions as those that looked at the Peru BIT; no significant investment flows to Canada, and therefore no significant environmental impact *for Canada*.[129]

4.3 Potential implications for environmental governance

As should be evident from the discussion in this chapter, standards of investment protection laid out in IIAs are often vague and imprecise and therefore open to a significant degree of interpretation. While Chapter 7 will explore how arbitrators have interpreted these standards in relation to environmental regulation in practice, it is worthwhile to first explore some of the potential implications of these standards that have been postulated in the literature.

4.3.1 Preferential treatment on environmental grounds

Observers have noted that discrimination (or 'preferential treatment', to use a less derogatory term) can, in some circumstances, be desirable from an environmental policy perspective.[130] Von Moltke also argues that given the limited resources of environmental authorities and the challenges of implementing environmental law, some degree of 'selective enforcement' is inevitable.[131] Criteria such as the nature of the environmental threat, the past history of a company, or public pressure may be of more relevance to an environmental regulator than nationality.[132] Examples of preferential measures that could conflict with the national treatment standard include:

(i) requiring higher environmental standards and cleaner technologies in foreign-owned operations than in domestic ones;[133]

---

[129] Final Environmental Assessment of the Canada-Madagascar Foreign Investment Protection and Promotion Agreement 2009, www.international.gc.ca.
[130] Downes 1999: 16; Clémençon 2000: 208; Mann and Araya 2002: 169.
[131] von Moltke 2002: 358.   [132] *Ibid.*   [133] Clémençon 2000: 208.

(ii) granting special land-use and resource exploitation rights to local communities and indigenous groups, in line with the Convention on Biological Diversity's measures to protect customary use;[134] and

(iii) requiring foreign investors to put up bonds or provide insurance guarantees to cover clean-up costs or reclamation efforts following the completion of the investment project (not required from domestic investors who cannot 'cut and run' before environmental requirements are fulfilled).[135]

With regard to most-favoured-nation treatment, Clémençon rightly points out that:

> Effective implementation of environmental agreements may depend on provisions that oblige Member countries to treat companies from non-Member countries (or from Member countries that are in violation of the agreement) differently from companies from complying Member countries.[136]

It is unclear whether tribunals will be willing to take such issues into account in the assessment of the 'circumstances' of different investors.

4.3.2   Environmental performance requirements

Provisions on performance requirements are not as widespread as those on standards of treatment, but when they are present in an IIA they may have implications for environmental governance. Freedman notes that prohibitions on performance requirements could affect environmental measures requiring the provision of certain emissions data and other environmental information.[137] According to a recent publication of the ILA International Law on Foreign Investment Committee:

> the scope of restrictions on entry and establishment rights may need to be considered further. A particular new issue here may arise in relation to environmental restrictions related to entry, such as, for example, a requirement for an environmental impact assessment of the proposed investment resulting in environmental performance requirements being imposed as a condition of entry.[138]

While, as noted above, provisions on performance requirements generally contain an exception clause, this still leaves open the possibility that

---

[134] Downes 1999: 16.   [135] Mann and Araya 2002: 169.
[136] Clémençon 2000: 205.   [137] Freedman 2003: 96.
[138] ILA International Law on Foreign Investment Committee 2006: 14.

tribunals will find that a given measure is not strictly *necessary* to protect the environment.

4.3.3   Environmental regulation that is 'unfair' or goes 'too far'

Measures to prevent discrimination and the use of performance requirements have potential implications for environmental governance, but it is the fair and equitable treatment standard and the notion of regulatory takings that have caused the greatest concern in civil society and generated the most discussion in academia. Perhaps the most significant problems with these provisions is that they have not been clearly defined.

According to some observers, the vagueness surrounding the fair and equitable treatment standard is intentional, in order to give arbitrators a certain amount of discretion.[139] Brower suggests that the inclusion of the reference to fair and equitable treatment in NAFTA Article 1105.1 'represents the exemplification of an intentionally vague term, designed to give adjudicators a quasi-legislative authority to articulate a variety of rules necessary to achieve the treaty's object and purpose in particular disputes'.[140] Despite, or perhaps because of the imprecise nature of the standard, the ILA International Law on Foreign Investment Committee has argued that fair and equitable treatment is 'currently the most important standard, from the perspective of investor protection'.[141] An UNCTAD report suggests it is the most likely standard to be relied upon by an investor in an arbitral claim.[142]

According to Freedman, because of the ambiguity of the standard, 'some environmentalists have expressed concern that it could be (and perhaps has been) interpreted expansively by an arbitral tribunal to second guess health and environmental regulations'.[143] Dolzer notes that:

> Certainly, the principle of fair and equitable treatment may, in practice, have wide-ranging repercussions for the sovereignty of the host state to determine and apply its administrative law, as it covers all phases of the investments and extends to all areas of domestic law affecting foreign investment. Depending upon how it is interpreted and applied by the tribunals, the principle has the potential to reach further into the traditional *domaine réservé* of the host state than any one of the other rules of the treaties.[144]

---

[139] Yannaca-Small 2004: 2.   [140] Brower 2001a: 78.
[141] ILA International Law on Foreign Investment Committee 2006: 16.
[142] UNCTAD 2007: 32. See also Subedi 2008: 63.   [143] Freedman 2003: 96.
[144] Dolzer 2005: 964.

In terms of expropriation, Gutbrod and Hindelang argue that if arbitral tribunals utilize the effects test, there could be serious implications for regulation:

> determining indirect expropriation only by diminution in property value might reduce national policy space to zero as, governments would then be confronted with claims for compensation any time they change policy, this would limit international law on foreign investment to an insurance policy against bad business decisions.[145]

However, even if a more balanced approach is adopted, there remains a broad remit for tribunals to interpret the actions of a government as arbitrary or unnecessary. In particular, it has been suggested that if there has been no substantial change in scientific knowledge or international environmental standards since the time when the state committed to the investment project, a policy change is more likely to be considered an expropriation.[146]

The priority for governments is the ability to establish at the policy development stage whether a measure constitutes a taking or not. However, a stable definition of regulatory takings is unlikely to emerge from investment arbitration in the near future, making such prediction extraordinarily difficult.[147]

4.3.4   Cosmetic changes

As noted, there have been efforts in recent IIAs to clarify certain substantive provisions that in theory would make it less likely that environmental regulations will be challenged in investor-state arbitration. Furthermore, many recent IIAs contain explicit provisions on the protection of the environment. However, these adjustments to the traditional model of IIAs are relatively minor and fail to address many of the issues raised in this study.

For example, some treaties, such as those based on the 2004 US Model BIT, now spell out in greater detail the distinction between expropriation and regulation. Gantz views the annex in the US Model as a 'truly remarkable effort to provide detailed guidance to future tribunals seeking to distinguish compensable expropriations from valid government regulations', and suggests that they 'unquestionably will make it more difficult

---

[145] Gutbrod and Hindelang 2006: 64.
[146] Fortier and Drymer 2004: 307; Wälde and Kolo 2001.
[147] Van Harten 2007a: 93.

for a foreign investor to claim successfully that any sort of government regulatory action is an expropriation, particularly if the regulatory action has any environmental or public health nexus'.[148] Others are less optimistic, and argue that the three-part test is too vague and is outdated in relation to both domestic and international jurisprudence.[149] Parisi suggests that the annex misses:

> critical limitations stating that an investor's expectations are a necessary, but not sufficient, condition for liability, that an investor's expectations must be evaluated as of the time of the investment or that an investor must expect that health, safety, and environmental regulations often change and become more strict over time.[150]

It has also been suggested that the use of the broad and vague 'rare circumstances' terminology will only encourage lawyers to develop creative arguments to test the boundaries of the exception.[151]

Provisions in 're-modelled' IIAs on fair and equitable treatment also remain open to a significant degree of interpretation. Furthermore, the new generation of agreements represents only a small subset of existing IIAs, and Europeans have failed to follow the North American lead in adjusting their models.[152] Gantz notes that, as a result, the American business community now feels that they are at a disadvantage compared to their European competitors.[153] Some arbitrators and authors have also taken exception with the changes introduced in the new generation of IIAs, in particular with the modifications to the fair and equitable treatment standard, arguing that it is an 'exercise which, in the large, constitutes a regressive, rather than progressive, development of international law'.[154]

As for environmental provisions, an UNCTAD report concludes that these types of clauses are mainly explanatory and meant as 'a tool for sending a message to civil societies that the contracting parties take environmental concerns into account'.[155] The use of language such as 'otherwise consistent' has led some observers to conclude that many of these provisions are solely tautological, and have no practical meaning whatsoever.[156] Hasic argues that the language in NAFTA pollution havens provision 'is

---

[148] Gantz 2004: 744–5.   [149] Muse-Fisher 2007: 509.   [150] Parisi 2005: 421–2.
[151] Edsall 2006: 958–9.   [152] Van Harten 2007a: 164.   [153] Gantz 2004: 764–5.
[154] Schwebel 2006.   [155] UNCTAD 2007: 89.
[156] Freedman 2003: 94; Baughen 2006: 222; Newcombe 2007a: 400.

simply not forceful enough to convey the impression of a serious commitment'.[157] Clémençon, commenting on the Draft MAI pollution havens provision, also expresses doubts about the value of such statements:

> It is important to recognize the limitation of such a provision – binding or non-binding. It would, in most cases, be impossible to prove that a country in effect had lowered environmental standards for the sole purpose of accommodating a particular foreign investor. Furthermore, such a provision does not address the problem that adequate environmental standards have still not been developed in many countries.[158]

In essence, the breach of environmental commitments in IIAs is likely to give rise to, if anything, no more than consultations among the parties.[159]

What is striking about all of the reforms that have been made is they appear to be motivated solely in response to developed country concerns and do little to address the disparities between developed and developing countries that are faced with disputes. This is particularly evident in the EIAs conducted by the US and Canada, which fail to even consider the environmental impacts of American and Canadian investments abroad, making them little more than a public relations exercise.

It is also notable that there has been no attempt to redress the fundamental imbalance between investor rights and responsibilities under IIAs. Shan notes that the new generation of American and Canadian IIAs:

> demonstrate only small changes ... [and] do not alter the fundamental character of these investment treaties as quintessential liberalist instruments, which only protect and 'empower' investors without sufficient consideration of the rights of host states and the duties of the investors.[160]

Similarly, Clémençon argues that the 'elimination of legal compatibility problems alone is not a panacea for making an investment agreement compatible with sustainable development'.[161]

---

[157] Hasic 2005: 154.   [158] Clémençon 2000: 218.   [159] Freedman 2003: 94.
[160] Shan 2007: 656.   [161] Clémençon 2000: 215.

5

Foreign investment contracts

The term 'foreign investment contract' is used in this book to refer to a legal agreement negotiated directly between a host government and a foreign investor. Countries may negotiate *ad hoc* contracts with investors, which are unique, or provide model contracts to establish the same conditions for several different projects, or employ a hybrid of these two options (where a model is provided but more specific terms can be negotiated).[1]

Foreign investment contracts may be classified into many different categories. However, there is a lack of consensus among authors about what the appropriate classifications are within one industry. When one looks at contracts across various sectors, the terminology is even more confusing. For example, 'concession agreement' is used as the designation for a wide range of contracts in the extractive industries, in infrastructure development, and in the context of the (partial) privatization of services and public utilities. In the extractive industries, concession agreements are the most straightforward type of contract. The basic structure of a concession involves a government granting certain rights (e.g., to exploit minerals) to a foreign investor in exchange for some form of royalty payment. In the context of infrastructure development and utilities, concession agreements are more complex. A Build-Operate-and-Transfer contract is an example. Under such a scheme, the government contracts a private sector enterprise to build something (e.g., a toll road) and operate it for a fixed period of time. The investor recoups his costs and potentially profits from the project during this period (e.g., by the collection of usage fees) and thereafter the project is transferred to the host government.[2] Variations on this model include Build-Operate-Own contracts, Build-Transfer-Operate contracts, Build-Lease-Transfer contracts and Build-Own-Operate-Transfer contracts.[3]

---

[1] Otto 1999: 30.   [2] Levy 1996: 102.   [3] *Ibid.*

Another major set of foreign investment contracts are those in which the government participates in the investment project, often through a state-owned enterprise.[4] In a joint-venture agreement, a locally incorporated entity is created with the investor and the host government acting as shareholders.[5] The government receives shareholder dividends, but may also collect royalties and taxes from the project. Another type of contract which has become common in the oil and gas sector is the production-sharing agreement. In this type of agreement, the foreign investor is contracted by the state to supply the funds, technology and expertise needed for the investment project.[6] The foreign investor is then entitled to a share of production, as stipulated in the contract.

In practice, these labels tend to be much less important than the specific content of a contract. As a UNCTC report has noted: 'Any mode of agreement can be highly rewarding or detrimental to the host Government's interest, depending on its provisions.'[7] This chapter looks at some provisions found in foreign investment contracts that are likely to have implications for environmental governance in the host state. A brief discussion of the process of negotiation and disclosure of contracts is also provided.

5.1   Key provisions

Foreign investment contracts serve more than one purpose. Most importantly, they set out the terms of the investment project, for example by stipulating the area of land that the contract covers and the period over which the investment is to take place. However, another key purpose of foreign investment contracts is to provide some level of assurance to foreign investors that once capital has been sunk into the project, and the relative power of the two parties has shifted, the government will not be able to change the 'rules of the game' unilaterally. While outright expropriations are now rare in most parts of the world, the risk of government interference in foreign investment projects remains. Despite the proliferation of IIAs, investors continue to demand clauses in their foreign investment contracts that will protect their investments. Yackee argues that contracts remain 'potentially the most effective investment protection instruments available because they allow investors to draft terms tailored to specific investment needs'.[8]

---

[4] Bernardini 1996: 166.   [5] Peter 1995: 21.   [6] Bernardini 1996: 167.
[7] UNCTC 1983: 72.   [8] Yackee 2008b: 133.

Foreign investment contracts vary widely by country and industry. Nevertheless, it is possible to discuss some aspects that are common across a range of sectors and jurisdictions. In this section, particular focus is given to two main types of provision found in foreign investment contracts: those dealing with stability of host country law; and those covering environmental issues. It should be noted that foreign investment contracts may also contain provisions on expropriation and discrimination. However, as these subjects have been addressed in the previous chapter, they will not be discussed here. Furthermore, like IIAs, foreign investment contracts often contain provisions delegating the settlement of disputes to international arbitral tribunals. This topic will be covered in the next chapter.

Most foreign investment contracts are not in the public domain. This section will draw on the academic literature on foreign investment contracts and on actual contracts or contractual provisions that are publicly available, have been disclosed through company filings to the Securities and Exchange Commission (SEC) or have been leaked to NGOs. Thus it must be recognized from the outset that it is not possible to determine whether the particular form of the provisions discussed herein are widespread, or are examples of best or worst practices.

5.1.1 Stability of host country law

Whilst investors in the modern period are less concerned that their contracts will be unilaterally altered or terminated by the host state than they were in the 1960s and 1970s, there remains a strong interest in mitigating the risk that changes in the host government's legislation will detrimentally affect the profitability, or even viability, of an investment project.[9] Stabilization clauses are one mechanism that investors use to deal with the problem of 'adverse change in law'.[10] Stabilization clauses were reported to have diminished in scope and frequency in the 1970s, but they now appear to be re-emerging in even more extensive forms than were previously observed.[11] In a recent study, Shemberg found that the use of

---

[9] An earlier version of this section was published in Tienhaara 2008.

[10] Pritchard 2005: 80. It should be noted that there is an important distinction to be made between stabilization clauses and 'intangibility clauses'. Intangibility clauses remove administrative interference in the contract (i.e., the government cannot modify or terminate the contract unilaterally), whereas stabilization clauses control legislative interference in the contract. See Montembault 2003.

[11] Wälde and N'Di 1996: 218.

stabilization clauses is widespread across industries and regions of the world.[12] Cotula notes that they are 'particularly common in large natural resource, energy and infrastructure projects, where high fixed costs require large capital injections in the early stages of the project and where long time frames are need for the economic viability of the project'.[13]

5.1.1.1   The purpose of stability

As Balasubramanyam clarifies, 'it is the stability of policies over time rather than the stability of governments and political regimes which weigh heavily in the FDI decision process of foreign firms'.[14] As mentioned in Section 4.1.4, many observers argue that provisions on fair and equitable treatment in IIAs require that host states provide a stable environment for investors. However, stabilization clauses are far more explicit in this respect. The purpose of a stabilization clause is 'to preserve the law of the host country as it applies to the investment at the time the state contract is concluded' and to ensure 'that the future changes to the law of the host country are inapplicable to the foreign investment contract'.[15] As Faruque illustrates, stability can be said to have both a temporal and an economic dimension:

> Stability has a temporal dimension to the extent that it requires the continuity of the contractual relationship towards its successful completion and the achievement of desired objectives as contemplated by the parties. The economic dimension, which is also regarded as the most important indicator of a stable contract order, implies maintaining the contractual equilibrium perceived by the parties throughout the duration of the contract.[16]

Notably, stabilization clauses are found almost exclusively in foreign investment contracts signed by developing and transition economies. Omalu and Zamora suggest that this is because the more a government is viewed by foreign investors as being 'volatile and unreliable', the more the use of stabilization methods will be 'desired and therefore in most cases required' by foreign investors.[17] In general, investors view developing and transition countries as more politically unstable than developed ones. Furthermore, the relative weakness of developing countries in terms

---

[12] Shemberg 2008. See also Maniruzzaman 2008.   [13] Cotula 2008: 160.
[14] Balasubramanyam 1999: 35.   [15] UNCTAD 2004b: 3.
[16] Faruque 2006a: 86.   [17] Omalu and Zamora 1998: 17.

of bargaining power, combined with a strong desire to attract investment, makes them accept conditions that developed countries would not
consider.[18]

5.1.1.2 Methods of achieving stability

Investment codes and national legislation in developing countries commonly contain provisions for the stability of investment contracts, and
some countries even have a stability guarantee included in their constitution.[19] Although a constitutional guarantee may have some weight,
legislative promises of stability are generally considered less enforceable
than a contractual clause or a separate stabilization agreement, since laws
can be modified at the will of the government. Nevertheless, legislative
promises may still be taken into consideration by an arbitral tribunal.[20]

One example of a national law that makes specific reference to the
stability of environmental regulations is Algeria's Mining Act of 2001.[21]
Article 84 sets out that a mining lease is to be accompanied by a mining
agreement, which should be concluded by the state and the investor, and:

> The mining agreement, after its effectiveness, can not be modified but by
> the written consent of parties. This amendment will be formalised by a
> rider approved by decree on proposal of the Minister in charge of mines.
> The mining agreement specifies the obligations and rights of the parties in
> relation with the legal, financial, fiscal, social and environmental conditions
> applying to exploitation during its term. It guarantees to the mining claim
> holder the stability of these conditions during the whole term of the claim
> according to this law provisions.

The Mining Act thus commits the government to stabilize all mining
agreements, which may also themselves contain stabilization clauses.

Traditionally, there were three main ways in which stabilization clauses
were formulated in foreign investment contracts.[22] The first option was to
prohibit the enactment of any legislation that would adversely affect the
investor's rights. This type of clause could even include the prohibition
of nationalization. The second type of clause provided that, in the event
of an inconsistency between any legislation enacted in the future and
the contract, the latter would prevail. Finally, the third type of clause
incorporated the host country's law into the contract and froze it at a

---

[18] Wälde and N'Di 1996: 223; Faruque 2006b: 323; Leader 2006: 659.
[19] Faruque 2006a: 105.   [20] Wälde and N'Di 1996: 240.
[21] Mining Act of the People's Democratic Republic of Algeria, Law no. 01-10 2001. For other
examples of stability provisions in recently enacted laws see Maniruzzaman 2007.
[22] Peter 1995: 215–17.

specific date, thus ensuring that legislative changes would not apply to the investment. These three formulations have been collectively referred to as stabilization clauses *stricto sensu*.[23]

Stabilization clauses *stricto sensu* are still employed in modern agreements. An example of a such a stabilization clause can be found in the 2005 Mineral Development Agreement between Mittal Steel and the Government of Liberia:

> In particular, any modifications that could be made in the future to the Law as in effect on the Effective Date shall not apply to the CONCESSIONAIRE and its Associates without their prior written consent, but the CONCESSIONAIRE and its Associates may at any time elect to be governed by the legal and regulatory provisions resulting from changes made at any time in the Law as in effect on the Effective Date.[24]

In addition to traditional stabilization clauses, there are also more modern clauses which require the 'economic equilibrium' of a contract to be restored following legislative change. As this type of clause does not seek to completely prevent the development or application of new legislation to the investment and favours renegotiation over arbitration (although arbitration is not precluded if the parties cannot come to an agreement), it is more compatible with the notion of state sovereignty and is likely to be preferable to host governments over traditional stabilization clauses.[25] However, restoring the economic equilibrium of a contract may still have significant implications for the state in terms of compensation to be paid to the investor or concessions to be made in other areas. Furthermore, determining what the economic impact of a regulation is and, therefore, how the investor should be compensated may be complex, making renegotiation difficult.

An example of an economic equilibrium clause is found in a contract between the State Oil Company of the Azerbaijan Republic (SOCAR) and a consortium of investors:

> The rights and interests accruing to Contractor (or its assignees) under this Contract and its Sub-contractors under this Contract shall not be amended, modified or reduced without the prior consent of Contractor. In the event that the Government or other Azerbaijan authority invokes any present or

[23] Montembault 2003: 600; Faruque 2006b: 319.

[24] Mineral Development Agreement between the Republic of Liberia and Mittal Steel Holdings N.V., Monrovia, 17 August 2005: Art. XIX, section 9. It is worth noting that this clause was substantially modified when this Agreement was renegotiated in 2006.

[25] Sornarajah 2004a: 408–9; Faruque 2006b: 321.

future law, treaty, intergovernmental agreement, decree or administrative order which contravenes the provisions of this Contract or adversely or positively affects the rights or interests of Contractor hereunder, including, but not limited to, any changes in tax legislation, regulations, administrative practice, or jurisdictional changes pertaining to the Contract Area the terms of this Contract shall be adjusted to re-establish the economic equilibrium of the Parties, and if the rights or interests of Contractor have been adversely affected, then SOCAR shall indemnify the Contractor (and its assignees) for any disbenefit, deterioration in economic circumstances, loss or damages that ensue therefrom. SOCAR shall within the full limits of its authority use its reasonable lawful endeavours to ensure that the Government will take appropriate measures to resolve promptly in accordance with the foregoing principles any conflict or anomaly between such treaty, intergovernmental agreement, law, decree or administrative order and this Contract.[26]

It is worth noting that it is also possible for a foreign investment contract to be stabilized even in the absence of an explicit stabilization clause. The strength of a contract depends both on the type of legal system in the country and the nature of the Act authorizing the agreement.[27] There are three main ways by which resource exploitation contracts are generally approved: by an Act of Parliament; by a decree of the executive or the responsible minister; or by the signature of the responsible minister. A contract enacted by Parliament provides the most protection to investors as it can effectively stabilize it, perhaps even against subsequent parliamentary actions. Indonesia is an example of a country that passes mineral contracts through Parliament (see Section 8.1.1).

Finally, in what appears to be a growing trend, many governments now offer investors the option to negotiate agreements separate from the main contract, to ensure stability. These agreements are variously termed 'stability agreements', 'development agreements' or '(legal) stability contracts'. Many of these agreements only stabilize the fiscal aspects of the investment (that is, taxes and royalties), while others stabilize the entire legal framework or other specific aspects of it. In Chile, stability contracts include stabilization of the legal, regulatory and policy regime in addition to fiscal and other incentives.[28] In Peru, the legal stability agreements are

---

[26] Agreement on the Joint Development and Production Sharing for the Azeri and Chirag Fields and the Deep Water Portion of the Gunashli Field in the Azerbaijan Sector of the Caspian Sea Among the State Oil Company of the Azerbaijan Republic and Amoco Caspian Sea Petroleum Ltd, BP Exploration (Caspian Sea) Ltd, Delta Nimir Khazar Ltd, Den Norske Stats Oljeselskap a.s., Lukoil Joint Stock Company, McDermott Azerbaijan, Inc., Pennzoil Caspian Corp., Ramco Hazar Energy Ltd, Turkiye Petrolleri A.O., and Unocal Khazar Ltd, 20 September 1994: Art. 23.2, http://subsites.bp.com/caspian/ACG/Eng/agmt1/agmt1.pdf.
[27] Barberis 1998: 41–3.   [28] UNCTAD 2006a: 26.

valid for ten years and are offered in a wide variety of sectors with variations in the terms of the agreement by sector. According to an UNCTAD
report, the mining, power, hydrocarbon and infrastructure sectors have
the most favourable arrangements.[29] Colombia also provides for legal stability contracts but takes a different approach than Chile or Peru. Direct
investments in certain sectors (including mining), which exceed about
US$1.2 million, can obtain contractual protection from adverse changes
in national legislation.[30] The contract can have a term of three to twenty
years, subject to negotiation. While in Chile and Peru, stability agreements can only cover a predetermined list of areas and there is no
option for negotiation of the scope of the terms, in Colombia the government has adopted a positive list approach, which means that they may
agree to stabilize any regulation, unless expressly excluded by law. An
UNCTAD report rightly points out that this approach will encourage
investors to maximize the regulations that will be covered by the contracts.[31] The report also suggests that this approach may foster disputes
and that the 'scope for future litigation could be immense'.[32]

5.1.1.3   The scope of commitments to stability

Promises of stability may be either restrictive or all-inclusive in their
application. A comprehensive stabilization clause that freezes the general
legislative framework 'attempts to insulate completely contractual undertakings from any change in the applicable law of a host state'.[33] Stabilization
clauses of limited scope may refer to one or more specific areas of legislation. Stabilization is often sought in the fiscal area (tax laws/royalties),
in labour legislation, in export-import provisions or in the free trans-
ferability of currencies.[34] Environmental regulations could fall into these
categories. Therefore, even if a stabilization clause does not explicitly refer
to environmental regulation, it could effectively cover it.[35]

   Additionally, there appear to be many cases where stabilization clauses
do explicitly refer to environmental regulation. Leading investment law
experts have suggested that after the fiscal regime, the environmental
management regime is perhaps the most relevant area in which to seek
stability.[36] It is not necessarily the stringency of environmental regulation
in the host country that concerns investors (as the controversial pollution
haven hypothesis would suggest; see Section 2.2), but rather uncertainty

---

[29] UNCTAD and Japan Bank for International Cooperation 2006: 18.
[30] UNCTAD 2006a: 25.   [31] Ibid: 27.   [32] Ibid.   [33] Faruque 2006b: 318.
[34] Ibid; Peter 1995: 221.   [35] Verhoosel 1998: 456.   [36] Wälde and N'Di 1996: 230.

regarding future changes to the law.[37] The existing environmental regulatory framework can be factored into a risk-profit assessment before the investment is made, whereas future changes cannot.[38] Investors want predictability and, particularly in developing countries, environmental regulation 'is currently one of the most unpredictable factors facing potential investors'.[39]

Finally, it is worth noting that stabilization clauses may apply to a broad range of government measures, including those taken in order to fulfil international legal obligations. For example, the host government agreements (HGAs) for the Baku-Tbilisi-Ceyhan (BTC) Pipeline project provide that:

> if any domestic or international agreement or treaty; any legislation, promulgation, enactment, decree, accession or allowance; or any other form of commitment, policy or pronouncement or permission has the effect of impairing, conflicting or interfering with the implementation of the Project, or limiting, abridging or adversely affecting the value of the Project or any of the rights, privileges, exemptions, waivers, indemnifications or protections granted or arising under this Agreement or any other Project Agreement, it shall be deemed a Change in Law under Article 7.2(x).[40]

Article 7.2(x) establishes an economic equilibrium clause. It is explicitly stipulated that the clause covers changes in taxes and regulations related to health, safety and the environment regardless of whether these changes are specifically aimed at the project or are of general application. States are obligated under this provision to restore the economic equilibrium of the contract 'promptly' and 'by whatever means may be necessary'.

The provisions are similar in the contracts for the West African Gas Pipeline (WAGP), a Build-Operate-Own project to develop a pipeline to transport natural gas from Nigeria to Ghana, Togo and Benin. This project is covered by an intergovernmental agreement (WAGP Treaty) and an International Project Agreement (WAGP IPA) between all of the governments and the West African Gas Pipeline Company Ltd (a consortium with

---

[37] Otto and Cordes 2002: IV–49.
[38] Bekhechi 2001: 86; Wälde 2001: 50.   [39] Verhoosel 1998: 454.
[40] Host government agreement between and among the Government of the Azerbaijan Republic and the State Oil Company of the Azerbaijan Republic, BP Exploration (Caspian Sea) Ltd, Stateoil BTC Caspian AS, Ramco Hazar Energy Ltd, Turkiye Petrolleri A.O., Unocal BTC Pipeline Ltd, Itochu Oil Exploration (Azerbaijan) Inc, Delta Hess (BTC) Ltd, 17 October 2000: Art. 7.2(vi).

Chevron as the primary shareholder). These agreements set out a legal regime that is harmonized across all four states and is stabilized for the duration of the project. This legal regime is referred to as the 'Agreed Regime'. The WAGP IPA defines 'Regime Failure' as including, *inter alia*:

> the entering by a State into any international agreement or similar or other commitment that conflicts with, impairs or interferes with, or adversely affects such State's performance of or ability to perform its obligations under, the WAGP Treaty or this Agreement or the implementation of the Project;

And further:

> any act or omission or series of acts or omissions by a State or any of its State Authorities or by the WAGP Authority of any nature whatsoever (including the coming in to force or application of any law, decree or regulation, or a failure to perform its obligations under this Agreement) which prevents or hinders completion of the Pipeline System according to schedule or the operation of the Pipeline System or which has a material adverse effect on the Company, or which causes the benefits derived by the Company from the Project or the value of the Company to the Shareholders to have materially decreased;[41]

If there is a 'Regime Failure', then the government is obliged to make its best efforts to restore the 'Agreed Regime'. If such efforts fail, the government will be required to compensate the consortium.

5.1.1.4   The validity and effect of commitments to stability

A long and divisive debate in academia about the validity of stabilization clauses has been largely drawn along ideological lines. While it is certainly important to acknowledge this division, one must also examine, from a practical perspective, the effect that a stabilization clause or agreement will have if it is deemed to be valid by an arbitral tribunal.

Three main positions have been taken by legal experts examining the validity of stabilization techniques: the acceptance of stabilization clauses as valid; the dismissal of stabilization clauses as invalid; and the 'middle ground' view, which accepts the validity of stabilization clauses but denies them full effect.

---

[41] West African Gas Pipeline Project International Project Agreement between the Republic of Benin, the Republic of Ghana, the Federal Republic of Nigeria, the Republic of Togo and the West African Gas Pipeline Company Ltd, 22 May 2003: Art. 36.1.

Those who uphold the validity of stabilization clauses emphasize the principle of sanctity of contract and argue that if a state can bind itself by a treaty with another state, then it may also bind itself by a contract with a private party.[42] Furthermore, they claim that the inclusion of certain clauses in a contract (particularly stabilization and arbitration clauses) has the effect of 'internationalizing' the contract (see Section 3.1.2.3).

Those who deny the validity of stabilization clauses generally focus on the principle of state sovereignty and the succession of laws principle.[43] They disagree with both the notion that a foreign investment contract can be equated with an inter-state treaty (as foreign investors do not have international legal personality) and the idea that state obligations rest in some 'external' system rather than in national law. It has even been suggested by one author that the theory of internationalization of contracts was only developed in order to give validity to stabilization clauses.[44] Furthermore, in the case of contracts in the natural resource sector, there is perhaps even more reason to doubt the validity of stabilization clauses, given the importance of the doctrine of permanent sovereignty over natural resources.[45]

Despite the seemingly intractable academic debate on this issue, tribunals have frequently affirmed the validity of stabilization clauses, although it is important to note that the early arbitrations on stability all dealt with expropriation rather than lesser forms of regulatory change.[46] Furthermore, notwithstanding the support for the principle of permanent sovereignty over natural resources, states continue to include commitments to stability in their national legislation and their foreign investment contracts. Given these realities, the critical issue would appear to be the extent of the effect of a commitment to stability, which is determined by several factors. First, the form of the commitment (that is, contractual clause versus national legislation) and its scope (all-inclusive versus restrictive) affects the strength of the commitment and determines its application. Second, the applicable law of the contract has an effect. If the contract is governed by national law, then the effect of a stabilization

---

[42] See Paasivirta 1989.

[43] Otto and Cordes 2002: IV–22, explain that the succession of laws principle provides that the 'legislative capacity of lawmakers cannot be bound, nor can the executive/public powers of the government be fettered by a contract with a private individual or corporation, i.e., no parliament can bind its successor through a contractual mechanism'.

[44] Sornarajah 2004a: 408.   [45] *Ibid.*

[46] Verhoosel 1998: 456; Cotula 2008: 164. For an overview of arbitration cases dealing with the issue of nationalization and stabilization, see Begic 2005.

clause may be limited or negated by constitutional constraints, whereas this is not an issue if international law is chosen as the applicable law of the contract.[47] However, even in the latter situation a complete guarantee of contractual stability will not exist, as it is recognized in international law that the state has the right to interfere in a contract when its vital interests are at stake.[48]

If a tribunal finds that a government has breached a promise of stability, what are the likely consequences? Some contracts stipulate that arbitrators are empowered to amend the contract, but other contracts are not clear on this issue.[49] The most accepted argument appears to be that while stabilization clauses cannot stop a government from 'doing what it pleases', the investor will be entitled to 'comprehensive compensation' in the instance of a breach.[50] Comeaux and Kinsella, for example, suggest that:

> Generally, arbitrators will not order specific performance of a concession agreement, even if it contains a stabilization clause, out of respect for state sovereignty and an inability to enforce such an award ... Instead a state's violation of a stabilization clause is more likely to affect the amount of damages awarded or the certainty that damages will be awarded.[51]

The effect of stability commitment on the amount of damages awarded to an investor has been referred to by Wälde and N'Di as a 'stabilization premium', the amount of which should be determined based on the legal weight of the stabilization promise.[52]

In addition to increasing the likelihood of receiving compensation, and potentially affecting the amount of compensation, several authors also suggest that there is a functional value to stabilization clauses since they can act as a 'bargaining chip' for investors in any re-negotiation of the terms of the contract.[53] There is also a potential 'deterrent effect' of the stabilization clause, which means that governments will be discouraged from committing a breach because it would damage the country's reputation with investors and could lead to arbitration before an international tribunal.[54]

Finally, it is worth noting that some observers have suggested that the existence of a stabilization clause in a contract may enhance a claim of expropriation or breach of the fair and equitable treatment standard in an IIA.[55] In this view, stabilization clauses provide investors with the

---

[47] Faruque 2006b: 333–4.   [48] *Ibid.*   [49] Maniruzzaman 2008: 132.
[50] Peter 1995: 227.   [51] Comeaux and Kinsella 1994: 25.   [52] Wälde and N'Di 1996: 267.
[53] Peter 1995: 228; Verhoosel 1998: 456.   [54] Faruque 2006b: 335.
[55] Cameron 2006: 74–5; Maniruzzaman 2008: 147.

legitimate expectation that regulation affecting their investment will not change over a given period of time.

5.1.2 Environmental issues

A 1983 report from the UNCTC suggests: 'Environmental protection was ignored under the traditional concession agreements and it continues to receive scant attention'.[56] Similarly, in a 1994 study, Gao found that environmental issues had not received much attention in foreign investment contracts in the oil and gas industry.[57] Some available information suggests that environmental provisions are now far more detailed in contracts in the extractive industries, as well as in other sectors. Nevertheless, questions remain as to the efficacy of these provisions.

5.1.2.1 Environmental standards

In Chapter 2 it was suggested that while foreign investors may employ international best practices in their operations, it cannot be assumed that they will do so automatically or consistently. Theoretically, foreign investment contracts could be a useful mechanism to translate voluntary self-regulatory standards into binding, enforceable obligations.

It would appear that, particularly in the extractive industries, reference is commonly made in contracts, not necessarily to international best practices, but at least to 'good' practices. According to Gao, a traditional requirement in oil and gas contracts in the 1970s and 80s was for operations to follow 'good petroleum industry practice'.[58] This type of provision is still employed in modern agreements. For example, a 2000 production sharing agreement between the Government of Georgia and Canargo Norio Ltd states that:

> In conducting Petroleum Operations, the Contractor shall operate according to Good Oilfield Practices and use best endeavors to minimize potential disturbances to the environment, including the surface, subsurface, sea, air, flora, fauna, other natural resources and property.[59]

But what does reference to 'good' oilfield or petroleum industry practice mean for environmental management? It is difficult to say. The first problem that one encounters is that the term is not typically defined in

---

[56] UNCTC 1983: 81.   [57] Gao 1994.   [58] *Ibid*: 50
[59] Production Sharing Agreement between State of Georgia and Canargo Norio Ltd, 12 December 2000.

contracts. However, Timor-Leste's 2005 Petroleum Act does provide a
definition that is potentially illuminating:

> Petroleum Operations shall be conducted in accordance with Good Oil
> Field Practice, that is, in accordance with such practices and procedures
> employed in the petroleum industry worldwide by prudent and diligent
> operators under conditions and circumstances similar to those experi-
> enced in connection with the relevant aspect or aspects of the Petroleum
> Operations, principally aimed at guaranteeing:
>
> (1) conservation of Petroleum resources, which implies the utilization of
> adequate methods and processes to maximize the recovery of hydro-
> carbons in a technically and economically sustainable manner, with a
> corresponding control of reserves decline, and to minimize losses at
> the surface;
> (2) operational safety, which entails the use of methods and processes that
> promote occupational security and the prevention of accidents;
> (3) environmental protection, that calls for the adoption of methods and
> processes which minimize the impact of Petroleum Operations on the
> environment;[60]

The first thing to note about this definition is that there is no reference
to a specific set of standards, even one developed by industry, that a government official or member of civil society could refer to as a benchmark
for investor compliance. Furthermore, it is clear that the appropriate comparator is the conduct of operators that experience similar 'conditions and
circumstances' to those found in the host state. Presumably this would
exclude the possibility of comparing the operations of a foreign investor
to those in, for example, its home country.

This type of vague, 'similar circumstances' provision is also evident in
foreign investment contracts outside of the petroleum sector. For example, the 2005 Concession Agreement between The Republic of Liberia
and Firestone Natural Rubber Company, LLC, and Firestone Plantations
Company states that:

> Firestone Liberia shall take reasonable measures to ensure that Production
> does not cause unreasonable risks to public health or unreasonable damage
> to the environment. Unless Firestone Liberia demonstrates that a particular
> measure is unreasonable, it shall employ measures as protective as those
> employed by Persons in Liberia and elsewhere engaged in the production
> and processing of Rubber on a basis similar to Production under this
> Agreement . . .[61]

---

[60] Art. 23.1. Available online at www.timor-leste.gov.tl/EMRD/p_law.htm.
[61] Art. 15(a).

If it is the case that environmental standards are universally low in rubber plantations, such a provision provides no scope for standards to improve. Furthermore, if one were to find a company elsewhere in the world producing rubber with higher environmental standards in its operations, Firestone could still argue that this was not 'on a basis similar to Production under this Agreement' or 'that a particular measure is unreasonable'.

Some contracts are somewhat more specific about the standards that are to apply in the environmental management of projects. For example, the Kashagan production sharing agreement between the Government of Kazakstan and a consortium of investors lists the following: Oil Industry International Exploration and Production Forum (later renamed the International Association of Oil & Gas Producers) guidelines on health, safety and environmental management systems; International Association of Drilling Contractors (IADC) safety and environmental guidelines; International Association of Geophysical Contractors (IAGC) safety and environmental guidelines; and The American Conference of Government Industrial Hygienists Threshold Limit Values for Chemical Substances in the Work Environment.[62] However, even when such lists of standards are provided, there remain, as Newell puts it, 'questions regarding the overall effectiveness of standards set by market actors for market actors, but which carry enormous implications for governments and publics alike'.[63] There is also the issue of public access to information; national legislation is usually freely available in the major language(s) of the host state, but industry guidelines, such as those listed above, may be difficult for even Internet-savvy English-speakers to track down.

On the other hand, one could argue that reference to industry standards allows some scope for change and evolution of the environmental management regime of an investment over time, thus providing a way around a contractual requirement for stability.[64] However, it is problematic that governments should be expected to wait for industry standards as a whole to shift before necessary regulations can be implemented. Furthermore, such an evolution in standards may be precluded in some instances. For

---

[62] Production Sharing Agreement In Respect of the North Caspian Sea (Kashagan) Among Agip Caspian Sea B.V.; BG Exploration and Production Ltd; BP Kazakstan Ltd; Den Norske Stats Oljeselskap a.s.; Mobil Oil Kazakstan Inc.; Shell Kazakstan Development B.V.; Total Exploration Production Kazakstan; JSC Kazakstancaspianshelf; The Republic of Kazakstan and JSC National Oil and Gas Company Kazakoil, 18 November 1997.

[63] Newell 2008: 83.   [64] Cotula 2008: 177.

example, the Koidu Kimberlite Project Mining Lease in Sierra Leone states that:

> Nothing in this mining lease or in the Decree or other legislation shall impose any liability whatsoever on the Lessee in respect of any pollution or loss or damage to the environment or the risk thereof, or other claim, where such pollution, loss, damage, risk or claim arises from, or in connection with, any acts or omissions in or with respect to the Mining Lease Area prior to the date of this Mining Lease, or *from the raising or extension of environmental standards generally accepted in the international mining industry above the level of such standards as prevailing as at the date hereof,* or as a result of scientific or technological information, analysis or findings not available at the date hereof, unless (i) such information, analysis or findings indicate the availability of effective preventative or remedial action and (ii) the Lessee fails to take such action notwithstanding that to do so would be financially and economically justified . . .[65]

Thus, in this case, even industry standards are effectively stabilized. Similarly, in a 1996 offshore oil agreement between Azerbaijan and a consortium of investors, it is stipulated that the investor and the government will jointly agree on a set of safety and environmental standards based on '(i) international Petroleum industry standards and experience with their implementation in exploration and production operations in other parts of the world and (ii) existing Azerbaijan safety and environmental legislation'.[66] However, once developed, this set of standards can only be altered through a written agreement and the company is not required to comply with evolving industry practice.

A slight improvement on this 'good industry practice' model is found in the BTC pipeline intergovernmental agreement, which states that the operations will be 'in accordance with international standards and practices within the Petroleum pipeline industry (*which shall in no event be less stringent than those generally applied within member states of the European Union*)'.[67] Nevertheless, this clause has been criticized by NGOs. For example, an Amnesty International UK report argues that reference to EU

---

[65] Koidu Kimberlite Project Mining Lease Agreement (Ratification) Decree, 1995: Art. 11.4.
[66] Agreement on the Exploration, Development and Production Sharing for the Shakh Deniz Prospective Area in the Azerbaijan Sector of the Caspian Sea between the State Oil Company of Azerbaijan and SOCAR Commercial Affiliate, BP Exploration (Azerbaijan) Ltd, Elf Petroleum Azerbaijan B.V., Lukoil International Ltd, Oil Industries Engineering and Construction, Statoil Azerbaijan A.S., Turkish Petroleum Overseas Company Ltd, 4 June 1996: Art. 26.1.
[67] Agreement Among The Azerbaijan Republic, Georgia and The Republic of Turkey Relating to the Transportation of Petroleum Via the Territories of The Azerbaijan Republic, Georgia and The Republic of Turkey Through the Baku-Tbilisi-Ceyhan Main Export Pipeline, 18 November 1999: Art. IV.

standards does not confer rights on individuals or citizens in the countries in which the project takes place (which are not currently EU member states) to sue the state or the consortium for breach of those standards.[68] The Center for International Environmental Law (CIEL) further points out that no reference is made to EU standards in the applicable HGAs between the consortium and each state.[69] Qualifying language used in the environmental provisions of the BTC HGAs, such as 'Best Endeavours', creates further uncertainty as to what is actually required of the investors.

5.1.2.2 Environmental impact assessments

EIAs and corresponding management plans have become a staple requirement in foreign investment projects in most sectors. EIAs may be prescribed under national legislation or by the policies of international financiers and insurers (see Section 2.3.2.5). Foreign investment contracts also often make reference to the requirement for investors to complete an EIA. However, it would appear that typically the EIA is to be completed *after* the contract has been signed. This suggests that regardless of the outcome of an EIA, an investment project is expected to proceed and the government is committed to ensuring that this occurs. Some contracts even spell out that governments are expected to approve the EIA in a timely manner:

> Government shall have 90 days thereafter to review and approve or reject the EMP [Environmental Management Plan], which approval shall not be unreasonably withheld and shall be deemed granted if Government has not denied approval by Notice to Firestone and Firestone Liberia and provided in writing full details of the basis for that denial. If in the opinion of Firestone or Firestone Liberia, Government wrongly withholds its approval of the EMP, then either Firestone or Firestone Liberia may invoke the provisions of Section 27 [Arbitration], and the standard for review shall be whether or not the proposed EMP complies with this Section, in which case it will be approved.[70]

The latter half of the above quoted provision illustrates a further problem; that disputes over the approval of an EIA may be delegated to arbitral tribunals. This is made explicit in other contracts as well. For example, a 1995 Mining Development Contract between Papua New Guinea and Lihir Gold Pty Ltd states that:

---

[68] Amnesty International UK 2003: 14. See also Ong 2008: 191.
[69] CIEL 2003a: 5–6.
[70] Concession Agreement between the Republic of Liberia and Firestone Natural Rubber Company, LLC and Firestone Plantations Company, 28 January 2005: Art. 15(b).

> In the event that there is a dispute in respect of any amendment [to the environmental plan] initiated by the Minister on behalf of the State in any of the circumstances set out in Clause 10.3, the dispute shall be referred to arbitration under Clause 21 and the amendment shall not become effective unless and until it is upheld by the resulting arbitration award.[71]

Arbitrators are not experts in environmental impact assessment, and contracts often provide little guidance on the required content of an EIA or management plan, let alone the parameters for its rejection or approval. There are also other concerns about the willingness and capacity of governments to engage in arbitration that are discussed further in the next chapter.

5.1.2.3   Environmental liability

As noted in Section 2.3.2.6, foreign direct liability is increasingly viewed as an important means of holding foreign investors accountable for environmental damage. It is also possible, of course, for cases on environmental liability (or other issues) to be brought against an investor in the local courts of a host state. Cases may also be brought against a government, by its own constituency or even by a foreign government in instances of transboundary environmental harm caused by the activities of an investor. Governments are often interested, therefore, in ensuring that investors will indemnify them for any claims that ensue as a result of an investor's operations. This is evidenced in clauses in foreign investment contracts such as the following:

> (a) Nothing in this Agreement shall exempt the Company from liability for any damage, loss or injury caused to any person, property or interest as a result of the exercise by the Company of any rights or powers granted to it under this Agreement.
> (b) The Company shall at all times indemnify the Government and its officers and agents against all claims and liabilities in respect of any loss suffered by or damage done to third parties arising out of the exercise by the Company of any rights or powers granted to it under this Agreement provided that the Company shall not so indemnify the Government, its officers and agents where the claim or liability arises out of the wrongful or negligent acts of the Government, its officers and agents.[72]

---

[71] The Independent State of Papua New Guinea and Lihir Gold Pty Ltd, Mining Development Contract for the Lihir Gold Project on Lihir Island, New Ireland Province, 17 March 1995: Art. 10.4.

[72] Mining Lease between the Government of the Republic of Ghana and Bogoso Gold Ltd, 29 June 2001: Art. 10.

However, in some cases this traditional indemnity clause is reversed, exempting the investor from liability and placing the onus of dealing with claims on the government:

> The Government shall for claims arising during the term of the Mining Lease and Additional Mining Leases indemnify the Company against such claims by owners or occupiers (including the Chiefdom Councillors) in respect of the Mining Lease Area other than claims for compensation made in accordance with the provisions of Section 26 of the Minerals Act but subject to Clause 10(b) of this Agreement.[73]

In at least one case, such a clause explicitly mentions claims of environmental damage:

> The Government covenants and agrees to waive, or cause to be waived, and indemnify the Producer against any private action under or with respect to, any and all environmental laws, rules or regulations now existing, or created hereafter, to which the Mollejon Project and the New Project may be subject, other than any laws, rules or regulations set forth in the Mollejon Project Compliance Plan and the New Project Compliance Plan, as the case may be, to which the Producer has agreed to be bound.[74]

This type of clause raises the legitimate concern that those who suffer from environmental damage will not be able to hold the perpetrators directly accountable. Furthermore, it suggests that poor countries that have agreed to such commitments will be expected to foot the bill for compensation and clean-up.

5.2   Contract negotiations and contract disclosure

While the content of contracts is of primary concern, it is clear that there is a close connection between content and the process through which contracts are developed. As noted in Chapter 1, there are issues about the capacity of developing countries to negotiate effectively with the sophisticated legal teams that often represent investors in contract talks. This section discusses two further issues: that typically only one sector of the government is involved in contract negotiations; and that contracts are generally not publicly disclosed even after negotiations are completed.

---

[73] The Sierra Rutile Agreement (Ratification) Act, 21 March 2002: Art. 2e.
[74] Third Master Agreement between Government of Belize, C.A. and Belize Electric Company Ltd and Belize Electricity Ltd, 21 November 2001: Art. 7.1.

5.2.1   Who negotiates foreign investment contracts?

Typically only a few high-level government officials, lawyers and company representatives are involved in contract negotiations, which are convened behind closed doors. Non-economic/industry sectors of government (e.g., environmental ministries) are often excluded from negotiations and may not even be aware of the content of contracts, which can, in turn, lead to policy incoherence and in some cases disputes. In many countries, contracts are negotiated and signed without the involvement of Parliament. When legislatures are involved in the process, it is often a matter of 'rubber-stamping' rather than genuine participation.[75]

An additional problem that has come to the fore in recent years is that foreign investment contracts are at times negotiated by authoritarian governments or transitional governments that lack accountability and are often corrupt. For example, mining companies acquired many favourable contracts in Indonesia in the years in which Suharto was in power. When Suharto was overthrown and a democratic government elected, the US government insisted that the original contracts be fulfilled.[76] In Liberia, the transitional government in place following the country's two civil wars concluded several major foreign investment contracts including a controversial agreement with Mittal Steel.[77] The UN Mission in Liberia (UNMIL) has questioned whether the transitional government actually had the authority to do this.[78] Some of the contracts have since been renegotiated.[79]

5.2.2   Who has access to foreign investment contracts?

Foreign investment contracts are typically not publicly disclosed. The production of model agreements provides some degree of transparency and opportunity for public scrutiny. However, model agreements are only common in the petroleum sector. Furthermore, these models may be substantially altered or ignored altogether in the negotiations of actual contracts.

The typical justification given by governments for confidentiality of contracts is that disclosure would negatively affect their bargaining power in future negotiations. However, as a guide produced by the IMF notes, the

---

[75] Ayine *et al.* 2005: 3. See also Global Witness 2006: 41.   [76] Stiglitz 2003: 71.
[77] See further discussion in Global Witness 2006.   [78] UNMIL 2006: 27–8.
[79] The Mittal contract was renegotiated in 2006. A contract with Firestone was renegotiated in 2008.

terms of a contract are likely to be widely known within the industry soon after signing.[80] In some sectors, such as petroleum and gas, contracts are available through expensive subscription services.[81] The IMF concludes that:

> Little by way of strategic advantage thus seems to be lost through publication of contracts. Indeed, it could be argued that the obligation to publish contracts should in fact strengthen the hand of the government in negotiations, since the obligation to disclose the outcome to the legislature and the general public increases pressure on the government to negotiate a good deal.[82]

It must also be considered that some government officials may have a vested interest in keeping contracts confidential. As Ayine *et al.* note: 'Lack of transparency is a breeding ground for corruption.'[83]

While traditionally NGOs such as Publish What You Pay and Revenue Watch have focused on the issue of transparency of government revenue from foreign investment projects, they are increasingly interested in the issue of contractual transparency. There are also indications of some degree of response from investors, governments and international organizations. For example, the BTC Pipeline contracts discussed above were made public after the outcry from civil society led the IFC to put pressure on BP to disclose them.[84] More recently, in response to the Extractive Industries Review (which recommended that the World Bank Group require the disclosure of contracts in the extractive sector) the IFC's Policy on Social and Environmental Sustainability was updated to include the following paragraph:

> Accordingly, IFC requires that: (i) for significant new extractive industries projects, clients publicly disclose their material project payments to the host government (such as royalties, taxes, and profit sharing), and *the relevant terms of key agreements that are of public concern, such as host government agreements (HGAs) and intergovernmental agreements (IGAs)*;[85]

Furthermore, in April 2008, the World Bank and a range of partners launched the Extractive Industries Transparency Initiative Plus Plus (EITI++). While the original EITI focused on the transparency in company

---

[80] IMF 2007: 14.

[81] See, e.g., the website of Barrows Company at www.barrowscompany.com.

[82] IMF 2007: 14.   [83] Ayine *et al.* 2005: 3.   [84] Reyes 2006: 846.

[85] IFC Policy on Social & Environmental Sustainability, April 2006, www.ifc.org/ifcext/ enviro.nsf/Content/SustainabilityPolicy, emphasis added.

payments and government revenues from oil, gas and mining, EITI++ goes further. According to the World Bank, the initiative will:

> provide governments with a slate of options including technical assistance and capacity building for improving the management of resource-related wealth for the benefit of the poor. Through technical assistance, EITI++ *aims to improve the quality of contracts for countries*, monitoring operations and the collection of taxes and royalties. It will also improve economic decisions on resource extraction, managing price volatility, and investing revenues effectively for national development.[86]

It is also worth mentioning that in 2004 the US Department of Treasury issued a statement in response to the Extractive Industries Review which noted that they 'would like there to be an *ex ante* presumption of disclosure of such documents as Host Government Agreements, Concession Agreements, and bidding documents, allowing for redaction of, or exceptions for, commercially proprietary information'.[87] Finally, some governments, such as Azerbaijan and Timor-Leste, have opted to publish their petroleum contracts.[88]

5.3   Potential implications for environmental governance

Foreign investment contracts could potentially be an important mechanism for ensuring that foreign investors adopt high environmental standards in their operations. However, many existing contracts appear to be structured in a manner that risks dissuading governments from improving environmental regulations and preventing citizens, who are almost always unaware of the content of the contracts when they are signed, from holding investors accountable for environmental damage.

5.3.1   *Flexibility vs stability*

Ong puts it well when he argues that foreign investment contracts are 'currently designed to operate within an artificially created and maintained legal lacuna, with the only exception being the laws and standards that the [multinational corporations] themselves are comfortable with and

---

[86] 'World Bank Group and Partners Launch EITI++, Turning Commodity Price Windfalls into Benefits for Poor People', *World Bank Press Release No:2008/269/AFR*, 12 April 2008, http://web.worldbank.org, emphasis added.

[87] US Department of Treasury Statement Concerning the Extractive Industries Review, From the Office of Public Affairs, 2 August 2004, www.treasury.gov/press/releases/js1841.htm.

[88] Muttitt 2007: 22.

willing to accept'.[89] When weak environmental provisions are combined with stabilization measures, there is the risk that low standards could be locked in for long periods of time. Foreign investment contracts rarely endure for seventy years or more, as was typical in colonial times, but they are still long-term in nature. For example, a thirty-year contract with renewal clauses would not be uncommon. One could argue that the long duration of foreign investment contracts is justified by the high costs and high risks that investors face. Nevertheless, it should also be recognized that this aspect of contracts may cause problems for the host state, as international and domestic political circumstances, government priorities, and indeed governments themselves, change over such periods of time.[90]

The need for flexibility to respond to change is particularly acute in the area of environmental policy-making. As von Moltke reasons:

> Environmental management is a dynamic activity, responding to growing knowledge concerning the environment and anthropogenic threats to it, as well as to changing perceptions concerning the seriousness of these threats . . . An added level of complexity derives from the continuous development of technologies designed to protect the environment. As these technologies become available, policy must adjust to reflect new capabilities.[91]

In addition to being pressured from below (from communities) to improve environmental standards, governments also have to implement their international commitments under multilateral environmental agreements. As noted above, the stabilization clauses in some contracts explicitly cover regulations that states develop in line with their international obligations. While Cotula suggests that states cannot 'contract out' of their commitments in international treaties, stabilization clauses could result in states having to pay investors compensation for their compliance with evolving international norms.[92] Leader summarizes the dilemma that governments face as a result of such contractual commitments:

> Poorer states which make such an agreement are thereby put before a difficult choice: either they fully implement into their domestic legal orders the international norms to which they are committed – with no exceptions carved out for the investor – and thereby pay the latter compensation for its lost profit; or else they permit the project to create a hazard to local populations, and find themselves in breach of international standards as a result.[93]

---

[89] Ong 2008: 205.   [90] Peter 1995: 14.   [91] von Moltke 2002: 357–8.
[92] Cotula 2008: 172.   [93] Leader 2006: 690.

In one case, this particular issue has sparked international concern, and eventually a response from the investors involved. Subsequent to substantial pressure from civil society groups, the BTC pipeline consortium adopted a 'Human Rights Undertaking'. In this unilateral deed, the consortium commits not to enforce the economic equilibrium clauses in its contracts when the actions taken by the host governments are 'reasonably required' to fulfil their obligations under human rights, labour, or health, safety and environmental protection treaties. While the Undertaking is seen as an important development, it has been criticized on several fronts. First of all, as a unilateral agreement rather than an amendment to the HGA, its legal status is somewhat questionable.[94] Secondly, as pointed out by CIEL, giving an arbitral tribunal the power to determine whether governmental actions are 'reasonably required' by international treaties is problematic.[95] Thirdly, government entities are still precluded from bringing claims against the consortium in the domestic courts, which means that disputes about human rights or the protection of the environment will still end up in arbitration.[96] As discussed in the next chapters, arbitrators are typically experts in commercial law and not in other areas such as human rights or environmental protection. Furthermore, there are serious concerns about the accountability of arbitrators and transparency in the arbitral process.

5.3.2   Reducing policy options and creating incoherence

Even when stabilization clauses do not preclude the application of new environmental regulations to an investment project outright, they may affect the options available to governments in the development of policy; in other words, the number of tools in the 'policy toolbox'. For example, stabilization of fiscal matters could also cover market-based environmental measures. While the use of measures such as environmental levies and taxes is not yet commonplace in developing countries, there is a global trend toward a greater use of such mechanisms and it can be expected that developing countries will adopt more of these types of instrument in the future.[97] If stabilization clauses limit the range of instruments available to regulators, then this may in turn result in a reduction of the effectiveness or efficiency of the policies produced.[98]

---

[94] Reyes 2006: 864.   [95] CIEL 2003a: 9.   [96] Leader 2006: 702.
[97] Verhoosel 1998: 457.   [98] Cotula 2008: 170.

Furthermore, if each foreign investment contract freezes the environmental legislation for one project at a given time, then it is possible for
different projects in the same sector to be governed by completely different sets of rules, creating policy incoherence. Domestic investors are
unlikely to be offered the stability that covers foreign investments and will
therefore also be covered by a separate set of rules. As Otto and Cordes
note:

> Stabilization clauses that attempt to immunize the contract from normal
> operation of the succession of laws principle raise serious practical and
> legal problems for host countries. If this limit on legislative discretion is
> effectively secured, ten or even thirty years later the project may operate
> under a legal regime very different from that governing all other economic
> activities. Moreover, different mining projects may operate under different
> investment terms. From political, economic, administrative and legal per-
> spectives the acceptability of this result is problematic. The concern is likely
> to be even greater when contracts freeze preferential terms not available to
> local investors.[99]

In sum, foreign investment contracts are likely to create a huge administrative burden for regulators. Many developing countries currently lack
well-established institutions for regulating foreign investors, particularly
on issues of environmental management. Contracts that establish mini-
enclaves for each investment project are likely to put further strain on the
already limited monitoring and enforcement capabilities of environmental agencies and the messy situation that results may not, in the end, be in
the best interests of foreign investors.

5.3.3   The cost of confidentiality

Confidentiality of contracts results in reduced accountability of both governments and foreign investors. As Ayine *et al.* note:

> Without public scrutiny of foreign investment contracts, it is impossible
> for citizens to judge whether or not their elected governments are acting
> in their best interests and effectively pursuing or meeting public policy
> goals. It is also impossible for them properly to hold their governments to
> account for consequences of foreign direct investment.[100]

Similarly, a Global Witness report notes that the lack of transparency
and scrutiny of contracts has serious implications: 'it curtails civil

---

[99] Otto and Cordes 2002: V–23.   [100] Ayine *et al.* 2005: 3.

society participation, it encourages lack of accountability and it provides an opportunity for corrupt behaviour'.[101]

While both investors and states argue that confidentiality allows them to maintain a competitive edge in negotiations, in reality the content of contracts is often well known within an industry. The current system of expensive subscription services to access contracts in the oil and gas sector is an example. This system ensures that companies and elite law firms will have access to contracts, while civil society and academic researchers will not. Furthermore, if contracts are only disclosed once they have been signed, public scrutiny will not result in changes to the terms of the contracts.[102]

Miranda argues that the lack of transparency and accountability in the development of foreign investment contracts is also problematic for investors as it is likely to exacerbate opposition to foreign investment projects from civil society.[103] In cases where pressure from NGOs or a local population is strong enough, governments may force renegotiation of the contract or, in extreme circumstances, cancel it outright. In several cases this has led to protracted and expensive arbitration proceedings, but it has also resulted in a significant amount of negative publicity for the corporations involved.

[101] Global Witness 2006: 41.   [102] Amnesty International UK 2005: 35.
[103] Miranda 2007.

6

International investment arbitration

Foreign investors have long argued that local courts in developing countries are incapable of fairly adjudicating claims brought against their own government. In response to their concerns, in the 1960s a system of dispute settlement emerged which allowed investors to initiate international arbitration proceedings with a host state. Investor-state dispute settlement mechanisms are now standard features of IIAs and foreign investment contracts.

An international 'investment court' to deal with investor-state disputes has not been established and, as there is no multilateral agreement on investment, nothing comparable to the WTO Dispute Settlement Understanding has been set up. Instead, IIAs and contracts refer to one or more sets of procedural rules, which can be used for the creation and function of one-off arbitral panels. While there are variations among the different sets of rules, some general statements about the set-up and operation of arbitration proceedings can be made. In this book a focus is given to arbitral rules developed by the International Centre for the Settlement of Investment Disputes (ICSID) and the United Nations Commission on International Trade Law (UNCITRAL).[1]

This chapter provides an overview of the most important procedural rules of investment arbitration. It then explores the issue of the confidentiality of proceedings and awards and assesses some of the developments that have occurred in recent years which have led to increased transparency in some disputes. Finally, an overall assessment of the potential implications of investment arbitration for environmental governance, particularly in developing countries, is given. It is argued that, despite some improvements in arbitral practice, the current governance of investor-state disputes is neither neutral, nor fair, nor democratic. The system is

---

[1] According to UNCTAD 2007: 110, ICSID and UNCITRAL Rules are the most commonly employed rules in investor-state disputes.

procedurally biased against states in general, and developing countries with limited resources in particular.

6.1   Introducing ICSID and UNCITRAL

Investor-state arbitration can be supervised by an administrative body (institutional arbitration) or can be unsupervised (*ad hoc* arbitration). The supervising body may assist in appointing arbitrators, determining the place of arbitration, determining costs and arbitrator fees, and will itself charge a fee for the performance of these functions.

The most important supervisory body referred to in IIAs and foreign investment contracts is ICSID, which is a part of the World Bank Group and is located in Washington, DC. ICSID was established in 1966, when the Convention on the Settlement of Investment Disputes between States and Nationals of Other States (ICSID Convention) came into force.[2] In order for a dispute to qualify for ICSID arbitration, it must be between a Contracting State and a national of another Contracting State. However, if one of the parties does not meet these criteria, then the Additional Facility, developed in 1978, may be utilized. The ICSID Rules and Additional Facility Rules are periodically revised; the most recent versions came into force in April 2006.[3] Some of the changes that were made in the latest update to the rules are discussed in Section 6.2.3.

More than 1,500 BITs provide for ICSID arbitration, as do important regional agreements such as NAFTA.[4] Unlike other supervisory bodies, ICSID was designed expressly for the purpose of handling investor-state arbitrations and does not handle disputes between firms. Although ICSID was established in 1966, the first ICSID arbitral tribunal did not convene until 1972, and the pace of cases brought before the Centre remained slow for decades.[5] It is only in the last decade that the case-load of ICSID has increased sharply. Between 2001 and 2006, the number of disputes filed under ICSID was 150 per cent of the total number of cases filed over the first thirty-five years that the Centre was in existence.[6]

---

[2] As of 1 August 2009, 156 states had signed the Convention and 144 had ratified it. These numbers will drop by one in January 2010 when Ecuador's denunciation of the Convention takes effect. See further Section 9.2.1.

[3] 'Rules of Procedure for Arbitration Proceedings (Arbitration Rules)', *ICSID Convention, Regulations and Rules*, April 2006, http://icsid.worldbank.org.

[4] 'Canada: ICSID at a Crossroads', *Mondaq*, 27 September 2006, www.mondaq.com.

[5] Egli 2007: 1063.

[6] 'Canada: ICSID at a Crossroads', *Mondaq*, 27 September 2006, www.mondaq.com.

In 1976, the most significant set of *ad hoc* arbitral rules was developed by UNCITRAL.[7] Established by the UN General Assembly in 1966, UNCITRAL was given the general mandate to further the progressive harmonization and unification of the law of international trade.[8] An integral part of the Commission's work is the promotion of the Convention on the Recognition and Enforcement of Foreign Arbitral Awards (1958 'New York Convention'), which is crucial to the enforcement of awards rendered under UNCITRAL Rules as well as other arbitral rules (see Section 6.1.2.6).[9] At the time of writing, discussions were taking place on a revision of the UNCITRAL Rules for the first time in their history (see Section 6.2.4).

6.1.1   Arbitral proceedings

According to the ICSID Convention, the host state (a contracting state) or the investor (of a contracting state) may initiate arbitration proceedings, but most IIAs only allow an investor to bring a claim.[10] IIAs and contracts may require that disputing parties enter into good faith consultations prior to the commencement of arbitration. This 'cooling off' period generally lasts six months.[11] Furthermore, there may be a period after which the dispute may no longer be brought to arbitration (i.e., a statute of limitations).[12]

6.1.1.1   Consent to arbitration and exhaustion of local remedies

There are a variety of ways in which a state may provide its consent to arbitration and this consent may refer to either a specific investor or a specific dispute or instead to a defined class of unknown investors and future disputes.[13] In the first instance, consent is generally given in a clause

---

[7] UNCITRAL Arbitration Rules, 28 April 1976, *Report of the United Nations Commission on International Trade Law on the Work of its Ninth Session*, UN Doc. A/31/17 (1976). Reproduced in 15 ILM (1976): 701.

[8] 'Origin, Mandate and Composition of UNCITRAL', UNCITRAL website, www.uncitral.org, accessed 17 December 2008.

[9] The New York Convention had 144 Parties as of 1 August 2009. The full text of the Convention and its membership status is found on the UNCITRAL website, www.uncitral.org/uncitral/en/uncitral_texts/arbitration/NYConvention.html.

[10] Choi 2007: 736.   [11] UNCTAD 2007: 105.

[12] For example, NAFTA Art. 1116.2 stipulates that a claim under Chapter 11 cannot be made 'if more than three years have elapsed from the date on which the investor first acquired, or should have first acquired, knowledge of the alleged breach and knowledge that the investor has incurred loss or damage'.

[13] Reed *et al.* 2004: 7.

within a foreign investment contract. In the second instance, the more general consent can be provided through a clause in an IIA or within national legislation. Consent in this form is referred to as 'arbitration without privity'.[14] It was only in the 1990s that the inclusion of general consent to arbitration in IIAs became widespread.[15] Van Harten notes that, unlike contractual consent where the state is only providing access to arbitration to specific investors with respect to specific investments, general consent in IIAs:

> incorporates within the system a broad class of potential claimants whose identity is unknown to the state at the time of the state's consent and a wide range of potential disputes arising from any exercise of sovereign authority that affects the assets of a foreign investor.[16]

Investors, not being party to IIAs, cannot provide such general consent and, therefore, consent to arbitration by initiating proceedings. The ICSID Convention stipulates that where both parties have consented to the jurisdiction of ICSID, neither party may withdraw its consent unilaterally.[17] Furthermore, consent to ICSID arbitration is at 'the exclusion of any other remedy' unless otherwise stated in a contract or IIA.[18]

Customary international law requires the exhaustion of local remedies before a foreign investor's claim may be brought to international arbitration, but holds that a domestic court's decision is not *res judicata*[19] for a subsequent international tribunal. Dodge summarizes the system well: 'It gives the foreign investor two "bites at the apple" but requires it to take the domestic bite first'.[20] However, the local remedies rule can be waived by international agreement. The ICSID Convention states that: 'A Contracting State may require the exhaustion of local administrative or judicial remedies as a condition of its consent to arbitration under this Convention.'[21] However, in contrast with treaties in other areas (e.g., human rights), IIAs rarely require that foreign investors first exhaust domestic legal remedies before proceeding to international arbitration.[22] As Horn points out, exhaustion of local remedies clauses 'are not very appreciated by investors who look for ways to immediately commence arbitration procedures'.[23]

---

[14] Paulsson 1995.   [15] Van Harten 2007a: 26.   [16] *Ibid*: 63.
[17] ICSID Convention: Art. 25.1.   [18] *Ibid*: Art. 26.
[19] A final judgment that is not subject to further appeal.
[20] Dodge 2000: 360.   [21] ICSID Convention: Art. 26.
[22] Peterson 2004b: 3, points out that the European Convention for the Protection of Human Rights and Fundamental Freedoms requires claimants to begin in local courts.
[23] Horn 2004: 25.

The issue of domestic versus international remedies can become particularly complex when an investor is pursuing both contract claims and treaty claims in relation to the same dispute. Some IIAs have so-called fork in the road provisions, which stipulate that if the investor submits a dispute before the local courts of the host state or to any other agreed dispute resolution procedure, he forever loses the right to submit the same claims to the international arbitration procedure in the IIA.[24] However, contract and treaty claims have been considered by some arbitration tribunals to be distinct.[25] Schreuer explains that the fork in the road clause may not be applicable in some circumstances:

> The loss of access to international arbitration applies only if the same dispute based on the same cause of action has previously been submitted to the domestic judiciaries of the host state. If the dispute before the domestic court concerns a contract claim or an appeal against the decision of a regulatory authority and the dispute before the international tribunal concerns a BIT claim, the fork in the road clause will not apply.[26]

Another provision, slightly different from the fork in the road, is the 'no U-turn' rule found in NAFTA and some BITs.[27] This type of provision allows investors to abandon domestic court proceedings, before or after a decision is rendered, in favour of submission to an arbitral tribunal, but prohibits an investor from returning to the domestic courts if it is unsuccessful in arbitration.

6.1.1.2 Arbitrators

While it is possible for a tribunal to consist of a sole arbitrator, or any uneven number of arbitrators, investment arbitration generally runs on a three-arbitrator model. Under this system, the respondent state appoints one arbitrator, the investor appoints one arbitrator and then the two parties jointly agree on a third, who will act as the 'president' of the tribunal.[28] If the parties cannot agree on the selection of the president, they may opt to have a supervisory body, such as ICSID, make the appointment on their behalf. This is possible even in instances where the tribunal is formed under non-ICSID rules. According to Van Harten, the importance of the power of appointment should not be underestimated: 'In tripartite

---

[24] Reed *et al.* 2004: 58.
[25] See the discussion of *Occidental* v. *Ecuador* in Blades 2006: 111.
[26] Schreuer 2005: 307.   [27] NAFTA: Art. 1121.2.
[28] Generally, the president cannot be a national of either of the contracting parties. See UNCTAD 2007: 113.

arbitration the decision-making process generally turns on the presiding arbitrator given that the party-appointed arbitrators are more likely to take opposing views and that the president usually drafts the award.'[29]

ICSID has a Panel of Arbitrators, from which appointments by the body must be made. However, parties may appoint arbitrators from outside the Panel, as long as they are: 'persons of high moral character and recognized competence in the fields of law, commerce, industry or finance, who may be relied upon to exercise independent judgment'.[30] It is not only barristers and retired judges that are frequently appointed as arbitrators, but also professors, who in many cases also have careers as leading private lawyers.[31] In fact, it is entirely possible for an individual to act as a legal representative for a respondent or claimant in one case, and an arbitrator in another.[32]

Either party may object to the appointment of an arbitrator or seek to have an arbitrator disqualified if he does not meet the criteria outlined in the ICSID Convention.[33] Decisions on disqualification are made by the other members of the tribunal, or if necessary, by the ICSID Secretariat. There are no criteria for the selection of arbitrators laid out in the UNCI-TRAL Rules, although an appointment can be challenged on the basis of lack of independence or impartiality.[34]

The selection of arbitrators is considered a key decision in winning or losing a case. As Dezalay and Garth note, the attorneys for each side 'well understand that the "authority" and "expertise" of arbitrators determine their clout within the tribunal'.[35]

6.1.1.3   Confidentiality

Investor-state arbitration has its origin in private firm-to-firm (commercial) dispute resolution. Commercial arbitration is cloaked in confidentiality to protect business interests, and this has carried over to investment arbitration. Consequently, there are no requirements in IIAs or in any of the *ad hoc* or supervised dispute settlement mechanisms for investors to signal their intention to launch a dispute. The ICSID Secretariat does keep a registry of all cases filed under its rules, which is published on the Internet and includes the names of the disputants, the date the case was registered and a short description of the dispute. However, the registry does not indicate whether the case was brought in relation to a contract,

---

[29] Van Harten 2007a: 169.   [30] ICSID Convention: Art. 40 and 14.1.
[31] 'Private Practices', *American Lawyer*, 2003, www.americanlawyer.com.
[32] Coe 2006: 1351–2.   [33] ICSID Convention: Art. 57.
[34] UNCITRAL Rules: Rule 10.1.   [35] Dezalay and Garth 1996: 8–9.

consent to arbitration under a national law, or to the provisions of a BIT or regional treaty. Other supervisory bodies do not have a public register and bodies such as UNCITRAL do not even keep track of arbitrations that make use of their *ad hoc* arbitral rules.

Proceedings of investment disputes are also held *in camera* and non-parties will not have access unless the disputants consent to open the proceedings.[36] There have been some developments in arbitral practice in recent years related to confidentiality, which will be discussed further in Section 6.2.

6.1.2 Arbitral awards

In the course of arbitral proceedings a tribunal may issue several awards, for example, on jurisdiction, merits, damages and costs. Awards on the merits of a case will address the substantive rules of investment protection that were discussed in the previous two chapters. This section briefly outlines the other types of awards as well as the issues of publication, annulment, enforcement and precedent.

6.1.2.1 Jurisdiction

There are several aspects that a tribunal must consider in order to determine whether it has jurisdiction over a dispute. The most critical concern whether the investment, the investor and the government measures fall within the scope of the IIA (see Section 4.1.1). It should also be noted that there may be temporal restrictions on the application of an IIA to a dispute. The majority of IIAs cover existing investments but do not retroactively apply to disputes that arose prior to the entry into force of the agreement.

6.1.2.2 Damages

Arbitral tribunals appear to be wary of awarding restitution to claimants, and prefer instead to only award monetary damages.[37] However, restitution is not definitively ruled out.[38] Some agreements, such as the 2004 US Model BIT, stipulate that the respondent state may pay monetary damages in lieu of restitution.[39] The ICSID Convention also strongly favours monetary relief over restitution.[40]

As mentioned in Chapter 4, articles on expropriation often contain references to the requirement for compensation, and may indicate whether

---

[36] ICSID Rules: Rule 32.2; UNCITRAL Rules: Rule 25.4. [37] Coe and Rubins 2005: 628.
[38] See generally, Endicott 2007. [39] Kantor 2004: 390. [40] ICSID Convention: Art. 54.1.

it is to be *prompt, adequate and effective* or only *appropriate*. Some IIAs also provide guidance on valuation. However, often the tribunal is left a significant degree of discretion to determine damages, which may include a company's lost future profits.[41]

In general, IIAs and contracts do not stipulate how compensation should be calculated for breaches that fall short of expropriation. According to the ILA International Law on Foreign Investment Committee, the method of assessing compensation in such cases is different than in expropriation cases and should be 'based on the actual market value of the damaged and lost property, taking into account the realities of the political and economic risks faced by the investor in the host country'.[42]

6.1.2.3   Costs

The ICSID Secretariat charges a fee for the lodging of a request for arbitration (US$25,000), for any interpretation, revision or annulment of an arbitral award rendered pursuant to the Convention (US$10,000), for the administration of a dispute (US$20,000 per year plus out of pocket expenses), and for the appointment of an arbitrator or decisions on the challenge of an arbitrator in arbitrations not conducted under the Convention or Additional Facility Rules.[43] ICSID Arbitrators receive reimbursement for any direct expenses reasonably incurred in the course of the arbitration, and unless otherwise agreed between them and the parties, a fee of US$3,000 per day of meetings or other work performed in connection with the proceedings. The tribunal in an ICSID case is free to determine how the costs of the arbitration, and the legal fees of the parties, should be distributed in the award.[44]

The UNCITRAL Rules provide that the arbitral tribunal shall fix the costs of arbitration in its award.[45] There is no ceiling for arbitrator fees under the UNCITRAL Rules, though it is stipulated that they 'shall be reasonable in amount, taking into account the amount in dispute, the complexity of the subject-matter, the time spent by the arbitrators and any other relevant circumstances of the case'.[46] It is also suggested that the 'costs of arbitration shall in principle be borne by the unsuccessful party'.[47] However, the arbitral tribunal may choose to divide the costs, including

[41] Subedi 2008: 126.
[42] ILA International Law on Foreign Investment Committee 2006: 17.
[43] This schedule of fees is effective as of 1 January 2008. The administration fee was previously only US$10,000 per year.
[44] ICSID Convention: Art. 61.   [45] UNCITRAL Rules: Rule 38.
[46] *Ibid*: Rule 39.   [47] *Ibid*: Rule 40.

legal fees, between the parties, taking into account the circumstances of the case.[48]

   According to an UNCTAD report, companies have been known to spend up to US$4 million on lawyers' and arbitrators' fees for an investor-state dispute, and countries can expect an average tribunal to cost US$400,000 or more in addition to the US$1–2 million in legal fees.[49]

6.1.2.4   Publication of awards

Not all arbitral awards are publicly disclosed. ICSID Rules require the consent of both parties to a dispute before a ruling will be published by the Secretariat (although either party may unilaterally publish it elsewhere), while under UNCITRAL Rules the award may only be published with the consent of both the investor and the state.[50]

6.1.2.5   Challenges and annulment procedures

The ICSID Convention excludes appeal and forecloses challenges to awards. The only remedies available to the losing party are interpretation of the scope and meaning of the award, revisions of the award based on discovery of a previously unknown factor of decisive importance, and annulment of the award in a limited number of circumstances.[51] An *ad hoc* committee chosen by the ICSID Secretariat rules on the annulment of an award.

   The ICSID annulment procedure is unique and available only for disputes that were brought under the ICSID Rules. Awards decided under the ICSID Additional Facility Rules or UNCITRAL Rules can be revised or set aside in the place of arbitration or in a court of the state 'under the law of which' the award was made.[52] Some states restrict the scope of court review of arbitral decisions within their territories, in part because tribunals generally seek to avoid siting proceedings in states where the scope for review of awards is broad.[53]

[48] For further discussion on the allocation of costs and fees see Rubins 2003.
[49] UNCTAD 2005b: 7.
[50] ICSID Rules: Rule 48.4; UNCITRAL Rules: Rule 32.5.
[51] The reasons, outlined in Arts. 50, 51, and 52 of the ICSID Convention, are: the tribunal was not properly constituted; the tribunal manifestly exceeded its powers; there was corruption on the part of a tribunal member; there was a serious departure from a fundamental rule of procedure; or the award failed to state the reasons on which it was based.
[52] New York Convention: Art. V.   [53] Gantz 2006: 52.

6.1.2.6 Enforcement of awards

It has been said that 'the awards of arbitrators are more widely enforceable than any other adjudicative decision in public law'.[54] There are several mechanisms which aid in the enforcement of arbitral awards. First, IIAs often explicitly obligate states to recognize awards, thus allowing investors to seek enforcement in the local courts of the host state.[55] Secondly, where an IIA or foreign investment contract provides for enforcement under the ICSID Convention, an investor can seek enforcement in the domestic courts of any state party to the Convention. Article 54 of the ICSID Convention stipulates that each Contracting State shall recognize an ICSID award as binding and enforce the pecuniary obligations imposed by that award within its territory as if it were a final judgment of a domestic court.

ICSID awards have a high execution rate, which some observers hypothesize is a result of the body's connection to the World Bank.[56] There is thought to be a perception amongst states that failure to enforce an ICSID award could lead to strained relations and a loss of credibility with the Bank.

Awards may also be enforceable under other arbitration treaties such as the New York Convention. The New York Convention is similar to the ICSID Convention in that it requires courts in contracting states to enforce arbitral awards. IIAs and foreign investment contracts will often stipulate that arbitration proceedings must be held in a country that is party to the New York Convention. Under the New York Convention, the recognition and enforcement of the award may be refused by a court under certain conditions, including when it would be 'contrary to the public policy' of the country.[57] However, the public policy exception is typically read quite narrowly by courts.[58]

6.1.2.7 Precedent

Awards rendered in investment arbitration are only binding on the parties involved in the dispute: the rulings of tribunals are said to have no *stare decisis*. Hence, tribunals do not have to base their decisions on the decisions of previous tribunals. However, Stone Sweet points out that this is also the case in the international trade regime, and yet nevertheless citations to past decisions are common and expected: 'Once constructed

[54] Van Harten 2007a: 5.   [55] *Ibid*: 118.
[56] Reed *et al.* 2004: 9; Franck 2007: 372; Van Harten 2007a: 118.
[57] New York Convention: Art. V.2.   [58] Harris 2007: 10.

as a precedent-based discourse about the meaning of GATT rules, panel decisions became a fundamental source of those rules.'[59] Citations to past rulings certainly also occur in investment arbitration, and Cheng argues that 'there is an informal, but powerful, system of precedent that constrains arbitrators to account for prior published awards and to stabilize international investment law'.[60] However, others have noted that a number of inconsistent awards have led to a 'legitimacy crisis' in international investment arbitration.[61]

6.2   Transparency and non-party participation

The system of investment arbitration has been criticized for adopting procedures that are well established in the realm of commercial arbitration, but that are considered inappropriate when applied to disputes involving the regulatory choices of states and, thereby, issues of public concern. Since 2001, there have been a number of changes to the investment arbitration process (in certain contexts) aimed at remedying the system's failings in this regard. The two developments of particular note are increased transparency and acceptance of non-party participation in disputes.[62]

Transparency relates not only to the publication of awards but also to access to pre-award submissions from the parties and to decisions made by the tribunal over the course of the proceedings. Furthermore, it also relates to public admittance to the tribunal hearings. As for non-party participation, in international tribunals this most commonly occurs through the submission of *amicus curiae* ('friend of the court') briefs. *Amicus curiae* submissions generally contain 'supplementary information on the case, particularly the occurrence of events or technicalities relating to the subject at hand'.[63] *Amici* are different from expert witnesses as they are not remunerated for their services and they are not in a contractual relationship with the parties to the dispute.[64] While historically there has been no role for *amici* in investor-state disputes, in recent years a trend of such participation has been emerging.

Transparency and non-party participation are intimately linked. Without public knowledge of the existence of disputes, *amici* will be precluded

[59] Stone Sweet 1999: 170.
[60] Cheng 2007: 1016. For a quantitative and qualitative assessment of citations in investment tribunal awards, see Commission 2007.
[61] Brower *et al.* 2003; Franck 2005.
[62] An earlier version of this section was published in Tienhaara 2007.
[63] Bennaim-Selvi 2005: 786.   [64] Mistelis 2005: 231.

from making submissions. Furthermore, it can be argued that without access to relevant documents and to the proceedings, non-parties will be incapable of formulating effective and worthwhile submissions.

6.2.1   Methanex and NAFTA FTC guidelines

The substantive aspects of the *Methanex Corporation v. United States of America* case will be discussed in Section 7.2.5; therefore this section will only discuss procedural decisions made by the tribunal.

In 2000, two requests were made by NGOs for permission to file *amicus curiae* briefs, to make oral submissions and have observer status at the oral hearings in *Methanex*.[65] The US and Methanex both filed submissions responding to the Petitioners' requests, as did the non-disputing parties of NAFTA (Canada and Mexico). Both Methanex and Mexico opposed the acceptance of *amicus curiae* briefs, while Canada and the US showed support. The US also indicated its willingness to open the proceedings and to disclose documents to the public.

The tribunal concluded that it had the power to accept *amicus curiae* submissions, but no power to authorize access to materials or to allow the petitioners to attend hearings.[66] The tribunal found that UNCITRAL Rule 15.1, which states that 'the arbitral tribunal may conduct the arbitration in such manner as it considers appropriate, provided that the parties are treated with equality and that at any stage of the proceedings each party is given a full opportunity of presenting his case', gave it the discretion to accept *amicus curiae* submissions. However, the tribunal made it clear that UNCITRAL Rule 25.4, which requires hearings to be private unless otherwise agreed by the parties, limits the flexibility of Rule 15.1. Furthermore, while indicating that it was minded to accept *amicus curiae* submissions in this case, the tribunal chose to delay its final decision until a later stage in the dispute.

It is clear that one of the reasons the tribunal was amenable to accepting briefs was that it believed that this would improve the public image of investment arbitration:

---

[65] Petition to the Arbitral Tribunal of the IISD, 25 August 2000, www.iisd.org; Amended Petition of Communities for a Better Environment, the Bluewater Network of the Earth Island Institute, and CIEL to Appear Jointly as *Amici Curiae*, 13 October 2000, www.earthjustice.org.

[66] *Methanex Corp. v. United States of America*, Decision of the Tribunal on Petitions from Third Parties to Intervene as '*Amici Curiae*', 15 January 2001: para. 47.

[the] arbitral process could benefit from being perceived as more open or transparent; or conversely be harmed if seen as unduly secretive. In this regard, the Tribunal's willingness to receive *amicus* submissions might support the process in general and this arbitration in particular; whereas a blanket refusal could do positive harm.[67]

On 7 October 2003, the NAFTA FTC, made up of representatives of the three NAFTA countries, issued a statement on non-party participation in Chapter 11 disputes.[68] The statement stipulated that any non-disputing party that is a person of a party (a NAFTA state), or that has a significant presence in the territory of a party, could apply for leave to file a submission. The statement also outlined guidelines for the acceptance of such submissions. According to these guidelines, in the application for *amicus* status the person or organization should disclose any affiliations or financial ties to either party in the dispute, indicate the nature of their interest in the dispute, and provide reasoning as to why the tribunal should accept the submission. Furthermore, the guidelines suggest that the tribunal, when making its decision, should consider the extent to which:

(a) the non-disputing party submission would assist the Tribunal in the determination of a factual or legal issue related to the arbitration by bringing a perspective, particular knowledge or insight that is different from that of the disputing parties;
(b) the non-disputing party submission would address matters within the scope of the dispute;
(c) the non-disputing party has a significant interest in the arbitration; and
(d) there is a public interest in the subject-matter of the arbitration.

It was also noted that in arbitrations to which they are a party, Canada and the US would consent to open the hearings to the public (the consent of the investor would also be required). Mexico announced its support for public hearings in investor-state disputes the following year.[69]

Shortly after the 2003 NAFTA FTC statement was issued, Methanex wrote to the tribunal, on behalf of both disputing parties, to suggest that the FTC guidelines for the acceptance of *amicus curiae* submissions be adopted. The tribunal did so in January of the following year and issued a press release outlining the procedures to be followed by potential

---

[67] *Ibid*: para. 49.
[68] 'Celebrating NAFTA at Ten', *NAFTA Commission Meeting Joint Statement*, 7 October 2003, Montreal, www.ustr.gov.
[69] 'A Decade of Achievement', *NAFTA Free Trade Commission Joint Statement*, 16 July 2004, San Antonio, Texas, www.ustr.gov.

amici. The original petitioners submitted their briefs in March 2004.[70] It is notable that the tribunal made reference to the *amicus curiae* brief of the International Institute for Sustainable Development (IISD) in its Final Award, describing it as 'carefully reasoned'.[71] The proceedings in *Methanex* were also eventually opened to the public, but only with the consent of both parties.

In the same period as *Methanex* was transpiring, another NAFTA tribunal (following UNCITRAL Rules) in *United Parcel Service (UPS)* v. *Canada* also found that it had the power to accept *amicus* briefs, and more recently the (NAFTA, UNCITRAL) tribunal in *Glamis Gold* v. *United States* has also done so.[72] It is interesting to note that, in the latter case, in addition to several NGOs and the Quechan Indian Nation, a business association was permitted to submit a brief.[73]

6.2.2   Provisions in recent BITs

In 2003 and 2004 respectively, the governments of Canada and the US released new versions of their model BITs.[74] The Canadian government had been a strong proponent of permitting non-party participation in NAFTA Chapter 11 disputes, and the government website notes that '[o]ne of the most significant improvements' made in the new Model BIT is the 'institutionalisation' of *amicus curiae* submissions.[75] The Model follows the NAFTA FTC guidelines on *amicus curiae* submissions quite

---

[70] Submission Of Non-Disputing Parties Bluewater Network, Communities For A Better Environment and CIEL, 9 March 2004, www.ciel.org; *Amicus Curiae* Submission by the IISD, 9 March 2004, www.iisd.org.

[71] *Methanex Corporation* v. *United States of America,* Final Award of the Tribunal on Jurisdiction and Merits, 3 August 2005: para. IV.B.27. Reproduced in 44 ILM (2005): 1345.

[72] *United Parcel Service (UPS)* v. *Canada,* Decision of the Tribunal on Petitions for Intervention and Participation as Amici Curiae, 17 October 2001; *Glamis Gold Ltd* v. *United States of America,* Decision on Application and Submission by Quechan Indian Nation, 16 September 2005.

[73] *Glamis Gold Ltd* v. *United States of America,* Application for Leave to File a Non-Disputing Party Submission by the National Mining Association, 13 October 2006, www.naftaclaims.com. The Association has direct ties with the Claimant, as Glamis Gold Ltd is an Association Member.

[74] Agreement between Canada and .... for the Promotion and Protection of Investments (Canadian Model BIT), 2003, www.international.gc.ca; Treaty between the Government of the United States of America and the Government of [Country] Concerning the Encouragement and Reciprocal Protection of Investment (US Model BIT), 2004, www.state.gov.

[75] 'Canada's Foreign Investment Protection and Promotion Agreements Negotiating Programme', *Foreign Affairs and International Trade Canada website,* www.international.gc.ca, accessed 17 December 2008.

closely.[76] The Model also stipulates that hearings will be open to the public and that all documents and awards will be freely available (with certain limits to protect confidential information).[77]

The US Model BIT has a less detailed provision on participation, which states: 'The tribunal shall have the authority to accept and consider *amicus curiae* submissions from a person or entity that is not a disputing party.'[78] The model also provides public access to all documents and awards and open proceedings.[79] These provisions have already been incorporated into the US-Chile FTA,[80] the CAFTA-DR,[81] the US-Morocco FTA,[82] the US-Singapore FTA,[83] the US-Uruguay BIT,[84] the US-Colombia Trade Promotion Agreement[85] and the US-Peru Trade Promotion Agreement.[86]

6.2.3 ICSID's rules, old and new

In 2006, ICSID updated its Rules of Procedure for Arbitration Proceedings. Changes to two rules in particular are relevant to the issues of non-party participation and transparency. The most significant change was to Rule 37 (Visits and Inquiries), where a second paragraph was added stipulating that, after consulting both parties, a tribunal could allow a non-disputing party to submit a written brief.

Rule 32 (Oral Procedure), which determines who may attend hearings, was also slightly modified. However, the change in wording is, in practice, very limited. Section 2 of the Rule formerly read: 'The Tribunal shall decide, with the consent of the parties, which other persons besides the parties, their agents, counsel and advocates, witnesses and experts during their testimony, and officers of the Tribunal may attend the hearings.' It now reads:

> Unless either party objects, the Tribunal, after consultation with the Secretary-General, may allow other persons, besides the parties, their agents, counsel and advocates, witnesses and experts during their testimony, and officers of the Tribunal, to attend or observe all or part of the hearings, subject to appropriate logistical arrangements.

---

[76] Art. 39. [77] Art. 38. [78] Art. 28.3. [79] Art. 29. [80] Art. 10.19 and 10.20.
[81] Art. 10.20 and 10.21. [82] Art. 10.19 and 10.20. [83] Art. 15.19 and 15.20.
[84] US-Uruguay BIT, 4 November 2005, Mar del Plata: Art. 28 and 29.
[85] US-Colombia Trade Promotion Agreement, 22 November 2006, Washington, DC: Art. 10.20 and 10.21.
[86] US-Peru Trade Promotion Agreement, 12 April 2006, Washington, DC: Art. 10.20 and 10.21.

The bottom line is that not all proceedings will be opened to the public under the new Rules.

Prior to the change in the ICSID Rules there were several cases that dealt with the issue of non-party participation[87] and since the adoption of the new Rules there has been a further case in which NGOs have petitioned for *amicus curiae* status.

6.2.3.1   Testing the water: Biwater and the application of the new rules

The *Biwater Gauff Ltd* v. *United Republic of Tanzania* case is worth reviewing, as it displays some of the limitations of the changes to ICSID's Rules, as well as the tension between transparency and confidentiality in proceedings.

In 2005, the Government of Tanzania cancelled a contract of the private utility City Water, owned by British company Biwater. The contract was to supply water to the country's commercial capital, Dar es Salaam. The Government claimed that the reason for the cancellation was that the residents have had to cope with erratic supplies and water shortages.[88] In August of 2005, the company filed a request for arbitration based on a UK-Tanzania BIT and under ICSID Rules. By the time that the case had begun, the new ICSID Rules had come into effect and the tribunal determined that they would govern the proceedings.

In July 2006, Biwater wrote a letter to the tribunal claiming that the Government of Tanzania had unilaterally disclosed certain documents to an 'unrelated' third party.[89] Subsequently a procedural order and the minutes of the first session were published on the Internet. According to Biwater, the dispute was attracting public interest which had led to, for example, a campaign by the World Development Movement (an NGO based in London) to discontinue the proceedings. In a second letter, the company filed a request to the tribunal for provisional measures

---

[87] *Aguas del Tunari, S.A.* v. *Republic of Bolivia*, ICSID Case No. ARB/02/3, Decision on Respondent's Objections to Jurisdiction, 21 October 2005; *Suez, Sociedad General de Aguas de Barcelona S.A. and InterAguas Servicios Integrales del Agua S.A.* v. *The Argentine Republic*, ICSID Case No. ARB/03/17, Order in Response to a Petition for Participation as Amicus Curiae, 17 March 2006; *Suez, Sociedad General de Aguas de Barcelona, S.A. and Vivendi Universal, S.A.* v. *The Argentine Republic*, ICSID Case No. ARB/03/19, Order in Response to a Petition for Transparency and Participation as Amicus Curiae, 19 May 2005.

[88] 'Tanzania Ditches Private Water Supplier', *BBC News*, 18 May 2005.

[89] *Biwater Gauff Ltd* v. *United Republic of Tanzania*, ICSID Case No. ARB/05/22, Procedural Order No. 3 (*Biwater* Procedural Order No. 3), 29 September 2006.

on confidentiality.[90] The request, which according to the company was based on the need to preserve the procedural integrity of the proceedings and to avoid aggravation or exacerbation of the dispute, called for the following:

(i) discussion on a case-by-case basis of the publication of all Decisions other than the Award (if mutual agreement cannot be reached then tribunal should make the decision);
(ii) no disclosure of the pleadings to non-parties;
(iii) no disclosure of any documents produced in the first and second rounds of disclosure to non-parties; and
(iv) no disclosure of any correspondence between the parties and/or the tribunal in respect of the arbitral proceedings to non-parties.

The tribunal noted that Biwater considered these measures to be necessary as they concerned the company's 'ability to rely on the private nature of the oral hearings, and its ability to present its case and accompanying evidence without the threat of increased harassment and interference from third parties'.[91]

In its decision on provisional measures, the tribunal suggested that what was required was 'a careful balancing between two competing interests: the need for transparency and the need to protect the procedural integrity of the arbitration'.[92] It commented: 'Without doubt, there is now a marked tendency towards transparency in treaty arbitration, which is reflected in the changes to ICSID's Rules.'[93] The tribunal reasoned that the provisions that continue to limit the publication of documents apply to the actions of the ICSID Secretariat, rather than to the parties themselves. However, the tribunal also agreed with Biwater that:

> the prosecution of a dispute in the media or in other public fora, or the uneven reporting and disclosure of documents or other parts of the record in parallel with a pending arbitration, may aggravate or exacerbate the dispute and may impact the integrity of the procedure.[94]

Furthermore, the tribunal stated that placing restrictions on disclosure for the duration of the dispute is not necessarily inconsistent with the objective of transparency, as these restrictions can be removed upon the conclusion of the dispute.[95]

---

[90] The letter, dated 17 July 2006, is referred to in *ibid*.
[91] *Biwater* Procedural Order No. 3: para. 38.   [92] *Ibid*: para. 112.
[93] *Ibid*: para. 114.   [94] *Ibid*: para. 136.   [95] *Ibid*: para. 140.

The tribunal determined that decisions on the publication of certain documents during the proceedings (decisions, orders, or directions) would be made on a case-by-case basis. Minutes or records of hearings would not be disclosed unless agreed by both parties or directed by the tribunal and, furthermore, any documents produced by one party would not be disclosed by the opposing party. Pleadings, written memorials, witness statements and expert reports (which could all contain details of the contents of other non-disclosed documents) would also be kept confidential pending the conclusion of the proceedings. Finally, correspondence between the parties and/or the tribunal would not be disclosed as these documents 'will usually concern the very conduct of the process itself, rather than issues of substance, and as such do not warrant wider distribution'.[96] The tribunal emphasized that parties were permitted to 'engage in general discussion about the case in public' as long as this was 'restricted to what is necessary' and not used to 'antagonise' or 'unduly pressure' the other party or exacerbate the dispute, or make the resolution of the dispute more difficult.

In November 2006, five NGOs (three Tanzanian and two international) jointly petitioned for *amicus curiae* status in this case.[97] The petitioners argued that the arbitration 'raises a number of issues of vital concern to the local community in Tanzania, and a wide range of potential issues of concern to developing countries' and 'also raises issues from a broader sustainable development perspective and is potentially of relevance for the entire international community'.[98]

Interestingly, the petitioners appear to have anticipated some of the possible objections to their participation in the dispute, pointing out that by acting together they had reduced the burden of additional *amicus curiae* submissions on the proceedings. The petitioners also argued that without greater transparency, it would not be possible for them to meaningfully participate in the dispute, nor would it be possible for the tribunal to even determine whether they passed the *amicus curiae* test provided by the ICSID Rules:

---

[96] *Ibid*: para. 161.
[97] Petition for *Amicus Curiae* Status of the Lawyers' Environmental Action Team, the Legal and Human Rights Centre, the Tanzania Gender Networking Programme, CIEL and IISD, 27 November 2006, www.ciel.org/Publications/Tanzania_Amicus_1Dec06.pdf.
[98] *Ibid*.

it is not possible for the Petitioners to fulfill all the conditions necessary to allow the Tribunal to fully apply this test. The reason for this impossibility is the impact of the confidentiality order contained in Procedural Order No. 3 of the Tribunal. By precluding the release to the public of the documents that detail the facts and legal issues in dispute, the Petitioners cannot describe the scope of their intended legal submissions, and hence the extent to which the tests set out in Rule 37.2 are fully met.[99]

The petitioners, therefore, suggested that the tribunal could either accept the petition and provide them with the legal documents needed to make a submission, or provide them with the legal documents in order that they might be able to prove that they meet the requirements of the *amicus curiae* test.

In response, Biwater argued that the petitioners had mistakenly assumed that the arbitration should concern them simply because the dispute related to water.[100] Biwater disagreed that environmental issues and issues of sustainable development were relevant to the case.

The tribunal's decision on *amicus curiae* was issued in February 2007.[101] In line with previous decisions, submissions were allowed but access to documents and hearings was not permitted. The tribunal reasoned that the petitioners had 'a sufficient interest' in the proceeding, and that their submission had the potential to assist the tribunal in the proceedings, by providing a perspective or knowledge that was different from that of the disputing parties. The tribunal also noted 'that allowing for the making of such submission by these entities in these proceedings is an important element in the overall discharge of the Arbitral Tribunal's mandate, and in securing wider confidence in the arbitral process itself'.[102] In terms of access to documents, the tribunal suggested that the dispute had been very public and widely reported, and that the 'broad policy issues' that the petitioners would address in their brief did not require access to documents from the arbitration.[103] However, it was also noted that the issue might be revisited in the future, given the fact that the limitations on disclosure were put in place to preserve 'procedural integrity' and not necessarily to ensure confidentiality *per se*.[104] Finally, with regard to the request to open the proceedings, the tribunal reasoned that Rule 32.2 was very clear

---

[99] *Ibid*: 11.
[100] The claimant's response is referred to in *Biwater Gauff Ltd* v. *United Republic of Tanzania*, ICSID Case No. ARB/05/22, Procedural Order No. 5 (*Biwater* Procedural Order No. 5), 2 February 2007.
[101] *Biwater* Procedural Order No. 5.   [102] *Ibid*: para. 50.   [103] *Ibid*: para. 65.
[104] *Ibid*: para. 66.

on this matter. As the claimant had voiced its objection to opening the proceedings, the tribunal had no option but to reject the request.[105]

In the Award, released in July 2008, the *Biwater* tribunal makes extensive reference to the *amicus curiae* submission. The tribunal notes that they 'found the *Amici's* observations useful' and that the submission 'informed the analysis of claims'.[106] In certain instances the tribunal directly references the brief in its analysis.

6.2.4   *Revision of the UNCITRAL Rules*

Although it was under UNCITRAL Rules that the tribunal in *Methanex* first determined that it had the power to accept *amicus curiae* submissions, it is important to remember that Rule 15.1 which provides this power is discretionary and is subordinated to other provisions in the Rules (the requirements that hearings will be held *in camera* unless the parties agree otherwise,[107] and that the award may only be made public with the consent of both parties).[108] Some observers argue that the power to consider *amicus curiae* submissions should be made explicit, mandatory, and coupled with increased transparency.[109]

In 2006, at its thirty-ninth session, UNCITRAL agreed that its Working Group II on International Arbitration and Conciliation should prioritize the revision of the UNCITRAL Arbitration Rules. In a report prepared by the Secretariat, several possible amendments were contemplated. Of relevance here are the following options for consideration: an express provision on non-party intervention; explicit rules regarding the confidentiality of the proceedings as such, or of the materials (including pleadings) before an arbitral tribunal; and rules addressing the situation where a party is under a legal duty to disclose an award or its tenor (for example under access to information legislation).[110]

In September of the same year, an unofficial UNCITRAL report was released, authored by two investment arbitration experts, with more specific recommendations for the revision of the Rules.[111] In terms of the

---

[105]   *Ibid*: paras. 70–2.
[106]   *Biwater Gauff (Tanzania) Ltd* v. *United Republic of Tanzania*, ICSID Case No. ARB/05/22, Award, 24 July 2008: para. 392.
[107]   UNCITRAL Rules: Rule 25.4.   [108]   *Ibid*: Rule 32.5.   [109]   See Marshall and Mann 2006.
[110]   United Nations Commission on International Trade Law Working Group II (Arbitration) Forty-fifth session Vienna, 11–15 September 2006, A/CN.9/WG.II/WP.143, www.uncitral.org.
[111]   Paulsson and Petrochilos 2006.

express provision on non-party access, the report recommended inserting a new Rule 15.5 that would read:

> Unless the parties have agreed otherwise, the Arbitral Tribunal may, after having consulted with the parties, and especially in cases raising issues of public interest, allow any person who is not a party to the proceedings to present one or more written statements, provided that the Tribunal is satisfied that such statements are likely to assist it in the determination of a factual or legal issue related to the proceeding by bringing a perspective, particular knowledge or insight which the parties are unable to present. The Arbitral Tribunal shall determine the mode and number of such statements after consulting with the parties.[112]

With regard to the inclusion of an explicit confidentiality clause, the authors noted that there had been substantial discussion on this issue during the revision of the ICC Rules in 1998. In that case, it was decided that a general clause should not be included and that tribunals should make these decisions on a case-by-case basis. However, with regard to the documents and evidence produced in the course of the arbitration, the authors did feel the need to propose a new clause, which would state that:

> Unless the parties have agreed otherwise, all materials in the proceedings which are not otherwise in the public domain, including materials created for the purpose of the arbitration and all other documents or evidence given by a party, witness, expert, [or any other person,] *shall be treated as confidential*, save and to the extent that disclosure may be required of a party by legal duty, to protect or pursue a legal right, and in bona fide legal proceedings before a state court or other judicial authority in relation to an award.[113]

Finally, the report suggested an amendment to the clause on the publication of the award to allow for publication with the consent of both parties (as before) or when 'disclosure is required of a party by legal duty, to protect or pursue a legal right or in relation to [bona fide] legal proceedings before a State court or other judicial authority'.[114] This clearly does not go as far as the ICSID Rules, where either party is permitted to publish the award unilaterally.

Two NGOs, which have been involved as *amici* in several investor-state disputes, also made a proposal to UNCITRAL in which they argued that a separate set of arbitration rules should be developed to govern disputes

---

[112] *Ibid*: 72.   [113] *Ibid*: 79, emphasis added.   [114] *Ibid*: 135.

that involve a state as a party. One of their suggestions was that in this separate set of rules, acceptance of *amicus curiae* briefs should be made explicit through a new Rule 15.4 along the lines of Rule 37.2 of the new ICSID Rules and the NAFTA FTC guidelines.[115] The NGO report also strongly cautioned against the adoption of a confidentiality clause, stating that in the case of proceedings involving a state such a clause 'would fly in the face of principles of good governance and human rights, and thus undermine the credibility and legitimacy of the arbitral proceedings'.[116]

In February 2007, member-governments rejected the idea of including a general provision on confidentiality in the UNCITRAL Rules, but delayed the decision on whether or not to develop a separate set of rules for disputes involving states.[117] At its forty-first session in New York in 2008, the Commission decided that:

> it would not be desirable to include specific provisions on treaty-based arbitration in the UNCITRAL Arbitration Rules themselves and that any work on investor-State disputes that the Working Group might have to undertake in the future should not delay the completion of the revision of the UNCITRAL Arbitration Rules in their generic form. As to timing, the Commission agreed that the topic of transparency in treaty-based investor-State arbitration was worthy of future consideration and should be dealt with as a matter of priority immediately after completion of the current revision of the UNCITRAL Arbitration Rules. As to the scope of such future work, the Commission agreed by consensus on the importance of ensuring transparency in investor-State dispute resolution.[118]

6.3   Potential implications for environmental governance

The role of arbitration in the institution of investment protection is particularly significant because, as noted in Chapters 4 and 5, the regulative norms and rules of investment protection are often vague and imprecise, requiring a significant amount of interpretation. Thus, as argued in Chapter 3, investment arbitration is best thought of as a form of transnational governance. Furthermore, it is a system that effectively governs areas of public policy. As such, it is appropriate to address how this system of governance measures up to other systems in terms of democratic values and fundamental issues of neutrality and fairness.

---

[115] CIEL and IISD 2007: 4.   [116] *Ibid*: 10.
[117] 'Governments Punt Discussion of Special UNCITRAL Rules for Investor-State Disputes', *Investment Treaty News*, 14 February 2007.
[118] UNCITRAL 2008: para. 314.

6.3.1 Arbitral bias

International arbitration is commonly framed in the literature as a neutral and depoliticized forum for dispute resolution.[119] However, in recent years scholars, states and NGOs have begun to question this depiction.

The international arbitration community is a relatively small and tightly knit group, often referred to as a 'mafia' or 'club'.[120] As Dezalay and Garth argue:

> Only a very select and elite group of individuals is able to serve as international arbitrators. They are purportedly selected for their 'virtue' – judgment, neutrality, expertise – yet rewarded as if they are participants in international deal-making. In more sociological terms, the *symbolic capital* acquired through a career of public service or scholarship is translated into a substantial cash value in international arbitration.[121]

Commission's data substantiates this claim: he found that in 115 concluded ICSID cases, forty-three arbitrators accounted for 49 per cent of appointments, and that in 103 pending ICSID cases, thirty-two arbitrators accounted for 54 per cent of appointments.[122]

This elite group shares 'common commercial values'[123] and often uses a 'property friendly approach' when making decisions.[124] The *culture* of commercial arbitration may be of concern for environmental advocates. As Wälde, an academic and arbitrator notes:

> the human rights 'topoi' get recognized in the like-minded human rights discourse community or environmental 'topoi' in the environmental lawyer's club but it is much harder to get a hard-nosed GATT or [Energy Charter Treaty] arbitral panel to accept what may be fully recognised in another club, not in the international trade lawyers' community.[125]

The arbitration world is, furthermore, perceived as a 'first world club'.[126] Appointing institutions, which have considerable influence over the overall direction of investment arbitration, are in some cases seen as being controlled by powerful developed countries. This is particularly the case with ICSID, given its intimate ties with the World Bank. In any case, a

---

[119] See Coe 2005: 925, who notes that former Secretary General of ICSID, Ibrahim Shihata, described the key objective of the organization as being to to depoliticize the resolution of investment disputes by providing access to a neutral forum and precluding the involvement of home states. For other examples see: Alvarez and Park 2003: 369; Legum 2006: 526.

[120] Dezalay and Garth 1996: 10.   [121] *Ibid*: 8.   [122] Commission 2007: 138–9.
[123] Wälde 1998a.   [124] Horn 2004: 19.   [125] Wälde 1998b: 244.   [126] Cutler 2001: 489.

disproportionate number of investor-state arbitrators come from the US, UK, France, Switzerland and Canada.[127] According to Garcia:

> the president of the arbitral panel will likely hail from an OECD-member state in continental Europe, and may not be sensitive to or cognizant of the legal, economic, cultural, political and commercial mores at work in the host state that are the necessary context to any evaluation of investor treatment.[128]

The means by which arbitrators are chosen and rewarded for their services also creates the appearance of a biased system. Court judges have no financial stake in the outcome of disputes. Arbitrators, on the other hand, are not only chosen by the parties to the dispute, they are also paid by the hour with no time-limits on proceedings. Such incentives inevitably favor the party advancing the claim (i.e., the investor), even if unintentionally.[129] Van Harten further notes that:

> the lack of security of tenure of arbitrators in a one-sided system of state liability, in which only investors bring the claims and only states pay damages for breach of the treaties, makes the adjudicator dependent on prospective claimants and thus biased, in an objective sense, against respondent governments.[130]

Wälde also suggests that while arbitrators may fear not being reappointed if they decide against an influential party, decisions against weaker parties (including weaker states) 'possibly count less'.[131]

The fact that individuals can act as both arbitrators and counsel is also problematic, as they may 'consciously or unconsciously' make decisions as arbitrators that will further their client's interests in another case.[132] Furthermore, even when such a direct conflict of interest does not exist, it remains the case that a large number of arbitrators work for law firms with corporate clients that have a direct stake in the interpretation of investment provisions.[133]

Otto and Cordes conclude that while in theory arbitration is a neutral forum for the amicable settlement of disputes, this is only possible when the 'process and decisional rules are mutually perceived as fair'.[134] This is often the case in private contractual disputes, but much less so in disputes involving states, particularly those from the developing world.

[127] For statistics on frequently appointed arbitrators and their nationalities see Commission 2007: 138–40.
[128] Garcia 2004: 363. [129] *Ibid*: 352.
[130] Van Harten 2007a: 5. [131] Wälde 2007: 51.
[132] Buergenthal 2006: 498. [133] Mann 2006: 76. [134] Otto and Cordes 2002: V–26.

6.3.2   *Making decisions behind closed doors*

While some progress has been made in the area of transparency, as noted above, problems remain, particularly with regard to non-ICSID cases outside of the NAFTA region. As Blackaby succinctly summarizes: 'the current opacity occurs at various levels: first, the knowledge of the dispute's existence; secondly, the access to the process itself and finally the access to the resulting decision'.[135] Confidentiality makes it impossible for there to be an accurate assessment of how many cases even exist, let alone to know their substantive content. Peterson suggests that there is a 'legal iceberg' where an unknown proportion of cases remain hidden from view.[136]

Those who argue in favour of increased transparency and non-party participation suggest that due to the public-interest nature of investor-state disputes, the confidentiality that applies to private firm-firm disputes is inappropriate. As Legum notes, there are in fact a number of different kinds of 'interest' implicated in investor-state disputes, including:

> specific interest in the measure that is challenged in the case; general interest in the appropriate functioning of the investment protections; interest in the domestic law analogues of the treaty provision invoked [e.g., regulatory takings]; interest in the appropriate interaction between federal, state and local government authorities; and many others.[137]

There are also several different types of 'public'. Mistelis argues that in addition to the 'general public', which has an interest in investment disputes, there is also the 'specialist public' (practising lawyers and academics), which also has an interest in knowing how treaty provisions are interpreted by arbitration tribunals.[138] Limiting disclosure effectively privileges a small subset of the specialist public (arbitrators and lawyers participating in cases) whilst increasing transparency would expand the range of actors which could potentially participate in and report on disputes.

Some observers take issue with the notion that the existence of a 'public interest' justifies non-party participation. In this view, it is the respondent state that should act in the public interest, and there is no further need for any other actor to do so. Some take this argument even further by questioning the legitimacy of NGOs, or other non-state actors, to act in the public interest. Brower, for example, suggests that 'many NGOs have

[135] Blackaby 2004.   [136] Peterson 2004a: 129.
[137] Legum 2003: 145.   [138] Mistelis 2005: 230.

very specific agendas and are not accountable to their own members, much less to the general public'.[139]

However, even if NGOs do not represent the general public interest, other arguments have been made in favour of non-party participation. One is that non-party participation can improve arbitral decisions by adding an extra layer of expertise or perspectives on issues that would not be provided by the disputing parties.[140] The counter-argument to this is that interested non-parties can petition the parties to the dispute directly to make claims on their behalf. However, if investors are to be given their own voice in these disputes, it seems only fair that other non-states actors also maintain independence.[141]

One of the most salient claims of those who support non-party participation is that it may help to allay public disquiet about 'secret trade courts',[142] and contribute to a higher level of accountability in the arbitration process. In several cases tribunals have noted the potential benefits of providing greater openness as well as the potential negative implications of not doing so. While this argument may hold when one is defending increased transparency in arbitration, it may be questioned whether the participation of private actors (which are not accountable to the public) actually increases the legitimacy of investment arbitration.

There appears to be a significant amount of support for the participation of *amici* and for increased transparency, from states and other observers. Nonetheless, there are still those who do not view the trends in this area as positive. Cook notes that confidentiality serves the parties' interests in several ways:

> By keeping proceedings confidential, parties are able to keep allegations of bad faith and bad business practices from the public, thus enabling the party to maintain a good business reputation. Furthermore, the public remains unaware of losses suffered resulting from adverse tribunal decisions. In addition, party autonomy inherent in arbitral proceedings allows parties to agree on the level of confidentiality so that they are able to keep from the public, and sometimes the other party, information critical to the livelihood of a business like trade secrets and other sensitive business information.[143]

However, it can be argued that information about bad business practices is precisely what the public should be privy to, and that 'trade secrets' can

---

[139] Brower 2003: 73. See also Knahr 2007: 327.   [140] Buckley and Blyshak 2007: 360.

[141] See also Mistelis 2005: 223 on the need for independent *amici*.

[142] As an editorial famously termed them; see 'The Secret Trade Courts', *New York Times*, 27 September 2004.

[143] Cook 2007: 1100.

be dealt with quite easily, as it is in other fora, by redaction in documents released to the public and *in camera* restrictions when discussions of this nature arise in the proceedings.

Another criticism of non-party participation is that it will increase the length and cost of arbitration.[144] Investor-state disputes already run, on average, several years and entail substantial costs for both claimants and respondent states. However, there are two counter-arguments here:

(i) the cost and delay in proceedings can be minimized by clear procedures for when and how *amici* may participate (e.g., only in the merits phase, limits to length of submission, etc.); and

(ii) the tribunal is receiving additional information at no direct cost to either party (as *amici*, unlike experts, are not remunerated for their services).[145]

Related to the issues of the cost and the time burden to the parties is the notion that allowing non-party participation will 'open the floodgates' to a large number of submissions. However, this is unlikely to occur in practice; there has been no flood of submissions in other bodies that accept *amicus curiae* briefs, and the experience thus far in investment disputes suggests that, in fact, NGOs are likely to make joint submissions rather than duplicative ones.

The position of the claimant in *Biwater* indicates another concern about greater transparency and disclosure. This is the notion that opening up arbitration to the 'court' of public opinion will lead to the 're-politicization' of investor-state disputes.[146] While in *Biwater* it was the investor that was concerned about negative publicity, Rubins suggests that the re-politicization of disputes is likely to be most costly for the host state, which runs the risk of losing credibility as an investor-friendly country.[147] This is likely to be an issue of particular concern for developing countries. Egonu notes that in *Amco* v. *Indonesia*, an early ICSID case, Indonesia requested confidentiality because the government was concerned that negative publicity related to the case might discourage foreign investment in the country.[148] In *Metalclad*, the respondent country (Mexico) also argued for confidentiality in the proceedings.[149] However, an obvious counter-argument is that some information about investor-state disputes is likely to reach the public domain whether investment arbitration is open or not. Increased transparency will result in the public having access

---

[144] Knahr 2007: 351–2.   [145] See Bennaim-Selvi 2005: 804.   [146] Rubins 2006.
[147] *Ibid.*   [148] Egonu 2007: 485.   [149] *Ibid.*

to more accurate and balanced information, thus decreasing the opportunity for smear campaigns against either the respondent state or the claimant.

It should be mentioned that the notion of permitting *amicus curiae* submissions has been viewed with some scepticism in the developing world, and not only because of concerns about the increased burden on the parties to the dispute in terms of the financial and reputational costs of arbitral proceedings. The South Centre, an intergovernmental body of developing countries, argues: 'Permitting *amicus* submissions effectively disadvantages developing countries because the civil society and industrial organisations in the developed countries are more experienced, better organised and equipped as well as better funded.'[150] However, the experience thus far has been that local NGOs in developing countries (e.g., Bolivia, Tanzania) have been involved and have benefited from support and cooperation with Northern-based NGOs.

6.3.3   The lack of capacity of developing countries

The cost of arbitration and the technical capacity of developing countries to effectively represent themselves is a critical issue that is often ignored in discussions of investor-state dispute settlement. As Salgado notes, 'a tribunal's ability to reach fair and just results largely depends on its ability to consider all interests affected by the proceeding', which in turn depends on the parties being well represented.[151] In any form of litigation, the level of expertise of a party's lawyers will likely be a decisive factor in the outcome of the dispute, but in the specialized area of investment arbitration the importance of having access to legal expertise is magnified.[152]

While developed countries will likely have sufficient in-house expertise, developing countries will generally not. Hiring representation from an international law firm that has specialists in the field of investment arbitration can overcome this problem and also has a number of other advantages. For example, as a result of the fact that not all awards are published, firms that are regularly involved in investment arbitrations are likely to have access to a broad range of tribunal decisions on which to base their case, while government counsel are forced to rely on 'scattered and incomplete sources'.[153] However, while hiring outside counsel can

---

[150] South Centre 2005: 10.   [151] Salgado 2006: 1036.   [152] Gottwald 2007: 252.

[153] Cosbey *et al.* 2004: 7. Similarly, Gottwald 2007: 256, suggests: 'Developing country counsel seeking to find relevant precedent are forced to engage in a kind of legal scavenger hunt through scattered and incomplete sources for past arbitral awards'.

be advantageous, it may not always be a feasible option for developing countries. Large law firms often have long-term relationships with TNCs. Such relationships may prevent a firm from representing a developing country in an investor-state dispute if there is a direct conflict of interest or if the retainer between the law firm and the TNC prevents the former acting against the latter in the absence of express consent.[154] If a law firm is available, the next question becomes whether a developing country can afford its services. Gottwald notes that the hourly rates for lawyers in elite firms can range from US$400 to US$600.[155] When a team of lawyers is retained for an arbitration proceeding that is drawn out over a period of several years, the result can be a 'staggering' legal bill.[156] The Czech Republic is reported to have spent US$10 million to defend itself against two particular treaty claims and announced that it would spend US$3.3 million in 2004 and US$13.8 million in 2005 on its defence against more than a half-dozen new claims.[157]

As a result of these obstacles, developing countries often rely on government attorneys regardless of their experience or access to necessary resources. As Gottwald has found in a recent study, 'this can lead to shocking disparities in the quality of legal representation between investor claimants and developing nation defendants'.[158] Gottwald discusses one example where the Attorney General for the Seychelles, who had no prior experience with investor-state arbitration, defended an ICSID claim without access to a reliable Internet connection, Westlaw or Lexis-Nexis, or basic treatises on ICSID or investment arbitration. Similarly, at the commencement of the onslaught of claims against Argentina there was no access to fundamental substantive law or arbitration doctrine in the government legal office. While Argentina can now claim to have considerable expertise in the area, this is only as a result of having to defend numerous claims. According to Coe, an anecdotal survey of recent investor-state disputes 'confirms that not infrequently one disputant faces significant resource limitations reflected in modest libraries, small teams of lawyers, and difficult choices about the use of counsels' time'.[159] It is important to note that this is an issue that will only become more critical in the near future. As Subedi notes, 'the decisions of ICSID or other international arbitrations are becoming more complex; the decisions of arbitral tribunals are getting longer and the issues involved are getting more sophisticated'.[160]

---

[154] Personal communication with Mahnaz Malik of Mahnaz Malik International Law Counsel, 14 December 2008.
[155] Gottwald 2007: 254.   [156] *Ibid.*   [157] *Ibid.*   [158] *Ibid.*
[159] Coe 2006: 1359–60.   [160] Subedi 2008: 179.

Even assuming that developing countries have the resources to effect-ively defend their actions in arbitration, if they lose they may face consider-able difficulty in paying damages awarded to the investor. While it is rather an extreme case, by 2006, Argentina was facing more than thirty claims for an estimated US$17 billion in compensation, amounting to nearly the entire annual budget of the national government.[161] The Czech Republic was obliged to pay more than US$350 million in compensation to a Dutch investor, which according to one report meant a near doubling of the country's public sector deficit.[162] The cost of losing a case only reinforces the need for developing countries to have effective representation.

[161] Van Harten 2007a: 2. On the Argentine cases, see Kentin 2007; Schill 2007.
[162] IISD 2007: 1.

7

Investor-state disputes

A plethora of investor-state disputes have been resolved in international arbitration in the last decade. The cumulative number of all *known*[1] treaty-based cases was 317 as of the end of 2008.[2] This can be compared to the end of 1994 when there were only five known treaty-based cases. At least 77 governments (47 in the developing world) have faced investment arbitration.[3]

The cases assessed in this chapter are restricted to those that involve environmental policy explicitly.[4] Limitations of time and space prevent consideration of the numerous cases that are of relevance to the elucidation of the norms and rules discussed in the previous chapters, even though some of these cases may be considered to border on environmental concerns.[5] Furthermore, there are several cases that directly relate to environmental regulation that will not be considered here because at the time of writing they had not yet proceeded past the stage of the investor submitting a notice of intent or a notice of arbitration.[6]

The disputes that are reviewed cover a wide range of regulatory actions and several different environmental issues (e.g., hazardous waste, biodiversity loss, air and water pollution). Cases from developed countries (Canada and the US) are discussed, as are cases from the developing world

---

[1] As discussed in Chapter 6, not all cases are disclosed to the public.

[2] UNCTAD 2009a: 2. This does not include cases brought on the basis of a foreign investment contract.

[3] *Ibid.*

[4] Environmental policy is defined broadly to cover instances, e.g., where a contract is cancelled for environmental purposes, or a permit is denied to an investor for reasons related to the environmental impact of the investment project.

[5] E.g., *Azinian et al.* v. *United Mexican States* ICSID Case No. ARB(AF)/97/2, *Waste Management Inc.* v. *United Mexican States* ICSID Case No. ARB(AF)/00/3, *Emilio Agustín Maffezini* v. *The Kingdom of Spain* ICSID Case No. ARB/97/7.

[6] E.g., *Chemtura Corp.* v. *Government of Canada, Dow AgroSciences LLC* v. *Government of Canada, Clayton/Bilcon* v. *Government of Canada, V.G. Gallo* v. *Government of Canada* (all notices are available at www.international.gc.ca) and *Pac Rim Cayman LLC* v. *Republic of El Salvador* (Notice of Arbitration available at www.pacrim-mining.com).

(Peru, Costa Rica and Mexico). Detailed descriptions of the cases are provided in order to avoid over-simplification of the complex issues that are
involved.

The purpose of this chapter is to identify the types of environmental
measures that may be subject to arbitration and to glean from the decisions
the possible range of interpretations of the norms and rules of investment
protection in relation to environmental matters. While there is no attempt
made in this chapter to judge whether a decision in a given case was *good*
or *bad*, an appraisal is made of the tribunal's attempt to balance public
and private interests.

The cases are divided into three types:

(i) concluded cases where the jurisdictional phase of arbitration was
    completed;
(ii) concluded cases where the jurisdictional phase and the merits phase
    of arbitration were completed; and
(iii) cases that, at the time of writing, were pending conclusion.

7.1   Cases completing the jurisdictional phase

7.1.1   *Ethyl* v. *Canada*

This dispute, the first filed under NAFTA's Chapter 11 to be resolved,
concerned a Canadian law banning internal and international trade
in a gasoline additive. An American investor claimed that the ban
amounted to expropriation and discriminatory treatment, and that it
further constituted a prohibited performance requirement. The tribunal, following UNCITRAL Rules, determined that it had jurisdiction
to hear the case despite the objections of Canada. The Canadian government opted to settle rather than to proceed to the merits phase of
arbitration.

7.1.1.1   Background

Methylcyclopentadienyl manganese tricarbonyl (MMT) is a fuel additive
used to increase the level of octane in unleaded gasoline. The combustion
of MMT releases airborne respirable manganese and unburned MMT into
the atmosphere.[7] The environmental and health effects of these releases
are disputed. The automotive industry has also argued that deposits of

---

[7] *Ethyl Corporation* v. *Government of Canada*, Statement of Defence (*Ethyl* Statement of
Defence), 27 November 1997.

manganese residues disrupt the proper functioning of emission control and monitoring systems in cars, resulting in increased emissions of air pollutants.

In May 1995, the Government of Canada introduced Bill C-94, an act to regulate the importation of, and interprovincial trade in, certain manganese-based substances. Bill C-94 failed to pass through Parliament before the session ended in January 1996, but was reintroduced in April of that year as Bill C-29. Bill C-29 was enacted into law on 24 June 1997, banning the import and interprovincial trade of MMT except in cases where it would not be used as a gasoline additive. As MMT is not produced in Canada, the ban ensured the removal of MMT from all Canadian gasoline. Although in theory a company could establish manufacturing plants to produce MMT for sale within a single province, this would be highly unlikely to occur in practice. The particular approach of a trade ban was adopted by the government because it had been determined that MMT did not meet the requirements for prohibition under the Canadian Environmental Protection Act.[8]

7.1.1.2 The dispute

Ethyl Corporation (Ethyl), incorporated under the laws of the State of Virginia and sole shareholder of Ethyl Canada Inc., was the developer and sole importer of MMT into Canada at the time of the ban. Ethyl filed a Notice of Intent to Submit to Arbitration under Chapter 11 of NAFTA and the UNCITRAL Rules on 10 September 1996 (prior to Bill C-29 being passed into law), and a Notice of Arbitration on 14 April 1997 (more than two months before the MMT Act came into force). Ethyl's Statement of Claim nevertheless relied on the MMT Act as the source of breach of several provisions of NAFTA. Specifically, Ethyl argued that the ban amounted to expropriation of its investment, as well as breach of the national treatment standard and the prohibition on performance requirements.

Interestingly, in addition to claiming expropriation of its 'enterprise' (i.e. Ethyl Canada), Ethyl also claimed an expropriation of its 'goodwill'.[9] Ethyl maintained that MMT was not harmful to public health or to the environment.[10] The company argued that by making public (and

---

[8] Gantz 2001: 665.

[9] *Ethyl Corporation* v. *Government of Canada*, Notice of Intent to Submit Claim to Arbitration (*Ethyl* Notice of Intent), 10 September 1996: 6.

[10] *Ibid*: 4.

according to the company 'unfounded') statements about the harmful effects of MMT, the government had created public fear and uncertainty about the product that in turn 'substantially interfered with the corporate reputations, images and goodwill associated with Ethyl Corporation and Ethyl Canada' both within Canada and globally.[11]

In terms of performance requirements, Ethyl suggested that the ban was intended to act as an incentive to encourage local production of MMT.[12] The company argued that it would have had to set up a plant in each Canadian province in order to sustain its share of the Canadian market.[13] Ethyl further argued that the ban did not meet the stipulations of the exception to the prohibition on performance requirements.[14] Ethyl claimed, based on GATT/WTO jurisprudence, that even if scientific evidence proving that MMT was a threat to health or the environment existed, in order for the ban to qualify as a *necessary* measure, it would have to be proved that it was the *least-trade restrictive* measure available to the Canadian government.

Ethyl also argued that the measure was designed to discriminate between foreign and domestic investors, contrary to the national treatment standard.[15] Ethyl claimed that it was in 'like circumstances' with producers of other gasoline additives such as ethanol because the end products were indistinguishable to consumers.[16]

The company claimed US$201 million in damages plus 'costs associated with efforts to prevent the Government of Canada's breach of its NAFTA obligations', costs associated with the arbitration proceedings and interest.[17] In the Notice of Arbitration the company raised its damages claim to US$250 million plus costs.[18] In its Statement of Claim the damages were again raised to US$251 million plus costs.[19]

Canada challenged the jurisdiction of the tribunal to hear Ethyl's claims, which it argued were outside the scope of Chapter 11. First, Canada claimed that Ethyl's action was premature, because at the time of Ethyl's notice of arbitration, the MMT Act had not yet come into

[11] *Ibid*: 6–7.   [12] *Ibid*: 7.

[13] *Ethyl Corporation* v. *Government of Canada*, Statement of Claim (*Ethyl* Statement of Claim), 2 October 1997: 12.

[14] *Ethyl Corporation* v. *Government of Canada*, Notice of Arbitration (*Ethyl* Notice of Arbitration), 14 April 1997: 14.

[15] *Ethyl* Notice of Intent: 10.   [16] *Ethyl* Statement of Claim: 9.

[17] *Ethyl* Notice of Intent: 11.   [18] *Ethyl* Notice of Arbitration: 19.

[19] *Ethyl* Statement of Claim: 13.

effect.[20] Secondly, Canada argued that Ethyl had failed to correctly follow the procedures for launching an arbitration laid out in NAFTA.[21] Canada also put forth that the MMT Act could not be considered a *measure relating to an investment*.[22] Furthermore, the Government argued that if it was to be considered a measure under NAFTA, it would have to be considered as relating to trade in goods, rather than relating to an investment, and thus subject to Chapter 3.[23]

In its Statement of Defence, the government acknowledged that while high doses of airborne respirable manganese are known to be toxic, the environmental and health impacts of low-dose, long-term, exposure are unknown.[24] Nevertheless, Canada argued that clean air is an 'exhaustible natural resource' and that, by damaging emission control technologies, MMT could increase the amount of airborne pollutants such as nitrous oxides, volatile organic compounds and carbon monoxide.[25] The government also noted its international commitments to reducing emissions of such pollutants.[26] According to Canada, the 'indirect potential effects' of MMT on the environment and health made it inappropriate to regulate it through the Canadian Environmental Protection Act, but the government argued that 'the absence of a pre-existing federal statutory authority to address the indirect hazards and risks associated with MMT use does not signify, as Ethyl infers, the absence of any environmental or health hazard'.[27]

In response to the substantive claims of Ethyl, Canada pointed out that there was no distinction made in the MMT Act between nationals and non-nationals (all were prevented from importing or interprovincially trading in MMT) and argued that the 'substance of the measure, not solely the relevant industry structure at a given point in time, must be assessed to determine its effect on national treatment obligations', otherwise every measure affecting a foreigner that was a sole supplier in a given

---

[20] Ethyl commenced Chapter 11 proceedings before the legislative process was complete and before the MMT Act had come into force. Even the Parliamentary debate on the Bill did not begin until fifteen days after Ethyl submitted its Notice of Intent. The Notice of Arbitration was delivered after the third reading of the MMT Act in the Senate, but before the legislative process was complete. The NAFTA procedures require that the Claimant wait six months following the events that give rise to a claim before submitting the claim to arbitration.

[21] Specifically Arts. 1119–1121 and 1137.

[22] NAFTA Art. 1101.1 states that Chapter 11 'applies to measures adopted or maintained by a Party *relating to*: (a) investors of another Party [or] (b) investments of investors of another Party in the territory of a Party' (emphasis added).

[23] *Ethyl* Statement of Defence: 10–12.

[24] *Ibid*: 13.   [25] *Ibid*: 17–18.   [26] *Ibid*.   [27] *Ibid*: 26.

market would be considered a breach of the national treatment standard.[28] Canada also rejected the claim that Ethyl was in 'like circumstances' with producers of other gasoline additives.[29] With regard to the claim that the MMT Act constituted a prohibited performance requirement, Canada argued that the purpose of the trade ban was to remove all MMT from gasoline in Canada, not to give preference to domestic production of the additive.[30] In the event that the tribunal nevertheless found the ban to constitute a performance requirement, Canada argued that the exception *was applicable*, as the measure was necessary to prevent a negative impact on clean air (an exhaustible natural resource) and life and health.[31] In response to the claim of expropriation, Canada argued that there had been no taking, and that in promulgating the MMT Act the country had exercised its 'police powers' as recognized in international law.[32]

On 11 March 1998, Mexico made a submission to the tribunal supporting the position of Canada.[33] Mexico argued that the dispute was not a Chapter 11 dispute (but rather related to issues of trade), and further noted that Chapter 11 does not apply to *proposed* legislation.[34]

Prior to the release of the tribunal's award, another dispute on the MMT Act outside of NAFTA, initiated by several Canadian provinces, was concluded. The dispute settlement panel in that case found the MMT Act to be inconsistent with the Federal Government's obligations under Canada's Agreement on Internal Trade.[35]

7.1.1.3   The outcome

The NAFTA tribunal produced its Preliminary Award on Jurisdiction on 24 June 1998.[36] The tribunal found that the claims Canada had made with regards to procedural failings on the part of Ethyl did not amount to a jurisdictional challenge. In the view of the tribunal, under the UNCITRAL Rules the fundamental jurisdictional issue is consent to arbitration, which Canada had provided when it ratified NAFTA.[37] The only relevant question, therefore, was whether the claims made by Ethyl fell within

---

[28] *Ibid*: 29.   [29] *Ibid*: 30.   [30] *Ibid*: 31.   [31] *Ibid*: 32.   [32] *Ibid*.

[33] Under NAFTA Art. 1128, non-disputant parties to the agreement may make submissions on the interpretation of the treaty.

[34] *Ethyl Corporation* v. *Government of Canada*, Article 1128 Submission of the United Mexican States, 11 March 1998, www.economia-snci.gob.mx.

[35] Swan 2000: 160.

[36] *Ethyl Corporation* v. *Government of Canada*, Preliminary Award on Jurisdiction, 24 June 1998. Reproduced in 38 ILM (1999): 700.

[37] *Ibid*: para. 60.

the bounds of what Canada had consented to submit to arbitration. The tribunal agreed with Canada and Mexico that a proposed piece of legislation did not constitute a 'measure'. Nevertheless, as the MMT Act had subsequently come into force, the only problem was that Ethyl had not waited the required six months to initiate proceedings, which the tribunal viewed as a procedural rather than a jurisdictional issue.[38] This conclusion was drawn despite the tribunal's acknowledgement that Ethyl 'may have "jumped the gun" for tactical reasons relating to the legislative process', and 'may have decided to file its Notice of Intent on 10 September 1996 *for the purpose of affecting that debate*'.[39]

The tribunal joined the issues of whether the MMT Act related to trade in goods or to an investment and whether Ethyl could claim damages to its goodwill and reputation outside of Canada to the merits phase of the proceedings, dismissing all other jurisdictional challenges.[40] However, the tribunal did place the burden of the costs of the jurisdictional phase that were related to the debate over procedural issues on Ethyl.[41]

Canada settled with Ethyl in July 1998, less than one month after the tribunal made its award on jurisdiction. Canada agreed to reverse the ban on MMT, to pay Ethyl US$13 million in legal fees and damages and to issue a statement declaring that current scientific information did not demonstrate any harmful effects of MMT to health or automotive systems.

One of the explanations given for why Canada chose to settle is that it had already lost the domestic challenge to the ban.[42] However, the panel in the internal trade case expressly stated that the withdrawal of the MMT Act was not recommended, and furthermore that case did not relate to the international ban, but only to the interprovincial one.[43] Others therefore hypothesize that the Canadian government settled because it was concerned about the large amounts of money that it had spent on the arbitration and the huge damages it could be expected to pay Ethyl if it lost the case.[44]

7.1.2 Lucchetti v. Peru

This case concerns the construction and operation of a pasta factory adjacent to an ecological reserve in Peru. Local governments revoked the operating licence for the Chilean-owned factory, forcing it to close,

---

[38] *Ibid*: para. 69.   [39] *Ibid*: para. 87, emphasis added.   [40] *Ibid*: para. 96.
[41] *Ibid.*   [42] Gudofsky 2000: 303; Gaines 2002: 110.
[43] Mann 2001: 73.   [44] Jones 2002: 542.

following allegations of environmental misconduct. The investor brought a claim under a BIT between Chile and Peru. The ICSID tribunal found that it did not have jurisdiction to hear the merits of the case because the dispute had 'crystallized' prior to the entry into force of the BIT. An annulment committee declined to overturn the tribunal award.

7.1.2.1   Background

Empresas Lucchetti, S.A., a Chilean company, is the majority shareholder of Lucchetti Perú, S.A., (collectively 'Lucchetti') which was the owner of an industrial plant for the manufacture of pasta situated in the district of Chorrillos in the City of Lima, Peru. The plant was situated close to, but not within, a protected wetland called Pantanos de Villa.

In August 1997, the Municipality of Chorrillos issued a stop work notice to Lucchetti, followed on 25 September by Decree 111, issued by the Council of the Municipality of Lima, which ordered work on the construction of the plant to cease immediately. The Decree also established a Commission, which reported in October that Lucchetti had 'violated specific provisions of the National Construction Regulations, the Environmental Code, rules and agreements on environmental protection and the Regulations on Construction Licenses'.[45] The Commission also suggested that the plant posed 'an imminent environmental threat to the Natural Protected Area of Pantanos de Villa'.[46] The Council of the Municipality of Lima followed up on the Commission's report with a further Decree (126) on 21 October, which established a 'Special Regulatory Zone of Pantanos de Villa' and suspended all construction permits and licences within that zone. A further Decree (01) on 2 January 1998 annulled Lucchetti's permits.[47]

The company challenged the annulment of the permits and the grounds on which they were based in the domestic courts of Peru.[48] Four separate judgments resulted, all in favour of Lucchetti.[49] The company was granted suspension of Article 4 of Decree 01, Decree 126, and the stop work notice. Thereafter, on 4 September 1998, the Council of the Municipality of Lima promulgated Ordinance 184, which established a comprehensive environmental regulatory scheme for the area and required company activities to be brought into compliance within five years. Lucchetti successfully challenged the Ordinance in the courts. Work was permitted to proceed and

---

[45] Qtd in *Empresas Lucchetti, S.A. and Lucchetti Perú, S.A. v. Republic of Peru*, ICSID Case No. ARB/03/4, Award (*Lucchetti* Award), 7 February 2005: para. 29(ii), http://icsid.worldbank.org. Reproduced in 19 *ICSID Review* (2004): 359.

[46] *Ibid.*   [47] *Lucchetti* Award: para. 19.   [48] *Ibid*: para. 31.   [49] *Ibid*: para. 32.

in December 1999, the Municipality de Chorrillos granted Lucchetti its construction and operating licences.

In August 2001 the Council of the Municipality of Lima promulgated Decrees 258 and 259. Decree 258 was designed to establish a regulatory framework for the permanent protection of the Pantanos de Villa as an ecological reserve. It authorized the municipal authorities of Lima to adopt measures to achieve that objective and contained a provision charging the Mayor of Lima to present the Peruvian legislature with proposals for the expropriation of all areas necessary for the permanent preservation, main-tenance and protection of the Ecological Reserve.[50] Decree 259 specifically revoked the operating licence of Lucchetti, and required that the plant be closed and demolished within twelve months. The Decree lists the follow-ing reasons for this action: Lucchetti's failure to comply, since 1997, with the legal rules applicable to the construction of the plant near the Pantanos de Villa, thus endangering that ecological reserve; Lucchetti's attempts to thwart the municipality's efforts to protect the region's environment in the courts; and the evidence (contained in testimony before a congressional committee) indicating that there was corruption in the procurement of the court judgments in Lucchetti's favour.[51]

7.1.2.2   The dispute

Lucchetti submitted a Request for Arbitration, on the basis of a BIT between Peru and Chile,[52] to ICSID on 24 December 2002. Lucchetti alleged that Peru had breached Article 3.2 of the Peru-Chile BIT on the promotion and protection of investments, Article 4.1 on fair and equitable, national and most-favoured-nation treatment and Article 6.1 on expro-priation. The company sought damages, costs and interests, and indi-cated that their investments in Peru had been worth more than US$150 million.[53]

Peru objected to the jurisdiction of the tribunal on the following grounds: the dispute arose in 1997, while the Chile-Peru BIT did not enter into force until 3 August 2001, and the provisions of the BIT do not apply to disputes that arose before the BIT entered into force (Article 2); the dispute was previously submitted to the domestic courts of Peru and the BIT has a 'fork in the road' provision (Article 8); and the plant is not covered as a protected 'investment' under the BIT because the investors

---

[50] Qtd in *Lucchetti* Award: para. 20.   [51] *Ibid*: para. 21.
[52] Convenio Entre el Gobierno de la República del Perú y el Gobierno de la República de Chile para la Promoción y Protección Recíproca de las Inversiones, 2 February 2000.
[53] *Lucchetti* Award: para. 17.

violated the laws and regulations of Peru governing the construction and operation of their plant (Articles 1 and 2).[54] With regards to the latter point, Peru contended that the company had commenced construction:

> without obtaining the necessary urban habilitation and environmental approvals and that their approach throughout the construction process was to build their plant quickly, without regard for Peruvian laws and regulations, in the expectation that they could then present a *fait accompli* to the municipal authorities who would feel pressured to approve the project and grant the necessary permits after the fact.[55]

Peru also made claims that the circumstances under which the company had attained favourable judgment in the domestic courts were 'corrupt and egregious' and suggested that for the tribunal to attribute 'any preclusive significance to those illicitly obtained judgments for purposes of permitting claimants to gain access to the ICSID forum would constitute a gross miscarriage of justice and subvert the rule of law'.[56]

Lucchetti countered that the dispute did not relate to the annulment of their permits in 1997–8, an issue which had been dealt with in the domestic courts, but related only to Decrees 258 and 259 which were promulgated by the Municipality of Lima in 2001, following the entry into force of the BIT. This dispute had not been taken before the domestic courts and therefore, in Lucchetti's view, the fork in the road provision did not apply. The company also denied that their investment in Peru had violated any national laws or regulations.[57] They further suggested that the opposition to the plant of the Mayor of Lima was motivated by political considerations, rather than concern for the environment.[58]

7.1.2.3   The outcome

The tribunal issued its Award on 7 February 2005. The tribunal decided that the dispute had 'crystallized' in 1998, and was not a 'new dispute' as claimed by Lucchetti.[59] The tribunal based this decision on the fact that the reasons for the adoption of Decrees 258 and 259 in 2001 were:

> directly related to the considerations that gave rise to the 1997/98 dispute: the municipality's stated commitment to protect the environmental integrity of the Pantanos de Villa and its repeated efforts to compel Claimants to comply with the rules and regulations applicable to the construction of their factory in the vicinity of that environmental reserve.[60]

---

[54] *Ibid*: para. 25.   [55] *Ibid*: para. 28.   [56] *Ibid*: para. 37.   [57] *Ibid*: para. 25.
[58] *Ibid*: para. 28.   [59] *Ibid*: para. 53.   [60] *Ibid.*

The tribunal rejected the claimant's argument that Decree 01 and Decrees 258/259 were substantially different, the former dealing with the issue of construction, and the latter addressing environmental concerns, finding that all dealt with environmental issues in both the construction and operation of the plant.[61] They also rejected the notion that the time lag between the court judgments and the 2001 Decrees made the disputes distinct.[62] Finally, they dismissed the argument that the dispute should be seen as discrete from the one resolved in Peru's courts because it concerned a violation of treaty rights. The tribunal noted that the company could hardly claim that it had made its investment with the expectation that it could rely on access to arbitration, given that such a remedy was unavailable 'until years after Lucchetti had acquired the site, built its factory, and was well into the second year of full production'.[63] While the tribunal did not delve into the question of whether the domestic court judgments in favour of Lucchetti had been tainted by corruption, they did note that if such corruption could be proved it would provide an independent ground for the conclusion that the court proceedings had not terminated the original dispute.[64] The tribunal concluded that because the dispute had 'crystallized' prior to the entry into force of the BIT, it had no jurisdiction to hear the merits of Lucchetti's claim. The tribunal decided that the costs of the arbitration should be borne equally by the parties.

On 6 June 2005, Lucchetti submitted to ICSID a Request for Annulment of the tribunal's Award. Lucchetti argued for the annulment of the Award on three grounds, which found their basis in the ICSID Convention:

(i) manifest excess of powers;
(ii) failure to state reasons; and
(iii) serious departure from a fundamental rule of procedure.[65]

A committee was formed to rule on the annulment.

---

[61] *Ibid*: para. 55.   [62] *Ibid*: para. 56.   [63] *Ibid*: para. 61.   [64] *Ibid*: para. 57.

[65] *Industria Nacional de Alimentos, S.A. and Indalsa Perú, S.A. v. Republic of Peru*, ICSID Case No. ARB/03/4, Decision on Annulment, 5 September 2007. The companies involved in the dispute changed their names to Industria Nacional de Alimentos, S.A. (previously Empresas Lucchetti, S.A.) and Indalsa Perú, S.A. (previously Lucchetti Perú, S.A.), but in the Decision the two claimants are treated as one unit, and the name 'Lucchetti' is used to refer to both of them.

With regard to the last charge, Lucchetti argued that the tribunal's approach departed from the 'fundamental rule of procedure in international cases under which jurisdiction is to be based on the claimant's formulation of its claims, not on the respondent's defence'.[66] Lucchetti suggested that it had not been given the opportunity to prove that the stated reason for Decree 259 (i.e., environmental concern) was mere pretext, disguising ulterior motives. As such, the tribunal based its assumption that the dispute was a continuation of the previous one only on the statements of Peru. Furthermore, Lucchetti argued that in implicitly accepting the allegations of corruption, the tribunal violated the company's right to be presumed innocent of a criminal offence.

For its part, Peru argued that the tribunal had not manifestly exceeded its powers, departed from fundamental rules of procedure or failed to state its reasons in the Award. Furthermore, Peru argued that what Lucchetti was seeking was not an annulment, but an appeal.

The Decision on Annulment was dispatched to the parties on 5 September 2007. The committee for the most part agreed with the position of Peru, and made it clear that it was not its task to determine whether or not the tribunal had interpreted the BIT correctly. The committee suggested that 'treaty interpretation is not an exact science, and it is frequently the case that there is more than one possible interpretation of a disputed provision, sometimes even several'.[67] The committee highlighted that rather than assessing a tribunal's reasoning, the purpose of an annulment proceeding is to examine the *process* by which a tribunal arrived at its decision. The committee, while finding flaws in the Award, did not find that an annulment was justified. One arbitrator dissented, finding that there were sufficient grounds for an annulment.[68] The costs of the annulment proceeding were divided between the parties.

7.2 Cases completing the merits phase

7.2.1 *Santa Elena* v. *Costa Rica*

This case is distinguishable from the rest of the cases discussed in this section by the fact that it involves a *direct* expropriation of property for the purpose of the protection of the environment. The issues in this case revolve only around the appropriate level of compensation to be provided to the aggrieved investor. Costa Rica argued that a number of factors, including the purpose of the measure and the development status of the

---

[66] *Ibid*: para. 46.   [67] *Ibid*: para. 112.
[68] The dissenting opinion is attached to the Decision on Annulment.

country, should be taken into account in the calculation of damages. However, the ICSID tribunal disagreed, and found that the duty to pay compensation is unaffected by such considerations.

7.2.1.1   Background

In 1978, the Costa Rican government expropriated a property in the north-west corner of the country owned by a Costa Rican company, Compañía del Desarrollo de Santa Elena, S.A. (Santa Elena), the majority of whose shareholders were American citizens. The company had intended to develop the property, which it had acquired for a sum of approximately US$395,000, as a tourist resort and residential community.[69]

The area expropriated was composed of tropical dry forest, known to contain 'flora and fauna of great scientific, recreational, educational, and tourism value' as well as beaches of particular importance for nesting sea turtles.[70] The area was also adjacent to the Santa Rosa National Park. The stated purpose of the expropriation was the expansion of the park for the preservation of biodiversity. The area of the park prior to the expansion was insufficient to maintain stable populations of large feline species such as pumas and jaguars.[71]

Costa Rican law requires that a property expropriated for a public purpose must be dedicated to that purpose within ten years, and thus the government issued a decree on 25 July 1987, expanding the boundaries of the park so as to incorporate the Santa Elena property.[72]

7.2.1.2   The dispute

After making an appraisal of the value of the property, Costa Rica initially offered Santa Elena the sum of approximately US$1.9 million.[73] This proposal was rejected, and the company countered with a proposed sum of approximately US$6.4 million, in accordance with an appraisal of the property that they had commissioned.[74] A long period of domestic court battles ensued. The company sought annulment of the 1978 Decree and separately petitioned against the 1987 Decree. The company pursued these claims as far as the Supreme Court of Costa Rica, but lost in every instance.[75] In 1992, negotiations on a settlement for compensation

---

[69] *Compañía del Desarrollo de Santa Elena, S.A. v. Costa Rica*, ICSID Case No. ARB/96/1, Final Award (*Santa Elena* Final Award), 17 February 2000: para. 16, http://icsid.worldbank.org. Reproduced in 39 ILM (2000): 1317.
[70] Expropriation Decree, qtd in *ibid*: para. 18.   [71] *Ibid*.
[72] *Santa Elena* Final Award: para. 22.   [73] *Ibid*: para. 17.   [74] *Ibid*: para. 19.
[75] Brower and Wong 2005: 751.

were recommenced and a new appraisal was conducted on behalf of the government in 1993, which valued the property at US$4.4 million.[76]

In May 1995, the company filed a Request for Arbitration with ICSID, which was officially lodged with the Centre in March 1996 (the delay was at the request of Santa Elena). Costa Rica was not obliged to participate in international arbitration under an IIA, but agreed to do so in response to diplomatic pressure and economic sanctions (specifically the delay of a US$175 million Inter-American Development Bank loan at the behest of the US government).[77]

There was no disagreement between Costa Rica and Santa Elena that the expropriation had been lawful. What was in dispute was the amount of compensation owed to Santa Elena. The parties agreed that the appropriate standard of compensation was the fair market value of the property.[78] However, the parties were not in agreement on the appropriate method to calculate the fair market value or the date on which this value was to be assessed, as this depended in part on the law applicable to the dispute. Under Costa Rican law, the value of an expropriated property is determined at the time that compensation is provided. Under international law, the value of expropriated property is assessed at the time of the expropriation, which in this case would be 1978. The former method would likely yield a higher value for the property, and thus a greater amount of compensation, and was therefore favoured by Santa Elena.[79] For the same reasons, Costa Rica favoured the application of international law. Costa Rica also argued that if the tribunal found that Costa Rican law was applicable to the case, environmental legislation developed since 1978, that would significantly restrict, if not prohibit outright, the commercial development of the property should be taken into account in the valuation. In particular, Costa Rica noted that the Guanacaste Conservation Area (which surrounded the expropriated area) was listed as a World Heritage Site in 1999.[80] Costa Rica also provided detailed evidence of its international obligations to protect the environment, including those found in the 1940 Western Hemisphere Convention.[81] The country argued that setting

[76] *Ibid.*
[77] *Santa Elena* Final Award: para. 24. Brower and Wong 2005: 751, suggest that it is likely that the company would have actually preferred to rely on the pressure imposed by US to reach a favourable settlement, rather than having to pay for an expensive and lengthy arbitration, and that it was rather Costa Rica that pushed for the latter option in order to avoid an unfair settlement.
[78] *Santa Elena* Final Award: para. 70.   [79] Brower and Wong 2005: 757–8.
[80] Brower and Hellbeck 2001: 25.   [81] *Ibid*: 764.

the level of compensation too high would discourage states (particularly those in the developing world) from adopting environmental
objectives.

The claimant requested an award in the amount of US$41.2 million
plus interest and other amounts (later revised to US$40,337,750).[82] Costa
Rica proposed an alternative sum of US$1,919,492 or, in the event that
Costa Rican law was applied, US$2,965,113.68.[83]

7.2.1.3   The outcome

The tribunal rendered its Final Award on 17 February 2000. The tribunal
accepted that the expropriation occurred on 5 May 1978 (the date the
Decree was in effect), arguing that there was no evidence that the property
was devalued by any prior public knowledge that it was about to be
expropriated. The tribunal further decided that in the absence of an explicit
agreement on what law would govern the dispute, international law would
be applied.

The tribunal found that it need not take into consideration the purpose
of the expropriation in the calculation of damages:

> While an expropriation or taking for environmental reasons may be clas-
> sified as a taking for a public purpose, and thus may be legitimate, the
> fact that the Property was taken for this reason *does not affect either the
> nature or the measure of the compensation to be paid for the taking.* That
> is, the purpose of protecting the environment for which the Property was
> taken does not alter the legal character of the taking for which adequate
> compensation must be paid. *The international source of the obligation to
> protect the environment makes no difference.*[84]

The tribunal also stated that:

> Expropriatory environmental measures – no matter how laudable and
> beneficial to society as a whole – are, in this respect, similar to any other
> expropriatory measures that a state may take in order to implement its
> policies: where property is expropriated, even for environmental purposes,
> whether domestic or international, the state's obligation to pay compensa-
> tion remains.[85]

The tribunal found that the reasonable and fair approximation of the
value of the property lay somewhere between the 1978 estimates of Costa
Rica (US$1.9 million) and Santa Elena (US$6.4 million) and thus came
to the amount of US$4,150,000.[86] Taking into account interest, the final

---

[82] *Santa Elena* Final Award: para. 29.   [83] *Ibid*: para. 35.
[84] *Ibid*: para. 71, emphasis added.   [85] *Ibid*: para. 72.   [86] *Ibid*: para. 95.

sum that the tribunal arrived at was US$16 million.[87] The costs of the arbitration were borne equally by the parties.

7.2.2   Metalclad v. Mexico

This is quite possibly the most controversial of any investor-state dispute concluded to date. The case revolves around the construction and operation of a hazardous waste facility in Mexico. The American investor involved in the dispute sought compensation for breach of the minimum standard of treatment (including fair and equitable treatment and full protection and security), national treatment, most-favoured-nation treatment, as well as expropriation and use of prohibited performance requirements, following the denial of a municipal construction permit and public demonstrations against the company's operations. An ICSID Additional Facility tribunal ruled in favour of the investor. Mexico challenged the award in a Canadian court, which partially annulled the award but still required Mexico to compensate the investor.

7.2.2.1   Background

In 1993, Ecosistemas Nacionales, S.A. de C.V., a Mexican corporation wholly-owned by Eco-Metalclad, which in turn is a subsidiary of Metalclad Corporation, incorporated in the US (collectively 'Metalclad'), purchased the Mexican company Confinamiento Técnico de Residuos Industriales, S.A. de C.V. (Coterin), which operated a hazardous waste transfer station in the Municipality of Guadalcázar in the State of San Luis Potosi.[88] Metalclad endeavoured to expand the transfer station into a toxic waste processing plant and landfill. Coterin had also attempted to develop a landfill when it was Mexican-owned, but the Municipality of Guadalcázar had turned down its applications for a permit because of community opposition and existing contamination problems on-site.[89] As part of the purchase agreement, Metalclad required that Coterin obtain a Municipal construction permit for the landfill or a court judgment declaring that such a permit was not required. However, the company completed its purchase of Coterin without such a permit or a court judgment in hand,

[87] *Ibid*: para. 107.
[88] *Metalclad Corp.* v. *United Mexican States*, ICSID Case No. ARB(AF)/97/1, Award (*Metalclad* Award), 30 August 2000: paras. 2, 28 and 29, http://icsid.worldbank.org. Reproduced in 40 ILM (2001): 36.
[89] Tollefson 2002: 188.

apparently after being assured by the federal government that all permits would be issued in due course.[90]

Metalclad began work on the development of the landfill in May 1994. In October of the same year, the Municipality of Guadalcázar ordered the cessation of all building activities due to the absence of a municipal construction permit.[91] Metalclad subsequently applied for the permit but resumed construction on the site without yet receiving it, completing the landfill in March 1995.[92]

The landfill's inauguration ceremony was blocked by public demonstrations. Metalclad claimed that it was thenceforth effectively prevented from opening the landfill.[93] The company entered into negotiations with the National Ecology Institute (INE) and the Mexican Federal Attorney's Office for the Protection of the Environment (PROFEPA) to resolve the problem, resulting in an agreement (the Convenio) in November 1995.[94] The Convenio stated that an environmental audit of the site had been carried out from December 1994 through March 1995. The audit detected certain deficiencies, and Metalclad was required to submit an action plan to correct them including a corresponding site remediation plan. The Convenio also required PROFEPA to create a Technical-Scientific Committee to monitor the remediation. The Convenio provided for a five-year term of operation for the landfill, renewable by the INE and PROFEPA. The Governor of San Luis Potosí denounced the Convenio shortly after it was publicly announced, and it was also the subject of a court action and a complaint by the NGO Greenpeace.[95]

On 5 December 1995, Metalclad's application for a municipal construction permit was denied.[96] From May 1996 through December 1996, Metalclad and the State of San Luis Potosí attempted to resolve their issues with respect to the operation of the landfill, but these efforts failed. On 23 September 1997, three days before the expiry of his term, the Governor issued an Ecological Decree declaring a Natural Area (encompassing the landfill site) for the protection of rare cactus.[97] The Decree preserved any existing permits and also allowed for new businesses to be established in the area on the condition that the sustainability of natural resources was ensured.[98]

---

[90] *Ibid*: 189.   [91] *Metalclad* Award: para. 40.   [92] *Ibid*: para. 45.
[93] *Ibid*: para. 46.   [94] *Ibid*: para. 47.
[95] *Metalclad Corp.* v. *United Mexican States*, ICSID Case No. ARB(AF)/97/1, Counter-Memorial (*Metalclad* Counter-Memorial), 17 February 1998: para. 65.
[96] *Metalclad* Award: para. 49.   [97] *Ibid*: para. 59.   [98] Tollefson 2002: 191.

7.2.2.2   The dispute

In 1996, Metalclad notified Mexico of its intention to file a dispute under NAFTA Chapter 11, which it did in January of the following year. Metalclad's request for US$90 million in compensation was based on a claim of expropriation (Article 1110), a breach of the minimum standard/fair and equitable treatment (Article 1105), a breach of the national treatment (Article 1102) and most-favoured-nation treatment (Article 1103) standards and use of prohibited performance requirements (Article 1106). The tribunal operated under the rules of the ICSID Additional Facility, as Mexico had not ratified the ICSID Convention, and the proceedings took place in Vancouver, British Columbia, Canada.

In its Memorial, Metalclad argued that NAFTA provided guidance on the interpretation of the international minimum standard in its preamble which states that the purpose of the agreement is to 'ensure a *predictable* commercial framework for business planning and investment'.[99] Metalclad further argued that the standard should be read in light of the objectives of NAFTA laid out in Article 102. In Metalclad's view, the minimum standard thereby also enveloped the principles of non-discrimination and *transparency*. Having established an interpretation of Article 1105, Metalclad proceeded to argue that Mexico's conduct had not met the requirements of the standard, leaving the company 'in a tenebrous investment climate, full of bewilderment, bereft of predictability'.[100] The company also claimed that it had been denied full protection and security.[101]

The claims regarding breach of Articles 1102 and 1103 were based on the fact that the Municipality of Guadalcázar did not require construction permits from any national investors or other foreign investors.[102] In terms of performance requirements, Metalclad argued that it had effectively been forced to provide proprietary information to the state government on how to construct a landfill, as well as to offer certain services to the local community, such as free medical care and free consultations for the government regarding hazardous waste matters.[103]

Finally, Metalclad addressed the issue of expropriation, arguing that the deprivation of its vested right to operate the landfill was irreversible. Metalclad further suggested that the taking had not been for a public purpose, noting that at best it had been for a 'political purpose' and at

---

[99] *Metalclad Corp. v. United Mexican States*, ICSID Case No. ARB(AF)/97/1, Memorial (*Metalclad* Memorial), 13 October 1997: para. 162, emphasis added by Metalclad.
[100] *Ibid*: para. 165.   [101] *Ibid*: para. 212.   [102] *Ibid*: paras. 214 and 228.
[103] *Ibid*: para. 235.

worst for personal gain. In Metalclad's view, the taking had also been discriminatory and implemented without due process.[104] While arbitration proceedings were initiated prior to the Governor issuing the Ecological Decree, Metalclad nevertheless subsequently sought to have this measure considered by the tribunal as an expropriation. In terms of compensation, Metalclad argued that the fair market value of the investment included lost future profits.[105]

Mexico disputed many of the facts raised in the Metalclad's Memorial, pointing out that Coterin had been denied a municipal construction permit in 1991, prior to Metalclad's purchase of the site, and arguing that it was always clear to the company that it would have to acquire the necessary permits and solicit local approval for the project.[106] Mexico further argued that the company had misrepresented itself to various levels of government, engaged in unethical and at times unlawful behaviour and was neither competent nor financially capable of running a hazardous waste landfill in a safe and effective manner.[107]

In terms of the relevant provisions of NAFTA, Mexico first argued that it could not be held liable for any actions taken prior to the entry into force of the agreement in 1994, or for anticipated actions (the Ecological Decree which was enacted following the Notice of Intent), or for the actions of non-state actors (e.g., the NGOs and the local community who staged protests). In response to the claim of discriminatory treatment, Mexico argued that Metalclad was not in 'like circumstances' with other investors in the state or municipality; no other hazardous waste landfills existed in the area, in fact the closest thing in the municipality to an 'industrial site' at the time was a gas station.[108] Other hazardous waste sites did exist within the country at the time, but because of the environmental liability issues unique to the Guadalcázar landfill and the local opposition to the project, Mexico argued that these sites were not an appropriate comparator.[109] Mexico suggested that Metalclad's treatment should only be compared with that of Coterin when it was wholly Mexican-owned. With such a comparison, there was clearly no discrimination.[110] Mexico further argued that Metalclad had provided no evidence that it had been forced to provide the state government with information or services, and that even if it had, these did not qualify as performance requirements under Article 1106.

---

[104] *Ibid*: para. 253.   [105] *Ibid*: para. 255.
[106] *Metalclad* Counter-Memorial: paras. 45–52.   [107] *Ibid*: paras. 77–129.
[108] *Ibid*: para. 814.   [109] *Ibid*: para. 813.   [110] *Ibid*: paras. 815–6.

In its discussion of the minimum standard and fair and equitable treatment, Mexico pointed out that the standard should be interpreted in light of the North American Agreement on Environmental Cooperation (NAAEC), a side-agreement of NAFTA. Among other things the NAAEC acknowledges the rights of states to set high standards for environmental protection, and requires them to enforce their own environmental laws. Mexico further argued that there was no authority on which to base an interpretation of fair and equitable treatment that required transparent and predictable behaviour on the part of the host state.[111] Additionally, as no damage had been caused by the demonstration put on by local opponents to the landfill (who were not connected with any level of government in Mexico), Metalclad's claim that full protection and security had not been provided could not be upheld.[112]

Finally, with regard to the claim of expropriation, it is worth quoting directly from Mexico's Counter Memorial:

> A finding of expropriation on the facts of this case would lead to an unprecedented result. In the Respondent's submission, it would be surprising to all three NAFTA Parties that where a foreign investor sought to make a high risk investment in a highly regulated field, where public opposition to its project was widely known and the investor knew of both prior to making its investment, a NAFTA Party could be held responsible for that calculated business decision to proceed in the face of known risks.[113]

Both the US and Canada made written submissions to the tribunal as permitted under Article 1128. Canada cautioned against any equation of the expropriation standard in NAFTA with the jurisprudence of either the US domestic courts or the Iran-US Claims Tribunal.[114] The US submitted that NAFTA Article 1110's reference to measures 'tantamount' to expropriation addressed both measures that directly and indirectly expropriate, but rejected the suggestion that the term was intended to create a new category of expropriation not previously recognized in customary international law.[115]

7.2.2.3   The outcome

The tribunal issued its Award on 30 August 2000. In a very controversial decision, the tribunal incorporated a provision on transparency from

---

[111] *Ibid*: para. 860.   [112] *Ibid*: paras. 876–9.   [113] *Ibid*: para. 905.
[114] *Metalclad Corporation* v. *United Mexican States*, ICSID Case No. ARB(AB)/97/1, Submission of the Government of Canada, 28 July 1999.
[115] *Metalclad Corporation* v. *United Mexican States*, ICSID Case No. ARB(AB)/97/1, Submission of the Government of the United States of America, 9 November 1999.

another chapter of NAFTA into its interpretation of Article 1105 on the
minimum standard/fair and equitable treatment.[116] The tribunal argued
that 'transparency' meant that 'all relevant legal requirements for the
purpose of initiating, completing and successfully operating investments
made, or intended to be made . . . should be capable of being readily known
to all affected investors [of a NAFTA Party]' and that there 'should be no
room for doubt or uncertainty on such matters'.[117] The tribunal went on
to conclude that:

> The absence of a clear rule as to the requirement or not of a municipal
> construction permit, as well as the absence of any established practice
> or procedure as to the manner of handling applications for a municipal
> construction permit, amounts to a failure on the part of Mexico to ensure
> the transparency required by NAFTA.[118]

This led the tribunal to the decision that Metalclad had not been treated
fairly or equitably.[119]

The tribunal's determination on expropriation was directly connected
to its finding of a breach of Article 1105. The tribunal argued that in
permitting or tolerating the conduct of the Municipality of Guadalcázar,
Mexico had taken a measure tantamount to expropriation. The tribunal
also relied on the absence of a timely, orderly and substantive basis for
the denial of the construction permit by the Municipality in making its
assessment that an indirect expropriation had occurred.

The tribunal determined that consideration of the Ecological Decree
was within its jurisdiction but chose not to attach to this particular measure
any 'controlling importance', meaning that their finding that the Decree
qualified as expropriation did not affect the Award (as the tribunal had
already found that other measures met the standard of expropriation).[120]
Despite its irrelevance to the Award itself, the tribunal made a significant
statement that it '*need not decide or consider the motivation or intent* of the
adoption of the Ecological Decree' in finding that it constituted a taking.
Metalclad was awarded US$16,685,000.[121]

Mexico petitioned the Supreme Court of British Columbia (the seat of
the arbitration) to annul the *Metalclad* award on the basis that the tribunal
had acted in excess of its jurisdiction by applying transparency provisions
as the basis for finding a breach of Article 1105. The Attorney General
of Canada intervened to support Mexico's petition. The court agreed
with Mexico and Canada that the tribunal should not have considered

---

[116] NAFTA: Art. 102.1.   [117] *Metalclad* Award: para. 76.   [118] *Ibid*: para. 88.
[119] *Ibid*: para. 101.   [120] *Ibid*: para. 69.   [121] *Ibid*: para. 131.

provisions on transparency found in NAFTA, but outside of Chapter 11, which are subject only to state-state disputes. While Chapter 11 is meant to be interpreted in light of 'international law', the court argued that this meant customary international law, not 'conventional international law' (i.e., treaties such as NAFTA).[122] The court struck down some aspects of the Award, but concurred with the tribunal that the actions of Mexico constituted an expropriation and calculated damages of US$15.6 million. Mexico eventually reached a settlement with Metalclad for an undisclosed amount of compensation.[123]

7.2.3   Tecmed v. Mexico

This case is similar to the *Metalclad* case (it concerns the operation of a hazardous waste facility in Mexico), although it was brought under a BIT rather than NAFTA. Following the denial for renewal of its operating permit, the Spanish investor in this case argued that Mexico had discriminated against it, had not provided fair and equitable treatment and had expropriated its investment. The tribunal found in favour of the investor.

7.2.3.1   Background

In 1996, an agency in the Municipality of Hermosillo auctioned a hazardous waste landfill located in the State of Sonora, Mexico.[124] The landfill had been built in 1988. Prior to privatization, the landfill had been run by a municipal government entity, which operated under a licence issued by the Hazardous Materials, Waste and Activities Division of the INE on an indefinite basis.[125]

Técnicas Medioambientales, Tecmed S.A. de C.V. (Tecmed), a company incorporated under Mexican law and owned by a Spanish parent company, made a successful bid on the site. The company set up a subsidiary, Cytrar, S.A. de C.V., to run the landfill operations. In 1996, Tecmed made a request to the INE for a change in the name on the operating licence to reflect the new ownership of the property.[126] The Municipality of Hermosillo

---

[122] *United Mexican States* v. *Metalclad Corporation*, Supreme Court of British Columbia, Reasons for Judgment, 2 May 2001: para. 62. Reproduced in 5 *ICSID Reports* (2002): 238.

[123] González de Cossío 2002: 236.

[124] *Técnicas Medioambientales Tecmed, S.A.* v. *United Mexican States*, ICSID Case No. ARB (AF)/00/2, Award (unofficial English translation from Spanish original) (*Tecmed* Award), 29 May 2003: para. 35, http://icsid.worldbank.org. Reproduced in 19 *ICSID Review* (2004): 158.

[125] *Ibid*: para. 36.   [126] *Ibid*: para. 38.

supported this request. However, rather than changing the name on the licence, the INE issued a new licence which, unlike the the previous one, was not indefinite and had to be renewed each year. The alteration of permit duration was a part of a general regulatory change implemented by the Mexican government to enable action to be taken against non-compliant landfill sites.[127]

In July 1997, a new Mayor of the Municipality of Hermosillo was elected.[128] Tecmed and the newly elected Mayor faced mounting opposition to the landfill from the local population. On several occasions there were demonstrations and blockades involving several hundred people. In late 1997, the municipal government and the company began negotiations on the relocation of the landfill.[129]

In December 1997, the association Academia Sonorense de Derechos Humanos (Sonora Human Rights Academy) filed a criminal complaint against Cytrar for 'environmental crimes'.[130] The main concern with the landfill was its close proximity to the urban centre of Hermosillo (8 km), which was in violation of Mexican regulations requiring hazardous waste to be sited at least 25 km from any settlement of more than 10,000 residents.[131] However, these regulations were put in place after the landfill had been established, and were not retroactive. Another concern was the transportation of contaminated soil from a plant in Baja California to the landfill.[132] On several occasions inspections conducted by PROFEPA had revealed that there were open hazardous material packaging bags in the trucks transporting the waste.[133] In April 1998, PROFEPA cited further irregularities and levied a fine against the company stating that 'there are circumstances that pose or may pose a risk to the environment or to health'.[134] A similar situation occurred in May 1998.[135]

In November 1998, the INE released a Resolution denying Cytrar a renewal of its permit and further requesting that the company submit a programme for the closure of the landfill. The Resolution based the non-renewal of the permit on the following three grounds:

(i) while the company had only been authorized to store agrochemicals and pesticides at the site, it had also been disposing of biological and infectious wastes;

(ii) the volume of waste confined at the site far exceeded the limits established for one of the landfill's active cells; and

---

[127] Newcombe 2007b: 408.   [128] *Tecmed* Award: para. 42.   [129] *Ibid*: para. 110.
[130] *Ibid*: para. 108.   [131] *Ibid*: para. 106.   [132] *Ibid*: para. 49.
[133] *Ibid*: para. 107.   [134] *Ibid*.   [135] *Ibid*.

(iii) the landfill had operated as a 'transfer centre' (temporarily storing hazardous waste destined for disposal outside the landfill), an activity for which the company did not have the required authorization.[136]

Tecmed argued that these infringements had already been investigated by PROFEPA, which had found that they were not egregious enough to justify the immediate cancellation, suspension or revocation of the permit, and had fined the company instead.[137] After the Resolution was issued, discussions on the possible relocation of the landfill site continued, but they ceased prior to the commencement of arbitration.

7.2.3.2   The dispute

On 28 July 2000, Tecmed filed with ICSID an application for approval of access to the Additional Facility and a request for arbitration based on the Spain-Mexico BIT, which entered into force on 18 December 1996.[138] Tecmed alleged that Mexico had violated the following provisions of the Spain-Mexico BIT: Article 2.1 on the promotion and admission of investments; Article 3 on the protection of investments (including full protection and security); Article 4.1 on fair and equitable treatment; Article 4.2 on most-favoured-nation treatment; Article 4.5 on national treatment; and Article 5 on expropriation.[139] The company sought damages, including compensation for harm to its reputation, and additionally requested restitution in kind through the granting of permits to the company to enable it to operate the landfill until the end of its useful life.[140] Tecmed assessed the market value of the landfill at US$52 million.

Tecmed argued that when it bid on the landfill, it bid not only on the land and tangible materials, but also on intangible assets, most importantly the existing operation permits.[141] However, the permits that were eventually granted to the company were different (in terms of their duration as well as the conditions to which they were subject) from the permit that was present at the time that the bid was made. Tecmed suggested that, while it was not central to their case, it wished to highlight the permit issue as evidence of a string of actions that amounted to discriminatory treatment.[142] Mexico, for its part, denied that the tender and subsequent award to Tecmed included intangible assets such as licences or permits,

---

[136] *Ibid*: para. 99.   [137] *Ibid*: para. 100.

[138] Agreement on the Reciprocal Promotion and Protection of Investments signed by the Kingdom of Spain and the United Mexican States, 22 June 1995.

[139] *Tecmed* Award: para. 93.   [140] *Ibid*: para. 184.   [141] *Ibid*: para. 40.

[142] *Ibid*: para. 40.

and argued that it was rather solely concerned with certain facilities, land, infrastructure and equipment.[143] Mexico suggested that it was always clear to Tecmed that it would require its own licences, authorizations or permits in order to operate the landfill.

The central issue for Tecmed was not the limited nature of the permit that Cytrar had been granted, but rather the refusal of the INE to renew it. Tecmed argued that the federal government had yielded to the combined pressure of the municipal authorities of Hermosillo and the State of Sonora along with the community movement opposed to the landfill.[144] The company denied any misconduct or violation of the operating permit that could justify a refusal to renew it.[145] Tecmed argued that it had not received: national treatment, noting that all the previous owners of the landfill (government entities) were provided with operation permits; or most-favoured-nation treatment, pointing out that another foreign investor had been granted an operation permit of unlimited duration for a similar landfill.

In terms of fair and equitable treatment, Tecmed argued that the standard 'encompasses the duty to act transparently and respecting the legitimate trust generated in the investor'.[146] The company claimed that the Mexican government had not acted transparently (it was not clear that the indefinite permit would be replaced with one of limited duration) and that the 'legitimate trust' that had been generated, inducing the company to make the investment in the first place, had been 'violated and seriously trampled upon'.[147] Tecmed also alleged that Mexican municipal and state authorities had encouraged the community protests against the landfill and that the authorities did not act 'as quickly, efficiently and thoroughly as they should have to avoid, prevent or put an end to the adverse social demonstrations'.[148] The company viewed this as a violation of Article 3.1 of the Spain-Mexico BIT, which provides for full protection and security.

Mexico responded that the INE Resolution was neither arbitrary nor discriminatory and furthermore that it was a 'regulatory measure issued in compliance with the State's police power within the highly regulated and extremely sensitive framework of environmental protection and public health'.[149] Mexico argued that the landfill was denied its permit and shut down for the following reasons:

[143] *Ibid*: para. 47.   [144] *Ibid*: para. 43.   [145] *Ibid*.
[146] *Ibid*: para. 58.   [147] Qtd in *Tecmed* Award: para. 58.   [148] *Tecmed* Award: para. 175.
[149] *Ibid*: para. 97.

(i) the site of the landfill did not comply with applicable Mexican regulations in terms of its location and characteristics;

(ii) in 1998, a number of irregularities occurred in the operation of the landfill, and these irregularities triggered strong community pressure against the landfill;

(iii) Mexican authorities, mainly from the Municipality of Hermosillo, expressed their doubts as to the safety of the landfill's operations; and

(iv) there was the risk that community pressure might increase if operation of the landfill continued.[150]

7.2.3.3   The outcome

In 2003, the tribunal issued its award, finding that Mexico had expropriated Tecmed's investment and had failed to provide the company with fair and equitable treatment.

In determining whether or not the INE resolution constituted an expropriation of Tecmed's investment, the tribunal adopted a two-part test. In the first part, they assessed whether the company had been 'radically deprived of the economical use and enjoyment of its investments, as if the rights related thereto – such as the income or benefits related to the landfill or to its exploitation – had ceased to exist'.[151] The tribunal suggested that this was:

> one of the main elements to distinguish . . . between a regulatory measure, which is an ordinary expression of the exercise of the state's police power that entails a decrease in assets or rights, and a *de facto* expropriation that deprives those assets and rights of any real substance.[152]

They went on to suggest that:

> the measures adopted by a State, whether regulatory or not, are an indirect *de facto* expropriation if they are irreversible and permanent and if . . . the economic value of the use, enjoyment or disposition of the assets or rights affected by the administrative action or decision have been neutralized or destroyed.[153]

Most significantly, they argued that the 'government's *intention is less important than the effects of the measures* on the owner of the assets or on the benefits arising from such assets affected by the measures'.[154]

However, the tribunal did look at the Mexican government's intentions in the second part of its test. The tribunal suggested that there must be a 'reasonable relationship of *proportionality* between the charge or

---

[150] *Ibid*: para. 105.   [151] *Ibid*: para. 115.   [152] *Ibid*.   [153] *Ibid*: para. 116.   [154] *Ibid*.

weight imposed to the foreign investor and the aim sought to be realized by any expropriatory measure'.[155] The tribunal determined that the INE Resolution was not designed to protect the environment, but rather issued as a response to the 'political circumstances' surrounding the dispute.[156] The tribunal noted that:

> The absence of any evidence that the operation of the Landfill was a real or potential threat to the environment or to the public health, coupled with the absence of massive opposition, limits 'community pressure' to a series of events, which, although they amount to significant pressure on the Mexican authorities, do not constitute a real crisis or disaster of great proportions, triggered by acts or omissions committed by the foreign investor or its affiliates.[157]

Thus, they concluded that there was not sufficient justification for Mexico to expropriate Tecmed's property without compensating the company, particularly as it had not been proved that Tecmed's behaviour was the cause of the political pressure or the demonstrations.[158]

The tribunal commenced its evaluation of fair and equitable treatment by noting that 'bad faith' on the part of a state was not required for a breach of this principle.[159] In the tribunal's view, the provision requires that states provide 'treatment that does not affect the *basic expectations* that were taken into account by the foreign investor to make the investment'.[160] They went on to note that the foreign investor expects the state to act in a 'consistent manner' and:

> *free from ambiguity and totally transparently* in its relations with the foreign investor, so that it may know beforehand any and all rules and regulations that will govern its investments, as well as the goals of the relevant policies and administrative practices or directives, to be able to plan its investment and comply with such regulations.[161]

The tribunal found that the behaviour of the INE conflicted 'with what a reasonable and unbiased observer would consider fair and equitable'.

The tribunal did not find that Tecmed had proved that the Mexican authorities encouraged, fostered, supported or participated in the protests against the landfill or that they had failed to deal with the protests in an acceptable manner.[162] The tribunal noted that the 'guarantee of full protection and security is not absolute and does not impose strict

---

[155] *Ibid*: para. 122, emphasis added.   [156] *Ibid*: para. 127.   [157] *Ibid*: para. 144.
[158] *Ibid*: para. 147.   [159] *Ibid*: para. 153.   [160] *Ibid*: para. 154, emphasis added.
[161] *Ibid*, emphasis added.   [162] *Ibid*: para. 176.

liability upon the State that grants it'.[163] The tribunal also found that
there was insufficient evidence indicating that Tecmed had been discriminated against or had received less favourable treatment than that
afforded to nationals or investors of any third state.[164] The tribunal further
decided that Mexico had not breached Article 2.1 (on the promotion and
protection of investments), and that if such a violation had occurred,
it would be the subject of a state-state dispute rather than an investor-
state dispute.[165] Finally, the tribunal ruled that the INE's refusal to renew
Tecmed's permit did not amount to a violation of Article 3.2 of the Spain-
Mexico BIT, pursuant to which each contracting party 'within the local
legal framework' shall grant the necessary permits with regard to the
investments from the other non-party.[166]

The tribunal chose not to consider the option of restitution in kind
and rather focused on monetary damages. The tribunal awarded Tecmed
approximately US$5.5 million plus interest.[167]

7.2.4   S.D. Myers v. Canada

This case concerns the movement of hazardous wastes across the Canada-
US border. Following an opening of the border from the American side,
Canada temporarily prohibited the transboundary movement of certain
hazardous wastes in order to ensure compliance with its obligations under
a multilateral environmental agreement. The country was subsequently
sued by an American investor for breach of NAFTA Chapter 11 provisions
on national treatment, the minimum standard of treatment, performance
requirements and expropriation. The UNCITRAL tribunal found a breach
of the former two provisions and awarded the investor compensation.

7.2.4.1   Background

Polychlorinated biphenyls (PCBs) are highly toxic substances that have
been the subject of increasingly strict regulation in Canada and the US
since the 1970s. Their production was banned in both countries following

---

[163] *Ibid*: para. 177.
[164] *Ibid*: para. 181. In particular, the tribunal accepted Mexico's argument that the circumstances of another foreign investor operating a landfill were materially different from those
of Tecmed and, therefore, could not be compared.
[165] *Ibid*: para. 182.
[166] *Ibid*. The tribunal found no evidence showing that INE's refusal to renew the permit was
contrary to Mexican laws.
[167] *Ibid*: para. 197.

a 1973 OECD Council Decision on the issue.[168] The use of PCBs in products manufactured in or imported into Canada was banned in 1977.[169] In 1986, Canada and the US entered into the Agreement Concerning the Transboundary Movement of Hazardous Waste (Transboundary Agreement), although there was some confusion as to whether this agreement actually covered PCBs, which have never been classified as a hazardous waste in the US (see further below).[170] In 1988, PCBs were included in Schedule 1 on Toxic Substances in the newly developed Canadian Environmental Protection Act.[171] This legislation was supplemented by the PCB Waste Export Regulations in 1990, which effectively banned the export of PCB waste from Canada to all countries other than the US.[172] Under these regulations, exports to the US were only permitted with the prior approval of the US Environmental Protection Agency (US EPA). In the US, there are restrictions on the manufacture, sale, use, import, export and disposal of PCBs and PCB contaminated wastes under the Toxic Substances Control Act; however, the US EPA may grant an exemption from this Act if it is satisfied that the applicant's activities will not result in unreasonable risk to human health or the environment.[173]

In 1992, Canada ratified the Basel Convention on the Transboundary Movements of Hazardous Wastes.[174] The US also signed the Basel Convention in 1989, but as of two decades later, the country had not yet ratified the agreement. It is worth noting that the Basel Convention is mentioned in NAFTA Article 104 on the relation of the agreement to environmental and conservation agreements, but this provision is not effective unless the Convention is in force in all three NAFTA parties.

PCBs are listed in Annex 1 of the Basel Convention as 'waste to be controlled'. Under the Basel Convention, parties are required, among other things, to:

(i) reduce the production of hazardous waste;
(ii) ensure the availability of adequate disposal facilities, to the extent possible, within their own boundaries; and

[168] *S.D. Myers* v. *Government of Canada*, Partial Award (*S.D. Myers* Partial Award), 13 November 2000: para. 99. Reproduced in 40 ILM: 1408.
[169] *Ibid*: para. 100.
[170] Agreement Concerning the Transboundary Movement of Hazardous Waste, 28 October 1986, Ottawa, www.epa.gov.
[171] *S.D. Myers* Partial Award: para. 100.   [172] *Ibid*.
[173] *S.D. Myers, Inc.* v. *Government of Canada*, Notice of Intent to Submit a Claim to Arbitration (*S.D. Myers* Notice of Intent), 21 July 1998: 4.
[174] Basel Convention on the Transboundary Movements of Hazardous Wastes and their Disposal, 22 March 1989, Basel, www.basel.int. Reproduced in 32 ILM (1993): 276.

(iii) ensure that the transboundary movement of hazardous wastes and other waste is reduced to the minimum consistent with the environmentally sound and efficient management of such wastes and is conducted in a manner which will protect human health and the environment against the adverse effects which may result from such movement.[175]

The export and import of hazardous wastes to and from non-parties is also prohibited, unless an agreement exists between the party and non-party that is as stringent as the Basel Convention.[176]

In the early 1990s, S.D. Myers, Inc., an American waste treatment company, began a concerted lobbying effort aimed at acquiring permission from the US EPA to import PCBs and PCB waste from Canada.[177] Between 1991 and 1993 the company submitted four petitions to the US EPA, which rejected each after finding that S.D. Myers had failed to prove that there was no unreasonable risk to human health or the environment.[178] By the company's own estimates, the proposed importation would have exposed the US and Canada to the risk of approximately 2.5 PCB spills, including spills of high-concentration PCBs.[179] The US EPA determined that the better alternative was for the PCBs to be destroyed in Canada.

However, S.D. Myers eventually succeeded in its lobbying efforts and received an enforcement discretion valid from 15 November 1995 to 31 December 1997.[180] Under the terms of the enforcement discretion, the US EPA would not enforce the US regulations banning importation of PCBs against S.D. Myers provided that the company met certain conditions. Following this decision, further enforcement discretions were granted to nine other US companies.[181] This turn of events was apparently the result of intense political pressure on the US EPA, brought about as a result of the S.D. Myer's extensive lobbying.[182]

In the period that followed the US EPA's decision, the Canadian government struggled with several issues including:

(i) whether the enforcement discretion fully complied with US law;
(ii) whether exports of PCB wastes to the US, a non-ratifying-Party to the Basel Convention, would be in compliance with Canada's international commitments;

---

[175] *Ibid*: Art. 4.2(a), (b) and (d).   [176] *Ibid*: Art. 4.5, 11.
[177] *S.D. Myers* Partial Award: paras. 113–4.   [178] Hodges 2002: 375.
[179] *Ibid*: 376.   [180] *S.D. Myers* Partial Award: para. 118.
[181] *Ibid*: para. 119.   [182] Hodges 2002: 378.

(iii) whether PCBs would be disposed of in the US in an environmentally sound manner;

(iv) whether exports would be in compliance with Canada's policy of destroying Canadian PCBs *in Canada*;

(v) whether exports would threaten the long-term viability of domestic PCB disposal facilities; and

(vi) whether there would be sufficient options for disposal if US facilities subsequently became unavailable, or if the US border was again closed to imports.[183]

In terms of the issue of compliance with the Basel Convention, Canada was unclear as to whether the Transboundary Agreement actually covered PCBs and met the requirements of Article 11. It was not until three months after the US EPA granted the first enforcement discretion that Canada received notification by a diplomatic memo that the US took the position that the Transboundary Agreement did in fact cover PCBs.[184]

In November 1995, the Canadian Minister of the Environment signed an Interim Order, which amended the PCB Waste Export Regulations and had the effect of banning the export of PCBs and PCB wastes from Canada. The stated purpose of the Interim Order was 'to ensure that Canadian PCB Wastes are managed in an environmentally sound manner in Canada and to prevent any possible significant danger to the environment or to human life or health'.[185] On 26 February 1996, the Interim Order was converted into a Final Order. It would appear from a memorandum written by the Director of the Hazardous Waste Branch in Environment Canada that there was concern within the government that this action could be difficult to justify (in particular, that the opening of the US border posed a significant danger to the environment or health) and also that it could spark a NAFTA Chapter 11 dispute.[186]

In February 1997, having studied the issues and having determined that the country could permit exports of PCBs and still satisfy the requirements of the Basel Convention, Canada re-opened the border by a further amendment to the PCB Waste Export Regulations, allowing exports of PCBs for disposal at US EPA-approved sites. The border was thus closed

---

[183] *S.D. Myers, Inc.* v. *Government of Canada*, Statement of Defence (*S.D. Myers* Statement of Defence), 18 June 1999: para. 20.

[184] de Pencier 2000: 415–16.

[185] Explanatory note attached to the Interim Order, qtd in *S.D. Myers* Partial Award: para. 123.

[186] Qtd in Weiler 2001: 178.

to cross-border movement of PCBs and PCB waste by regulations introduced by Canada for a period of approximately sixteen months, from
November 1995 to February 1997.[187] Thereafter, the border was open
and there were seven contracts pursuant to which PCBs and PCB waste
material were exported from Canada to the US for processing by S.D.
Myers.

While these events were transpiring in Canada, across the border the
Sierra Club (an environmental NGO) was challenging the legality of the
US EPA enforcement discretion. In July 1997, the Ninth Circuit of the US
Court of Appeals overturned the enforcement discretions, finding that
the US EPA had violated its own rule-making procedures and the Toxic
Substances Control Act.[188] Thus, the border was closed once again from
the American side. In total, the border was open to the movement of PCBs
and PCB wastes for a period of five months, between February and July
1997.

7.2.4.2   The dispute

S.D. Myers filed for NAFTA Chapter 11 arbitration in 1998, seeking
US$20 million in damages.[189] S.D. Myers claimed that Canada had
breached the following articles of NAFTA: 1102 on national treatment;
1105 on the minimum standard; 1106 on performance requirements; and
1110 on expropriation.[190]

In terms of national treatment, S.D. Myers argued that the Interim
Order discriminated against US waste disposal operators and favoured
domestic companies.[191] S.D. Myers put forth that the true purpose of
the Interim Order was to protect a Canadian competitor called Chem-
Security, which had disposal facilities for PCBs located in the Province of
Alberta.[192] Canada suggested instead that the export ban merely established a uniform regulatory regime under which all companies were treated
equally: neither national nor foreign operators were permitted to export
PCBs.[193]

---

[187] *S.D. Myers* Partial Award: para 127.   [188] Hodges 2002: 379–80.
[189] *S.D. Myers, Inc.* v. *Government of Canada*, Notice of Arbitration, 30 October 1998: 4.
[190] *Ibid.*
[191] *S.D. Myers, Inc.* v. *Government of Canada*, Statement of Claim (*S.D. Myers* Statement of
Claim), 30 October 1998: 11.
[192] *S.D. Myers, Inc.* v. *Government of Canada*, Memorial (*S.D. Myers* Memorial), 20 July 1999:
9–13.
[193] *S.D. Myers, Inc.* v. *Government of Canada*, Counter-Memorial (*S.D. Myers* Counter-
Memorial), 5 October 1999: 81.

With regard to the minimum standard, the company claimed that the Interim Order was promulgated in a discriminatory and unfair manner that constituted a denial of justice and a violation of good faith under international law.[194] In particular, S.D. Myers pointed out that prior to the Interim Order being finalized there had been no consultation with the company or with the US government.[195] Canada rebutted that given the circumstances and the urgent need to respond to the sudden and surprising decision of the US EPA, it had no duty to consult the US government (which had not consulted Canada prior to the US EPA decision), let alone a company.[196] In any case, non-consultation would not amount to the kind of egregious behaviour required to breach the minimum standard, in the view of Canada.[197]

In terms of performance requirements, S.D. Myers claimed that the Interim Order effectively required it to dispose of PCB-contaminated waste in Canada.[198] The company argued that this resulted in a performance requirement for PCB disposal operators to accord preference to Canadian goods and services and to achieve a given level of domestic content.[199] Canada refuted this and pointed out that NAFTA lists all prohibited performance requirements and export bans are not so-listed. Furthermore, Canada argued that even if the Interim Order were classified as a prohibited performance requirement, the exception would apply because it is a measure necessary to protect human, animal or plant life or health or was necessary for the conservation of living or non-living exhaustible natural resource. The argument that the Interim Order was intended to protect the environment was challenged by S.D. Myers, who pointed to the fact that the majority of the PCB waste in Canada was located in Ontario and Quebec, making S.D. Myers facilities in Ohio significantly closer than those of Chem-Security in Alberta.[200] Assuming that the facilities in Alberta and Ohio were comparable (as S.D. Myers claimed), one would conclude that cross-border shipment was the more environmentally-sound option. However, as S.D. Myers reportedly planned to recycle the wastes in Ohio, but then ship them to Texas for final incineration, the distances for the movement of the wastes were actually much greater than S.D. Myers suggested.[201]

[194] S.D. Myers Memorial: 51–7.   [195] Ibid.
[196] S.D. Myers Counter-Memorial: 89–90; de Pencier 2000: 411–12.
[197] Ibid: 88.   [198] S.D. Myers Memorial: 62–6.   [199] Ibid.   [200] Ibid: 6.
[201] Hodges 2002: 383.

With respect to its final claim, S.D. Myers put forth that Canada had indirectly expropriated its investment without providing compensation.[202] Canada repudiated this claim, pointing to the fact that S.D. Myers's subsidiary in Canada had continued operations while the Interim Order remained in effect and that there was no evidence that S.D. Myers had sustained any loss as a result of the Interim Order.[203]

In addition to rebutting S.D. Myers's claims, Canada also argued that the Interim Order was not a measure that 'related to' an investor or an investment in Canada (as required for Chapter 11 to apply), and suggested that S.D. Myers did not in fact have an investment in Canada, as the shares of Myers Canada were owned by several members of the Myers family, rather than by S.D. Myers as a company.[204] Furthermore, Canada contended (as did Mexico in a Non-Party submission) that because S.D. Myers and Myers Canada were engaged in the trade in goods or cross-border services, Chapters 3 and 12 of NAFTA applied, which take precedence over Chapter 11.[205] Canada further argued that its other international obligations, including the Basel Convention and Transboundary Agreement, should prevail over Chapter 11 obligations in the event of any inconsistency.[206] Finally, Canada sought to establish that the US EPA Enforcement Discretion, which had provided the basis for the open border and thus the Interim Order and NAFTA dispute, had not been lawful.[207]

7.2.4.3   The outcome

On 13 November 2000, the tribunal delivered its First Partial Award. Although the tribunal was unanimous in its findings, one arbitrator also wrote a Separate Concurring Opinion.[208]

The tribunal found that S.D. Myers was an 'investor' and had an 'investment' under the definitions provided in Chapter 11, despite the previously mentioned issue of share ownership.[209] The arbitrators also concluded that S.D. Myers's plan to expand its Canadian operations was the specific inspiration for the Interim and Final Orders and that, therefore, the measures clearly *related to* the company and its investment in

---

[202] *S.D. Myers* Memorial: 74–5.   [203] *S.D. Myers* Counter-Memorial: 105.
[204] *Ibid*: 66–76.
[205] *Ibid*: 122; *S.D. Myers* v. *Canada*, Article 1128 Submission of Mexico on the Merits, 14 January 2000.
[206] *S. D. Myers* Counter-Memorial: 61–3.   [207] *S.D. Myers* Partial Award: para. 191.
[208] Under the UNCITRAL Rules (31 and 32) there can only be one award of the tribunal on any particular issue, and therefore a separate opinion is technically not part of an award and has no legal status.
[209] *S.D. Myers* Partial Award: paras. 320–1.

Canada.[210] The tribunal determined that Canada had breached Articles 1102 and 1105 (on national treatment and the minimum standard respectively).[211] They did not find that Canada had used a prohibited performance requirement or that it had expropriated S.D. Myers's investment.[212] In arriving at its decision, the tribunal found that the evidence presented by S.D. Myers established that the Interim and Final Orders were designed to a great extent with the 'desire and intent to protect and promote the market share of enterprises that would carry out the destruction of PCBs in Canada and that were owned by Canadian nationals'.[213] They argued that while other factors were considered, the 'protectionist intent of the lead minister ... was reflected in decision-making at every stage that led to the ban'.[214] In terms of the environmental justification for the measures, the tribunal found 'no legitimate environmental reason for introducing the ban'.[215] The tribunal suggested that the 'indirect environmental objective' of ensuring continued domestic capacity to dispose of PCBs and PCB wastes was legitimate but 'could have been achieved by other measures' (e.g., sourcing all government requirements, granting subsidies to the Canadian industry, etc.).[216] As for the Basel Convention, the tribunal determined that Article 11 clearly permitted the continuation of the Transboundary Agreement, which allowed for cross-border movements of hazardous waste between Canada and the US. However, they also noted: 'Even if the Basel Convention were to have been ratified by NAFTA parties, *it should not be presumed that Canada would have been able to use it to justify the breach of a specific NAFTA provision*.'[217] Thus, the tribunal concluded that 'where a state can achieve its chosen level of environmental protection through a variety of equally effective and reasonable means, it is obliged to adopt the alternative that is *most consistent with open trade*'.[218] The tribunal chose not to look into the issue of the legality of the US EPA enforcement discretion, arguing that Canada had never challenged the measure directly, and did eventually re-open the border (thus implicitly accepting the legality of the situation).[219]

In considering whether Canada had breached its commitment to provide national treatment, the tribunal looked at the broader legal context in

---

[210] *Ibid*: para. 234.   [211] *Ibid*: para. 322.   [212] *Ibid*: para. 323.   [213] *Ibid*: para. 162.
[214] *Ibid*.   [215] *Ibid*: para. 195.
[216] *Ibid*. Orellana 2007: 769, argues that it is highly debatable whether these alternatives would have been as (cost) effective as the Interim/Final Order, and furthermore suggests that they likely would have violated the WTO Government Procurement Agreement or the WTO Subsidies Agreement.
[217] *S.D. Myers* Partial Award: para. 215, emphasis added.
[218] *Ibid*: para. 221, emphasis added.   [219] *Ibid*: para. 191.

which Article 1102 is situated, including: the rest of NAFTA; the NAAEC; and principles that are affirmed by the NAAEC (including the Rio Declaration principles). The principles that the tribunal highlighted were the following:

(i) states have the right to establish high levels of environmental protection and they are not obliged to compromise their standards merely to satisfy the political or economic interests of other states;
(ii) states should avoid creating distortions to trade; and
(iii) environmental protection and economic development can and should be mutually supportive.[220]

The tribunal appeared to focus quite extensively on the interpretation of the phrase 'like circumstances' in respect of these principles. The tribunal suggested that:

> Article 1102 must take into account the general principles that emerge from the legal context of NAFTA, including both its concern with the environment and the need to avoid trade distortions that are not justified by environmental concerns. The assessment of 'like circumstances' must also take into account circumstances that would justify governmental regulations that treat them differently in order to protect the public interest.[221]

After establishing that S.D. Myers was in 'like circumstances' with Canadian competitors, the tribunal further assessed two factors: whether the practical effect of the measure is to create a disproportionate benefit for nationals over non-nationals; and whether the measure, on its face, appears to favour its nationals over non-nationals who are protected by the relevant treaty.[222] The tribunal concluded on the basis of its assessment that the issuance of the Interim Order and the Final Order was in breach of Article NAFTA 1102.[223]

The tribunal commenced its argument on the minimum standard with a precautionary statement that a tribunal 'does not have an open-ended mandate to second-guess government decision-making'.[224] They then went on to acknowledge that:

> Governments have to make many potentially controversial choices. In doing so, they may appear to have made mistakes, to have misjudged the facts, proceeded on the basis of a misguided economic or sociological theory, placed too much emphasis on some social values over others and

[220] *Ibid*: para. 220. [221] *Ibid*: para. 250. [222] *Ibid*: para. 252.
[223] *Ibid*: para. 256. [224] *Ibid*: para. 261.

adopted solutions that are ultimately ineffective or counterproductive. The *ordinary remedy, if there were one, for errors in modern governments is through internal political and legal processes, including elections.*[225]

[handwritten margin note: INTERNATIONAL-TION OF US TAKINGS LAW. SEE NOTES]

The tribunal thus appeared to be somewhat sympathetic to the position of states and further held that breach of fair and equitable treatment, as an integral part of the minimum standard, requires conduct that is so unjust or arbitrary that it can be deemed unacceptable from the international perspective, noting that 'determination must be made in the light of the high measure of deference that international law generally extends to the right of domestic authorities to regulate matters within their own borders'.[226] It is somewhat surprising that the tribunal followed these statements with its determination (by majority) that 'the breach of Article 1102 essentially establishes a breach of Article 1105 as well'.[227] This decision would later be rebuked by all NAFTA parties in an Interpretation of Article 1105 released by the NAFTA FTC.[228]

The tribunal agreed, by majority, with Canada that the Interim and Final Orders did not qualify as prohibited performance requirements under Article 1106.[229] The tribunal also rejected the interpretation provided by S.D. Myers that the phrase 'tantamount to expropriation' expanded the meaning of Article 1110 beyond the accepted definition in international law.[230] The tribunal argued that 'tantamount' meant 'equivalent to'.[231] The tribunal categorized the Interim Order and the Final Order as 'regulatory acts', noting the distinction between expropriations, which 'tend to involve the deprivation of ownership rights' and regulations, which are a 'lesser interference'.[232] They went on to note: 'Regulatory conduct by public authorities is unlikely to be the subject of legitimate complaint under Article 1110 of NAFTA, although the Tribunal does not rule out that possibility.'[233] However, the tribunal then proceeded to draw a different distinction, between permanent and temporary interferences in an investment. The fact that the closure of the Canadian border was temporary appears to have strongly influenced the tribunal's decision that it did not amount to an expropriation:

---

[225] *Ibid.*   [226] *Ibid*: para. 263.   [227] *Ibid*: para. 266.
[228] Paragraph B.3 of the Interpretation states: 'A determination that there has been a breach of another provision of NAFTA, or of a separate international agreement, does not establish that there has been a breach of Article 1105(1).' *[handwritten margin note: PAGE 182]*
[229] *S.D. Myers* Partial Award: para. 278. One arbitrator dissented, finding that the effect of the Orders was to require S.D. Myers to undertake all of its operations in Canada which amounted to a prohibited performance requirement.
[230] *Ibid*: para. 285.   [231] *Ibid*: para. 286.   [232] *Ibid*: para. 282.   [233] *Ibid*: para. 281.

In this case, the Interim Order and the Final Order were designed to, and did, curb [S.D. Myers's] initiative, *but only for a time*. CANADA realized no benefit from the measure. The evidence does not support a transfer of property or benefit directly to others. *An opportunity was delayed*.[234]

The tribunal deferred its final decision on damages to the Second Partial Award, where it concluded that the total compensation payable to S.D. Myers was CAD$6,050,000 plus compound interest.[235] The Final Award concerned the apportionment of legal fees and arbitration costs. Canada was required to pay CAD$850,000 plus compound interest in costs and fees.[236]

Canada sought judicial review of the First Partial Award in the Federal Courts of Canada (the arbitration had its seat in Toronto). Canada argued that the tribunal had exceeded its jurisdiction by deciding on a case in which no investment was involved and had incorrectly determined that S.D. Myers was in 'like circumstances' with Canadian waste disposal companies. Canada also argued that the First Partial Award violated the country's public policy.[237] The Court issued its judgment in January 2004, noting the limited scope of judicial review of tribunal awards and dismissing the case.[238] Of particular interest is the court's decision that review on the basis of conflicts with public policy is limited to cases of flagrant injustice, rather than mere conflicts with a government's 'political position'.[239]

7.2.5   *Methanex v. United States*

This case revolves around the production and sale of a gasoline additive in California. Following a university study that concluded that the additive was a significant source of potential water pollution and a threat to public health, the State of California phased out its use. A Canadian investor subsequently sued the US under NAFTA Chapter 11 for expropriation and breach of national treatment and the minimum standard of treatment. The tribunal in the case dismissed all claims and determined that the

---

[234] *Ibid*: para. 287, emphasis added.
[235] *S.D. Myers, Inc. v. Government of Canada*, Second Partial Award, 21 October 2002: paras. 311–12.
[236] *S.D. Myers, Inc. v. Government of Canada*, Final Award, 30 December 2002: paras. 53–5.
[237] Brower 2004: 342.
[238] *Attorney General of Canada v. S.D. Myers, Inc.*, 3 *Federal Court Reports* (2004): 368, http://reports.fja.gc.ca.
[239] *Ibid*: para. 55.

claimant should pay all of the costs and legal fees incurred in the course of the arbitration.

7.2.5.1   Background

Beginning in the late 1980s, studies were undertaken in the US to identify ways in which gasoline could be reformulated to help achieve certain air quality goals.[240] These studies found that the addition of oxygenated organic compounds, such as alcohols and ethers, to conventional gasoline resulted in a reduction in the emissions of carbon monoxide and other products of incomplete combustion.[241] The use of oxygenates in fuel subsequently became mandatory under US Federal law. In California, the 'oxygenate of choice' was methyl tertiary-butyl ether (MTBE). Thus, MTBE was initially brought into use in California (and in other locations) to bring about health and environmental benefits. However, improvements in the emission control technology used in newer cars have significantly reduced emissions of air pollutants and as a result, MTBE and other oxygenates no longer have significant effects on air quality.[242] On the other hand, they do pose environmental risks associated with groundwater contamination. MTBE is highly soluble in water and will transfer readily to groundwater from gasoline leaking from underground storage tanks, pipelines and other components of the gasoline distribution system.[243]

On 9 October 1997, the California Senate adopted Bill 521, which commissioned an assessment of the human health and environmental risks and benefits associated with the use of MTBE and other gasoline oxygenates, to be carried out by researchers at the University of California.[244] In 1998, the University of California released its five-volume, 600-page, report (the UC Report).[245] The UC Report concluded that California's

---

[240] *Methanex Corporation* v. *United States of America*, Final Award of the Tribunal on Jurisdiction and Merits (*Methanex* Final Award), 3 August 2005: para. III.A.4. Reproduced in 44 ILM (2005): 1345.

[241] *Ibid.*

[242] 'University of California Report MTBE Fact Sheet', UC Davis website, 12 November 1998: 1, http://tsrtp.ucdavis.edu/public/mtbe/mtberpt/index.php.

[243] *Ibid.*

[244] *Methanex Corporation* v. *United States of America*, First Partial Award (*Methanex* First Partial Award), 7 August 2002: para. 26.

[245] Health & Environmental Assessment of MTBE, Report to the Governor and Legislature of the State of California, Volume I, Summary & Recommendations, November 1998, https://tsrtp.ucdavis.edu/public/mtbe/mtberpt/vol1.pdf.

water resources were being placed at risk by the use of MTBE in gasoline. While the UC Report suggested that the risk of exposure to MTBE through ingestion or inhalation was low, they noted that there were significant gaps in the scientific understanding of the acute and chronic toxicity of MTBE.[246] The UC Report also suggested that the potential treatment costs of MTBE-contaminated drinking water could be enormous. Furthermore, the costs associated with remediating leaks and spills from underground storage tanks and pipelines could be in the order of tens to hundreds of millions of dollars per year.[247]

The UC Report recommended that California phase out the use of gasoline oxygenates. In order to do so, it would have to seek a waiver from the Federal Government requirements on the use of oxygenates in fuel. A second-best option, suggested in the UC Report, was the use of ethanol as an oxygenate to replace MTBE. The inadequate supply of ethanol in the state meant that an immediate ban on MTBE would have negative implications for consumers and disrupt gasoline production significantly, and the UC Report therefore recommended a scheduled phase-out, coupled with a careful study of the environmental and health impacts of alternative oxygenates, such as ethanol.[248]

In response to the UC Report, Gray Davis, then Governor of California, issued Executive Order D-5-99 on 25 March 1999.[249] The Order directed the relevant government bodies to:

(i)   develop a timetable for the phase-out of MTBE;
(ii) request from the US EPA a waiver of the Federal Government reformulated gasoline oxygenate requirement; and
(iii) conduct a study on the environmental and health impacts associated with the use of ethanol as an oxygenate in gasoline.

Furthermore, the Governor commissioned a study on the potential for the development of a California waste-based or other biomass ethanol industry and required that gasoline containing MTBE be labelled prominently at the point of sale (gas stations) to enable consumers to choose the type of gasoline that they wished to purchase.[250]

On 12 April 1999, Governor Davis wrote to the Administrator of the US EPA requesting a waiver from the reformulated gasoline oxygenate requirement. On 8 October 1999, Governor Davis signed into law California Senate Bill 989 placing into statute the previously issued Executive

---

[246] *Ibid*: 12.   [247] *Ibid*.   [248] *Ibid*: 13–14.
[249] *Methanex* First Partial Award: para. 29.   [250] *Ibid*: paras. 30–1.

Order (D-5-99) and enacting several other provisions designed to protect groundwater and drinking water from MTBE contamination.[251] In December 1999, the California EPA issued its report, entitled Health and Environmental Assessment of the Use of Ethanol as a Fuel Oxygenate.[252] Based on the report, the California Environment Policy Commission concluded that, although further research was warranted, the impacts associated with the use of ethanol as a fuel oxygenate would be significantly less, and that these impacts would also be more manageable, than those associated with continued use of MTBE.[253]

On 16 June 2000, the California Reformulated Gasoline Phase III Standards (CaRFG3), which prohibited the use of MTBE in gasoline beginning 31 December 2002, were adopted.[254] These regulations became effective on 2 September 2000, and were amended in 2001. The phase-out date was later postponed in response to the US EPA's denial of California's request for a waiver of the federal oxygenate requirement. Governor Davis felt that in light of the circumstances, in particular the fact that the current production, transportation and distribution of ethanol was insufficient to meet California's needs, keeping to the original timetable would cause economic hardship.[255]

7.2.5.2   The dispute

In December 1999, Methanex Corporation, a Canadian company that produces and markets methanol, served a Notice of Arbitration against the US under NAFTA Chapter 11 and the UNCITRAL Rules of Arbitration.[256] Methanex supplies the vast majority of methanol in California, which has no methanol industry of its own.[257] While Methanex does not produce or sell MTBE, approximately one-third of Methanex's methanol production at the time was directed at the fuel sector, principally for use in the production of MTBE.[258]

[251] *Methanex* Final Award: para. III.A.29.
[252] Health and Environmental Assessment of the Use of Ethanol as a Fuel Oxygenate, Report to the California Environmental Policy Council in Response to Executive Order D-5-99, State Water Resources Control Board of California, Air Resources Board, Office of Environmental Health and Hazard Assessment, UCRL-AR-135949 Vol. 1, www-erd.llnl.gov/ethanol/etohdoc/index.html.
[253] *Methanex* Final Award: para. III.A.31.   [254] *Ibid*: para. III.A.32.
[255] *Ibid*: para. III.A.34.
[256] *Methanex Corporation* v. *United States of America*, Notice of Arbitration, 3 December 1999.
[257] *Methanex Corporation* v. *United States of America*, Rejoinder to US' Reply Memorial on Jurisdiction, Admissibility and the Proposed Amendment, 25 May 2001: 27.
[258] *Methanex* First Partial Award: para. 24.

Subsequent to submitting its Statement of Claim,[259] the company changed its legal counsel and applied to the tribunal to amend the claim. Methanex's application substantially modified the legal and factual basis of its claim, and was apparently based on new information related to Governor Gray Davis (see below).[260] The tribunal allowed the amendment, with the caveat that Methanex should ultimately bear, regardless of the outcome of the arbitration, the costs related to the additional burden on the tribunal and the US in having to respond to the amendments to the claim.[261] Methanex submitted its Amended Statement of Claim in February 2001.[262]

In the Original Statement of Claim, Methanex argued that the State of California did not accord a minimum standard of treatment as required by Article 1105, and that various actions taken by the State of California and its Governor directly or indirectly constituted a measure tantamount to expropriation under Article 1110. Methanex claimed compensation from the US in the amount of approximately US$970 million (together with interest and costs).[263] In the Amended Statement of Claim, the company focused only on the California Executive Order and the CaRFG3 Regulations, and not the California Senate Bill.[264] Methanex added a new claim of discrimination on the basis of nationality as prohibited by Article 1102, as well as further claims for breaches of Articles 1105 and 1110.[265]

In its Statement of Defence, the US raised a series of objections about the admissibility of Methanex's claims.[266] The tribunal identified seven distinct challenges articulated by the US Government:

(i) no proximate cause (no connection between US measures and claimed damages);

(ii) no legal right impugned by US measures (customer base or goodwill or expectation of future profits from methanol sales cannot qualify as an investment under NAFTA);

(iii) no legally significant connection between US measures and Methanex or its investments;

---

[259] *Methanex Corporation* v. *United States of America*, Statement of Claim (*Methanex* Original Statement of Claim), 3 December 1999.

[260] *Methanex Corporation* v. *United States of America*, Notice of Change of Legal Council and Intent to File an Amended Claim, 30 November 2000.

[261] *Methanex* First Partial Award: para. 78.

[262] *Methanex Corporation* v. *United States of America*, Amended Statement of Claim (*Methanex* Amended Statement of Claim), 12 February 2001.

[263] *Methanex* Original Statement of Claim: 13.

[264] *Methanex* Amended Statement of Claim: 35.   [265] *Ibid*: 42–70.

[266] *Methanex Corporation* v. *United States of America*, Statement of Defense (*Methanex* Statement of Defense), 10 August 2000.

(iv) no loss; no claim for subsidiaries' losses (a procedural issue);
(v) no waiver (a procedural issue); and
(vi) no possible claim of discrimination (all methanol producers were treated the same, regardless of corporate nationality).[267]

The third challenge is particularly worth discussion. This challenge related to NAFTA Article 1101.1, which requires that measures subject to a dispute *relate to* an investor or investment. The US asserted that the Californian ban of MTBE did not relate to Methanex because it was not directed at methanol or methanol producers. The US contended that the phrase 'relating to' requires a *legally significant* connection between the disputed measure and the investor.[268] This excludes measures of general application, especially measures aimed at the protection of human health and the environment, which are likely to affect a vast range of actors and economic interests. The US argued that if such general measures were not excluded from consideration by tribunals, the NAFTA Parties could be subject to claims based on untold numbers of local, state and federal measures that merely have an incidental impact on an investor or investment.[269] Methanex, on the other hand, suggested that it should be sufficient that government measures *affect* an investor or its investment.[270] Furthermore, the company argued that the 'relating to' requirement is easily satisfied if there is discriminatory intent behind a measure.[271]

In its First Partial Award, the tribunal found that several of the US challenges were not *jurisdictional* challenges and that, even if they were, the issues were so tied up in the facts of the case that they would have to be dealt with in the merits phase of arbitration. However, the tribunal did extensively discuss the third challenge, concerning the connection required between a measure and an investment. The tribunal noted that:

> If the threshold provided by Article 1101(1) were merely one of 'affecting,' as Methanex contends, it would be satisfied wherever any economic impact was felt by an investor or an investment ... As such, Article 1101(1) would provide no significant threshold to a NAFTA arbitration ... Methanex's interpretation would produce a surprising, if not an absurd, result. The possible consequences of human conduct are infinite, especially when comprising acts of governmental agencies; but common sense does not require that line to run unbroken towards an endless horizon.[272]

[267] *Methanex* First Partial Award: para. 84.   [268] *Methanex* Statement of Defense: 28.
[269] *Methanex Corporation* v. *United States of America*, US Memorial on Jurisdiction, 13 November 2000: 48–9.
[270] *Methanex Corporation* v. *United States of America*, Counter-Memorial on Jurisdiction, 12 February 2001: 47–8.
[271] *Ibid*: 51–2.   [272] *Methanex* First Partial Award: para. 137.

As such, the tribunal determined that it had no jurisdiction to hear Methanex's case as laid out in the Original Statement of Claim. Similarly, it denied jurisdiction on the Amended Statement of Claim *as a whole*, but found that it had jurisdiction to hear *a part of that claim*. In particular, the tribunal found that Methanex's allegations relating to the *intent* underlying the Californian regulations could potentially meet the requirements of jurisdiction, but that without further evidence, this could not be definitively determined. Methanex was therefore invited to submit a fresh pleading setting out its specific factual allegations related only to the issue of intent, and the decision on jurisdiction was consequently postponed pending the conclusion of the merits phase of the arbitration.[273] Methanex submitted a Second Amended Statement of Claim in November 2002.[274]

In order to support its claims of breach of national treatment, which were largely based on the notion that California's actions were intended to favour the American ethanol industry, Methanex first had to establish that it was in 'like circumstances' with ethanol producers. The company's reasoning on this issue was based on the fact that ethanol, as an oxygenate, competes directly with MTBE. Methanex supported this claim with the expert opinion of Sir Robert Jennings and reference to WTO jurisprudence on the treatment of 'like products'.[275] Methanex contended that the burden of proof was on the US to justify its discriminatory treatment. It argued that under WTO jurisprudence this would require the US to show that the ban on MTBE was:

(i) necessary to protect the environment of California;
(ii) the least restrictive option available;
(iii) based on sufficient scientific evidence; and
(iv) not arbitrary or discriminatory.[276]

Methanex suggested that none of these requirements had been met. In the company's view, MTBE is safe and effective and any environmental problems associated with it are principally caused by leaking underground gasoline tanks. Consequently, according to Methanex, the appropriate

[273] *Ibid*: paras. 169 and 172.
[274] *Methanex Corporation* v. *United States of America*, Second Amended Statement of Claim (*Methanex* Second Amended Statement of Claim), 5 November 2002.
[275] *Ibid*: para. 300.
[276] *Methanex Corporation* v. *United States of America*, Reply to US Amended Statement of Defense (*Methanex* Reply), 19 February 2004: paras. 191–5.

solution was not to ban MTBE, but to repair and improve these storage tanks.[277]

Methanex further argued that, in any case, the MTBE ban was not motivated by the Government of California's desire to protect the environment. The company claimed that environmental protection was merely a convenient cover for measures that would significantly benefit the powerful US ethanol industry. In this respect, Methanex focused on one company in particular, Archer Daniels Midland (ADM), which produces more than 70 per cent of US ethanol. Methanex pointed to several contributions that ADM made to Gray Davis's gubernatorial campaign and to a supposedly secret meeting with Davis in 1998, when he was Lieutenant Governor of California and the California MTBE policy was being developed.

In response, the US argued that the appropriate comparator in the 'like circumstances' test was the substantial domestic methanol industry. As the California ban had precisely the same effect on American methanol companies as it had on Methanex, there could be no breach of national treatment. The US rejected Methanex's method of comparing methanol and ethanol, pointing out that they were different in several respects, and specifically that while ethanol can be used directly as an oxygenate additive to gasoline, methanol is prohibited from being used as such.[278] Methanex countered that the fact that they were in identical circumstances with domestic methanol producers was irrelevant.[279]

The US also challenged the allegations that the measures were not motivated by environmental concern, pointing out that the decision to ban MTBE was firmly based on the recommendations and findings of an extensive scientific study and consultation with stakeholders.[280] The US argued that:

> Methanex's claim *does not remotely resemble* the type of grievance for which the States Parties to NAFTA created the investor-State dispute resolution mechanism of Chapter 11. Methanex's case is founded on the proposition that, whenever a State takes action to protect the public health or environment, the State is responsible for damages to every business enterprise claiming a resultant setback in its fortunes if the enterprise can persuade an arbitral tribunal that the action could have been handled differently.

---

[277] *Methanex* Second Amended Statement of Claim: para. 199.
[278] *Methanex Corporation* v. *United States of America*, Amended Statement of Defense (*Methanex* Amended Statement of Defense), 5 December 2003: paras. 315–16.
[279] *Methanex* Reply: para. 173.
[280] *Methanex* Amended Statement of Defense: paras. 190–206.

> Plainly put, this proposition is absurd. If accepted by this Tribunal, *no NAFTA Party could carry out its most fundamental governmental functions unless it were prepared to pay for each and every economic impact occasioned by doing so.* The NAFTA Parties *never intended* the NAFTA to bring about such a radical change in the way that they function, and Methanex cannot show otherwise.[281]

Whereas Methanex's discussion of the discriminatory treatment that it had allegedly endured was quite extensive, its discussion of the minimum standard and expropriation was remarkably short, occupying only a few paragraphs each in the Second Amended Statement of Claim. This is likely due to the fact that Methanex viewed discrimination as intimately connected to the other standards. Methanex argued that a breach of Article 1102 also constituted a breach of Article 1105, citing the decision in *S.D. Myers* (see above).[282] In terms of expropriation, Methanex argued that a substantial portion of its investments, including its share of the California and wider US oxygenate markets, had been handed to the US domestic ethanol industry. In addition to having lost its share of the California market, Methanex claimed that the measures contributed to the continued idling of one of its plants in the US and resulted in an immediate drop in its share price.[283]

In 2001, the US submitted a copy of the Notes of Interpretation issued by the NAFTA FTC to the tribunal. The Interpretation clarified that Article 1105 did not require treatment beyond that prescribed in customary international law, and stipulated that the determination that there had been a breach of another provision of NAFTA did not establish a breach of Article 1105. Methanex challenged the Interpretation, arguing that it had been made with a clear purpose of affecting the outcome of the case.[284]

Canada and Mexico also made submissions to the tribunal, which supported the arguments of the US on both jurisdictional issues and the merits of the case.[285] For the first time in an investor-state dispute, non-parties (several NGOs) were also permitted to submit briefs to the tribunal (see Section 6.2).

[281] *Methanex* Statement of Defense: para. 2, emphasis added.

[282] *Methanex* Second Amended Statement of Claim: para. 315.

[283] *Methanex* Final Award: para. II.D.31.

[284] *Ibid*: para. II.B.14. Other investors made the same claim in other disputes that were proceeding at the time.

[285] *Methanex Corporation* v. *United States of America*, Article 1128 Submission of Canada on Jurisdiction, 30 April 2001; Article 1128 Submission of Mexico on Jurisdiction, 30 April 2001; Article 1128 Submission of Canada on the Re-Submitted Amended Claim, 30 January 2004; Article 1128 Submission of Mexico on the Re-Submitted Amended Claim, 30 January 2004.

7.2.5.3   The outcome

The Final Award of the tribunal was issued on 3 August 2005. As the majority of Methanex's arguments had focused on discriminatory treatment, and the First Partial Award had largely limited the case to an analysis of the motivation behind the Californian measures, the bulk of the Final Award also dealt with these issues.

In the tribunal's view, there was significant evidence that the measures in question were motivated by legitimate concern for the environment and the health and welfare of the population of California: 'This policy was motivated by the honest belief, held in good faith and on reasonable scientific grounds, that MTBE contaminated groundwater and was difficult and expensive to clean up.'[286] In particular, they found that the UC Report reflected 'a serious, objective and scientific approach to a complex problem in California'.[287] The tribunal also rejected Methanex's conspiracy theory about ADM and Governor Davis, pointing out that California Senate Bill 521, which mandated gubernatorial action regarding MTBE, was passed by the California legislature prior to the election and that once he was Governor, Davis had no discretion to deviate from the results and recommendations of the UC Report.[288] Furthermore, the tribunal noted that the evidence suggested that the Government of California, far from favouring ethanol, aimed to receive a waiver from the US EPA standards so that it could prohibit the use of *all* gasoline oxygenates.[289] The tribunal, therefore, found no breach of Article 1102.

With regards to Article 1105, the tribunal addressed the issue of whether a breach of Article 1102 (had a breach been found) would have constituted a further breach of Article 1105. The tribunal decided that Methanex's argument was untenable, even in the absence of the NAFTA FTC Notes of Interpretation, because the plain meaning of the minimum standard does not support the contention that it precludes discrimination.[290] As this was the entire basis of Methanex's claim on Article 1105, the tribunal found that it had failed to make its case for a breach of this provision.

Although the discussion of expropriation was not extensive in Methanex's pleadings, and its claim was largely based on the supposed discriminatory nature of the measures, the tribunal made an important decision on the issue, suggesting that:

> as a matter of general international law, a non-discriminatory regulation for a public purpose, which is enacted in accordance with due process and, which affects, inter alios, a foreign investor or investment is not deemed

---

[286] *Methanex* Final Award: para. III.A.102.2.   [287] *Ibid*: para. III.A.101.
[288] *Ibid*: para. III.B.54.   [289] *Ibid*: para. III.B.55.   [290] *Ibid*: para. IV.C.14.

expropriatory and compensable unless specific commitments had been given by the regulating government to the then putative foreign investor contemplating investment that the government would refrain from such regulation.[291]

The tribunal concluded that the California ban did not amount to an expropriation.

Having dealt with the merits of the claim, the tribunal returned to the issue of jurisdiction, which it had delayed in order to assess the issue of intent. The tribunal found, as it had in its discussion of national treatment, that Methanex had failed to prove its case in respect of malign intent on the part of the Government of California.[292] As such, it concluded that there was no legally significant connection between the Californian regulations and Methanex and its investments, and the US jurisdictional challenge was therefore upheld. Thus despite having determined that Methanex's claims had failed on the merits, the tribunal subsequently found that it lacked the jurisdiction to consider these claims, and dismissed the case accordingly.[293]

Finally, the tribunal dealt with the issue of costs. It found no compelling reason not to follow standard UNCITRAL practice, based on Rule 40.1, that the losing party should pay all of the costs of the arbitration. The amount that Methanex was required to reimburse the US in this respect amounted to nearly US$1.1 million.[294] The tribunal also held that Methanex should cover the nearly US$3 million that the US had incurred in legal fees.[295]

7.3 Pending cases

7.3.1 *Glamis Gold* v. *United States*

This case concerns California regulations requiring the reclamation of land following open-pit mining operations. A Canadian mining company filed for arbitration under NAFTA Chapter 11, arguing that the regulations amounted to expropriation and denial of fair and equitable treatment. As this book was going to press, the award in this case was released to the

---

[291] *Ibid*: para. IV.D.7. The effect of the caveat with regard to 'specific commitments' is unclear. Specific commitments could refer to a contract or stability agreement, but as noted in Chapters 4 and 5, there is continued debate about the relationship between breach of contract and breach of treaty. For further discussion of the caveat, see Mann 2005.

[292] *Ibid*: para. IV.E.18.   [293] *Ibid*: para.IV.E.22.   [294] *Ibid*: para. V.13.   [295] *Ibid*.

parties. Although the award was not immediately available to the public, media reports indicated that the US had prevailed.

7.3.1.1 Background

In 1987, Glamis Gold Ltd (Glamis)[296] began acquiring mining claims on federal public lands in the Imperial Valley of California. Under the General Mining Law of 1872, US citizens are allowed to acquire claims for mining on federal land simply by putting up posts and registering the claim with the Department of the Interior. An annual maintenance fee of US$100 per claim is required, but the federal government receives no rents or royalties from mining operations conducted on these lands.[297] Glamis established subsidiaries in the US to act as 'citizens' to acquire the claims. The Imperial Project consisted of approximately 187 mining claims.[298]

Prior to the development of any mineral operations, Glamis was required to submit several EIAs to the Bureau of Land Management (within the US Department of the Interior), which is responsible for the administration of mining claims on federal lands. There were numerous contentious issues surrounding the project, including the fact that the area of the proposed mine was 'adjacent to two formally designated wilderness areas, critical habitat for the federally-listed desert tortoise and an area designated as a place of critical environmental concern for Native American cultural values'.[299]

Following a six-year review of the project, the Bureau of Land Management decided that the no-action alternative was preferred (i.e., it recommended that there be no development of the mine) and in 2001 the Secretary of the Interior Bruce Babbitt officially denied the proposed plan of operations for the Imperial Project.[300] However, in late 2002, following a change of administration, the new Secretary of the Interior, Gale Norton rescinded the decision and the Bureau of Land Management initiated a

---

[296] At the commencement of this case, Glamis Gold Ltd identified itself as a publicly held Canadian corporation, incorporated under the laws of British Columbia. Glamis Gold Inc. was a wholly-owned subsidiary of Glamis Gold Ltd, and was incorporated under the laws of the State of Nevada. Glamis Imperial was a wholly-owned subsidiary of Glamis Gold Inc., and also a Nevada corporation. Glamis Gold Ltd merged with the Canadian company, Goldcorp Inc. in 2006.

[297] *Glamis Gold Ltd* v. *United States of America*, Statement of Defense (*Glamis* Statement of Defense), 8 April 2005: 3.

[298] *Glamis Gold Ltd* v. *United States of America*, Notice of Arbitration (*Glamis* Notice of Arbitration), 9 December 2003: 5.

[299] Non-Party Submission of the Quechan Indian Nation, 19 August 2005: 1.

[300] *Glamis* Statement of Defense: 11–12.

process for the project plan to be reconsidered. In anticipation of the possible approval of the Imperial Project, the State of California began to take steps to mitigate the potential impacts of this and other open-pit mine developments. In particular, California Senate Bill 22 was passed in 2003, stipulating that Californian authorities may not approve the reclamation plan for surface mining operations located within one mile of any Native American sacred site or located in an area of special concern,[301] unless it is stipulated that all excavations would be backfilled and graded to achieve the approximate contours of the land prior to mining. In addition to aiding in the restoration of the visual landscape, backfilling also reduces the potential environmental damage caused by cyanide leaching from waste rock piles.[302]

7.3.1.2   The dispute

On 31 July 2003, Glamis submitted a Notice of Intent to Submit a Claim under NAFTA Chapter 11.[303] In the Notice of Intent, Glamis argued that two Chapter 11 rules had been violated by California and thereby the US: the prohibition of expropriation (Article 1110) and the requirement to provide fair and equitable treatment to foreign investors (Article 1105). The company's Notice of Arbitration was filed in December 2003.[304] The dispute proceeded under the UNCITRAL rules of arbitration.

Glamis argued that the measures taken by the US and California individually and collectively amounted to an expropriation. Glamis focused on Senate Bill 22 in particular, stating that 'there was little doubt about the discriminatory and expropriatory purpose of this legislation'[305] and suggested that because the backfilling requirements are mandatory and non-discretionary, they resulted in the complete destruction of the economic value of the company's investment.[306] According to Glamis, the company 'undertook the significant investment necessary to establish and begin gold mining operation'[307] including 'less than 2 million in acquiring and developing the mineral rights' prior to 1994 and 'an additional 13 million . . . in the acquisition, exploration and development of the Imperial

---

[301] As defined by the California Desert Conservation Area Plan of 1980.
[302] *Glamis* Statement of Defense: 9.
[303] *Glamis Gold Ltd* v. *United States of America*, Notice of Intent to Submit a Claim to Arbitration, 21 July 2003.
[304] *Glamis* Notice of Arbitration.
[305] *Ibid*: 10.   [306] *Ibid.*   [307] *Ibid*: 6.

Project' as of December 2002.[308] However, Glamis's original claim was for a sum not less than US$50 million, based on the fair market value of the property interests owned by Glamis Imperial.[309] Glamis later amended its claim to not less than US$49.1 million in compensation for the loss of the property, plus further damages that 'the Tribunal may deem appropriate for the United States' failure to accord Glamis the minimum standard of treatment'.[310]

In addition to disputing Glamis's substantive arguments (see further below), the US raised the issue of Glamis's status as a *foreign* investor, pointing out that in the proposed mining plan, the subsidiary described its ultimate owner, Glamis Gold Ltd, as a 'publicly-owned US corporation'.[311] This issue was also a key point in the joint non-party submission of Friends of the Earth Canada (FOE-Canada) and Friends of the Earth US (FOE-US).[312]

On 31 May 2005, the tribunal issued a procedural order notifying the parties that it would address both jurisdictional issues and the merits of the case in its final award, despite the request of the US for a preliminary award on jurisdiction.[313]

In two sessions in August and September 2007, a total of nine days of hearings on the merits of the case were held. The hearings were open to the public.[314] During the hearings, the key points of contention between the parties were:

 (i) the property rights actually possessed by Glamis;
 (ii) the ripeness of the company's claim;
(iii) the interpretation of the two standards at issue; and
(iv) the application of these standards to the facts of the case.

With regard to the interpretation of measures tantamount to expropriation, both parties argued that the key issue was the economic impact of the measures. The US argued that this issue was paramount because without evidence of a full or nearly full deprivation of an investment, an expropriation claim must fail. On the other hand, Glamis argued that economic

---

[308] *Ibid*: 7. [309] *Ibid*: 10–11.
[310] *Glamis Gold Ltd* v. *United States of America*, Memorial (*Glamis* Memorial), 5 May 2006: 317.
[311] Qtd in *Glamis* Statement of Defense: 9, emphasis added by US.
[312] *Amicus Curiae* Submissions of Friends of the Earth Canada and Friends of the Earth United States, 30 September 2005.
[313] *Glamis Gold Ltd* v. *United States of America*, Procedural Order No. 2, 31 May 2005.
[314] The transcripts of the hearings can be found on the US State Department website, www.state.gov.

impact was the critical issue because if a total deprivation was shown to have occurred then no further analysis was required by the tribunal. While the US argued that because the denial of the project proposal by the Department of the Interior had been rescinded, Glamis could resume the approval process and eventually (theoretically) commence mine development, Glamis asserted that the California measures had made their project economically infeasible. The parties presented valuation reports to back up their claims about the economic impact of the California measures. The US presented a valuation study based on Glamis's own contemporaneous documents which indicated that the mining claims retained a significant value (US$9.1 million) after the California measures were adopted. The US further argued that by the time of the hearings in 2007, the value of the property had increased substantially to US$159 million as a result of the phenomenal rise in gold prices in the interim period. Glamis argued to the contrary that its property had a value of US$49.1 million prior to the enactment of the reclamation requirements, but retained no value thereafter. The company suggested that the US figures were preposterous and neglected important factors such as rising mine operation costs. Glamis also put forth that if the mining claims had retained any value, the company would have received purchase offers.

While both sides argued that the expropriation analysis should end with economic impact – the US because it had proved that there was none, and Glamis because it had shown that a full deprivation had occurred – they both also offered further steps of analysis in the event that the tribunal disagreed with their interpretation of the standard or with their valuation findings. Both parties suggested that two further analytical steps were well established in US and international takings jurisprudence:

(i) determination of the investor's reasonable investment-backed expectations; and
(ii) determination of the character of the measure(s).

Echoing the decision in *Methanex*, the US suggested that investors who operate in highly regulated industries, in highly regulated jurisdictions such as California, cannot have reasonable expectations that they will not be subject to extensions of those regulations, unless the government has made 'specific commitments' to the investor in that respect. The US pointed out that Glamis had no approved project plan or contract, which might qualify as specific commitments. On the other hand, Glamis argued that while specific commitments are a factor in the determination of reasonable expectations, their absence is not determinative.

✱ COMMON THEME

With regard to the assessment of the character of the measures, the US argued that numerous international arbitral tribunals have concluded that, except under rare circumstances, non-discriminatory regulations enacted for a public purpose will not be deemed expropriatory and compensable. While the US suggested that arbitral tribunals generally accept a government's characterization of a measure as 'regulatory', Glamis argued that the motivation of the government must be interrogated. In this respect, Glamis put forth that the California measures were not only discriminatory (because they did not apply to non-metallic mines) but also were specifically targeted at the company. Glamis further argued that even regulation that is intended to protect the public must not disproportionately burden individuals. In rebuttal, the US argued that the situations of metallic and non-metallic mines were distinct enough to justify their separate treatment and that, furthermore, the fact that an environmental regulation fails to address every environmental problem does not make the regulation discriminatory. In addition, the US argued that while Glamis's project might have been the impetus for the development of the California measures, those measures were not specifically targeted at the company and had in fact been applied to another mining project. Finally, the government argued that it was perfectly reasonable for a company to have to shoulder the burden of dealing with environmental damage that it had itself caused through its operations.

With respect to Article 1105, Glamis relied heavily on arbitral decisions that had interpreted 'fair and equitable treatment' as requiring governments to act transparently, to act in a manner that does not frustrate an investor's reasonable expectations, and to refrain from arbitrary conduct. The US first disputed that the requirements set forth by Glamis could be shown to be general and consistent state practice as required for them to amount to customary international law, and second objected to the notion that these requirements had, in any case, been breached.

The State of California expressed serious concerns about what a victory for Glamis in this case could have meant for their ability to regulate. In a letter to the US Trade Representative, the California Senate Select Committee on International Trade Policy and State Legislation wrote that the case 'provides a striking demonstration of the threats posed to the traditional regulatory power of state governments as a result of current models of trade and investment agreements'.[315] However, as this book

---

[315] Letter from California Senate Select Committee on International Trade Policy and State Legislation to Robert B. Zoellick, 17 November 2003, www.tradeobservatory.org.

was going to press, the outcome of the case was reported in the media. According to reports, all of Glamis's claims were unanimously rejected by the tribunal and the company was ordered to pay two-thirds of the arbitration costs.[316]

7.4   Analysis

The cases in this chapter illustrate that there is a wide range of environmental issues implicated in investment arbitration, and further that several different types of regulation (denial of permits, bans on trade, remediation requirements) have been claimed to be in breach of the rules and norms of investment protection. It would appear, from the limited number of cases reviewed, that breach of the national treatment standard, breach of the minimum standard/fair and equitable treatment and expropriation are the most common claims made by investors in environmentally relevant cases, and also are the claims that are most likely to be successful. While the interpretation of these standards remains a fluid process, several trends are discernible that are worthy of particular note.

7.4.1   Different circumstances or different interpretations?

In the accounts of academics and other observers, the cases detailed above are usually briefly summarized with the author very clearly taking a position on the outcome. For example, as Weiler notes:

> The 'story' of *Metalclad* v. *Mexico* has become quite well known in different circles; it just so happens that it has been told in dramatically different ways, depending upon the circle. In circles inhabited by the opponents of trade and investment liberalisation, as well as those who more generally profess an amorphous 'anti-globalisation' ethos, *Metalclad* is a story about the rights of foreign corporations trumping the popular will of the citizens of a small, Mexican municipality. For trade and investment lawyers, and associated policy analysts, it is just a familiar story – about international investment being held hostage to regulatory decision-making in a developing country.[317]

Despite acknowledging the disparate accounts of the case, Weiler himself professes that there is no middle ground to be taken, and that the trade and investment lawyer position is the correct one.

[316] 'Goldcorp loses bid for $50 mln NAFTA compensation', *Reuters*, 10 June 2009. At the time, the award remained unpublished, pending redaction of confidential information.
[317] Weiler 2005: 701.

It is argued here that the circumstances of each case and the interpretation of the standards in each case must be differentiated. Is it that observers view the facts of each case differently or do they take issue with the application of investment law to these facts by arbitral tribunals? Weiler, in the above quotation, is referring to the circumstances of the *Metalclad* case. However, even if one agrees with his argument that the investor was treated poorly by Mexico, one can still debate the specific interpretations of the regulative rules and norms of investment protection proffered by the *Metalclad* tribunal.

One can compare the *Metalclad* case with the remarkably similar (in terms of circumstances) *Tecmed* case. While the tribunal in each case found that the Mexican government had expropriated an investment, the *Metalclad* tribunal applied the effects test, and most controversially noted that it need not consider the motivation for the adoption of the measure establishing the ecological reserve. As Mann and Araya point out: 'By arguing that the purpose is simply not relevant, the tribunal established a precedent that could be interpreted as broadly limiting a state's authority to engage in environmental protection.'[318] In contrast, although the *Tecmed* tribunal also concluded that an expropriation had occurred, it applied a more balanced approach of considering the effect, purpose and proportionality of a measure. Similarly, the tribunal in *S.D. Myers* considered the purpose of the government measure. However, the focus given to the temporary nature of the ban on PCB exports leaves open the question of how the *S.D. Myers* tribunal would have assessed the measure had it not eventually been repealed. In contrast, the *Methanex* tribunal dealt with a permanent measure, but nevertheless found that it did not amount to an expropriation.

Even in a limited examination of only four cases one can find several distinct interpretations of one standard. These discrepancies are not solely the result of the different circumstances in each case, but also a consequence of the broad ambit given to tribunals to interpret standards. The same pattern is evident in a review of decisions on the scope of the minimum standard and fair and equitable treatment. Both the *Tecmed* and *Metalclad* tribunals read this standard very broadly to incorporate requirements for the government to act *transparently* and *consistently*. Behrens questions whether 'any government in the world' would be able to live up to the transparency requirement as it was defined in *Tecmed*.[319] The Supreme Court of British Columbia found that the *Metalclad* tribunal

---

[318] Mann and Araya 2002: 171.   [319] Behrens 2007: 175.

erred in incorporating transparency into the evaluation of fair and equitable treatment; however, this decision remains a topic of heated debate
amongst scholars.[320]

The discussion of the minimum standard/fair and equitable treatment
in the *S.D. Myers* and *Methanex* cases focused more on the issue of discrimination. The *S.D. Myers* tribunal found that breach of the national
treatment standard amounted to breach of the minimum standard as
well. In contrast, the *Methanex* tribunal disagreed with this interpretation.
While in the NAFTA context this issue appears to have been definitively
decided for future cases (through the FTC Notes of Interpretation), it is
questionable whether tribunals outside of NAFTA will agree with the *S.D.
Myers* interpretation or the *Methanex*/FTC interpretation.

It can be concluded, therefore, that the scope of an investment protection standard is not only determined on a *case-by-case basis* (according to
varying circumstances) but also on a *tribunal-by-tribunal basis* (according to varying interpretations). This makes the outcome of cases more
difficult for states to predict.

In light of the importance of the viewpoints of arbitrators, it is worth
reiterating that the majority of arbitrators are experts in commercial law
and have little or no experience with environmental law. A review of the
biographies and CVs of the arbitrators that decided the cases discussed in
this chapter indicates that they are all well-respected and eminent lawyers,
judges or academics in the field of commercial arbitration. However, of
the twenty-three arbitrators that served on these eight tribunals (one
arbitrator served on both the *Santa Elena* and *Metalclad* tribunals) there
are only two – the US-nominated arbitrator in *Glamis*, David Caron, and
the president of the tribunal in *Glamis*, Michael K. Young – that appear to
have any significant experience with environmental law.

7.4.2   Evolution of standards or double standards?

Many supporters of investment protection suggest that interpretations
of the regulative norms and rules are undergoing a natural process of
evolution and refinement as more cases are examined and as arbitrators
build on the decisions of previous tribunals. In particular, they point
to the *Methanex* Award as proof that the broad effects test adopted to
determine expropriation in the *Metalclad* case has been supplanted by a

---

[320] Weiler 2003: 47, argues that 'the local judge was wrong in substituting his uninformed
opinion for that of the tribunal'. See also Brower 2001a; 2002.

more reasonable interpretation, which Gaines argues sets 'a high bar for investor claimants to vault over to gain compensation from host states', reducing the chances for a successful claim 'and thus the incentive for investors to mount challenges to national regulatory actions'.[321]

However, other observers caution against premature jubilation, noting in particular that in the absence of a system of precedent, an arbitrator could just as easily follow the reasoning of the *Metalclad* tribunal as that of the *Methanex* tribunal.[322] Given the broad support that the *Metalclad* Award has received amongst many investment law experts, the possibility of future awards in the same line is not inconceivable. Furthermore, it does not appear that the *Methanex* decision has dissuaded investors from pursuing cases related to environmental regulation or from relying on pre-*Methanex* decisions.[323]

It has also been questioned whether greater deference was given to the Californian measures in *Methanex*, not because the understanding of the expropriation standard had naturally evolved over time, but because this case was against a large and powerful country. Sornarajah argues that '[o]ne has to wait until the rich states are affected before there can be change' and questions whether the change will be uniform, or whether a *double standard* will emerge.[324] Similarly, Van Harten cautions that:

> arbitrators may choose to limit state liability only where a damages award could provoke controversy among decision-makers and the public in the major states. If so, this would be the right result for the wrong reason. By encouraging adjudicators to tread softly on powerful governments while maintaining strict disciplinary standards for those less powerful, such reasoning jeopardizes the neutrality of treaty arbitration.[325]

Finally, while one could argue that the expropriation standard has been subjected to stricter, narrower, interpretations over time, it would seem that the opposite is true for the the minimum standard/fair and equitable treatment. Thus, the question arises as to whether investors will continue to challenge environmental regulation, but simply shift their focus to the latter standard.[326]

7.4.3   *Limits to investment protection?*

IIAs are developed in such a manner as to limit the protections that they offer to a specific group of investors and investments under a specific set of

---

[321] Gaines 2006: 689.   [322] Mann 2005: 9; Lawrence 2006: 293.
[323] See cases cited in note 6.   [324] Sornarajah 2006b: 33, emphasis added.
[325] Van Harten 2007a: 147   [326] Sornarajah 2006a: 345.

circumstances. However, several cases suggest that these limitations may be less effective than states had anticipated.

For example, the *Ethyl* tribunal accepted jurisdiction over Ethyl's claims despite its acknowledgement that the company had 'jumped the gun' in filing for arbitration before the MMT Act was in force. One NGO report referred to Ethyl's actions as a 'blatant attempt to intimidate a legislative body from taking action'.[327] In effect, the tribunal's decision sanctions Ethyl's behaviour, and thereby encourages other companies to act in the same manner. An NGO report suggests: 'Threats to use Chapter 11 are now a routine lobbying instrument.'[328] The use of the threat of arbitration to influence policy outcomes will be discussed much more extensively in Chapter 8.

Another example is the *Glamis* case, which raises questions about the limitations on investor nationality. Ochs points out that it is ironic that in this case the company claimed mining rights available only to US citizens at the same time as it invoked NAFTA-based rights available only to non-US investors.[329] If corporations are permitted to either shift nationalities at will or create multiple nationalities, it not only undermines the reciprocity aspect of IIAs, it also creates further uncertainty for governments about which investors are covered by treaty rights.[330]

In contrast, two other cases suggest that some limitations are being placed on the scope of investment protection. While in the *Lucchetti* case the decision on jurisdiction was largely based on technicalities, the fact that the tribunal acknowledged that corruption could be considered as a basis for why the dispute had not been definitively terminated prior to the entry into force of the BIT is somewhat encouraging. It suggests that tribunals are potentially willing to examine evidence on egregious conduct by foreign investors. The decision of the *Methanex* tribunal that a legally significant connection between a measure and an investment is required is also notable, as it rules out the possibility of investors only incidentally affected by regulation being granted protection.

7.5   Implications for environmental governance

This section moves from the general review of environmentally relevant investor-state disputes to an exploration of their implications for environmental governance, particularly in developing countries.

[327] Public Citizen and FOE 2001: vii.   [328] Mann 2001: 16.
[329] Ochs 2005: 511.   [330] Wallace 2005: 366.

7.5.1   Legitimate regulation and legitimate expectations

Legitimacy is currently a popular word in the political science literature, and it is also frequently used by states, investors and arbitrators in the context of investor-state disputes. In particular, it is employed with relation to the measures adopted by governments, and in regard to the expectations of investors (as mentioned in Sections 4.1.4 and 4.1.5). The cases in this chapter illustrate that tribunals feel justified in interrogating the legitimacy of government regulation and that they will assess the legitimacy of investor expectations to varying degrees. It appears in some cases that the actions of governments are scrutinized far more closely than those of investors.

Supporters of investment protection argue that legitimate regulation will not be found in breach of regulative rules and norms of investment protection and further that arbitral tribunals are equipped to make decisions on the legitimacy of government actions. Gantz notes: 'In theory at least, one of the strengths of the NAFTA legal system is to permit arbitral tribunals to distinguish between legitimate government regulatory activity and arbitrary, discriminatory or expropriatory actions, and to discourage (and require compensation for) the latter.'[331] Similarly, Brower argues that there is no support for the proposition that Chapter 11 undermines 'legitimate regulatory programs', and Wälde suggests that investment arbitration 'is about the dissection of national regulation to identify elements that can stand up to the sober examination of international law to distinguish what is legitimate regulation and what is excessive interference with proprietary and contractual rights'.[332]

The issue of the legitimacy of government policy in the environmental context primarily relates to the concern that regulation will be utilized as a cover for protectionism. There is evidence in each case discussed above that the governments involved had genuine concerns about the environment. However, there were also indications that other issues played a role, as is likely to be the case in practically all political decisions. For example, it has been suggested that the Canadian ban on PCB exports related to intense lobbying that the government had received on the part of S.D. Myers's Canadian competitors.[333] In *Methanex*, all of the investor's claims were built on the intent of California to favour domestic ethanol producers over foreign methanol producers. The question is whether the existence of multiple factors influencing a government, which is arguably inevitable given the complexity

---

[331] Gantz 2001: 655–6.   [332] Brower 2001a: 69; Wälde 2001: 30.   [333] Weiler 2001: 177.

of the issues raised in these disputes, provides proof that environmental concern is not legitimate. Loy makes the crucial point that: 'Virtually every piece of environmental or conservation legislation or regulation affects a commercial sector, and will thus be politically supported (or opposed) by private interest groups.'[334] He calls this the 'Baptist/Bootlegger' problem, and questions: 'How much should this possible duality matter?'[335] Kurtz makes a further relevant argument:

> The 'smoking gun' nature of protectionist statements should not be dispositive in themselves. Politicians will often engage in such populism for a variety of factors not least of which is the ever present desire for re-election. A test based on identification of protectionist intent cannot workably be based on the subjective intent of a single legislator.[336]

A second issue related to the legitimacy of environmental regulation concerns the role of science. In *S.D. Myers*, the tribunal appeared unconvinced that there was scientific evidence to support the fact that the transport of PCBs across the Canada-US border was potentially dangerous to the environment, and this scepticism factored into the decision that the Interim Order was motivated by protectionism rather than legitimate environmental concern. However, one could interpret the available scientific information differently, for example, by giving greater weight to the numerous decisions of the US EPA that stated it was preferable for PCB waste to be disposed of in Canada. The existence of an extensive scientific report from a respectable academic institution was given considerable weight by the *Methanex* tribunal in their determination that the California phase-out of MTBE was legitimate. The question which inevitably arises is, how much scientific evidence is required to convince a tribunal? Furthermore, will a government's capacity to gather sound scientific information factor into a tribunal decision on the legitimacy of a regulation? For example, if scientific evidence is contested, but the investor has access to more convincing scientific or technical studies, will this sway an arbitral tribunal against a developing country that adopted a regulation based on only the scientific information which it could gather with limited human and economic resources?[337]

It is argued here that the *precautionary principle* has not been incorporated into the reasoning of arbitral tribunals.[338] Jones notes the dilemma

WHAT'S STANDARD IN WTO

---

[334] Loy 2002: 24.   [335] *Ibid.*   [336] Kurtz 2007: 342.
[337] Alvarez-Jiménez 2006: 430. See also Orellana 2007: 745.
[338] For a different perspective see Newcombe 2007a.

that governments face in the absence of a clear adoption of the precautionary principle in the institution of investment protection:

> A government could forbid the use of the product as soon as it learns of its potential danger, but it would then face litigation by negatively affected foreign investors. Alternatively, the government could wait to amass more scientific evidence while hoping that the product is not later found to be dangerous. If the product were found to be harmful, the government would likely be criticized for not acting sooner to curtail use of the product and could then face litigation from its own injured citizens. Under either scenario the government risks substantial liability.[339]

While the tribunals in the cases discussed in this chapter have not addressed the issue of precaution, it is likely to emerge as a key issue in future disputes. For example, it will be an unavoidable topic in the dispute between Dow Agrosciences and the Government of Canada.[340]

Turning to the legitimacy of investor expectations, it would appear that tribunals are much more forgiving. The most critical example of this is *S.D. Myers*, where the tribunal awarded compensation to a company that had invested in an activity that, at the time, was completely illegal. The company was well aware of Canada's established policy of disposing of PCBs domestically and took on the significant risk that the US EPA would not provide it with an enforcement discretion. In such circumstances, how could the investor have had legitimate expectations that it could ship PCB wastes across the border? Similarly, Metalclad knowingly invested in a controversial landfill that had previously been denied permits. In *Methanex*, the existence of a highly regulated environment coupled with a lack of 'specific commitments' made to the investor that regulations would not change, led the tribunal to conclude that the company did not have legitimate expectations. However, one has to question whether the existence of a highly regulated environment is an appropriate standard against which to measure investor expectations. Does the presence of lax standards conversely legitimize an investor's expectations that regulation will not change? Given the low base level of regulation in developing countries, and the pressures from both domestic and international sources for governments to 'catch up' to international best practices, would it not be fair to assume that investors should expect regulation to change even more dramatically in developing countries than in developed ones?

---

[339] Jones 2002: 556.
[340] *Dow AgroSciences LLC v. Government of Canada*, Notice of Arbitration, 31 March 2009. The dispute concerns the Province of Quebec's ban on the cosmetic use of pesticides. See 'Ban on Pesticides May Face NAFTA Test', *The Globe and Mail*, 22 October 2008.

7.5.2   Positive obligations

An important trend visible in the *Metalclad* and *Tecmed* cases in particular, and also evident in the literature as discussed in Chapter 4, is the
growing acceptance of *positive obligations* of investment protection. Thus,
protecting investment no longer solely requires a state to *refrain* from taking certain actions, it also mandates compliance with 'good governance'
principles. As Reisman and Sloane argue, governments must 'establish and
maintain an appropriate legal, administrative, and regulatory framework,
the legal environment that modern investment theory has come to recognize as a *conditio sine qua non* of the success of private enterprise'.[341] Not
only is regulation subject to challenge, so too is the *failure* to regulate.[342]

The trend is certainly not universally accepted or welcomed. The expansion of the scope of the minimum standard was met with considerable
disquiet in all three NAFTA states, and resulted in the issuance of the
Notes of Interpretation. Outside of the NAFTA context, it may be more
difficult for governments to adopt an interpretation of the standard, and
furthermore, it is not even clear whether this type of response conclusively
resolves the issue. The promulgation of the Notes, when several Chapter
11 disputes were ongoing, caused consternation amongst many observers
who argued that not only was the timing inappropriate, but furthermore
that the Interpretation of Article 1105 in fact amounted to an amendment
of NAFTA.[343] Cook has gone so far as to claim that the Interpretation is
a 'severe curtailment of rights provided for under the "fair and equitable
treatment" clause' and 'is contrary to the plain meaning of the language'
and thus constitutes 'a violation of the Vienna Convention on the Law of
Treaties, which has risen to the level of customary international law and
requires treaties to be interpreted in accordance with their plain meaning'.[344] Despite the uproar, others suggest that the Interpretation, far from
amounting to an amendment, may not preclude the inclusion of elements
such as transparency in an analysis of the minimum standard at all. As
Kirkman has noted, equating fair and equitable treatment with the minimum standard may only serve to intensify the debate on the current status
of customary international law in the area; investors and many arbitrators
may argue that the standard has evolved (and expanded) considerably in

---

[341] Reisman and Sloane 2003: 117.   [342] *Ibid*: 129.
[343] See the discussion in *Pope & Talbot* v. *Government of Canada*, Interim Award on Damages,
31 May 2002. See also the submissions in *Methanex* of the investor, the US, Canada and
Mexico re: NAFTA FTC Statement on Article 1105.
[344] Cook 2007: 1112–13.

recent history.[345] This was the (apparently unsuccessful) strategy adopted by Glamis Gold.

What are the implications of an expanded minimum standard that imposes positive obligations on states? It certainly provides greater scope for investors to launch disputes, and therefore counteracts any narrowing of the definition of regulatory takings that may have occurred. It also arguably disproportionately affects developing countries. Many poor states are still struggling to establish the very fundamental elements of a functional democratic system. The imposition of 'good governance' requirements (transparency, accountability, etc.) in the form of aid conditionality has been fraught with difficulty and controversy.[346] It is fair to assume that this new form of *investment conditionality* will be equally contentious.

7.5.3 Multilevel governance

Another critical aspect to recognize in the cases described in this chapter is that in almost all instances they revolved around either measures taken by local or regional governments (*Lucchetti, Metalclad, Tecmed, Methanex, Glamis Gold*) or measures taken by a national government in pursuit of international objectives (*Santa Elena, S.D. Myers*). Thus, the cases reflect the now well-established phenomenon of 'multilevel governance' in the environmental field. They also raise cause for concern in this respect.

In investment arbitration, only the national level of government can be held liable for compensation, regardless of the level of government responsible for the offending action. As such, national governments have an incentive to prevent subnational governments from adopting laws that are prone to challenge.[347] Dhooge notes that the mandate of national governments is clear: they 'must establish the limits of subnational jurisdiction existing through the exercise of the police powers and stringently enforce those limits by taking prompt and effective action against non-complying state and local governments'.[348]

Multilevel governance may particularly complicate matters when it comes to the payment of monetary damages to a successful claimant. The Mexican government reportedly missed a payment deadline to Metalclad because of ongoing disputes with the various levels of government involved in the case about the appropriate division of the cost of the settlement.[349] In

[345] Kirkman 2002: 390; Westcott 2007: 430.   [346] See Doornbos 2001.
[347] Kelemen 2004: 273.   [348] Dhooge 2001: 264–5.   [349] Been and Beauvais 2003: 90.

Canada, the Federation of Canadian Municipalities has requested that the national government 'guarantee that it will never penalize municipalities for actions that are valid under domestic law but violate NAFTA'.[350] Been and Beauvais suggest that if the US government faced payment of an award based on local or state regulations it could adopt several different strategies, such as:

  (i)   suing the state or local government for the cost of compensation;
 (ii)   deducting the amount of the award from grants or other funds that it would have otherwise made available to the state or locality;
(iii)   conditioning future funding for the state or locality upon its agreement to rescind or modify the regulation; or
(iv)   preempting, or conditionally preempting, the state or locality's regulation.[351]

Concern about liability under investment agreements could lead to efforts to (re)centralize control over aspects of environmental governance, counteracting the recent trend of decentralization in developing countries.[352] While Kelemen rightly argues that centralization of power also results from the harmonization of social regulation, the consequences of sub-national governments deviating from such commitments are less immediate then in the case of violations of trade and investment agreements.[353]

With regard to the other end of multilevel environmental governance – international law developed under multilateral environmental agreements – the *Santa Elena* and *S.D. Myers* cases are particularly relevant. In *S.D. Myers* the tribunal suggested that it should not be presumed that a breach of a regulative rule of investment protection could be justified by the existence of an international environmental commitment, because the state is obliged to adopt measures that are least inconsistent with investment protection. While the argument that a state presented with a 'variety of equally effective and reasonable means'[354] to protect the environment should choose the one that is most consistent with investment protection does not appear unreasonable on its face, the notion that an arbitral tribunal is better equipped than a democratically elected

---

[350] Qtd in *ibid.*   [351] Been and Beauvais 2003: 135–6.
[352] Been 2002: 58; see also Luz and Miller 2002: 976, who argue that Chapter 11 will lead to an erosion of provincial power and authority in Canada. On the trend of decentralization see Larson and Ribot 2005.
[353] Kelemen 2004: 273.   [354] *S.D. Myers* Partial Award: para. 221.

government to decide what regulations are effective and reasonable is certainly contestable. In *Santa Elena*, the tribunal reasoned that the existence of international obligations to protect the environment did not affect the level of compensation owed to an investor. Wagner argues that requiring governments to pay compensation to implement measures developed in line with multilateral environmental agreements 'interferes with efforts to address global environmental problems through international consensus'.[355]

7.5.4   Paying the polluters?

Several NGO reports have suggested that the *S.D. Myers*, *Ethyl* and *Metalclad* cases have turned the polluter pays principle into 'pay the polluter' principle.[356] Similarly, Madalena suggests: 'Investment treaties do not follow the well-settled polluter pays principle, but impose a sacrifice on the community at large, in the detriment of sustainable development under the auspices of a broadly interpreted right to property.'[357] On the other hand, according to Kentin, the cases decided to date display 'a rather restrained attitude in awarding high amounts of damages with a few exceptions'.[358] Investors are generally awarded much less than they claim. Metalclad, for example, criticized the amount of damages that it received, calling it 'a token amount of money' that failed to reflect the actual value of the investment.[359] Nevertheless, it should be noted that it is quite possible that investors have significantly inflated their compensation claims in these cases, including speculations about future profits.

It is suggested here that what is more crucial is that there does not appear to be any acknowledgement of the principle of *common but differentiated responsibilities* in the institution of investment protection.[360] In fact, the purpose of investment protection arguably is to make the obligations of states uniform, despite varying levels of development. Neither Costa Rica nor Mexico's ability to pay was mentioned in the tribunal decisions in *Santa Elena*, *Metalclad* and *Tecmed*. Brower and Wong argue that the tribunal in *Santa Elena* did *implicitly* address this issue and:

> granted compensation in an amount that, on the one hand, would not 'break' Costa Rica, or worse still, tempt it for lack of funds to consider returning a World Heritage Site back to its owners for development into a

[355] Wagner 1999: 535.   [356] Mann 2001: 33; Public Citizen and FOE 2001: 9.
[357] Madalena 2003: 82. See also Hasic 2005: 155–6.   [358] Kentin 2004: 336.
[359] Dhooge 2001: 259.   [360] This point has also been argued by Alexander 2008.

'Disney-fied' golf-courses-and-hotels resort and, on the other hand, would not so far disappoint [the investor's] expectations as to cause it to seek annulment of the Award.[361]

However, without explicit recognition of this principle, developing country governments may be wary of the financial consequences of defending an environmental regulation in arbitration.

[361] Brower and Wong 2005: 774.

The threat of arbitration

While most research on the relationship between investment law and environmental policy focuses on disputes that are resolved in international arbitration, many conflicts between investors and states will never reach this stage. Arbitration is a high-risk, high-cost option for both governments and investors. As noted in Chapter 6, arbitration fees and legal fees can add up to several million dollars for each party.

In contrast, the *threat of arbitration*, in monetary terms, costs little or nothing. Otto and Cordes suggest that arbitration may be used as 'an offensive weapon to harass or intimidate'[1] and Peterson notes that 'practicing lawyers do admit that they hear rumours of investors applying informal pressure upon host states while brandishing an investment treaty as a potential legal stick'.[2] Even Wälde, a strong advocate of investment arbitration and sometime arbitrator, has noted that due to the high risks of litigation (for investors): 'The impact of the arbitration clause is . . . less in its actual use, as in its implicit threat to both parties.'[3]

This chapter provides a detailed examination of investor-state conflicts that were resolved without recourse to arbitration, but where the threat of arbitration may have played an important role in the outcome. Conflicts concerning both environmental policy (in Ghana, Indonesia and Costa Rica) and domestic court proceedings (in Indonesia and Ecuador) are examined.

8.1 Conflicts over policy

8.1.1 Open-pit mining in Indonesia's protected forests

This case concerns a law banning open-pit mining in Indonesia's protected forests.[4] Several mining companies holding contracts in areas of protected

---

[1] Otto and Cordes 2002: V-34. [2] Peterson 2004a: 139 [3] Wälde 1998a.
[4] An earlier version of this case study was published in Tienhaara 2006b.

forest threatened to take the government to arbitration if the ban was applied to their prospective mining operations. The conflict garnered significant attention from the public and was drawn out over several years. Eventually, the government exempted a number of companies from the ban.

8.1.1.1   Background

In 1999, following the fall of the New Order Regime, the Government of Indonesia passed a number of reform laws, including Law no. 41 Year 1999 Stipulation to the Act on Forestry. Article 1 provides several basic definitions, including the designation of various types of forest.[5] These include: 'production' forests, which are allocated mainly for the exploitation of forest products; 'protection' forests, which have the chief function of maintaining life-supporting hydrological systems, preventing floods, controlling erosion, etc.; and 'conservation' forests, which are principally aimed at preserving plant and animal diversity. Article 38 stipulates that open-cast mining is prohibited in protection forests. The reason for this prohibition is that to expose and mine the ore in an open-cast design, it is generally necessary to excavate a large area and to relocate a large quantity of 'waste rock'. Two of the main environmental concerns of the construction of open-pit mines are the disruption of the ecosystem where the mine is excavated, and the disposal of the waste rock. Other environmental impacts also ensue from the building of roads to service mines, and this requires the clearance of land, results in changes to the hydrological functioning of the ecosystem, and opens access to the area for exploitation from other sectors. In Indonesia, increasing the accessibility of protection forests to illegal loggers is a major concern.

At the time of the ban, mineral investment in Indonesia was organized under contracts-of-work (CoWs). In the early years of the CoW system (1967–70), the majority of the content in the contracts was negotiated, but later a standardized text was adopted on terms pertaining to technical, legal and general matters.[6] However, periodic changes to laws and regulations on taxation and financial matters required adjustment to the standardized terms, resulting in several 'generations' of contracts.[7] A CoW specifies land rents, royalties and other payments to be made by the

---

[5] An unofficial translation of the law was found on the Public Participation Forum website, www.fppm.org.

[6] Hoed 1997: 122.

[7] Between 1967 and 1998, 236 CoWs were signed, the majority in the fourth generation (1985–90) and sixth generation (1997).

investor to the government. In addition, it describes the environmental obligations of the company, although these are for the most part general statements which, as Hamilton remarks, 'lack the specificity required to allow effective inspection and enforcement of their terms'.[8] With regard to the settlement of disputes, there are options for arbitration under internationally accepted rules. In later generations, the contracts specifically make reference to UNCITRAL Rules.

Two further aspects of CoWs require further explanation: conjunctive title and *lex specialis*. Conjunctive title refers to the fact that if a commercial discovery is made, the CoW allows for the contractor to proceed from the initial stages of surveying and exploration all the way through to exploitation and marketing. *Lex specialis* in this instance refers to the fact that the terms and conditions of CoWs, which are passed into law, are not subject to changes in the general laws and regulations of Indonesia. As Barberis explains, 'the CoW, once approved by Parliament, has the status of law. Therefore in the case of conflict between the law and regulations of Indonesia and the CoW, the CoW supersedes'.[9]

8.1.1.2 The conflict

Prior to the entry into force of Forestry Law 1999/41, a number of CoWs had been signed covering areas of protection forests. In fact, over 150 companies were supposedly affected by the ban on open-cast mining. At first, the companies carried on with their activities as they presumed that the legislation would not be applied retroactively and that, in any case, the contracts were *lex specialis* and would therefore not be affected. The issue was eventually brought to the attention of the public and was taken up by a number of NGOs. The Forestry department stopped issuing permits to mining companies in protection forests and all affected contracts were effectively suspended.

In 2002, reports began to emerge that several foreign mining companies were threatening to bring the Government of Indonesia to international arbitration on the matter of the Forestry Law. Several NGOs declared that the threat of arbitration was without basis.[10] The following reasons were cited:

---

[8] Hamilton 2005: 38.   [9] Barberis 1998: 47.
[10] 'Mining Industry Threatens Indonesia with International Arbitration', *Friends of the Earth Indonesia (WALHI) and Mining Advocacy Network (JATAM) News Release*, 4 April 2002, www.jatam.org.

(i) all contracts state that companies must conform with the relevant environmental protection laws and regulations of Indonesia;

(ii) the law only prohibits surface mining, whereas underground mining is still permitted;

(iii) all the contracts in protected areas were signed during the period of authoritative government, and the Forestry Law was made under democratic rule;

(iv) the preservation of protected areas is an issue of global concern with popular support; and

(v) Indonesia is bound by international commitments including the provisions of the Convention on Biological Diversity[11] and the Statement of Forest Principles, and also participates in the United Nations Forum on Forests.

The issues raised by the NGOs are worth some further examination.

The first point, that companies must comply with the relevant environmental laws of Indonesia, is accurate. For example, the CoW of Pt. Nusa Halmahera Minerals (Australia) states that the company shall:

> In accordance with the prevailing Environmental protection and natural preservation laws and regulations of Indonesia from time to time in effect, use its best efforts to conduct its operations under this Agreement so as to minimize and cope with harm to the Environment and utilize recognized modern Mining industry practices to protect natural resources against unnecessary damage, to minimize Pollution and harmful emissions into the Environment, to dispose of Waste in a manner consistent with good Waste disposal practices, and in general to provide for the health and safety of its employees and the local community.[12]

The use of the terminology 'time to time in effect' suggests that investors should not expect regulations to remain frozen over the course of the contract. Gross argues that the clear requirement of companies to comply with environmental regulations, combined with the absence of stabilization clauses in the CoWs, rules out the possibility that the companies

---

[11] Togu Manrung, a professor at the Bogor Institute of Agriculture and Director of Forest Watch Indonesia, has suggested that allowing mining in protected forests would specifically violate Arts. 7 and 8. See 'Open Pit Mines Endanger Lives, Nature', *The Jakarta Post*, 21 September 2002.

[12] Contract of Work between the Government of the Republic of Indonesia and Pt. Nusa Halmahera Minerals, 17 March 1997, Jakarta: Art. 26. It should be noted that CoWs are not, in general, public documents, although model CoWs have been published. A copy of this specific CoW was obtained from an NGO in Jakarta. Several other CoWs were also retrieved by the author from company filings to the Securities and Exchange Commission (SEC), http://pro-edgar-online.com.

could effectively argue that there was a breach of contract by Indonesia.[13] Additionally, according to a report in *The Jakarta Post*, a noted lawyer told legislators that they should not worry about being sued for breach of contract because the Forestry Law had been ratified by the House of Representatives (DPR) and any agreements signed between the government and investors could not violate Indonesian law.[14] However, the investors argued that this conclusion failed to take into account the fact that CoWs also have the status of law in Indonesia, and are thus, effectively stabilized.

Whether the companies could have claimed breach of treaty standards, for example under the UK-Indonesia BIT, the Australia-Indonesia BIT or the 1987 Association of South-East Asian Nations (ASEAN) Agreement for the Promotion and Protection of Investments, is another question. Gross has analysed the various options and has concluded that: 'the Government of Indonesia could have likely beaten the mining companies' claims at a preliminary/jurisdictional phase, and certainly on the merits'.[15] If the companies were to argue that the Forestry law was a breach of treaty, then the second point in the NGO statement (that only one method of mining – surface mining – is banned) would likely be a key point for debate on whether the ban qualified as a taking. The mining companies rejected the notion that alternatives to open-cast mining exist, arguing that underground mining operations are not feasible because more than 90 per cent of Indonesia's mineral potential is found in the top soil layer (around 0–50 metres).[16] Thus, in the view of investors, a ban on open-cast mining is effectively a complete prohibition on all mining activities and thus a clear case of an expropriation. If the case had gone to arbitration, the companies would also likely have argued that the ban did not fall under Indonesia's police powers. As the forests in question are classified as protection rather than conservation forests, the mining companies argued that the issue of biodiversity conservation is not relevant.[17] However, Dr Hariadi Kartodiharjo, a lecturer at the Bogor Agricultural Institute, suggests that regardless of how the areas have been classified, mining in protection forests will result in permanent devastation of the environment,

---

[13] Gross 2003: 896.
[14] 'House Urged to Challenge Mining Ruling', *The Jakarta Post*, 2 July 2004.
[15] Gross 2003: 901.
[16] 'Minister of Forestry Ready to Implement DPR Decision on Mining', *MiningIndo*, 1 September 2003.
[17] 'IMA Responds to NGOs and Mining in Forestry Critics', *MiningIndo*, 30 July 2003.

a raised threat of extinction of rare species, and a decrease in water supply to the Barito River and millions of people living along the riverbank.[18]

The third point in the NGO statement (that the contracts were signed under a period of authoritarian rule) is rather beyond the scope of this study, but it is an issue that has been considered by others. Sornarajah notes that:

> It is an interesting point as to whether international lawyers who promote the norm of democracy would concede that concessions and other foreign investment agreements signed by dictators or unrepresentative governments should be considered invalid. It is possible to argue that the norm of self-determination, now having acquired a near *ius cogens* status would invalidate concession agreements signed by unrepresentative rulers.[19]

It seems unlikely that any arbitration panel would consider this issue, as government officials have consistently stated that contracts signed under the New Order Regime would be honoured.[20]

Finally, it is questionable whether the last two points in the NGO statement, relating to forest preservation as an issue of global concern and the obligations of the government under multilateral environmental agreements, would have any influence on an arbitral tribunal, given the conclusions drawn from the cases analysed in the previous chapter (see Section 7.5.3).

8.1.1.3   The outcome

In any event, discussion of how a tribunal would deal with this case will remain hypothetical. In 2002, the Government of Indonesia produced a list of twenty-two companies with CoWs signed prior to the promulgation of Forestry Law 1999/41 that they recommended be given approval to operate in protection forests. How this list was devised from the original 150 or so affected companies is not clear. Furthermore, the list did not remain constant over time; half of the companies were removed (due to gloomy business prospects) and a further eleven were added, leading State Minister for the Environment Nabiel Makarim to ask 'whether twenty-two was a sacred number'.[21] In November of 2003, it was reported that

---

[18] 'Government Warned of Catastrophe from Mining in Protected Forests', *MiningIndo*, 8 March 2004.

[19] Sornarajah 2004a: 42.

[20] Stiglitz 2008 (note 61) points out that the US Ambassador who insisted that the contracts should be honoured after the departure of Suharto was later named to the board of one of the mining companies whose contract was upheld.

[21] 'Government Questioned Over Mining in Protected Forest', *The Jakarta Post*, 19 July 2003.

thirteen 'prioritized' companies from the list of twenty-two would be allowed to continue operations with the issuance of a Presidential Decree, but the actual issuance of the Decree was put off until a later date.[22] These companies were apparently prioritized because their operations were seen to be economically viable. The nine companies on the original list of twenty-two that were not included on the prioritized list of thirteen were reported to have made continued threats to sue the government. In March 2004, Paul Louis Coutrier, an executive of the Indonesian Mining Association, was quoted as stating that the nine companies had strong grounds to file a lawsuit, though he hoped that the conflict would be settled out of court.[23]

On 11 March 2004, Perpu (government regulation substituting a law) no. 1/2004 was issued by the Government of Indonesia to add a new provision to the 1999 Forestry Law stating: 'All permits or contracts in mining in forest areas which were issued before the promulgation of Law 41 of 1999 on Forestry are declared to remain valid until the expiration date of the respective permit or contract.'[24] It also stated that further implementation of the Perpu would be determined by Presidential Decree.[25] The Indonesian Constitution of 1945 provides that a Perpu should be utilized only in 'a pressing matter of utmost urgency'. This type of measure had only been used once before by the Megawati administration, following the 2002 Bali terrorist bombings.[26] Many environmental groups questioned the 'utmost urgency' of the mining issue, but also pointed out that the Perpu did not actually change the position of the companies, whose contracts had never been declared invalid.

The Presidential Decree (41/2004) issued in May was more specific and named the thirteen companies that would be allowed to continue with open-pit operations in protection forests. The Decree also stated that the operations would be further regulated under a separate decree to be issued by the Ministry of Forestry. Immediately following the issuance of the Presidential Decree, a group of NGOs issued a statement that they would bring the Perpu, which had not yet been approved by Parliament, before the Constitutional Court for Judicial Review. Following the development

---

[22] '13 Mining Sites get Forest Status Changed', *MiningIndo*, 6 November 2003.
[23] 'Mining Firms Threaten to Sue Indonesian Government', *Bisnis Indonesia*, 12 March 2004.
[24] 'Indonesian Forestry Issue Resolved', *Weda Bay Minerals News Release*, 17 March 2004, www.allbusiness.com.
[25] 'Mining in Protected Forests – Government Gives Way to Mining Industry Pressure', *Down to Earth* No. 61, May 2004.
[26] 'Nickel Miner to Sue Indonesian Government', *Asia Times*, 17 March 2004.

of a special commission and much deliberation, the DPR finally voted on the Perpu in July. Initially it appeared that the emergency law would be rejected,[27] and the NGOs were confident that they 'had the numbers' needed to defeat it.[28] However, the Perpu was passed into law (Law no. 19/2004) by a vote of 131 to 102[29] amidst allegations of corruption. NGOs reported that they had been informed that the government would provide Rp1 billion for every faction in the national parliament that voted to allow the mining operations to go ahead.[30] These allegations were corroborated by several members of Parliament who came forward claiming to have been offered bribes.[31] The money for the bribes was allegedly solicited from the mining companies by the Department of Mines.[32]

In late September 2004, the Ministry of Forestry issued its Ministerial Decree (no. 12/2004), outlining restrictions on the operations of companies permitted in protection forests. According to a spokesperson for the Ministry: 'The Decree is designed to limit the potential destruction caused by mining operations on natural forests and the environment.'[33] Included in the Decree was a requirement for companies to pay a bond to cover the costs of rehabilitating areas following mine closures, and also to provide alternate areas of land for reforestation.

In 2005, in what appeared to be the last hurdle for the government, the Constitutional Court conducted its review of Perpu no.1/2004 and Law 19/2004. The Minister of Forests reportedly stated that he would be happy if the Court annulled the law,[34] but it did not. Instead the judges concluded that:

> Although this Court shares the opinion of all the experts brought by the appellants regarding the dangerousness and negative impacts of open pit mining in protected forests, nevertheless this Court also understands the reasoning for the need for transitional regulation which continues the

---

[27] Irwan Prayitno, Speaker of the Commission VIII of the DPR, reportedly stated that if the Perpu was passed to the DPR it would be rejected. See 'DPR to Decline Approval of Mining in Protected Forest', *MiningIndo*, 20 April 2004.

[28] Author's confidential interviews with NGO representatives (#1 and #7), Jakarta, July 2005.

[29] 'Disputed Mining Bill Endorsed', *The Jakarta Post*, 16 July 2004.

[30] 'NGOs Allege Bribery in Indonesian Government Bid to Allow Mining Permits to Resume in Protected Forest', *MiningIndo*, 13 November 2002; 'Lawmakers Smell Fishy Deal behind Mining Regulation', *The Jakarta Post*, 24 July 2004.

[31] *Ibid.*

[32] Author's confidential interview with a foreign embassy official (#4), Jakarta, July 2005.

[33] 'Forestry Ministry Softens Stance on Mining', *MiningIndo*, 1 October 2004.

[34] 'Constitution Court to Conduct Judicial Review over Mining in Protected Forest', *MiningIndo*, 17 February 2005.

legal status or rights gained by mining companies before the advent of the Forestry Law.[35]

The Constitutional Court president reportedly also stated: 'We can understand the government's argument that the regulation should be issued otherwise it would face difficulties in developing a *favorable investment climate*.'[36]

While the Minister of Environment has said that no more licences (beyond the thirteen) should be issued, there is certainly potential for further threats of arbitration. In fact, by singling out thirteen companies, the government has actually made the case of other companies far stronger as they could now also claim discriminatory treatment.[37] Furthermore, the additional requirements imposed on companies operating in protection forests included in the Ministerial Decree issued in late 2004 (later issued as Regulation No. 14/2006) may also be subject to challenge. The Chair of the Indonesian Mining Association, Jeffrey Mulyono, was reported to be particularly upset with the requirement that mining firms operating in protection forests would have to provide a 'compensatory site' twice as large as the mining concession. According to Mulyono, the requirements will cause unnecessary problems for mining firms and could deter future investment in the sector.[38] An Inco report to the US Securities and Exchange Commission (SEC) also alludes to this issue:

> While PT Inco continues to believe that the terms of its Contract of Work provide it with all authorizations needed to conduct mining activities in the areas covered by its Contract of Work and any disputes relating to its Contract of Work are *subject to arbitration* under international conventions, if the Forestry Regulation restricts PT Inco's ability to mine in certain areas, it could reduce PT Inco's estimated ore reserves and adversely affect PT Inco's long-term mining plans.[39]

[35] Conclusions of the Judgment of the Constitutional Court, qtd in 'Constitutional Court Rules no to BHP *et al.* in Indon Protected Forests', NGO Forum for Protected Forests News Release, 8 July 2005, www.eng.walhi.or.id.

[36] 'Mining in Protected Forests Legalized', *The Jakarta Post*, 8 July 2005, emphasis added.

[37] Author's confidential interviews with an NGO representative (#7), and a mining investor (#9), Jakarta, July 2005.

[38] 'Mining Group Objects to New Forest Guidelines', *The Jakarta Post*, 31 May 2006.

[39] Inco Ltd. 2005. Quarterly Report Pursuant to Section 13 or 15(d) of the Securities Exchange Act of 1934 for the quarterly period ended June 30, 2005. Commission file number 1-1143, Washington DC, emphasis added.

8.1.1.4   Epilogue: Indonesia's new mining law

Indonesia has been in a protracted debate over the development of a new mining bill for several years. The Bill on Mineral and Coal Mining, intended to supersede Law No. 11/1967 on mining, was finally passed by the DPR on 16 December 2008. The Bill replaces the CoW system with exploration and production licences to be awarded by local administrations in line with the regional autonomy law.[40] Exisitng CoWs will remain legal, but will be adjusted slightly to be brought into line with the new law.[41]

Throughout the process, foreign investors have made it abundantly clear that they do not favour the move from contracts to licences. International accounting and consulting firm PricewaterhouseCoopers called on the government to keep CoWs, noting that the proposed change to the system 'hasn't been well received by foreign investors' and would deter investment in the sector.[42] The managing director of mining giant Rio Tinto has declared: 'It would be of interest to Indonesia to keep its [CoW] for long-life, large-scale projects.'[43] A group of major mining companies issued a 'white paper' in March 2007, calling on the government to retain the CoW system.[44] The Indonesian Mining Association also urged the government to keep the CoW system as, in their opinion, it provides greater legal certainty than the licensing system.[45]

It is clear that the ability to access international arbitration is a key concern for investors.[46] One observer has noted:

> If one were to strip away the rhetoric and get right down to the issue that really has industry concerned about the mining law being debated in the House of Representatives (DPR), it would be the proposed shift from independent international arbitration to a local government decision as a dispute settlement mechanism.[47]

According to a brief prepared by the law firm Allens Arthur Robinson, it is as yet unclear as to whether the dispute settlement provision in the

---

[40] 'Lawmakers Debate New Mining Bill to Install New System', *The Jakarta Post*, 6 February 2006.

[41] 'New Indonesian Mining Law', *Focus*, December 2008. Allens Arthur Robinson website, www.aar.com.au.

[42] 'Lingering Legal Concerns Deter Mining Investors', *The Jakarta Post*, 23 January 2006; 'Don't Scrap CoW for Mining Licenses', *The Jakarta Post*, 1 March 2007.

[43] 'Mining Law Must Provide Certainty and Equality', *The Jakarta Post*, 20 February 2007.

[44] 'Miners Issue "White Paper" Against Draft Mining Law', *The Jakarta Post*, 21 March 2007.

[45] 'Don't Scrap CoW for Mining Licenses', *The Jakarta Post*, 1 March 2007.

[46] *Ibid.*

[47] 'Dispute Resolution and the Environment', *The Jakarta Post*, 25 April 2007.

new law 'will be implemented (in combination with existing Indonesian investment laws) in a manner that permits foreign investors sufficient scope to resolve disputes through international arbitration'.[48]

8.1.2 Mining in Ghana's forest reserves

This case concerns a conflict over a moratorium on mining activities in forest reserves in Ghana.[49] The moratorium was put in place in 1996, but at that point several mining companies had already carried out exploration activities in the reserves and wished to proceed with mine development. The conflict pitted the Forestry Commission against the Minerals Commission and garnered significant attention from NGOs. There were indications that the government was threatened with arbitration from the affected investors. The government eventually allowed five companies to carry out mine operations within the forests, subject to specific environmental guidelines.

8.1.2.1 Background

Ghana has a very long history of mining, particularly of gold, dating back to pre-Christian times; in the colonial period it was known as the 'Gold Coast'. Mining law in Ghana was reformed under a World Bank structural adjustment programme in the 1980s. The 1986 Minerals and Mining Law provided for the referral of disputes to arbitration in accordance with the UNCITRAL Rules or within the framework of a BIT. Ghana has concluded 21 BITs; some of the agreements had been ratified while others were still awaiting ratification.[50]

The 1986 Minerals and Mining Law recognizes three stages of mineral development, and an investor requires a separate licence for each stage: reconnaissance, prospecting and mining. In terms of mineral tenure, there is no automatic right for the holder of a reconnaissance licence to acquire a prospecting licence, but there is an automatic right for the holder of a prospecting licence to obtain a mining lease.[51] Mining leases are valid for

---

[48] 'New Indonesian Mining Law', *Focus*, December 2008. Allens Arthur Robinson website, www.aar.com.au.

[49] An earlier version of this case study was published in Tienhaara 2006a.

[50] 'Treaties of Ghana', ICSID website, http://icsid.worldbank.org, accessed 17 December 2008. The US has also signed three agreements with Ghana – the OPIC Investment Incentive Agreement, the Trade and Investment Framework Agreement, and the Open Skies Agreement – but these are not traditional BITs.

[51] Addy 1999: 237; Omalu and Zamora 1998.

up to thirty years, and generally include renewal clauses.[52] Negotiations for licences and leases are normally led by the Minerals Commission, and the country's Constitution requires any contract or undertaking to be ratified in Parliament by a two-thirds voting majority. However, ratification has little impact on the substantive content of agreements.[53] According to Ayine *et al.*: 'Whether and when contracts become available to the wider public depends on whether the Parliamentary Committee invites public comments on the contract document; for most agreements placed before Parliament this does not happen.'[54]

In the course of this research, three mining leases[55] were obtained from company filings to the SEC in Washington, DC.[56] These examples give some insight into the substantive content of Ghanaian mining leases, although it should be cautioned that other leases may differ significantly. Furthermore, it should be noted that in addition to mining leases, a more recent trend has been for companies to sign more general 'investment agreements' with the government. For example, in 2003, Newmont Mining Corp. signed an investment agreement that covered its investments under three mining leases.[57] This trend is in line with Ghana's new mining law, which will be discussed further below.

Returning to the content of the leases, it can be noted that with regard to environmental provisions, they are quite general:

> The company shall adopt all necessary and practical precautionary mea-
> sures to prevent undue pollution of rivers and other potable water and to
> ensure that such pollution does not cause harm or destruction to human
> or animal life or fresh water or vegetation.[58]

In terms of dispute settlement, the 1987 and 1988 leases refer to the jurisdiction of ICSID for settlement by reconciliation or arbitration, while the more recent 2001 lease refers to UNCITRAL Rules. All three leases also

---

[52] Addy 1999: 237.   [53] Ayine *et al.* 2005.   [54] *Ibid*: 3–4.

[55] Mining Lease signed between the Government of the Republic of Ghana and Canadian Bogosu Resources Ltd, 21 August 1987. Mining Lease signed between the Government of the Republic of Ghana and Canadian Bogosu Resources Ltd, 16 August 1988. Mining Lease signed between the Government of the Republic of Ghana and Bogoso Gold Ltd, 29 June 2001.

[56] All three leases are now under the control of Golden Star Resources Ltd. The 1987 and 1988 leases can be found in Golden Star Resources Ltd, SEC Form 10-K (Annual Report) Filed 29 March 2006, for Period Ending 31 December 2005, and the 2001 lease can be found in Golden Star Resources Ltd, SEC Form 8-K Filed for Period Beginning 25 October 2001, http://pro-edgar-online.com.

[57] 'Newmont Joins Mining List', *Ghana News Agency*, 19 December 2003.

[58] Art. 8b of all three leases.

have a second section to the arbitration clause, which provides for some stability for the investor but favours renegotiation. For example, the 2001 Mining Lease with Bogoso Gold Ltd states that:

> The Parties acknowledge and agree that this Agreement was made on the basis of the laws and conditions prevailing at the date of the effective conclusion of the negotiation of this Agreement and accordingly, if thereafter, new laws and conditions come into existence which unfairly affect the interest of either party to this agreement, then the party so unfairly affected shall be entitled to request a re-negotiation and the parties shall thereupon re-negotiate. The parties hereby undertake and covenant with each other to make every effort to agree, co-operate, and negotiate and to take such action as may be necessary to remove the causes of unfairness or disputes.[59]

Mining activities in Ghana are concentrated in the south of the country, as this is where the most substantial mineral deposits are found. Incidentally, this is also the area within which the majority of Ghana's remaining forestland is located.

Permanent forest estate, in the form of reserves, was developed by the colonial government in the early part of the last century, in recognition of the increasing pressures on Ghana's forests. The intention was to maintain climatic quality, protect watersheds and ensure an environment conducive to cocoa production.[60] The demarcation of the forest estate was largely completed by 1939. While it is widely acknowledged that much of the forest estate has been degraded despite the reserve status, it has also been suggested that without the reserves 'Ghana wouldn't have any forest left'.[61] Ghana has an estimated 5.5 million hectares of forest, which the Food and Agriculture Organization (FAO) of the United Nations reports it is losing at a rate of two per cent per year.[62] According to one report, 10–12,000 people depend on forest reserves directly for their food and livelihood.[63] The reserves are also significant stores of biodiversity, containing over 700 types of tropical trees and many endangered species including: 34 species of plant, 13 species of mammal, 23 species of butterfly and 8 species of bird.[64]

---

[59] Art. 35(d).   [60] Kotey *et al.* 1998: 23.
[61] Author's confidential interview with an NGO representative (#3), Accra, June 2005.
[62] FAO 2007: Annex Table 2.
[63] 'Mining Takes Heavier Toll on Ghana's Biodiversity', *Ghanaian Chronicle*, 27 September 2006.
[64] *Ibid.*

8.1.2.2   The conflict

Following the promulgation of the 1986 Minerals and Mining Law, several gold mining companies were granted permission by the National Defence Council (NDC) government to carry out exploration activities within forest reserves. As early as 1992, the Forestry Commission was raising concerns about the potential impacts that mining could have on the reserves:

> Mining in forest reserves will imply abandonment of scientific management of forest reserves and consequently loss of goods and services derived from our forest heritage set aside 60–70 years ago. Ghana could be sanctioned by the International Conservation organizations, which have credited Ghana with a long history of responsibility for tropical forest conservation and management.[65]

In 1996, based on the apprehension about the depletion of the permanent forest estate and the potential for mineral activities to accelerate this depletion, the Ministry of Lands and Forestry placed a moratorium on mineral operations in forest reserves.[66]

At the time of the moratorium, some mining companies had already reached advanced stages of exploration in forest reserves. The government selected seventeen companies, apparently on the basis of the level of investment incurred and the state of exploration that had been achieved, and determined that they should be allowed to continue with their exploration activities.[67] In 1997, the *Operational Guidelines for Mineral Exploration in Forest Reserves for Selected Companies* were produced and put in place to regulate exploration activities and the selected companies were invited to reapply for Forest Entry Permits.[68]

Up until this point, the issue had not been widely publicized. However, in 1998, Friends of the Earth (FOE)-Ghana began to investigate further. The group visited the exploration sites and spoke with companies, who claimed that if they found economically viable deposits they would be given mineral leases.[69] FOE-Ghana expressed alarm over the potential

---

[65] Tuffuor 1992.
[66] Newmont Ghana Gold Ltd, Environmental and Social Impact Assessment: Ahafo South Project, Accra, 2005, www.newmont.com.
[67] Chirano Gold Project Scoping Report & Terms of Reference, Prepared by SGS Environment, Project No. B246. Available in the Ghana EPA Library, Accra.
[68] Environmental Guidelines for Mining in Productive Forest Reserves in Ghana, May 2001: 1.
[69] Author's confidential interview with an NGO representative (#3), Accra, June 2005.

consequences for forest conservation and founded a Coalition of Civil Society Groups Against Mining in Ghana's Forest Reserves (FOE-Ghana Coalition).

In response to the concerns that were increasingly being raised over the possibility of mining in forest reserves, and in preparation for the expected transition from exploration to mine development, the Ghana Chamber of Mines, an association of representatives of mining companies operating in Ghana, took a fact-finding mission to South Africa and Australia, bringing with them representatives of the Forestry Commission, Environmental Protection Agency and other institutions. The purpose of the trip was to view successful mining operations in forests in these countries. Upon return from the trip, the Chamber commissioned the preparation of the *Environmental Guidelines for Mining in Productive Forest Reserves.*

8.1.2.3 The outcome

By the time that the *Environmental Guidelines* had been published in 2001, a new government under the New Patriotic Party (NPP) had been elected, and had thus, 'inherited the problem' of the mining in reserves debate.[70] Under increasing public pressure, the list of proposed operations was decreased to five[71] and the government undertook visits to the proposed mine sites. The final approval for these operations came on 12 February 2003, in a letter issued by the Ministry of Mines to the Ghana Chamber of Mines.

The Ministry of Mines (now Ministry of Lands, Forestry and Mines) defended its decision to allow mining in forest reserves with several key arguments:[72]

(i) the companies had invested substantial sums of money and, if they were not allowed to proceed with mine development, the government would have to pay them compensation;

---

[70] Mr Kwadjo Adjei Darko, former Minister of Mines, qtd in 'Golden Greed: Trouble Looms over Ghana's Forest Reserves', *World Rainforest Movement News Release*, n.d., www.wrm.org.uy.

[71] The companies were Newmont (US), Nevsun Resources (acquired by Anglogold Ashanti/South Africa), Birim Goldfields (acquired by Goldenstar Resources/Canada), Chirano Goldmines (acquired by Redback Mining/Canada) and Satellite Goldfields (acquired by Goldenstar Resources/Canada).

[72] This summary of arguments is based on Tetteh 2004, various news articles quoted elsewhere in this section, and the author's confidential interviews with mining investors (#1 & #20), government officials (#2 & #12), NGO representatives (#3, #4, #8 & #11), a representative of an international organization (#6), and academics (#9, & #18), Accra, Kumasi and New Abirim, June 2005.

(ii) not allowing the companies to proceed would discourage future investments in the industry;

(iii) the benefits of mining in terms of jobs and local infrastructure and royalties to the government outweigh the environmental consequences of mine development;

(iv) the forest reserves earmarked for mining are not pristine, rather they have already been degraded; and

(v) stricter environmental controls will be placed on companies operating in forest reserves (the *Environmental Guidelines*) and they will be required to plant trees outside of their concessions in addition to rehabilitating the mine area.

With regard to the first argument, according to several sources in Ghana, the threat of international investment arbitration was clearly made by companies with interests in the forest reserves, although there is disagreement from the sources over whether the government took the threat seriously,[73] or merely used it as a convenient excuse to defend its position.[74] The main companies involved in the conflict were based in Canada, the US and South Africa. Canada does not have a BIT with Ghana, there is no record of a South African BIT ever having been ratified, and the American agreements (a framework Agreement Concerning the Development of Trade and Investment Relations and an Investment Incentive Agreement) do not provide for investor-state dispute settlement. Therefore, it is unlikely that any of the companies could have brought a claim based on treaty rights. If the companies had mineral leases or investment agreements, they could bring a contract claim. However, even without leases, the investors could access arbitration through the consent in Ghana's national legislation.

As for the second argument made by the Ministry of Mines, about the value of the mining industry for the country, this is also disputed. Ghana is the second largest producer of gold in Africa (after South Africa), and gold has replaced cocoa as the leading foreign exchange earner.[75] However, a calculation by UNCTAD based on 2003 government figures showed that in that year Ghana earned only about 5 per cent of the total value of mineral exports – about US$46.7 million out of a total value of US$893.6

---

[73] Author's confidential interviews with a government official (#7), an academic (#9), and an NGO representative (#11), Accra, June 2005.

[74] Author's confidential interviews with an NGO representative (#8), and academics (#9 & #18), Accra and Kumasi, June 2005.

[75] Awudi 2002: 1.

million.[76] Furthermore, according to Awudi, the increased activity in the sector has not led to a significant increase in employment.[77]

The Ministry's third claim, that the forest reserves to be mined were degraded, is also contested. According to one publication 'Ghana mine operators roll their eyes at the "reserve" designations because locals have already plundered them'.[78] Even the former Minister of Mines, Cecilia Bannerman, has reportedly stated that 'many of these reserves are reserves only on paper'[79] and the Minister of Lands, Forestry and Mines at the height of the conflict, Prof. Dominic Fobih, had also referred to the forests in question as 'so-called reserves'.[80] However, others have taken a different view, disputing the notion that the reserves in question were degraded and suggesting to the contrary that there were still areas of virgin forest.[81] It has also been suggested that it is illogical to conclude that because an area is degraded it should be 'offered up for further degradation'.[82] Even a representative of one of the mining companies involved in the debate admitted that it was understandable that there was controversy over mining, even if the forests were degraded, because there is not much forest left in Ghana.[83] The FOE-Ghana Coalition further argued that allowing mining in forest reserves contravened various national policies and the principles underlining the establishment of forest reserves in Ghana as well as international commitments that the government had made, for example in the Convention to Combat Desertification and the Convention on Biological Diversity.

The government's final argument, that the companies operating in forest reserves would be more strictly regulated, could be seen as a compromise between the position of the investors/Minerals Commission and that of the environmentalists/Forestry Commission (with the two sides ironically brought together at the Ministry level with the amalgamation of the Forestry Ministry and the Mining Ministry). However, members of the FOE-Ghana Coalition charged that, in the development of the *Environmental Guidelines*, there had been no consultation with communities directly affected by mining or forestry or with civil society

[76] UNCTAD 2005a: 50.   [77] Awudi 2002: 1.
[78] 'Country Winds up for Enviro-Mining Clash', *Mineweb*, 4 September 2003.
[79] *Ibid.*
[80] 'Minister Rekindles Mining in Forest Reserve Controversy', *Public Agenda*, 8 September 2003.
[81] Author's confidential interviews with a government official (#2), and NGO representatives (#3, #4, #8, & #11), Accra, June 2005.
[82] Author's confidential interview with an NGO representative (#11), Accra, June 2005.
[83] Author's confidential interview with a mining investor (#20), New Abirim, June 2005.

organizations.[84] The *Environmental Guidelines* listed twelve organizations as key contributors,[85] all of which are either representatives of the mining industry or government agencies, and the funding for the project came entirely from foreign mining companies, leading one observer to conclude that: 'the production of the document was funded by the mining industry and it cannot be trusted since it merely parrots the wishes of the mining industry.'[86] In any event, the *Environmental Guidelines* are non-binding, and provisions are frequently qualified by language such as 'where practicable'. The companies operating in forest reserves would not be permitted to build any additional facilities within the reserves and would also be required to reforest the areas that they cleared.[87] However, according to one forestry official, the idea of restoring forests in Ghana is a myth: 'You fell tropical trees and in place you plant grass and ornamental trees – you fell mahogany and plant cassia – it is not the same. After mining the soil is unable to sustain indigenous species.'[88] Officials from international organizations operating in Ghana were even more pessimistic: 'Resources from mining will never be reinvested in forestry; rehabilitation doesn't happen in Africa.'[89]

8.1.2.4   Epilogue: Ghana's new mining law

When it was drafted, the 1986 Minerals and Mining Law was considered very attractive for investors. However, times change and, in an attempt to regain the country's competitiveness *vis-à-vis* other regimes, the Government of Ghana enacted a new Minerals and Mining Act (Act 703) in March 2006.

The key provisions which could have implications for the regulation of the environment are found in Sections 45 and 46, where investors are given the opportunity to sign 'stability agreements' and 'development

---

[84] 'National Coalition of Civil Society Groups Against Mining in Ghana's Forest Reserves: A Presentation to the Ghanaian Media', 31 March 2004, Old Press Centre, Accra, www.bicusa.org/Legacy/Coalition_press_statement_March04.pdf.

[85] Abosso Goldfields Ltd (South Africa), Ashanti Goldfields Company Ltd (South Africa), Birim Goldfields Inc. (Canada), Environmental Protection Agency, Forestry Commission, Forestry Services Division, Ghana Chamber of Mines, Knight Piesold Consulting (global consulting firm, with representatives from Australia and South Africa), Minerals Commission, Mines Department, Ministry of Lands and Forestry, and the Wildlife Division.

[86] 'Golden Greed: Trouble Looms over Ghana's Forest Reserves', *World Rainforest Movement News Release*, n.d., www.wrm.org.uy.

[87] 'Only Proper Mining to Be Allowed in Forest Reserves', *Ghana News Agency*, 13 June 2006.

[88] Author's confidential interview with a government official (#13) Accra, June 2005.

[89] Author's confidential interview with a representative of an international organization (#14), Accra, June 2005.

agreements' with the government. These agreements are binding and are subject to international arbitration. A stability agreement ensures that:

> the holder of the mining lease will not, for a period not exceeding fifteen years from the date of the agreement
>
> (a) be adversely affected by any new enactment, orders, instruments or other actions made under a new enactment or changes to any enactment, orders, instruments that existed at the time of the stability agreement, or other actions taken under these that have the effect or purports to have the effect of imposing obligations upon the holder or applicant of the mining lease.[90]

According to the Minister of Lands, Forestry and Mines at the time the law was enacted, Prof. Dominic Fobih, the 'essence' of this provision is to 'protect the holder of a mining lease for a period not exceeding fifteen years from being adversely affected by future changes in laws that result in heavier financial burdens being imposed on the holder'.[91] In addition to a stability agreement, an investor may also enter into a development agreement, if the proposed investment will exceed US$500 million. Such an agreement may contain provisions:

> (a) relating to the circumstance or manner in which the Minister or the Commission will exercise a discretion conferred by or under this Act;
> (b) relating to the mineral right or operations to be conducted under the mining lease;
> (c) on stability terms as provided under section 45;
> (d) *relating to environmental issues and obligations of the holder to safeguard the environment in accordance with this Act or other enactment*; and
> (e) dealing with the settlement of disputes.[92]

A former Minister of Mines, Cecilia Bannerman, has stated that stability and development agreements 'are mutually beneficial to investors and government as they enable both parties to negotiate and agree on specified commitments and expectations'.[93] The Ghana National Coalition on Mining (a group of organizations, communities and individuals)

---

[90] Ghana Minerals and Mining Act: Section 45.
[91] Memorandum to the draft Minerals and Mining Bill, 17 May 2005.
[92] Ghana Minerals and Mining Act: Section 46, emphasis added
[93] Speech by Cecilia Bannerman, Ghana Minister of Mines, at the Conference of Montreal's CIDA/IDRC International Forum Bringing the Best of the Private Sector to Development, 7 June 2004, www.idrc.ca/en/ev-61467-201-1-DO_TOPIC.html.

is not convinced of this and strongly opposed the inclusion of stability or development agreements in the new Bill.[94]

The next step for Ghana is to develop a model stability agreement. UNCTAD has recommended that this model be drafted in close consultation with industry and Parliament and suggests that the stability agreements of Chile and Peru would provide useful models (see Section 5.1.1.2).[95]

8.1.3   Open-pit mining in Costa Rica

Two cases in Costa Rica are presented in this chapter. The first case involves a Canadian company that held a mineral exploration licence in the country. In 2002, the Costa Rican government placed a moratorium on oil and gas exploration and open-pit mining. The Canadian mining company's concession was not directly affected by the moratorium, but the company faced difficulty in the approval of its EIA. The company threatened to take the government to arbitration under the terms of the Canada-Costa Rica BIT, but was eventually permitted to proceed with mine development.

8.1.3.1   Background

In the late 1990s, Placer Dome Inc. of Canada explored for minerals on two properties in the far north-west corner of Costa Rica, near the Nicaraguan border.[96] Subsequently, these properties were acquired by Lyon Lake Mines Ltd, another Canadian company. In June 2000, Lyon Lake sold the rights to Vannessa Ventures, also incorporated in Canada.[97] The Crucitas project developed by Vannessa consisted of ten gold mining concessions covering an area of 176 square km.[98] Vannessa set up a subsidiary in the country, Industrias Infinito, S.A., submitted a feasibility report to the government in 2001 and received an exploitation permit in 2002, only days before a presidential election.[99]

Oil and mining were hot campaign issues in the election. All three of the leading candidates for office voiced their opposition to oil exploration

[94] Memorandum on the Minerals and Mining Bill 2005, Submitted by the National Coalition on Mining to the Select Parliamentary Committee on Mines and Minerals, 8 June 2005.
[95] UNCTAD and Japan Bank for International Cooperation 2006: 21.
[96] Doan 1998: 1.   [97] Velasco 2000: 2.
[98] 'Multi-Million Ounce Crucitas Gold Project Acquired', *Vannessa Ventures News Release*, 17 May 2000, www.vannessaventures.com.
[99] 'Vannessa Advances Multi-Million Ounce Crucitas Gold Project', *Vannessa Ventures News Release*, 22 January 2002.

in the country.[100] Abel Pacheco was elected in a close fought race, and in his inaugural address in May, he declared 'peace with nature'. On Earth Day, he placed a moratorium on future oil and gas exploration as well as on large-scale open-pit mining projects.

Assuming that it would not be retroactively affected by the moratorium, Vannessa Ventures continued with the development of its project. The company contracted a Costa Rican consulting company to produce an EIA, and submitted it to the country's environmental agency (SETENA) in March 2002.[101] In August of that year, the Sala IV ruled on an appeal of the open-pit mining moratorium brought by Franz Ulloa, a representative of the Costa Rican Chamber of Mines. While the court upheld the moratorium, it affirmed the legality of concessions which were issued before the moratorium was put in place. The Environment Minister said that he would respect the decision, but also indicated that the government was ill-equipped to properly regulate and monitor large-scale gold mines.[102]

8.1.3.2 The conflict

Vannessa Ventures was confident that its mining licence was valid, based on the court decision, but it still faced a second hurdle: the approval of its EIA. In March 2003, a year after it had submitted the EIA, Vannessa filed an injunction to obtain a resolution on its approval or rejection. SETENA responded that the EIA was below standards and would not be approved. Vannessa subsequently filed an appeal with SETENA and requested that the Supreme Court review the decision.

The company declared that 'the political environment that manifests itself in the declarations and actions of the President and Minister may have involuntarily influenced the legal and administrative process and resulted in unfair treatment of Infinito and its shareholders'.[103] As a result, the company felt that the principles of fairness, transparency and non-discrimination found in the Canada-Costa Rica BIT had been violated.[104] The definition of investment under the BIT covers 'rights, conferred by law or under contract, to undertake any economic and commercial activity, including any rights to search for, cultivate, extract or exploit natural

---

[100] 'Texas Oil a Slippery Issue in Costa Rica', *CNN*, 5 February 2002.
[101] 'Vannessa Submits Crucitas Environmental Impact Study', *Vannessa Ventures News Release*, 19 March 2002.
[102] 'High Court Gives Go-Ahead to Open-Pit Mine in North', *Tico Times*, 25 October 2002.
[103] *Ibid.*
[104] Agreement between the Government of Canada and the Government of the Republic of Costa Rica for the Promotion and Protection of Investments, 18 March 1998, San José.

resources'.[105] The company also suggested that they had been discriminated against: 'The negative viewpoints of the President and the moratorium against mining singles out open pit gold mining and excludes
non-metallic mines altogether.'[106] Erich Rauguth, a senior mining consul-
tant for Vannessa, further stated: 'In reality we've been expropriated.'[107]
The company noted in a news release that, if it proceeded with international arbitration under the BIT, '[e]ffective compensation would be
based on the loss of return on investment that can reasonably be expected
to materialize', which Vannessa estimated at the time to be approximately
US$200 million.[108]

Despite its bold statements, the company continued to pursue a
response from SETENA on its appeal and took the issue to the local
courts. The Sala IV found in their favour, requiring SETENA to respond
to Vannessa's appeal within five days.[109] The permitting process thereafter
recommenced and in March 2004 the company appointed a technical
commission to deal with additional issues raised by SETENA.[110]

In late 2004, environmentalists brought a case to the country's Constitutional Court, arguing that Vannessa was awarded its Exploitation
Permit prior to receiving the required environmental approvals and that,
as such, it should be annulled.[111] In December 2004, the court upheld
the injunction, finding that the mining concession was in violation of the
Central American Biodiversity Agreement and Article 50 (on the right to
a healthy environment) of Costa Rica's Constitution.[112] The court ordered
the state to pay costs, damages and compensation to the permit holder
but, to the confusion of Vannessa, apparently stated that the EIA process
should move ahead. The company once again began openly discussing the
option of international arbitration. John Morgan, president of Vannessa
Ventures, explained why the company was not going to give up without a
fight: 'These projects are not that easy to find. When you look at whether
we should persevere with these existing projects versus the other option

---

[105] *Ibid*: Art. 1(g)(vi).
[106] 'Crucitas Update', *Vannessa Ventures News Release*, 14 April 2003.
[107] 'High Court Sides with Gold Mining Company', *Tico Times*, 13 June 2003.
[108] *Ibid.*   [109] *Ibid.*
[110] 'Vannessa Ventures Updates Shareholders on its Activities', *Vannessa Ventures News Release*, 26 April 2004.
[111] 'Clarification of Supreme Court Decision on Crucitas Concession', *Vannessa Ventures News Release*, 5 December 2006.
[112] 'Court Annuls Gold Mining Concession', *Associated Press*, 12 December 2004.

of going out and trying to find another million ounce project, I'd take the former.'[113]

In April 2005, the company asked the Constitutional Court to reconsider, clarify and add to its ruling. Vannessa also filed a request to advance the international arbitration process with ICSID in July 2005. In a news release, the company stated that it sought restitution of its contractual rights and US$5 million in legal and administrative costs. In lieu of restitution it sought lost profits of US$240 million, plus US$36 million in expenses and compound interest.[114] The company made it clear that it was advancing the arbitration process in order to protect its claim under the time requirements of the BIT, and that it would halt the process if SETENA provided approval of the EIA in the interim.[115]

8.1.3.3 The outcome

In September 2005, SETENA approved the EIA for the company, which could thereafter proceed with mine development.[116] Industrias Infinito's Chief Executive Officer (CEO), Jesus Carvajal, noted that the arbitration request to ICSID had helped Vannessa's case, stating: 'This kind of pressure helped SETENA resolve the issue.'[117] The company reported that the approval of the EIA was 'sufficient reason for the investor Vannessa Ventures, to consider the withdrawal of the arbitration presented before [ICSID]'.[118]

8.1.4 Offshore oil exploration in Costa Rica

The second case in Costa Rica involves an American oil company that held several land and offshore concessions in the country. The oil company's land concessions were annulled and it encountered problems in the approval of its EIA for the offshore concessions. This latter issue led to a conflict with the government and a filing to initiate investment arbitration

---

[113] 'Vannessa to Seek International Arbitration if Necessary', *Business News Americas*, 24 January 2005.

[114] 'Vannessa Updated Crucitas Developments', *Vannessa Ventures News Release*, 22 July 2005.

[115] *Ibid.*

[116] 'Crucitas Environmental Submission Approved', *Vannessa Ventures News Release*, 1 September 2005.

[117] 'Vannessa Secures Crucitas Enviro Permit', *Business News Americas*, 1 September 2005.

[118] 'Mining Company Considers Withdrawal of International Arbitration', *Infinito News Release*, 2 September 2005, http://infinito.co.cr.

under the terms of a foreign investment contract. The company eventually withdrew its arbitration request.

8.1.4.1   Background

In 1994, the Government of Costa Rica passed a Hydrocarbons Law as part of a series of measures designed to implement a structural adjustment programme. This law opened Costa Rica to foreign interests in oil and gas exploration. In 1997, the Ministry of Environment and Energy (MINAE) opened a round of bidding for oil and gas exploration concession blocks on land and offshore. In 1998, MKJ Xploration, a Lousiana-based company, acquired four concession blocks – two on land and two offshore.[119] Texas-based Harken Energy later purchased an 80 per cent stake in the project under the subsidiary Harken Costa Rica Holdings (collectively 'Harken'). In 1999, protests began over the seismic tests that were being carried out in one of Harken's offshore concessions. Environmentalists expressed alarm over the potential impacts on marine life, and noted that wildlife reserves existed close by, including two sites registered under the Ramsar Convention on Wetlands.[120] Fishermen and members of the tourism industry also voiced concerns about the impacts that oil exploration could have on their livelihoods.[121]

Meanwhile, communities in the area of the land concessions filed a petition with the country's Constitutional Court, claiming that the bidding process had been flawed as there had been no prior consultation with them.[122] In 2000, the Constitutional Court ruled in favour of the petitioners, citing irregularities in the bidding process and a lack of public consultation.[123] The decision annulled Harken's concessions and called on the government to consult with indigenous communities.[124] Opposition groups, which had banded together under the Acción de Lucha Antipetrolera, celebrated the decision. However, Harken maintained that the project was still viable as the Court had not made a decision on the validity of oil exploration, but only on the way that the contract had been

---

[119] 'The Case of Oil Exploration in the Caribbean off Costa Rica: Legal Background', *Environmental Law Alliance Worldwide*, n.d., www.elaw.org.

[120] 'Oil Exploration Protested', *Tico Times*, 10 December 1999; 'Costa Rica Rejects Oil Exploration Near Ramsar Sites', *Ramsar News Release*, 3 March 2002, www.ramsar.org.

[121] 'Oil Drilling Plans Denounced', *Tico Times*, 1 September 2001.

[122] 'The Case of Oil Exploration in the Caribbean off Costa Rica: Legal Background', *Environmental Law Alliance Worldwide*, n.d., www.elaw.org.

[123] 'Oil Drilling Plans Denounced', *Tico Times*, 1 September 2001.

[124] 'Court Orders Halt to Oil Drilling', *Tico Times*, 14 September 2000.

awarded.[125] The company filed a motion for relief, claiming that it had been denied the opportunity to make its case heard before the Court. Subsequently the Court amended its decision so that only the two land concession blocks held by Harken were annulled, leaving the marine concession blocks unaffected.[126] The company welcomed this decision, as it had conducted the bulk of exploration work in the offshore blocks, and it later decided to give up its contractual rights in the land blocks rather than proceed with consultations with the indigenous communities.[127]

8.1.4.2   The conflict

While Harken's offshore concessions had not been annulled, the company still had to obtain approval for its EIA. In 2001, SETENA outlined numerous legal and technical elements that were missing from Harken's EIA. These included the failure to address the potential effects of an oil spill and to provide measures for containment in the event of a spill.[128] Environmentalists sought the assistance of the International Union for the Conservation of Nature, who in turn hired two independent experts to review the EIA. The consultants also reviewed an Addendum to the EIA which the company produced in response to SETENA's concerns, and found that it failed to adequately address the potential scope and cumulative effects of oil exploration in the area.[129]

In February 2002, the Constitutional Court ruled that the part of the Hydrocarbons Law relating to the EIA process was not in compliance with Article 50 of the Constitution guaranteeing the right to a healthy and ecologically balanced environment. The main problem with the Law was that approval of a comprehensive EIA was not required before a contract was signed.[130] The court also noted that SETENA was ill-equipped to deal with the review of these studies. A push to repeal the law entirely began, which the CEO of Harken Costa Rica Holdings argued would 'send a terrible, tragic and devastating message to the international business community'.[131]

In late February, SETENA made its final decision, providing fifty-five reasons for rejecting Harken's EIA. The reasons provided by SETENA

---

[125] 'Oil Firm: Project Not Dead Yet', *Tico Times*, 29 September 2000.
[126] 'Oil Firm Faces Deadline to Clarify Report', *Tico Times*, 2 February 2001.
[127] 'Oil Firm Out of Indian Land', *Tico Times*, 23 March 2001.
[128] 'Oil Firm Faces Deadline to Clarify Report', *Tico Times*, 2 February 2001.
[129] *Ibid.*
[130] 'High Court Dampens Oil Plans', *Tico Times*, 15 February 2002.
[131] 'Hydrocarbons Law Stirs Furor', *Tico Times*, 22 February 2002.

relied heavily on the precautionary principle, international agreements such as Ramsar, the Constitutional Court decisions, the lack of resources in the country to deal with oil spills, and the deficiencies in the company's application. Harken maintained that the decision to reject the EIA was based on a lack of understanding about the technology that would be employed in the operation and filed an appeal.[132]

In October 2003, the company submitted a request for arbitration to ICSID. Harken claimed it had lost US$9–$12 million in exploration activity and costs related to administrative and legal procedures, but the company sought US$57 billion in damages and lost future profits. President Pacheco flatly refused to consent to arbitration and pointed out that Harken's contract required the company to exhaust local remedies.[133] Furthermore, he argued that the company had not met its environmental requirements, which was ground for termination of the contract. On the other hand, Harken Costa Rica Holdings' CEO suggested that SETENA's decision had been politically motivated, that a fair hearing in Costa Rica would be impossible, and that the company 'would prefer to reserve the decision to the panel of unbiased and fair international arbitrators'.[134] A representative of the NGO OilWatch Costa Rica suggested that the threat of arbitration was 'a bluff intended to give the company a stronger negotiating position', and a lobbyist of the company admitted that the company would be willing to back down for a US$10 million settlement.[135]

8.1.4.3   The outcome

Only seventeen days after the initial request to ICSID, Harken dropped the case as a 'good faith' act and sought negotiations.[136] President Pacheco called the withdrawal a 'triumph for reason and justice'.[137] Negotiations ensued, and at one point Costa Rica was apparently willing to pay Harken between US$3–11 million, as this was 'cheaper than being sued' and

---

[132] Harken Energy Corporation, SEC Form S-3 (Registration Statement for Securities Offered Pursuant to a Transaction), Filed 3 June 2002, www.secinfo.com.

[133] 'The Threat to the Environment from the Central America Free Trade Agreement (CAFTA): The case of Harken Costa Rica Holdings and Offshore Oil', Natural Resources Defense Council and Friends of the Earth US (FOE-US) Fact Sheet, n.d., www.foe.org/camps/intl/harken.pdf.

[134] 'Pacheco Stands Firm Against Oil Drilling', *Tico Times*, 3 October 2003; 'U.S. Oil Company Withdraws Request', *Tico Times*, 10 October 2003.

[135] 'Pacheco Stands Firm Against Oil Drilling', *Tico Times*, 3 October 2003.

[136] 'Harken Stopped Arbitration', *La Nación*, 4 October 2003.

[137] 'U.S. Oil Company Withdraws Request', *Tico Times*, 10 October 2003.

'preferable to facing retaliatory sanctions from the US government'.[138] In the end, the negotiations were unsuccessful and in a resolution signed by the President in 2005, the government of Costa Rica formally cancelled Harken's concession contract.[139]

8.1.5 *Analysis*

This section assesses the role that the threat of arbitration played in the outcome of each conflict. It also compares the factors that contributed to the efficacy of the threat of arbitration in each case.

8.1.5.1 The threat of arbitration

The role that a threat to arbitrate plays in the outcome of a conflict depends, first of all, on the credibility of the threat. However, this is not always a straightforward issue. There were clearly differing opinions in Indonesia on whether the CoWs, as *lex specialis*, were exempt from the Forestry law. One interviewee in Ghana suggested that many observers were not convinced that the threat of arbitration was serious in the forest reserves case.[140] In Costa Rica, the threat from Harken to arbitrate was taken by the government to be a hollow one, as the contract stipulated a requirement to exhaust local remedies, and no BIT or regional investment agreement was (yet) in place. If CAFTA-DR had already been in place, it is possible that the outcome of the conflict might have been different. Indeed, the outcome was different in the Vannessa Ventures conflict, where the threat of arbitration could be backed up by the Canada-Costa Rica BIT.

A second issue is the confidence (or lack thereof) of a government that it could win if it was taken to arbitration. NGOs in both Ghana and Indonesia expressed considerable confidence that their governments would be successful in the event of an arbitration. In Ghana they argued that it was clear in the country's laws that mining in forest reserves was not permitted, and that therefore both the former government and the companies were at fault for breaching the law.[141] In Indonesia, NGOs argued that the contracts stipulated that mining companies must comply with

---

[138] 'Government, Harken to Negotiate Settlement', *Business News Americas*, 13 January 2004.
[139] 'Government Cancels Harken Exploration Concession', *Business News Americas*, 3 March 2005.
[140] Author's confidential interviews with an NGO representative (#4), Accra, June 2005.
[141] *Ibid.*

environmental law.[142] However, in both cases the governments appeared less confident of a successful outcome.

The threat of arbitration appeared to have the greatest influence in Indonesia. After having done little to resolve the conflict for a quite some time, the government responded quite dramatically with the Perpu following the threat of arbitration. Furthermore, the fact that the companies that threatened arbitration were also the ones which were exempted from the law is unlikely to be mere coincidence.[143] The need to avoid arbitration was also mentioned by the Parliament in their discussions on the issue and by the judges in the Constitutional Court decision.[144] Furthermore, the fact that the government subsequently tried to move away from the CoW system in the drafting of a new mineral law, and specifically tried to remove recourse to international arbitration for mineral investors, suggests that the threat of a formal dispute was a serious concern of the administration (although it also relates to efforts to decentralize oversight of mineral projects).

In Ghana, the role that the threat to arbitrate played in the outcome of the conflict is less clear-cut, particularly in light of a recent development. Following the effective resolution of the debate on mining in reserves, reports began to emerge that Alcoa, a multinational bauxite mining company, was seeking access to explore in the Atewa forest reserve.[145] It was later confirmed that the government had permitted the company to undertake exploration activities there.[146] This development suggests that the claim used by the government that its hands were tied by its obligations to the initial five mining companies was an excuse used to quell domestic and international opposition to the decision. It appears evident that the Minerals Commission is keen to move ahead with more projects in forest reserves despite the objections of the Forestry Commission and the concerns of the Ghana EPA, and that it has benefited from the threat of arbitration in this regard.

Finally, in Costa Rica, the differing treatment of Harken and Vannessa Ventures appears to correspond directly to the government's assessment of the potential outcome of each case, suggesting that a threat of arbitration

---

[142] 'Mining Industry Threatens Indonesia with International Arbitration', *WALHI and JATAM News Release*, 4 April 2002, www.jatam.org.

[143] Gross 2003: 895.

[144] Author's confidential interview with an NGO representative (#7), Jakarta, July 2005.

[145] 'Price Tag on Atewa Forest as Alcoa Eyes Bauxite', *Public Agenda*, 7 August 2006.

[146] 'Minister Commends Bauxite Exploration at Atiwa', *Ghana News Agency*, 11 September 2006.

does have considerable influence when it has a firm basis. However, there are also alternative explanations for the discrepancy in the treatment of these two investors (see below).

8.1.5.2   Factors that contributed to the efficacy of the threat

The available evidence suggests that governments faced with a threat of arbitration are primarily concerned with the financial consequences of losing in arbitration as well as the reputational consequences of participating in arbitration. Additionally, it would appear that divisions within a government can contribute to the efficacy of a threat. Finally, a threat of arbitration may be more disquieting for a government that has had a negative experience with the process in a previous case.

In terms of financial concerns, it is the very substantial claims of compensation that are particularly troubling for governments. The Indonesian Minister for Environment, Nabiel Makarim, stated that the decision to allow the 13 companies to mine in protection forests was 'hard luck'[147] and only taken to avoid paying compensation for which funds were not available.[148] The Indonesian government reportedly received legal advice that it could be sued for up to US$31 billion.[149] While that is a very large sum compared to any of the awards reviewed in Chapter 7, one has to remember that there were several companies involved in the conflict. For any country, such a sum would be significant, but particularly for a country with a gross domestic product (GDP) of US$364 billion (making the potential award worth 8.5 per cent of GDP). While it is clear from Chapter 5 that investors are usually not awarded as much as they seek, even if this estimate were double or triple what could foreseeably be awarded, the cost would still be considerable. The sum of more than US$275 million in compensation claimed by Vannessa Ventures would also surely have been a daunting figure for the Costa Rican government, although obviously less so than the US$57 billion claimed by Harken. It should be noted that Costa Rica's annual GDP at the time was only about US$17 billion, and the government budget about US$5 billion. There were no reports in Ghana that suggested a possible figure for the amount of compensation that the government might be expected to pay, but it was implied that there had

---

[147] 'No More Mining Permits in Protected Forests', *MiningIndo*, 16 March 2004.
[148] 'State Minister for Environment: Issuing Mining Licenses for 13 Companies was a Mistake', *Tempo Interactive*, 15 March 2004.
[149] 'Indonesian Government Can't Bury Mining Conflicts', *Asia Times*, 10 January 2004. Other analysts have estimated the potential costs and compensation payments closer to US$22.8 billion.

been significant investments made by the mining companies.[150] One publication in Ghana argued that 'it is better for the government to refund the money to the companies, rather than giving out concessions for them to destroy the remaining forest reserves in the name of investment'.[151] However, others suggested that the government simply could not afford to do so.[152]

In terms of reputational concerns, it should be noted that these will exist even in the absence of investment protection; a conflict can be detrimental to the investment climate whether the investor is protected by a contract or IIA or not. However, the elevation of a conflict to formal dispute resolution is considered to be particularly damaging to a country's image in the eyes of foreign investors.[153] Concerns about reputation were particularly evident in Ghana and Indonesia. Indonesia's mineral sector ranked twenty-seventh out of thirty-five countries assessed for 'attractiveness' in a 2001–2 industry survey.[154] The low attractiveness ranking is not based on resource limitations (minerals are in abundance in the country), but rather relates to problems in the investment climate.[155] The mining in protected forests debate certainly affected investors' perceptions of the country. Mélanie et al. suggest that:

> The conflict between provisions of the Forestry Law of 1999 and the mining industry has probably created more uncertainty for investors in Indonesia's mining sector than any other legal or regulatory provision and is one of the key reasons for the decline in investment activity in recent years.[156]

Hence, the desire to keep existing mineral investments and attract further ones was a likely factor in the Indonesian government's decision to issue the Perpu. Even greater concern about this issue was evident in Ghana, a country that is generally perceived as quite 'investor-friendly'. It has been suggested that the initial indecision over whether to open the forest reserves to mining contributed to dwindling investment in the country.[157] In addition, at least one company that was seeking a

---

[150] 'Only Proper Mining to be Allowed in Forest Reserves', *Ghana News Agency*, 13 June 2006.
[151] 'Whither the Mining Industry?', *Public Agenda*, 12 May 2003.
[152] Author's confidential interviews with government a official (#7), and an academic (#9), Accra, June 2005.
[153] Otto and Cordes 2002: V-16.
[154] 'Indonesian Government Can't Bury Mining Conflicts', *Asia Times*, 10 January 2004.
[155] PricewaterhouseCoopers 2004.   [156] Mélanie *et al.* 2005: 13.
[157] 'Ghana Lures Miners with New Laws Opening Forests', *Reuters*, 20 February 2003.

concession inside a reserve made it clear that its other potential investments in the country would be impacted by the government's decision.[158]
Several interviewees suggested that the government feared arbitration
not because they feared losing, but because they feared the impact that
denying the leases and proceeding to arbitration would have on their reputation with foreign investors.[159] In contrast, Costa Rica was obviously
not concerned about lost future investments in the extractive industries.
Unlike the bans in Ghana and Indonesia, the moratorium in Costa Rica
did not apply only to certain areas, but to the entire country. This is
clearly a part of Costa Rica's broader strategy to focus on tourism, particularly eco-tourism, as a source of economic development, rather than the
exploitation of natural resources.

In terms of internal government politics, it is evident that there are
often disagreements on how conflicts with investors should be resolved,
and how threats to arbitrate should be dealt with. In both the Ghanaian and Indonesian cases, ministries responsible for mining and those
responsible for forests and environment were pitted against one another.
This clearly would make the position of the government much weaker
in an arbitration, and thus the threat of arbitration more potent. While
the government would have to present a united front if it proceeded in
arbitration, an investor would be able to refer to statements previously
made by its supporters in government. Ministries that are closely tied with
foreign investors often have more clout in the government, and can put
substantial pressure on government leaders and legislatures. They also
have more knowledge of contracts and IIAs, which they can exploit to
their advantage.

Finally, it is evident in the Indonesian case that the government's past
experience with international arbitration may have been an important
factor in the outcome of the conflict. According to several observers, the
government had been 'burned' in previous arbitrations and was not eager
to try its luck again.[160] *The Jakarta Post*, in an article on the mining

---

[158] When Newmont found gold in two locations, one inside a reserve, it was reported that the
company wanted 'both concessions or nothing'. See 'Ghana's Gold Dilemma', *BBC News*,
4 February 2003.

[159] Author's confidential interviews with an NGO representative (#4), a representative of an
international organization (#6), a government official (#13), and an academic (#18), Accra
and Kumasi, June 2005.

[160] Author's confidential interviews with foreign embassy officials (#4, #10), an NGO representative (#7), and a mining investor (#9), Jakarta, July 2005.

in forests case, noted that government officials frequently referred to the *Karaha Bodas* dispute in particular.[161]

8.1.5.3   Alternative scenarios

While it would appear that there is substantial evidence that the threat to arbitrate played a significant role in the outcome of the cases discussed, other explanations cannot be ruled out. For example, diplomatic pressure on governments, applied by the home state of the investors, could have also contributed to the outcome in each case. Indonesia was apparently subject to informal pressure applied by the home governments of the investors through their embassies.[162] Vannessa Ventures enlisted the support of the Canadian Embassy 'to encourage transparency and due process from the Costa Rican government'[163] and there were reports that the US Embassy had become involved in the Harken case. Although the US Ambassador to Costa Rica maintained that he was only assisting the company in so far as to ensure that it was treated fairly by the government, activists remained suspicious.[164] Their suspicions were fuelled by the fact that US President George W. Bush was a former Harken board member. However, others believed that the US pressure was actually on Harken to withdraw its arbitration request, as it could have complicated the negotiations for CAFTA-DR.[165] Thus, the discrepancy in the treatment of Harken and Vannessa Ventures might be explained by the fact that Canada urged the government to resolve the conflict, while the US instead might have pressured the investor to drop its arbitration request.

[161] In the mid-1990s, two American companies – Florida Power & Light and Caithness Energy – formed Karaha Bodas Company, incorporated in the Cayman Islands. Karaha Bodas entered into a joint operation contract with the state-owned oil company Pertamina to develop a geothermal project in West Java. When the Asian currency crisis hit in 1997, the project was postponed. By the spring of 1998, the company had filed for arbitration under UNCITRAL Rules, as provided for in their contract. The tribunal found that Pertamina was liable for losses incurred by Karaha Bodas as a result of the economic crisis, and awarded the company US$261.1 million in damages, including sunk costs and lost profits. Pertamina attempted, unsuccessfully, to have the award set aside in the Swiss Supreme Court (Switzerland was the seat of the tribunal). Karaha Bodas, for its part, began actions to enforce the award against Pertamina's assets in foreign countries. Pertamina has made several attempts in Indonesian and foreign courts to block the enforcement of the award. See further: Chung 2007; Wells and Ahmed 2007.

[162] See, e.g., 'Indonesia: Mining and Forestry (Question No.1662)', *Australian Senate Official Hansard* No. 11, 2003, 15356–57, http://parlinfoweb.aph.gov.au.

[163] 'Crucitas Update', *Vannessa Ventures News Release*, 14 April 2003.

[164] 'Costa Rica Just Says No to Oil Development', *Environmental News Network*, 20 September 2002.

[165] 'Pacheco Wins One With Reversal by Harken Energy', *A.M. Costa Rica*, 6 October 2003.

One can also not rule out the possibility that corruption was involved in the outcome of these conflicts; it was certainly alleged to be a factor in the Indonesian case.

8.2   Conflicts over domestic court proceedings

8.2.1   Liability for marine pollution in Buyat Bay, Indonesia

This case concerns a civil liability suit brought by the Indonesian Ministry of Environment against an American mining company for allegedly breaching the country's environmental laws in the course of its operations. The suit was brought in an Indonesian court but was dismissed because the court found that all disputes between the government and the investor should be resolved through investment arbitration, as stipulated in the company's contract.

8.2.1.1   Background

Newmont Mining Corporation's 80 per cent-owned subsidiary, PT Newmont Minahasa Raya, operated the Mesel Gold Mine in North Sulawesi, Indonesia, from 1996–2004, when it was closed due to depletion of gold ore at the mine. In that period, the company was authorized by the Indonesian government to use submarine placement of tailings.[166] The tailings were placed on the seabed at a depth of 82 metres via a pipeline that extended 900 metres into the sea at a location known as Buyat Bay.[167] The tailings contained insoluble mercury and arsenic compounds. Submarine tailings disposal is effectively illegal in Canada, the US and Australia.[168]

Local communities and NGOs claimed that the tailings had polluted Buyat Bay and were responsible for adverse health effects experienced by local residents. Subsequently, several studies were carried out, commissioned by both the Indonesian government and Newmont. Local police found elevated levels of arsenic and mercury in the water; however a World Health Organization study found the levels to be within normal parameters.[169] Finally, a study by the Indonesian Ministry of Environment found

---

[166] Tailings are finely ground rock from which minerals such as gold have been recovered.
[167] 'Buyat Bay: History and Status', Newmont Brochure, May 2006, www.newmont.com.
[168] 'Submarine Tailings Disposal', Mineral Policy Institute website, www.mpi.org.au, accessed 17 December 2008.
[169] Mercury Pollution: Buyat & Totok Bay, North Sulawesi, Indonesia. Final Report. Prepared by Mineshi Sakamoto, Institute for Minamata Disease, Ministry of Environment Japan, for the World Health Organization Indonesia, 8 September 2004.

that the waste from the gold mine left high levels of arsenic and mercury in the sediment on the floor of the bay, which then entered bottom-feeding organisms known as benthos that provide food for fish.[170] For its part, Newmont claimed that the arsenic was not the kind that would dissolve in water, and would not enter the food chain. Newmont admitted that it released 17 tons of waste mercury into the air and 16 tons into the water over five years, but argued that these releases were well within the range allowed under national law.[171] The Ministry of Environment countered that the company had not been authorized to release that amount of waste.

8.2.1.2   The conflict

On 9 March 2005, the Ministry of Environment filed a civil lawsuit against PT Newmont Minahasa Raya in the South Jakarta District Court, seeking US$133.6 million in damages. The Ministry also filed separate criminal proceedings against the company, and its President Richard Ness, for the pollution of Buyat Bay. The Ministry stated that in the civil lawsuit it was seeking damages to pay for the restoration of the environment in Buyat Bay and the relocation of local residents, while the purpose of the criminal prosecution was to deter others from breaching the country's environmental laws.[172]

According to the legal representation for Newmont, in filing the civil suit the Ministry had 'not complied with the prevailing provisions under the Contract of Work', which 'stipulates that all disputes between the parties will be settled by conciliation or arbitration in accordance with the international arbitration rules'.[173] The company's attorney went on to say that Newmont would 'have to consider filing for international arbitration to follow the CoW' and noted his confidence that the company would win both the court case and the arbitration, concluding that the Environment Ministry had 'made a blunder'.[174]

In October 2005, Newmont filed an objection to the court's jurisdiction, contending that the Indonesian government had previously agreed to

---

[170] 'U.S. Mine to Pay Jakarta $30 million to Settle Suit', *The New York Times*, 16 February 2006.

[171] 'Govt, Newmont Seek Amicable Deal', *The Jakarta Post*, 9 July 2005.

[172] *Ibid.*

[173] 'Newmont to Submit Case to International Arbitration', *Newmont News Release*, 9 March 2005, www.newmont.com.

[174] *Ibid.*

resolve any disputes through conciliation or arbitration.[175] Prosecutors insisted that the dispute resolution clause in the contract was only applicable in business disputes, but not in a case of breach of environmental law.[176]

8.2.1.3   The outcome

In November 2005, the Jakarta District Court dismissed the Ministry of Environment's civil claim against against Newmont on the grounds that the parties had agreed, in the CoW, to settle disputes in investment arbitration. Newmont hailed the court ruling as well reasoned, with President Richard Ness stating that the verdict was both 'fair' and 'good for the investment climate'.[177] Environmentalists urged the Ministry to appeal the decision, arguing that the court had erred in finding that a pollution case should be resolved in investment arbitration.[178] WALHI asserted that a provision in the Environment Law (23/1997) gave the government the right to sue companies for environmental damage and suggested that the court decision elevated commercial mining contracts over national law.[179] WALHI later lodged its own civil lawsuit against the company.[180]

On 16 February 2006, the government settled with Newmont for US$30 million and entered into a 'Goodwill Agreement'. In the Agreement, the Indonesian government agreed that further scientific investigation into whether Newmont's operations had caused any adverse environmental impacts in Buyat Bay or adverse health impacts in local residents would be undertaken by an independent panel of six scientists over a period of up to ten years. Newmont agreed to the establishment of a charitable foundation to oversee the dispersal of the funds to support the scientific panel as well as other projects in the local community.[181] State Minister of the Environment, Rachmat Witoelar, when defending the settlement remarked: 'If there's someone who's upset about the ruling, why don't they ask the presiding judge [in the original civil suit]? The settlement

---

[175] Newmont Mining Corporation Notes to Condensed Consolidated Financial Statements (Unaudited), SEC Form 10-Q, 27 July 2006, http://sec.edgar-online.com.
[176] 'Court Dismisses Civil Suit Against Newmont', *The Jakarta Post*, 16 November 2005.
[177] *Ibid.*
[178] 'Environmentalists Urge Indonesia to Appeal Court Ruling on Newmont Lawsuit', *Associated Free Press*, 17 November 2005.
[179] 'WALHI Sues Newmont', WALHI News Release, 22 March 2007, www.eng.walhi.or.id.
[180] *Ibid.*
[181] 'Buyat Bay: History and Status', Newmont Brochure, May 2006, www.newmont.com.

occurred because the court dismissed our demand. I've suffered because the court trampled on me.'[182]

Newmont and Richard Ness were acquitted of all criminal charges on 24 April 2007.[183]

8.2.2 Liability for oil pollution in the Ecuadorian Amazon

In this case, an American oil company attempted to take the Government of Ecuador to arbitration to ensure that it would not be held liable for any compensation awarded to the claimants in a class action lawsuit. The lawsuit was brought by the residents of Ecuador's Amazon region who had allegedly suffered from the impact of oil pollution. Ecuador challenged the arbitration and successfully blocked the proceedings in the courts of New York. The class action lawsuit, which was originally filed in the US but later refiled in Ecuador, was proceeding at the time of writing. While the company argued against the suit being tried in the US courts, it has recently suggested that the trial in Ecuador is unfair and that it amounts to a denial of justice, in contravention of international law.

8.2.2.1 Background

Kimerling remarks that the discovery of commercial quantities of oil in the Ecuadorian Amazon in the 1960s 'was heralded as the salvation of Ecuador's economy, the product that would, at last, pull the nation out of chronic poverty and "underdevelopment"'.[184] Texaco was one of the companies that first discovered oil in the region. The company began exploring for oil in Ecuador in 1964 under a subsidiary called Texaco Petroleum Company, often referred to as 'TexPet'. In 1965 Texaco signed a joint operating agreement (JOA) with the Gulf Oil Company covering a block of land known as the Napo Concession.

In 1972, Ecuador's military assumed control of the government and, in an effort to nationalize the state's oil industry, issued Supreme Decree No. 430, which required both TexPet and the Gulf Oil Company to agree to relinquish a substantial percentage of the Napo Concession. In 1973, the government published Decree No. 925, which established a new contract

---

[182] 'Rachmat Says $30 Million Newmont Deal No Slap in the Face', *The Jakarta Post*, 18 February 2006.
[183] 'Indonesian Court Clears U.S. Mining Firm', *Associated Press*, 25 April 2007.
[184] Kimerling 2006: 414–15.

for the concession.[185] The contract was signed by Ecuador, TexPet and Gulf Oil, and mandated that Compañía Estatal Petrolera Ecuatoriana, a state-run oil company later renamed Petroecuador (which is the name that will be used hereafter in order to avoid confusion), be given the option to purchase a stake in the Napo Concession. The 1973 contract did not contain an arbitration clause.[186]

While the 1973 contract did not anticipate Petroecuador's participation in the concession until 1977, the government sped up the process and in 1974 another contract was signed, giving Petroecuador 25 per cent of Gulf Oil's stake in the concession. This contract did not contain an arbitration clause, but stated: 'The totality of the activities that will develop in the Joint Operation will be regulated by an operating agreement entered into by the parties.'[187] Petroecuador subsequently assumed all Gulf Oil's remaining interest in the concession in 1976.[188] From that point on, Petroecuador had a majority (62.5 per cent) interest in the consortium, although Texaco remained the operational partner.[189] Petroecuador never signed the 1965 JOA and although negotiations were held for the development of a new JOA, they were never successfully concluded. In 1990, Texaco sold its interest in the concession to Petroecuador.[190]

In the operation of the concession, Texaco used a controversial but cost-saving method of bringing a mixture of oil and water to the surface before separating the two, and leaving the water to run-off into rivers and streams.[191] According to one report, Texaco intentionally dumped more than 19 billion gallons of toxic wastewater into the region and was responsible for 16.8 million gallons of crude oil spilling from the

[185] *The Republic of Ecuador and Petroecuador, Claimants,* v. *ChevronTexaco Corporation and Texaco Petroleum Company, Defendants,* and *ChevronTexaco Corporation and Texaco Petroleum Company, Counterclaim Plaintiffs,* v. *The Republic of Ecuador and Petroecuador, Counterclaim Defendants,* United States District Court, South District New York, 27 June 2005. Reproduced in 376 *Federal Supplement Second Series*: 334. Subsequently referred to as ROE I.
[186] *Ibid.*   [187] Qtd in *ibid*: 340.
[188] 'Chevron Warns Ecuador on BIT Claim as Contract and Environmental Disputes Persist', *Investment Treaty News,* 26 July 2006.
[189] 'Arbitration Proceedings', ChevronTexaco website, www.texaco.com/sitelets/ecuador, accessed 17 December 2008.
[190] 'ChevronTexaco and Texaco Petroleum Company File Arbitration Claim to Enforce Petroecudor's Obligations under Joint Operating Agreement', *Chevron Texaco News Release,* 15 June 2004, www.texaco.com/sitelets/ecuador.
[191] 'Chevron Warns Ecuador on BIT Claim as Contract and Environmental Disputes Persist', *Investment Treaty News,* 26 July 2006.

main pipeline into the forest.[192] The resulting ecological damage has been referred to as an 'environmental disaster 30 times larger than the Exxon Valdez spill', and the cost of clean-up has been estimated at between US$16–27 billion.[193]

In 1994, TexPet, Petroecuador, and Ecuador signed a Memorandum of Understanding, followed in 1995 by a contract, relating to the remediation of areas that had been polluted by oil operations. Under this settlement, TexPet agreed to perform specified environmental remedial work (for an estimated US$40 million) in exchange for being released from liability for any claims by the Government of Ecuador or Petroecuador.[194] In 1998, following the remedial work, TexPet was released of liability for such claims.

8.2.2.2   The conflict

In 1993, two class action lawsuits were filed against Texaco under the Alien Tort Claims Act in a federal court in New York on behalf of an estimated 30,000 Amazon residents.[195] The court determined that New York was not the most convenient forum for the cases, which was confirmed by a US appeals court in 2002.[196] However, the judgment in the appeals court was subject to the condition that Texaco agree to submit to the jurisdiction of Ecuador's courts, and the claims were subsequently refiled in Ecuador. President Rafael Correa has publicly sided with the plaintiffs in their case.[197]

On 11 June 2004, ChevronTexaco[198] filed a claim with the American Arbitration Association (AAA) under the terms of the arbitration clause in the 1965 JOA. In the claim, the company asserted that Petroecuador is 'responsible for all fees, costs and expenses incurred by ChevronTexaco

---

[192] The 1993 report 'Crudo Amazónico' (Amazon Crude) by the environmental lawyer Judith Kimerling is qtd in 'Chevron (CVX) in the Amazon: Oil Rights or Human Rights?' Amnesty International USA website, www.amnestyusa.org.

[193] 'Expert Asks Ecuador Court to Fine Chevron $7–$16 bln', *Reuters*, 2 April 2008; 'Texaco Toxic Past Haunts Chevron as Judgment Looms', *Bloomberg*, 30 December 2008.

[194] ROE I: 341–2.

[195] *Aguinda* v. *Texaco, Inc.*, United States Court of Appeals for the Second Circuit, 16 August 2002. Reproduced in 303 *Federal Reporter Third Series* (2002): 470; *Jota* v. *Texaco, Inc.*, Court of Appeals, Second Circuit, 5 October 1998. Reproduced in 157 *Federal Reporter Third Series* (1998): 53.

[196] 'US Court Sides with Chevron in Amazon Case', *Energy Compass*, 23 August 2002. For further discussion of these cases see Kimerling 2006.

[197] 'Chevron Says Victim of Unfair Trial in Ecuador', *Reuters*, 2 July 2007.

[198] In 2001, Chevron Corporation merged with Texaco.

and TexPet related to the pending litigation against the companies, including any final judgments that may be rendered against ChevronTexaco in Ecuador'.[199] In ChevronTexaco's view, even though Petroecuador did not sign the 1965 JOA, it knowingly accepted benefits from the agreement and behaved as if the agreement controlled its relationship with TexPet. As such, the company argued that Petroecuador should be bound by the arbitration clause within the 1965 JOA.[200]

Ecuador subsequently filed a suit with the New York Supreme Court to stop the arbitration proceedings in the AAA. The case was later moved to the New York Southern District Court. Chevron filed a counterclaim, arguing that the company had been released from all liability by the 1995 remediation agreement. In response, Ecuador argued that Texaco concealed from the government the true extent of the contamination in order to obtain an agreement at a lower cost than was actually necessary for the remediation.[201]

8.2.2.3 The outcome

On 19 June 2007, the New York Southern District Court ruled that the JOA was not applicable to the Government of Ecuador or Petroecuador, because neither was a signatory to the agreement.[202] The contract, as mentioned above, was signed between the Gulf Oil Company and Texaco. ChevronTexaco claimed that the terms of the JOA had been transferred to Petroecuador when it bought Gulf Oil's stake, but the Judge ruled that Ecuadorian law in the 1970s was too 'unsettled' to assume that it would support this claim.[203]

---

[199] 'ChevronTexaco and Texaco Petroleum Company File Arbitration Claim to Enforce Petroecuador's Obligations under Joint Operating Agreement', ChevronTexaco News Release, 15 June 2004, www.texaco.com/sitelets/ecuador.

[200] ROE I: 352.

[201] The remediation settlement became the subject of an official corruption investigation in Ecuador. Two of Chevron's lawyers and seven former Ecuadorian government officials were indicted on fraud charges in September 2008. See: 'Chevron Faces Fraud Charges in Ecuador Over Flawed Environmental Remediation, Amazon Watch Says', PR Newswire, 8 November 2006; 'Ecuador Seeks Chevron Probe: U.S. Officials Asked to Look at Rain Forest Contamination Claim', San Francisco Chronicle, 23 December 2006; 'Chevron Lawyers Indicted by Ecuador in Oil-Pit Cleanup Dispute', Bloomberg, 13 September 2008; 'Chevron's Troubles in Ecuador Continue to Mount with Fraud Indictment of High-level Executive', Amazon Defence Coalition Press Release, 18 September 2008.

[202] Republic of Ecuador and Petroecuador, Plaintiffs, Counterclaim Defendants, v. Chevron-Texaco Corporation and Texaco Petroleum Company, Defendants, Counterclaim Plaintiffs, United States District Court, South District New York, 19 June 2007.

[203] 'New York Court Rules Against Chevron in Environmental Dispute with Ecuador', Investment Treaty News, 31 May 2006.

According to the company:

> The Court did not rule on the fundamental issue related to Chevron's claim for arbitration – that Petroecuador is obligated to indemnify TexPet (and Chevron) for any claims against it. Rather, the Court simply ruled that, in its opinion, this was not an issue that should be addressed by arbitration in New York.[204]

ChevronTexaco subsequently filed a notice of appeal of the New York District Court ruling. However, the original ruling was upheld in a summary order released by the appeals court in October 2008.[205] A further appeal to the Supreme Court was rejected in June 2009.

8.2.2.4 Epilogue: Chevron's claims of denial of justice

The arbitration proceedings in the AAA are under an injunction, and meanwhile the liability case against ChevronTexaco in Ecuador continues. Despite having pushed for the case to be heard in Ecuador, rather than the US, Chevron has been very critical of the judicial process in the country and has indicated that it may pursue investment arbitration on the basis of denial of justice and lack of due process. According to Chevron's managing counsel for Latin America, Ricardo Viega, the company 'will not hesitate to go to international tribunals to review what we believe is an unfair trial and lack of due process in this country'[206] and Kent Robertson, a Chevron spokesman, has stated: 'Chevron ultimately expects to defeat the unfounded claims at issue in this litigation, whether in the courts of Ecuador or in some other tribunal that will hold Ecuador to account for its flagrant failure to live up to its legal commitments and its disregard for the rule of law.'[207]

In October 2007, Chevron's legal team submitted a petition to dismiss the case to the President of the Superior Court of Justice of Nueva Loja.[208] The petition outlines a long list of actions during the trial that when taken together, according to the company, constitute a denial of justice. An English translation of the petition states that:

[204] 'Chevron Responds to Comments by Amazon Defense Front Regarding U.S. Court Decision', *ChevronTexaco News Release*, 22 June 2007, www.texaco.com/sitelets/ecuador.
[205] *Republic of Ecuador and Petroecuador, Petitioners-Counter-Defendant-Appellees*, v. *ChevronTexaco Corporation and Texaco Petroleum Company, Respondents-Counter-Claimants-Appellants*, United States Court of Appeals for the Second Circuit, 8 October 2008.
[206] 'Chevron Says Victim of Unfair Trial in Ecuador', *Reuters*, 2 July 2007.
[207] 'Chevron Expects to Defeat Ecuador in Amazon Cleanup Litigation', *MarketWatch*, 27 March 2008.
[208] 'Chevron Calls for Dismissal of Ecuador Lawsuit', *Chevron News Release*, 8 October 2007, www.chevron.com.

International law imposes on Ecuador, at a very minimum, an obligation to maintain and make available to aliens such as Chevron a fair and effective system of justice. A failure of this universal obligation to provide a capable and impartial judiciary results in a denial of justice, an international violation by a State's judiciary for which the State is held responsible. If this Court continues on its present, unjust path and ultimately issues a final judgment in the Plaintiffs' favor, Chevron will take the necessary steps to seek redress against Ecuador under international law.[209]

It goes on to state that the lawsuit, 'as it has transpired, constitutes a flagrant and grotesque violation of Ecuadorian law, a farce of the judicial system, as well as a violation of the most basic and fundamental principles of universal justice to which Chevron is entitled'.[210]

A lawyer for the plaintiffs in the class action suit, Alejandro Ponce, highlights: 'It is ironic that Chevron, which argued in New York for over a decade that this trial should be held in Ecuador, is now trying to avoid responsibility by questioning the fairness of the trial here.'[211] Another lawyer for the plaintiffs, Steven Donzinger, has pointed out that when the case was in New York, Chevron filed ten separate expert affidavits praising Ecuador's courts as impartial and transparent.[212]

Given the state of the contract-based arbitration, an important question that arises is whether the company would have access to arbitration for their claim of denial of justice through the US-Ecuador BIT, signed in 1993 and in force as of 1997.[213] According to the terms of the BIT, it applies only to 'investments existing at the time of entry into force as well as to investments made or acquired thereafter'.[214] As already mentioned, Texaco left Ecuador in 1992, and even the settlement agreement on remediation was signed before 1997. However, in December 2008 an UNCITRAL-based arbitral tribunal, administered by the Permanent Court of Arbitration in The Hague, found that it had jurisdiction over a US$1.6 billion BIT-claim filed by Chevron against Ecuador.[215] Although the claim relates primarily

---

[209] English translation of the original Spanish petition: 46, www.texaco.com/sitelets/ecuador.

[210] *Ibid*: 46–7.

[211] 'Chevron Increasingly Desperate in $6 Billion Environmental Lawsuit in Amazon Rainforest: Chevron Seeks to Avoid Judgment it Requested in 2002', *Amazon Watch News Release*, 2 July 2007, www.amazonwatch.org.

[212] 'Chevron Is to Blame for Ecuador's Oil Pollution', *The Wall Street Journal*, 26 April 2008.

[213] Treaty between the United States of America and the Republic of Ecuador Concerning the Encouragement and Reciprocal Protection of Investment, 27 August 1993, Washington, DC.

[214] *Ibid*: Art. XII.1.

[215] 'Tribunal to Hear Chevron's Claim that Ecuador Lacks Judicial Independence', *Investment Arbitration Reporter*, 11 December 2008.

to the company's difficulties in resolving a number of unrelated contract disputes in the Ecuadorian courts, it is a denial of justice case and there are also numerous connections to the environmental lawsuit. It is worth noting that the company relies in part on the 'environmental remediation work related to TexPet's operations that continued into 1998', as the basis for its claim that it continued to have investments in the country after the entry into force of the US-Ecuador BIT. For its part, Ecuador views the arbitration as a ploy, designed in part to affect the outcome of the class action lawsuit:

> Consistent with its original strategy of using the underlying seven lawsuits as "bargaining chips" in negotiations, Chevron has now found a new use for them. Having prevailed in persuading the courts of the United States to dismiss a lawsuit brought by Ecuadorian citizens for environmental damage they suffered as a result of Chevron's oil drilling activities on the very basis that the Ecuadorian courts were an adequate forum Chevron now faces the prospect of liability in the resurrection of that lawsuit in Ecuador. To a large extent, the present claim is merely a component of Chevron's broader litigation strategy to undermine any judgment of its liability that may emerge in that case by an award in this case condemning the Ecuadorian court system.[216]

8.2.3   Analysis

This section assesses the role that the threat of arbitration played in the outcome of each conflict. It also compares the factors that contributed to the efficacy of the threat of arbitration in each case.

8.2.3.1   The threat of arbitration

In these cases the threat of arbitration must be assessed by two different sets of actors: judges and government officials.

In the Buyat Bay case, the Indonesian judge was faced with the prospect of the state being taken to arbitration if he did not dismiss the civil suit against the company. However, it cannot be stated definitively that the judge based his decision on the threat of arbitration. It is possible that the judge found Newmont's legal argument (that arbitration was the proper forum) to be sound, even though NGOs and officials from the Environment Ministry were of the opinion that it was not. In the ChevronTexaco case there does not appear to be any evidence, as of

---

[216] Qtd in *Chevron Corporation and Texaco Petroleum Corporation v. The Republic of Ecuador,* Interim Award, 1 December 2008: 18.

yet, that threats from the company to sue Ecuador for denial of justice have impeded the progress of the class action case against the company. However, the threat has only very recently become more palpable, with an UNCITRAL tribunal accepting jurisdiction over Chevron's denial of justice claims in several contract disputes.

As for the assessment of threats to arbitrate by government officials, it should be emphasized that the Indonesian government was not faced with a typical threat of arbitration in the Buyat Bay case, as the company was not seeking damages. The government was given the option to pursue its liability case in arbitration, but chose instead to settle. In the ChevronTexaco case, government officials took the threat of arbitration very seriously. However, rather than settling with the company or submitting to arbitration, the government initiated court proceedings in the State of New York. The government was successful in blocking the arbitration in this instance, but it is important to recognize that its victory was based on technicalities; the status of the contract and the absence of an applicable BIT or regional agreement barred ChevronTexaco from arbitration. Had there been a contract signed by both parties, or had their been an IIA in place at the time of investment, the outcome of the conflict could have been quite different.

8.2.3.2   Factors that contributed to the efficacy of the threat

In these cases, concerns about the cost of compensating investors were not significant. In the Buyat Bay case it was the government that was seeking compensation, thus at most it would have been concerned with the cost of arbitration and the potential that it would have to pay Newmont's legal fees if suffered a defeat. Similarly, the Ecuadorian government could not stop or interfere with the class action lawsuit against ChevronTexaco, and would have likely faced a comparable compensation claim in either a settlement or an arbitration (i.e., it would be based on the amount that ChevronTexaco was found liable for in the lawsuit). Hence, the potency of the threat was not enhanced by financial concerns.

In terms of reputational concerns, the story is less clear-cut than in the cases related to environmental policy. In the Buyat Bay case, it was the government that took the initiative to take Newmont to court in both civil and criminal proceedings. This move, in itself, might appear to negate any interest by the government in achieving an investor-friendly reputation. In particular, many reports on the criminal proceedings suggested that investors were closely watching the case, and the chairman of the Indonesian Mining Association stated that a guilty verdict would have sent a

negative message to all investors.[217] However, when one recognizes that
it was not the Indonesian government as a whole but rather the Ministry
of Environment that took the case to court, then it becomes clear that
domestic political factors explain the apparent incongruity. The Ministry
of Environment is chiefly concerned with its own mandate, which does
not involve the attraction of foreign investment, but this does not mean
that other government departments and ministries do not prioritize this
issue.

The Government of Ecuador arguably had no control over the reputational effect of the class action lawsuit against ChevronTexaco, as it was
brought to the local courts by individuals. Thus, regardless of whether
the government was concerned with the implications of the lawsuit for its
reputation with investors, there is very little that it could do to remedy the
situation except to offer to pay the company compensation in the event
of a ruling in favour of the plaintiffs. However, at this point the government does not appear to be particularly interested in an investor-friendly
image, but instead is aligning with other leftist governments in Latin America who have rebelled against neo-liberal economic policies (see Section
9.2.1). Thus, the decision of the government to fight Chevron's move to
arbitrate is unsurprising in this regard.

In addition to the reputational concerns of governments, one could also
hypothesize that the judges in each case have concerns about their own
reputations and about the reputation of the country's judicial system as
a whole. To have a ruling criticized by a respected group of international
arbitrators could be embarrassing and damaging for a judge's career. To
have a proceeding deemed a denial of justice could harm the reputation of
the entire court system of a country. Hence, it is possible that the judges
in each case might have been influenced by such concerns.

Finally, the domestic politics in each case should be emphasized. The
Ecuadorian government was unified in its opposition to arbitration proceedings, and the President even openly supported the plaintiffs in the
lawsuit against ChevronTexaco. This no doubt limited the efficacy of the
threat to arbitrate. In contrast, the divisions in the Indonesian government
likely contributed to the decision to settle with Newmont. The original
case in the domestic courts was brought by the Ministry of Environment.
The Ministry of Mines was not in favour of litigating against Newmont,
but evidently it cannot stop the Ministry of Environment from launching

[217] 'Newmont Boss Could Face Three Years for Pollution', *The Jakarta Post*, 11 November
2006; 'Indonesian Court Acquits Newmont, Ness of Pollution', *Bloomberg*, 24 April 2007.

a case in the local courts. However, the arbitration process is significantly different, and cannot be initiated by an individual ministry unless it has the support of the executive.

8.2.3.3 Alternative scenarios

As noted above, it is possible that the threat of arbitration was not a motivating factor for the Indonesian judge to dismiss the case against Newmont: he may have simply agreed with the legal argument. However, it is clear that the institution of investment protection was central in this case. While the Buyat Bay civil lawsuit may have eventually been either dismissed or amicably settled for any number of reasons, the case would not have been dismissed for the reason that the domestic courts were an incorrect forum had there not been a CoW which stipulated that all disputes should be settled in arbitration. Even if corruption was involved, the judge would not have been able to employ his particular reasoning for the dismissal in the absence of a CoW.

As for the Ecuadorian case, it appears that the outcome in this case is a result of the absence of investment protection. It is interesting to consider what might have happened if the JOA had been applicable or if the US-Ecuador BIT had been in force. In the case of the contract being valid, the dispute would have ended up in the AAA, an arbitral body with much less transparency than ICSID and Ecuador could have been held liable for any compensation awarded against Chevron.

8.3 Implications for environmental governance

While the concerns over tribunal decisions made in the investor-state disputes discussed in the previous chapter are merited, given the weak bargaining position of many states, negotiated outcomes to conflicts may be as, or even more, undesirable from an environmental policy perspective. Furthermore, as threats of arbitration are very difficult to track and may never even be made known to the public, they represent, as MacArthur puts it, a 'more insidious danger'.[218]

In some of the cases discussed in this chapter, governments did not bow to pressure to settle or arbitrate (e.g., Costa Rica in the Harken case) or they actively fought arbitration proceedings in the courts (e.g., Ecuador in the ChevronTexaco case). However, the states in these cases were arguably successful because the investors were not actually protected by contracts

---

[218] MacArthur 2003: 945.

or treaties. This suggests that similar cases could emerge under different circumstances with much more significant implications.

8.3.1   Maintenance of the status quo

Several of the cases in this chapter illustrate that, in addition to fearing industrial flight as the traditional regulatory chill hypothesis (see Section 2.2.2) assumes, governments maintain the status quo in environmental regulation out of fear of being sued by foreign investors in investment arbitration, and these two fears are tightly intermingled.[219] The main factors that contribute to regulatory chill appear to be the level of government concern about the country's reputation with investors, the potential cost of compensating investors, and prior negative experience in arbitration.

Some observers question the logic of applying the regulatory chill hypothesis to investment arbitration. Coe and Rubins, for example, point out that the hypothesis makes assumptions about the level of awareness that regulators have on issues of international law, which they suggest is likely to be limited.[220] The argument is that if regulators are not aware of the ramifications of their actions, it will not be possible for their behaviour to be affected. While Coe and Rubins are correct in assuming that many environmental regulators would be unaware of the commitments made in IIAs and foreign investment contracts (as these agreements are generally negotiated by separate ministries), this argument ignores the fact that regulators can be *made aware* of the relevant points of international investment law by investors and their lawyers when it is in their interests to do so. In fact, *a lack of knowledge* about the specificities of investment law makes the threat of arbitration all the more potent, because regulators will be less likely to recognize when an investor is bluffing.

Another aspect of the regulatory chill hypothesis that Coe and Rubins critique is the notion that concerns about compensation will prevent states from producing or enforcing regulation:

> While the apprehension of international liability may prompt reflection and careful tailoring of means to ends, it seems less likely to cause abandonment of legislation at the heart of a government's mandate. Indeed, to the extent a government *has the machinery* to defend such claims, it might well expect victory, since expropriation claims often fail.[221]

---

[219] See also Mann 2001: 34; Neumayer 2001a: 87; Gray 2002: 311; Cosbey *et al.* 2004.
[220] Coe and Rubins 2005: 599.   [221] *Ibid*, emphasis added.

This statement seems to have been written with developed countries in mind; these countries would have little difficulty in making compensation payments, and certainly possess the 'machinery' to defend claims. However, it is a different story for developing countries. Although threats of investment arbitration have occurred in developed states,[222] such threats are likely to be a much greater problem in developing countries where there is less willingness to devote scarce resources to engage in arbitration.[223] Furthermore, the statement that a government 'might well expect victory' assumes an awareness of the international jurisprudence, which is in contradiction to the earlier statement that regulators will most likely be unaware of the nuances of international law. This statement also fails to acknowledge that the jurisprudence in the area is small and inconsistent, and this creates uncertainty rather than the confidence implied by Coe and Rubins.

It is not suggested here that regulatory chill occurs in all cases. At the other end of the spectrum, governments arguably might use the existence of commitments to investment protection as an excuse for the maintenance of the status quo in environmental policy. For example, Allee and Huth have argued that political leaders 'will seek legal dispute settlement in situations where they anticipate sizeable domestic political costs should they attempt to settle a dispute through the making of bilateral, negotiated concessions'.[224] The authors refer to this as 'political cover'. Through political cover, a leader can use the existence of an international constraint as a defence for a politically unpalatable position. In a similar vein, Brewster has assessed how international constraints can benefit certain divisions of government, resulting in a shift of power (e.g., from the legislature to the executive) and a change in the results of the domestic political process.[225] Her insights could equally apply to different sectors of government (see further below). In summary, a government (or part of a government) could use the spectre of international arbitration as political cover for a controversial decision – an 'our hands are tied', 'we can't afford to be sued' argument. The existence of a stability promise in a foreign investment contract with binding arbitration clauses could be used quite effectively in this way, particularly if a previous government was responsible for the negotiation and signing of the contract.

---

[222] For example, Schneiderman 2001: 524, claims that the Government of Canada has received threats to arbitrate from investors in relation to a public auto insurance plan, proposals on cigarette packaging, and the cancellation of plans to privatize an airport. He expands on these cases in Schneiderman 2008. See also Section 7.1.1.

[223] Romano 2002: 552.   [224] Allee and Huth 2006: 219.   [225] Brewster 2006: 283.

Discerning when a government is being genuinely constrained by a commitment to investment protection (regulatory chill), and when it is instead using that commitment as a convenient defence for a politically unpalatable position (political cover), is difficult in practice. For example, in the Ghanaian case it initially appeared that the government had experienced regulatory chill, until it subsequently began to offer new contracts in forest reserves. In either case, the end result remains negative from the perspective of environmental policy development.

8.3.2   Domestic political divides

While the cases in the previous chapter indicated that investment arbitration can create tension between different levels of government (e.g., federal v. provincial or municipal), the cases in this chapter illustrate that the complex relations between departments and ministries within a level of government are also affected by the institution of investment protection and may partially determine the response of governments to threats of arbitration.

Each ministry, agency, or even department within a ministry, may have an agenda that is particular to its mandate. It is rare that the separate interests of various branches of government are coordinated with one another to guarantee the perfect compatibility of these agendas.[226] In the context of investment protection, contracts and IIAs are not likely to be negotiated by the ministries/agencies that make the social and environmental policies which are affected by them. While environmental ministries may seek to be progressive in policy development and may seek to redress environmental harm through court action, it may be in the interests of other ministries (mining, economic, foreign, etc.) to ensure the maintenance of the status quo in order to secure a friendly investment climate.

Ministries involved in investment and economic development are likely to hold a stronger position in the government hierarchy than environmental ones, and the existence of a strong institution for investment protection may serve to reinforce or even exacerbate these power structures. With their position 'backed-up' by a strong international enforcement mechanism, these interest groups have an advantage over environmental ministries, which can only point to the existence of vague and unenforceable commitments in multilateral environmental agreements. Furthermore, savvy foreign investors can strategically exploit these domestic divides by

---

[226] Leon and Terry 2006: 71.

targeting their lobbying efforts at specific ministries, departments and agencies which are most likely to support them.[227]

8.3.3   Justice denied?

Several of the cases in this chapter, particularly the final two, illustrate how international arbitration can affect domestic judicial processes.

In the Buyat Bay case, the existence of a contract with an arbitration clause determined the outcome of the civil court proceedings, despite the fact that the case related to a breach of Indonesia's national environmental law rather than a breach of contract. As mentioned previously, a CoW specifies the environmental obligations of the company in general terms; basically the company must comply with laws and regulations. Thus, if an arbitration panel were expected to rule on whether Newmont should be found liable for environmental damage in Buyat Bay, they would have to look to, and interpret, Indonesian environmental law. This is a significant outcome, regardless of what one makes of the merits of the Ministry of Environment's case against Newmont. Aside from the fact that arbitrators are generally experts in investment and commercial law rather than environmental law (let alone the specific environmental law of Indonesia) one also has to consider the additional consequences of this shift from domestic courts and to international arbitration: it entails significant costs for states and is customarily non-transparent and closed to non-disputing parties.

The Ecuador case also has several important implications. The initial conflict over who (ChevronTexaco or Petroecuador) was liable for the pollution in the Ecuadorian Amazon was based on a contract and is perhaps less broadly applicable to other situations. However, the later claims of 'lack of due process' and 'denial of justice' could have significant implications for environmental liability cases in many developing countries. While there have been extensive discussions in the literature about foreign direct liability and the problem of *forum non conveniens*, there does not appear to have been significant attention paid to the threat of BITs and other IIAs to the pursuit of environmental liability claims in the host state.

While courts in developing countries are often claimed to be biased and unreliable, it is worth noting that developed country courts have not escaped the scrutiny of arbitral tribunals. In this respect, two NAFTA cases that were not discussed in the previous chapter (as they did not

---

[227] *Ibid.*

directly relate to environmental regulation) are worth mentioning. In the *Mondev* case, a Canadian real-estate development corporation submitted a claim based in part on a decision by the Supreme Judicial Court of Massachusetts.[228] Although the *Mondev* tribunal dismissed the investor's claims on the merits, Amirfar and Dreyer suggest that 'its recognition that liability may result from a breakdown of judicial function is itself notable'.[229] In the Loewen case, a Canadian investor brought a suit against the US based on the conduct and verdict of a Mississippi State Court.[230] The *Loewen* tribunal determined that it did not have jurisdiction over the dispute because the investor had not exhausted local remedies. While under NAFTA there is no general requirement to exhaust local remedies, it was determined by the tribunal that in cases where the measure concerned is a ruling of a lower court, the higher courts must have an opportunity to review the case before it can be elevated to international arbitration. Despite the fact that the *Loewen* tribunal did not make a decision on the merits of the case, they did express their opinion that, had domestic remedies been exhausted, they would have had competence to review the Mississippi court's actions and likely would have found them in breach of NAFTA. Hill suggests that 'the threat to domestic sovereignty presented by *Loewen* is difficult to overstate'.[231]

Other arbitral tribunals outside of NAFTA have also found states responsible for the losses suffered by foreign investors because they found domestic court decisions to amount to a denial of justice.[232] Although the standard of denial of justice should be difficult to meet, it can be hypothesized that the threat of arbitration may nevertheless influence a state, or indeed a court, leading to *judicial chill*. This can also be seen as a denial of justice; not for corporations, but for vulnerable populations that are directly affected by environmental degradation.

---

[228] *Mondev International Ltd* v. *United States of America*, ICSID Case No. ARB(AF)/99/2, Award, 11 October 2002, www.state.gov. Reproduced in 42 ILM (2003): 85.

[229] Amirfar and Dreyer 2007: 44.

[230] *The Loewen Group, Inc. and Raymond L. Loewen* v. *United States of America*, ICSID Case No. ARB(AF)/98/3, Award, 26 June 2003, www.state.gov. Reproduced in 42 ILM (2003): 811.

[231] Hill 2006: 168.   [232] Cheng 2005: 508–9.

9

Conclusions

Traditionally, the resolution of conflicts between investors and governments has been kept largely within the purview of the political and judicial organs of the state. With the advent of the institution of investment protection, and with the expansion of substantive norms and rules of this institution to cover aspects of environmental protection, elements of environmental governance have arguably been *expropriated* by international arbitral tribunals. While the term expropriation is most commonly associated with the actions of states, its plain meaning refers to any action to deprive another of a possession (including intangibles such as rights or ideas).[1] To expropriate is to annex, to appropriate, to commandeer, to confiscate, to dispossess, to sequester, to take, or to take over.[2] Arbitral tribunals have expropriated the authority to determine when an environmental policy or court decision is legitimate. This is not necessarily a role that was freely bestowed upon arbitrators; in fact, many observers suggest that at least some of the effects of the institution of investment protection were unintended and unanticipated by states.

This chapter summarizes the main problems with the institution of investment protection and explores the consequences of the expropriation of environmental governance for policy-makers and the public. Additionally, the backlash to the institution that is developing in some parts of the world is reviewed. The chapter concludes with potential options for moving forward.

9.1 The bigger picture

Some observers suggest that the concerns of environmentalists over investment arbitration are unnecessarily alarmist, and liken them to those of

---

[1] 'Expropriation', *Merriam-Webster Online Dictionary*, www.merriam-webster.com/dictionary.
[2] *Roget's New Millennium Thesaurus*, first edn, 2007.

Chicken Little, who declared that the sky was falling when it was not.[3] By focusing on individual cases and arguing either that the tribunal made a *good decision* or that the dispute was *not really about the environment*, these observers tend to miss the bigger picture. As Sornarajah has pointed out in the context of the trade regime, the fact that a decision in a given case is supportable from an environmental perspective is immaterial: 'The point is whether the dispute was one which should have been disposed of by a trade tribunal when it raised issues which transcended trade matters and implicated interests of concern to the international community at large.'[4] A *fortiori*, this concern exists with regard to the institution of investment protection where issues of accountability are manifold. Arbitrators in the WTO system are not chosen by the parties to the dispute and cannot act as the legal representation for the parties in other arbitral proceedings. Furthermore, in the trade regime, disputes can only be brought by states who bear an equal risk of having disputes brought against themselves, unlike the one-way system of investment arbitration, in which only states are punished and private actors rewarded.

It is argued here that the most critical problem with the institution of investment protection is that it lacks balance. In fact, it is suggested in this section that the institution of investment protection actually produces or exacerbates power differences between certain individuals and groups both within a state and in the international context.[5] There are several important consequences of this for policy-makers and the broader public.

9.1.1   The asymmetry of investment protection

The asymmetry of investment protection is most evident in the comparison of the benefits and consequences of the institution for:

(i) foreign investors and states;
(ii) foreign investors and 'everyone else';
(iii) arbitral tribunals and governments;
(iv) national and lower levels of government within a state;

---

[3] Laird 2001; Lilley 2002: 728. See also Behrens 2007: 178, who notes that the 'popular fears that host states who have tied their hands by investment protection treaties might be limited to promote, e.g., environmental protection only at the cost of compensating foreign investors, are entirely unjustified'.

[4] Sornarajah 2002: 99.

[5] For an alternative view of the asymmetries of investment arbitration, see Wälde 2007: 54–67.

(v) economic and environmental ministries within a state; and
(vi) developed and developing countries.

9.1.1.1   Foreign investors and states

The first asymmetry produced, that between foreign investors and states, concerns an imbalance between rights and obligations. In this study, the numerous IIAs, foreign investment contracts and the system of investment arbitration have been classified as comprising the institution of *investment protection* because this title conveys the fundamental one-sidedness of *protecting* investors but not *obliging* them to take on any responsibilities, and conversely *obliging* states to behave in a given manner, but not *protecting* them from harm that an investor may cause. This asymmetry is often justified as a means to redress the existing imbalance between the power of states and the power of investors. In this view, the state as 'leviathan' can easily crush the unsuspecting foreign investor. However, in reality the picture is quite dramatically different; over one-third of the world's 100 largest economies are corporations, not states.

Wälde argues that large corporations rarely use investment arbitration because they don't need to (i.e., they have leverage to negotiate and expertise in the management of risks) and they don't want to (i.e. because it may poison their relations with host states).[6] However, he does admit that arbitration can be useful as a 'bargaining card' for TNCs. The fact that many large TNCs may only use investment protection as a bargaining card does not eliminate this asymmetry. Indeed, the cases discussed in this study have shown that the *threat* of arbitration can be just as or even more, obstructive to policy development than its *actual use*. Arbitration is expensive, but just initiating a claim, or threatening to do so, costs very little.

9.1.1.2   Foreign investors and everyone else

The second fundamental asymmetry that is brought about by investment protection occurs between foreign investors and everyone else, including domestic investors. Domestic investors are not offered the same level of protection as foreign investors who are entitled to fair and equitable and most-favoured-nation treatment in addition to national treatment. Domestic investors are also not offered contracts with stabilization clauses,

---

[6] Wälde 2007: 62.

which arguably could give foreign investors a marked competitive advantage. Finally, domestic investors are not provided with access to international arbitration in the event of a conflict.[7] Thus, for all the emphasis on non-discrimination, the institution of investment protection clearly discriminates against domestic investors in favour of foreign ones. Again, the arguments to justify this, that domestic investors are familiar with the local court system and will therefore fare better in it, or that domestic investors are more likely to curry favour with their own government, and in any case have the right to vote in general elections, are not particularly convincing. Xenophobia may certainly work against foreign corporations, but domestic companies also face their own challenges and are generally smaller and less powerful than TNCs.

However, it is not only domestic investors who are disenfranchised in international law. Even more significant are the indigenous peoples, local communities and other individuals who suffer human rights abuses (including the denial of the right to a healthy environment) at the hands of either a state or a corporation but lack the necessary means to redress the wrongs that are committed against them. Human rights treaties are not nearly as prevalent as IIAs, are much more difficult for individuals to access, require the exhaustion of local remedies, and do not hold non-state actors accountable for violations.[8] While it is not suggested here that the institution of investment protection should be designed to redress all wrongs done to all peoples, a greater balance – achieved either through a strengthening of the rights of others or a reduction of the rights of investors – would contribute to the maintenance of a stable international order. The current asymmetry leaves open the question of why one class of individuals is singled out for preferential treatment. Furthermore, if the institution of investment protection results in regulatory or judicial chill, or decreases the efficiency and effectiveness of environmental regulation, then it is not only that foreign investors are given more favourable treatment, it is that this treatment is given *at the expense* of the well-being of others.

9.1.1.3   Arbitral tribunals and governments

A third asymmetry exists in what is expected of arbitral tribunals and of governments in the institution of investment protection. It has frequently been argued that the obligations of states under the institution of

---

[7] However, it is worth noting that domestic investors at times have changed their nationality in order to bring a claim as a foreign investor against their previous home state. See Subedi 2008: 183.

[8] Kriebaum 2007: 186; Sornarajah 1997: 134.

investment protection are the 'ingredients of good governance'.[9] Such an analysis is appealing. Who, after all, can argue with the need for greater accountability and transparency in governance? However, a more critical evaluation reveals that the ingredients of good governance are *selectively applied* in the institution of investment protection. In particular, it does not appear that the principles of transparency, accountability and participation must apply in contexts that would be disadvantageous to investors, such as in the negotiation of foreign investment contracts or, crucially, in the resolution of disputes.

Van Harten points out that governing is an inherently complex and contentious activity:

> Governments are often required to make difficult and controversial decisions when exercising public authority and their policy choices may in some cases appear to misapprehend facts, apply misguided theories, emphasize wrong-headed priorities, or create more problems than they solve. This is in many ways inherent to the dilemmas of governing.[10]

It is also the case that, as governors themselves, arbitrators make mistakes, interpret the rules and norms of investment protection in controversial ways, and apply theories about international law that are not universally accepted. However, while states are to be held accountable to tribunals, it would appear that arbitrators are accountable to no one. While states must govern in a transparent and predictable manner, tribunals may operate behind closed doors and do not have to ensure that their decisions are consistent with those made in substantively similar cases.

9.1.1.4   Levels and sectors of government within a state

The fourth and fifth asymmetries that are produced, or perhaps more accurately *exacerbated*, by the institution of investment protection occur between different levels and sectors of governance within a state. The national government representatives that negotiate foreign investment contracts and IIAs are unlikely to be knowledgeable on environmental issues or sympathetic to the concerns of environmental agencies and ministries.[11] Most environmental regulators will be unaware of the implications of these agreements until a conflict arises. The already complex balance of power that exists between various levels and sectors of governance

---

[9] Dolzer 2005: 972. See also Wälde 2004: 475; Gutbrod and Hindelang 2006: 82; ILA International Law on Foreign Investment Committee 2006: 16; Newcombe 2007a: 393; Schill 2007: 285.

[10] Van Harten 2007a: 89.   [11] Tabb 2004: 27.

is upset by the the investment arbitration system that targets one level (national) and reinforces the power of one sector (economic/industrial).

While state, provincial and municipal levels of government are often accorded a substantial degree of competence over environmental matters, and although decentralization is a process occurring in many developing countries, only national governments have standing in international law. This creates difficulties for both upper and lower levels of government. Although they are uninvolved in the negotiations of foreign investment contracts and IIAs, unaware of the policy implications of these agreements, and potentially unable to participate in arbitration, lower levels of government may be pushed to reverse policies or to pay compensation to foreign investors who claim breach of treaty or contract. Despite the potential negative implications for multilevel governance, it must also be acknowledged that it is understandable that national governments are concerned about being held accountable in international arbitration for the actions of lower levels of government over which they may have little control.

In addition to creating tension between levels of governance, conflicts with investors may also result in ministries and agencies being pitted against one another. A savvy foreign investor will exploit such divisions to his advantage. The existence of the institution of investment protection gives the investor and his government supporters a distinct advantage over the opposition; even if environmental regulators are well advised on the nuances of investment law, they are provided with little certainty that their policies will stand up under the scrutiny of an arbitral tribunal. Without strong and enforceable international agreements on the environment or on corporate conduct, environmental regulators are left with no comparable clout to bolster their position and must rely solely on public pressure and NGOs for support.

9.1.1.5 Developed and developing countries

The final, and perhaps most critical, asymmetry relates to the implications of the institution of investment protection for developed and for developing countries. While arguably such asymmetry will exist in any international arrangement involving developed and developing countries, it is much more conspicuous in IIAs. This is particularly true for those IIAs that are negotiated bilaterally, leaving developing countries in the weakest possible bargaining position.[12]

---

[12] Ekwueme 2006: 170–1.

Developing countries are far more likely to face conflicts with investors over environmental issues than are developed countries for several reasons. First, environmental policy is more likely to *change* in developing countries. Continuous change is an integral part of environmental governance in any country, but it is commonly accepted that developing countries, in general, have a lower base-line of environmental regulation. As a result, there is a greater likelihood of rapid, and possibly radical, regulatory change in these countries, as awareness increases and as governments are asked by the international community to 'catch up' with developed country standards. At the same time, it has been emphasized by experts that it is change in policy, rather than its absolute level, that is the most significant problem for investors. Thus, change in policy is likely to lead to conflict. A statement by a Chilean trade official exemplifies this predicament:

> Chile is a country where probably there will be quite a lot more regulatory changes in the future. There is still a lot of work to be done in that area, and to expose ourselves to the kind of demands by U.S. investors like what has happened with NAFTA, where the investors say regulatory changes have been tantamount to indirect expropriation and have demanded huge compensation involving many millions of dollars, well that would be very difficult for Chile.[13]

Secondly, there is less policy *coherence* in developing countries, meaning that effective communication between different ministries and different levels of government is often lacking. Policy incoherence may certainly also exist in developed countries, but it is commonly acknowledged that government agencies in developing countries are especially underfunded and overstretched, particularly in the environmental sector. Developing countries that are undergoing a process of decentralization are also likely to experience a number of glitches (governance gaps and overlaps) before the process of multilevel governance starts running smoothly. Policy incoherence inevitably leads to conflict. If an investor's 'legitimate expectations' are based on the assurances of one governing body, which has not consulted with other relevant bodies, then these expectations are unlikely to be met.

Thirdly, there is a higher instance of *corruption* in developing countries. Corruption can result in investors receiving very favourable treatment, particularly under foreign investment contracts that are negotiated in the absence of transparency. The country is subsequently locked into this

---

[13] Qtd in Been and Beauvais 2003: 126.

standard of treatment by the institution of investment protection, even if a new (less corrupt) government is elected. Corruption, or even the perception of corruption, can also inflame public hostility to investment projects, which may lead to public protests and, subsequently, conflicts between the investor and the host state.

Finally, the *courts* in developing countries are less respected and trusted by the international community. This is arguably the primary justification for the development of international investment arbitration in the first place. As a result, claims brought against foreign investors in domestic courts, for environmental liability for example, are more likely to be challenged in investment arbitration for a lack of due process or denial of justice.

In addition to the fact that developing countries are expected to be confronted with more conflicts related to the environment, it is also argued here that it is more probable that these conflicts will be resolved in investment arbitration, or that their resolution will be influenced by the threat of arbitration. Because they are more desperate for capital, developing countries make more *commitments* to investment protection, in the hopes that it will foster increased FDI flows. Furthermore, these commitments are categorical, while developed country commitments are illusory so long as IIAs are only negotiated on the basis of asymmetric flows of FDI. In this respect, NAFTA is an anomaly. Developing countries are also more likely to be influenced by the threat of arbitration because of concerns about the *cost* of the arbitral process, both in terms of actual financial costs of lawyer and arbitrator fees and in terms of the cost to their reputation as an investor-friendly host state. Their susceptibility to threats of arbitration is also affected by their lower technical *capacity*, which makes it more difficult for them to effectively defend themselves in arbitration. For these reasons, developing countries are also more likely to lose the cases that are brought against them by investors.

The discrepancy in the obligations of developed and developing countries under IIAs has been justified by supporters of investment protection by the fact that, in theory, developed countries already possess a 'civilized' system of law and therefore do not have to be held accountable under international law. Aside from the extreme arrogance of this claim and the lack of deference that it indicates for the special situation of developing countries, it also appears to be disproved by the fact that foreign investors appear eager to pursue arbitration claims against 'civilized' countries such as Canada and the US, in the rare instances when they *have the opportunity* to do so.

9.1.2   Consequences for policy-makers and the public

9.1.2.1   Less democratic accountability

The expansion of the institution of investment protection to the point where it may interfere with public policy development has not only taken environmental regulators unawares, it has also shocked the general public, who expect their governments to be accountable to them rather than to foreign corporations and enigmatic tribunals. Traditionally, in international law and international relations states are considered the loci of power and authority. The protection of foreign investment through international, regional and bilateral agreements and through foreign investment contracts shifts some of this power and authority to arbitral tribunals.

That arbitrators are resolving disputes of great public importance is not novel *per se*; they have had a long and significant role in the resolution of both inter-firm (commercial) and inter-state disputes. However, what is novel is the ease by which private actors, vested with international legal rights but not responsibilities, are able to directly initiate arbitration against sovereign states. Of further significance is the breadth of the investment arbitrators' jurisdiction and the elevation of dispute resolution to a governance system aimed at 'regulating the regulators'.[14]

It is acceptable in democratic countries for domestic courts to check the power of the legislature, because the judiciary is considered reasonably free from political influence.[15] On the other hand, as a governance system investment arbitration is fundamentally undemocratic and its neutrality is questionable. The procedural rules and norms of investment protection were established to deal with commercial disputes where confidentiality was considered paramount, and consistency irrelevant. Such a system is inappropriate when states are involved in disputes and especially when sensitive issues of public policy, such as environmental regulation, are at stake. How can a system, that is itself experiencing a 'legitimacy crisis', possibly be suited to evaluating the legitimacy of decisions made by democratically elected governments and domestic courts? Supporters may argue that the system of investment arbitration is, despite having existed for decades, still in its infancy (or at most early childhood) given that it has only been frequently put to use in the last ten to fifteen years. However, while some procedural flaws may be eliminated with time, and while the reasoning of tribunals may become more nuanced with the increased scrutiny that awards are likely to receive, a 'wait and see' attitude is cold

---

[14] Head 2007: 515.   [15] Van Harten 2007a: 168.

comfort for states faced with the prospect of (numerous) economically significant awards being decided against them.

While there has been considerable focus on the lack of transparency and participation in the arbitration process in this study, it must also be emphasized that these elements are absent or limited in other areas as well. As noted in Chapter 5, foreign investment contracts are frequently negotiated and signed without the involvement of parliament or the disclosure of the agreement to the public. In addition to being negotiated in fundamentally undemocratic ways, IIAs and foreign investment contracts also bind governments for long periods of time. Hence, the ministries that sign these agreements are locking in other ministries and future governments to the institution of investment protection. Governments may therefore be legitimately constrained in their responses to democratic demands. However, commitments to investment protection also give governments a way to avoid domestic political backlash to unpopular decisions. The ability of governments to utilize commitments to investment protection as political cover, which is enhanced when the details of commitments are not publicly disclosed from the outset, arguably reduces the democratic accountability of government decisions.

9.1.2.2 Less certainty for regulators

While it is certainly not possible to predict with perfect accuracy the outcome of dispute resolution in any context – if it were, we would not need judges – uncertainty in the system of investment arbitration is particularly pronounced. The regulative rules and norms of investment protection are ambiguous and vary in their specific wording from treaty to treaty and contract to contract. When arbitral tribunals attempt to throw light upon the meaning of these rules and norms, their interpretations are controversial and inconsistent. Transparency is increasing, but confidentiality is still ubiquitous, making it more difficult for states to evaluate how disputes have been treated in arbitration. Furthermore, states may not even be aware when an investor is actually protected by an IIA, as opposed to when a threat of arbitration is a bluff. While foreign investment contracts are made directly with a specific investor, regarding a specific project, IIAs cover a vast number of unknown potential investors. With mergers, frequent changes in ownership, and TNCs able to relocate to take advantage of 'flags of convenience', states may be understandably uncertain about the validity of investor claims.

As a result of decreased certainty, a substantial portion of the risk that is associated with investing abroad, particularly in developing countries, has been shifted to regulators. Of course, investors cannot be certain that they will succeed in arbitration or that, if they are successful, the level of compensation will be fair and promptly paid. Arbitration is also risky for investors who wish to continue operating in a specific country, or region: just as governments can acquire a bad reputation with investors, so too can investors acquire a bad reputation with governments. However, clearly the risks of investing have been diminished. Risks for foreign investors are also minimized by investment insurance and other mechanisms. On the other hand, states that already risk the loss of resources (with often unfair returns), and serious environmental harm, now additionally risk being sued in international arbitration. When the outcome of arbitration is uncertain, states that are faced with a threat of arbitration are more likely to settle, often at the expense of public policy.

9.1.2.3   Less (effective) environmental regulation

Environmental regulators appear to be particularly susceptible to conflicts with investors because environmental standards do, and must, constantly change and evolve, and because the implementation of environmental policy often involves significant costs. The institution of investment protection does not categorically reject the right of states to regulate investment for the protection of the environment, and in fact, some IIAs explicitly confirm this right. However, arbitral tribunals have taken on the role of deciding *how* and *when* a government should enforce this right. In the view of many tribunals, governments should only adopt policies that are the *least inconsistent* with investment protection, that have been developed through a process that is *predictable* and *transparent*, and that are supported by a substantial amount of *scientific evidence*. These criteria are not universally accepted amongst arbitrators, but governments that do not follow this formula risk being disciplined in arbitration.

Additionally, investment protection, and stabilization clauses in particular, may limit the number of tools in the 'policy toolbox'. For example, a fiscal stabilization clause in a foreign investment contract could preclude the use of a market mechanism to tackle environmental pollution. If investment protection limits the range of instruments available to regulators, then this may in turn result in a reduction of the effectiveness or efficiency of the policies produced.

Finally, in addition to directly castigating states, arbitrators also *influence* regulators and judges. Just as any good judicial system will *prevent* as well as *punish* crime, the system of investment arbitration dissuades regulatory or judicial misconduct by states. The problem is that it may also deter policy development and court proceedings that are in the interests of the public good. Environmental ministries, agencies and even domestic courts may be relinquishing some degree of responsibility for the protection of the environment out of fear that their policies and decisions will be challenged in arbitration (regulatory and judicial chill). Those wishing to maintain the status quo in environmental policy, whether it be investors or non-environmental government agencies, can exploit these fears to their advantage.

9.1.2.4   Compensation?

One could nevertheless conclude that the transfer of some authority to international tribunals is a 'small price, if any price at all, to pay for the numerous benefits of international trade and investment'.[16] But where is the proof of the benefits of investment protection? Establishing a causal connection between the conclusion of IIAs and increased foreign investment flows is riddled with difficulty and remains contested in the literature (see Section 3.3.1). Furthermore, any gains made by developing countries in attracting investment through IIAs will be largely at the expense of other developing countries, because the system is based on competition, and thus overall welfare will not improve even if specific flows increase.[17]

Then there is the question of the actual benefit to the host state of increased inflows of foreign investment if they do materialize. In particular, there is the issue of the value of foreign investment in the form that is promoted in IIAs and foreign investment contracts, given the fact that these agreements seem to emphasize the encouragement of foreign investment as if it were *an end in itself*, rather than a means to achieving sustainable development.[18] As argued in Chapter 2, it cannot be assumed that foreign investors will automatically contribute to sustainable development: states must retain the policy space necessary to regulate investors to ensure the achievement of this goal.

9.2   Once BITten, twice shy?

The case studies presented in this book have illustrated that a threat to arbitrate can be an effective tool for foreign investors when they are in a conflict with a host state. However, the cases also indicate that states do not uniformly capitulate to investor demands when faced with the prospect of arbitration. States challenge the jurisdiction of tribunals and they use

[16] Laird 2001: 229.   [17] Guzman 1998: 688.   [18] García-Bolívar 2005: 754.

local and foreign courts to block proceedings and to annul or prevent the enforcement of awards. They also sometimes attempt, often with the help of NGOs, to shame foreign investors in the media.

Some states have gone even further and have attempted to extricate themselves from the 'spaghetti bowl' of investment protection. This is one of the 'perils of success' for international investment law, according to van Aaken.[19] This section examines the strategies of the developing countries that have been most vocal about their disenchantment with investment protection. It also notes the weakening support for the institution amongst its traditionally most avid champions: developed countries and TNCs.

9.2.1 Opting out in the periphery

It has been argued by Werner that:

> One of the great fallacies of international relationships is a determinist belief that economic and political circumstances in fact dictate countries' policies, leaving them with no real choice. Quite to the contrary. Countries, like people, always have choices even if some are more difficult and painful than others, and countries dissatisfied with the way investment arbitration functions can *opt out* of it.[20]

In recent years, several governments have indicated that they may do just that. A significant degree of unease with the institution of investment protection has arisen in several states, largely a result of the precipitous rise in investor-state disputes. However, in some areas of the world, such as Latin America, this development also reflects broader political and ideological shifts that have taken place.

Argentina has faced more arbitration cases and awards against it than any other country in the world. It is therefore unsurprising that the government has begun to assess the options for avoiding the payment of current awards and precluding the possibility of future ones.[21] At first the government adopted a legal strategy, cancelling the national decree that authorized the submission of disputes to international arbitration and proposing a bill that would give ultimate control of cases to the national courts.[22] The country is now also adopting a diplomatic strategy and has

---

[19] van Aaken 2008.   [20] Werner 2003: 769, emphasis added.
[21] As of October 2007, awards against the country totalled US$750 million and more than thirty claims remained outstanding. See 'Argentina Seeks Diplomatic Exit From ICSID Suits', *Dow Jones Newswires*, 12 October 2007.
[22] Shan 2007: 643. See also Ryan 2008.

announced that it will request that the US, the home-state of a number of investors currently pursuing arbitration, 'formally recognize Argentina's right to declare its 2001–2 financial meltdown an emergency event that permitted it to break contracts otherwise protected by a US-Argentine investment treaty'.[23]

The government of Bolivia has announced its desire to renegotiate investment treaties with twenty-four countries, including the US, Brazil and France.[24] Bolivia is also the first country to formally withdraw from the ICSID Convention.[25] In explaining the withdrawal, the country's trade ambassador, Pablo Solon suggested that ICSID arbitration is expensive and biased against developing countries.[26] Ryan notes that 'if Bolivia is able to attract investment after withdrawing from the Washington Convention, other developing countries may follow in its wake'.[27]

The Bolivian President, Evo Morales, has certainly been encouraging his neighbours, particularly Venezuela and Ecuador, to follow suit. In a statement made at a meeting of the leaders of the three countries, Morales stated: '[We] emphatically reject the legal, media and diplomatic pressure of some multinationals that . . . resist sovereign rulings of countries, making threats and initiating suits in international arbitration'.[28] Venezuelan President Hugo Chávez has vowed to withdraw from ICSID as well as from the rest of the World Bank and the IMF.[29] Ecuador's former President Alfredo Palacio very vocally rejected arbitration in a case with a US oil company, and the US froze talks on a free trade agreement with the country as a result.[30] In May 2007, President Rafael Correa announced that he would not renew the BIT between Ecuador and the US. Ecuador's Foreign Minister said that the treaty had caused problems for the country

[23] 'Argentina Seeks Diplomatic Exit From ICSID Suits', *Dow Jones Newswires*, 12 October 2007.
[24] 'Bolivia Plans to Renegotiate Investment Protection Pacts with 24 Countries', *Forbes*, 9 May 2007.
[25] The World Bank received a written notice of denunciation of the Convention from the Republic of Bolivia on 2 May 2007. In accordance with Art. 71 of the ICSID Convention, the denunciation took effect six months after the receipt of Bolivia's notice of withdrawal (3 November 2007).
[26] 'Bolivia Will Withdraw from Dispute Panel, Solon Says', *Bloomberg*, 31 May 2007.
[27] Ryan 2008: 752.
[28] 'Latin Leftists Mull Quitting World Bank Arbitrator', *Reuters*, 30 April 2007.
[29] 'World Bank Withdrawal Latest Latin Headache for Big Oil', *MarketWatch*, 30 May 2007.
[30] 'Ecuador Prez: No Oxy Arbitration', *Prensa Latina*, 9 September 2006; 'Ecuador Rejects Arbitration Demand by Occidental', *MarketWatch*, 23 May 2006; 'US-Ecuador FTA Talks on Hold After Ecuador Cancels Occidental Contract', *Bridges Weekly Trade Digest*, 17 May 2006.

and did not respect national interests.[31] Ecuador has also terminated other BITs and in July 2009 became the second country to withdraw from the ICSID Convention.[32] Finally, Ecuador's constitution has been amended; it is now unconstitutional for the country to submit to arbitration unless it is with a Latin American citizen and in a Latin American forum.[33]

Countries in Eastern Europe and Central Asia have also been the target of numerous arbitral claims. In 2006, the Czech Republic announced its intention to terminate or renegotiate its investment agreements with other EU members as well as forty BITs with non-EU countries.[34] In November 2006, a posting on a government website reportedly stated that Uzbekistan would not recognize rulings made by international arbitral tribunals. The Constitutional Court apparently adopted an amendment to the 1994 law on foreign investment that would invalidate rulings made outside the country and without the consent of the government. The move followed a threat of arbitration from the American mining company, Newmont.[35]

9.2.2 Weakening support in the core

It is not only developing and transition countries that are increasingly concerned about arbitration. Shan argues that there has been a resurgence of the Calvo doctrine and a weakening of the neo-liberal high standard investment protection agenda even in the US.[36] At one point in the 2008 Democratic primaries, both Hillary Clinton and Barack Obama claimed that, if elected, they would renegotiate NAFTA. At a debate in February, Clinton stated:

> It is not enough just to criticize NAFTA, which I have, and for some years now. I have put forth a very specific plan about what I would do. And it does include telling Canada and Mexico that we will opt out unless we renegotiate the core labor and environmental standards. Not side agreements, but core agreements. That we will enhance the enforcement mechanism, and

[31] 'Ecuador Won't Renew U.S. Investment Deal', *Associated Press*, 7 May 2007.
[32] Ecuador's denunciation of the ICSID Convention was received on 6 July 2009 and will take effect on 7 January 2010.
[33] 'Merits of Investor-State Arbitration Debated at International Arbitration Seminar Hosted by Ecuador's Attorney General', *Investment Treaty News*, 8 December 2008, www.investmenttreatynews.org.
[34] 'International Investment Arbitration', *Mondaq*, 9 October 2006.
[35] 'Uzbekistan Dismisses International Arbitration Courts and Foreign Miners', *Resource Investor*, 24 November 2006.
[36] Subedi 2008: 145; Shan 2007: 650.

32ar.3

that we will have a very clear view of how we're going to review NAFTA going forward to make sure it works. *And we're going to take out the ability of foreign companies to sue us* because of what we do to protect our workers.[37]

The renegotiation of NAFTA also became an issue in the 2008 Canadian elections, with the leader of the New Democratic Party, Jack Layton, promising to add environmental safeguards and remove Chapter 11 if he was elected Prime Minister.[38] Gagné and Morin further point out that in the negotiations for the US-Australia FTA, the Australian government 'consistently rejected US demands for an investor-state mechanism' and apparently the US conceded to this position without much resistance.[39]

Shan argues that the debate has shifted in recent years from '"strong states" versus "weak states" (i.e., a "North-South divide"), towards "state sovereignty" versus "corporate sovereignty" (i.e., a "Private-Public debate")', and reasons that this shift offers an opportunity for states to agree to a multilateral deal that strikes a better balance between investment protection and investment regulation.[40] However, others suggest that the North-South divide remains, and that what is in fact emerging is a double standard: in developed countries, arbitration is still viewed as 'good' when it corrects misbehaviour by foreign (developing) host states, but is seen as undesirable when their own behaviour is challenged.[41] The absence of an investor-state mechanism in the US-Australia FTA exemplifies this double standard.

Foreign investors may also be starting to question the value of international arbitration. Peterson argues that Bechtel, an American engineering and construction company that sued Bolivia over a failed privatization of water services, 'bought themselves at least $25 million worth of bad publicity'.[42] When the arbitration became known to the public, the company was 'bombarded with thousands of emails and letters, facing scores of protests outside their headquarters along with receiving largely negative coverage in the international media'.[43] A UK supermarket chain that pursued arbitration against the impoverished country of Guyana dealt with

[37] Presidential Debate at Cleveland State University, 26 February 2008, transcript available at www.msnbc.msn.com/id/23354734/.
[38] 'Layton Would Reopen NAFTA Negotiations to Safeguard Environment, Jobs', *Canwest News Service*, 23 September 2008.
[39] Gagné and Morin 2006: 372.   [40] Shan 2007: 664.   [41] Alvarez and Park 2003: 368–9.
[42] 'There are no Winners in Bolivia's Water War', *Embassy*, 1 February 2006.
[43] 'Bechtel Case Sends Warning to Oil and Gas Multinationals', *OneWorld UK*, n.d., http://uk.oneworld.net/article/view/125938/1/5795.

a similar backlash, and eventually dropped its case as a result.[44] As civil society becomes more aware of international investment arbitration, the negative implications of bringing claims, particularly for large TNCs, are likely to increase.

9.3   Moving forward

Despite the increasing disenchantment with the institution of investment protection, for many countries 'opting out' is not an attractive or practical option. Investment protection is often integrated into important trade agreements, and furthermore, many developing countries do not want to disrupt their relationships with powerful developed economies. It is important, therefore, to offer options for *reform* of the institution that would make it more compatible with the goals of sustainable development.

9.3.1   *Existing proposals for institutional reform*

As has been noted throughout this book, there have been many small reforms made to the institution of investment protection in the last few years. The most dramatic changes have occurred in the procedures of investment arbitration. Many arbitral awards are now made publicly available, and *amicus curiae* submissions to tribunals are becoming more frequent. Some countries, such as Canada and the US, have also revised their model BITs and have taken up the practice of conducting EIAs of new investment agreements. However, these changes are largely cosmetic and fail to address the key issues of accountability, predictability and the capacity of developing countries to handle disputes.

Several proposals have been made for more substantial reform of the institution. Three main ones are discussed here.

9.3.1.1   An appellate body

While hardly revolutionary, the development of a system for appeals of arbitral awards would require significant initiative. It is perhaps the most frequently recommended reform in the literature on investment arbitration, though it is not a universally supported concept.[45]

---

[44] The Big Food Group sought compensation for a sugar business that was nationalized in 1975. See Hamilton and Rochwerger 2005: 22–3.

[45] In support see: Knull and Rubins 2000; Brower 2003; Franck 2005; Wells and Ahmed 2007; Subedi 2008.

A permanent appellate body could ensure consistency in tribunal decisions and provide some predictability for regulators. As mentioned in
Section 6.1.2.5, the only remedies that can be sought at present under
ICSID, for example, are the interpretation of the meaning or scope of an
award, the revision of an award based on the discovery of new information, or the annulment of an award. An annulment is only possible in
rather extreme circumstances. The purpose of an appeal is also fundamentally different from that of annulment. In an appeal, a tribunal may
reverse or substitute a new decision for the one appealed against, whereas
in an annulment the tribunal may only nullify or invalidate a decision.
An annulment committee is only concerned with the process leading to
a tribunal decision, whereas an appellate panel is additionally concerned
with the substantive correctness of an award.[46]

The push for an appellate body appears particularly strong in the US.
Recent US FTAs such as the US-Chile FTA, the US-Singapore FTA and the
US-Morocco FTA provide that the parties will consider the establishment
of an appellate body within three years after the date of entry into force of
the agreement.[47] The CAFTA-DR has a much more detailed provision on
the development of an appellate mechanism, requiring the establishment
of a negotiating group on the issue within three months of entry into force
of the agreement.[48] Gantz notes that a CAFTA-DR appellate mechanism
could be a 'significant first step' toward a broader appellate body.[49]

The ICSID Secretariat also raised the issue of the development of an
appellate body in a 2004 discussion paper.[50] However, the comments that
the ICSID Secretariat received from governments, business and civil society groups, generally indicated that the establishment of such a mechanism
was premature.[51]

One of the main problems with developing an appellate mechanism
is that, if it is going to have any chance of enhancing the consistency of
awards, it should bring all, or at least most, existing IIAs under its umbrella.
With the prospects for a multilateral agreement on investment exceedingly
dim, it is difficult to imagine how broad negotiations on the development
of such a body could be initiated. Gantz notes further legal and practical
challenges such as: the choice of the appropriate standard of review; the
power of the appellate mechanism to confirm, set aside and remand;

[46] Ekwueme 2006: 187.
[47] US-Chile FTA: Annex 10-H; Side Letter to the US-Singapore FTA; US-Morocco FTA: Annex 10-D.
[48] CAFTA-DR: Annex 10-F.   [49] Gantz 2006: 48.   [50] ICSID Secretariat 2004.
[51] Gagné and Morin 2006: 378.

issues relating to choice of law; the relationship of the appellate mechanism process to national court review; and transparency considerations.[52]

As mentioned above, not all observers view an appellate mechanism as a solution to all, or even most, of the important problems with investment arbitration and it has been argued by some that such a mechanism will create new problems. From the perspective of investors, the main objection to an appellate mechanism is that it will slow the arbitration process down and give the outcome of a dispute less finality.[53] As Werner notes:

> While it was recognized by the business community that arbitrators were just humans who could fail in their decisions, the consensus was that it was more important to have a one-stop shop, enabling the parties to put the disputes behind them once and for all without having to go through lengthy appeal proceedings.[54]

Finality of awards may also be an issue for states, particularly in the NAFTA context where several awards have been decided in favour of states, and the US has yet to lose even one claim.[55] Furthermore, Foy suggests that, in the NAFTA context at least, agreeing to an appellate body would require some further ceding of authority, given that at present the parties possess the ability to issue their own interpretations of the agreement.[56]

9.3.1.2   An international investment court

If the other problems inherent in investment arbitration (transparency, accountability, etc.) are not dealt with prior to, or in concordance with, the development of an appellate body, it is hard to imagine that the issues for environmental governance that have been raised in this study would disappear. Rulings would likely become more predictable, but that doesn't mean that they would be consistent with the objectives of sustainable development. In this respect, Van Harten has a far more interesting proposal. Rather than advocating an appellate body, he suggests the adoption of a multilateral code that would establish an international investment court with comprehensive jurisdiction over the adjudication of investment claims.[57] In this model, judges would be appointed for set terms, which Van Harten attests is critical for making them independent, and they

---

[52] Gantz 2006: 57.

[53] 'Wanted: A World Investment Court', *American Lawyer*, 2004, www.americanlawyer.com.

[54] Werner 2003: 783.   [55] Amirfar and Dreyer 2007: 54.   [56] Foy 2003: 104–5.

[57] Van Harten 2007a: 180.

would be appointed by states, which is 'essential to make them account-able'.[58] Van Harten suggests that an international investment court would benefit both capital-importing and capital-exporting states:

> For capital-importing countries, an international court in which they have some say in the appointment process is much preferable to a system of private arbitration, biased against host governments, in which they have little say at all. For the major capital-exporting states and their firms, the proposal asks them to sacrifice little in exchange for an international judicial body that is more likely to have political staying power than the current system.[59]

9.3.1.3 An investment agreement for sustainable development

While the proposals for an appellate body or investment court are intended to deal with the procedural failings of investment arbitration, other pro-posals for reform aim more squarely at addressing the imbalance between the rights and duties of investors, host states and home states. There are two main approaches to addressing this imbalance: the 'complementary approach' of developing codes of investor conduct in parallel with IIAs; and the 'consolidated approach', which instead incorporates provisions on the responsibilities of foreign investors directly into IIAs.[60]

While the complementary approach has largely prevailed in the mod-ern period (see Section 2.3.2), the consolidated approach now appears to be gaining favour in some quarters. For example, Clémençon notes that 'a multilateral investment agreement offers many opportunities for linking the pursuit of economic and development objectives directly with environmental protection objectives'.[61]

The IISD has gone so far as to develop a Model International Investment Agreement for Sustainable Development.[62] The IISD Model Agreement makes many clarifications of the standard provisions on investment pro-tection, several of which are similar to those that have been incorporated in recent US and Canadian BITs (see Chapter 4). In addition, there is clarification of 'like circumstances' with respect to national and most-favoured-nation treatment, requiring that the tribunal must take into account certain factors, including the effects of the investment on the

---

[58] *Ibid*: 182.   [59] *Ibid*: 183.   [60] Shan 2007: 656–7.   [61] Clémençon 2000: 205.
[62] IISD Model International Investment Agreement for Sustainable Development, 2005, www.iisd.org/investment/model_agreement.asp.

environment.[63] The Model Agreement also delves into issues of procedural reform with provisions on the development of a standing roster of arbitrators, an appellate body, and a legal assistance centre.

Far more innovative than the textual clarifications and procedural reforms in the IISD Model is the addition of a section on investor obligations as well as one on home state obligations. With regard to the environment, the obligations include compliance with environmental screening criteria and EIA procedures, and maintenance of an environmental management system (e.g., ISO 14001).[64] Such measures are, of course, open to criticism (see discussion in Section 2.3.2). On the most fundamental level one has to question whether these provisions will achieve anything more than the status quo. Many corporations already hold ISO 14001 certification, and EIAs are commonly required by the institutions that finance and insure investment projects.

Salgado concludes that the IISD Model is 'not a panacea to all legal challenges in international investment law', but is certainly 'the best alternative currently available'.[65] Most significantly, while it is unlikely to be adopted at the multilateral level in the near future, it may have value as a template for the development of more balanced bilateral and regional agreements.[66]

While the IISD Model is perhaps the best-known initiative in the area, it is not the only one. The Alternativa Bolivariana para las Américas (ALBA) is an international cooperation organization based upon the idea of social, political and economic integration between the countries of Latin America and the Caribbean. Largely a vision of Venezuelan president Hugo Chávez, the ALBA was initially proposed as an alternative to the FTAA. As a first step toward greater integration, a trade agreement known as the People's Trade Agreement (PTA or TCP in Spanish) has been signed by Bolivia, Venezuela and Cuba. The PTA is aimed not at liberalizing trade or reducing tariffs, but at lowering poverty rates and spurring sustainable development.[67] Tockman argues that the agreement 'reasserts public control over the economy and attempts to recast the role of the corporation from that of "master" to "partner" in a process of sustainable development'.[68] As one

---

[63] IISD Model Agreement: Art. 5E.   [64] *Ibid*: Art. 12 and 14.   [65] Salgado 2006: 1066.

[66] According to the IISD, cited in Anderson and Grusky 2007: 25, a number of developing countries are looking carefully at the Model, with a view to incorporating the provisions into BITs.

[67] 'Bolivia Advocates Alternative Vision for Trade and Integration', Upside Down World website, 11 July 2006, www.upsidedownworld.org.

[68] *Ibid*.

would expect, there is no recourse to international arbitration for investors provided in the agreement; disputes are to be resolved in local courts. On a broader level, the agreement addresses the issue of state capacity through the transfer of resources to the most underdeveloped countries through a Compensatory Fund for Structural Convergence.[69]

9.3.2   Recommendations

The proposals discussed above are certainly worth further discussion and study. However, in order to be implemented they require broad agreement at the international level, and this is unlikely in the near future. On a more practical level, this section provides several recommendations that states can implement in at least all future contracts and IIAs and potentially also in renegotiations of existing agreements.

It is recommended that states:

   (i) omit access to investor-state arbitration;
  (ii) omit reference to the international minimum standard/fair and equitable treatment;
 (iii) omit stabilization clauses; and
  (iv) add reference to principles of environmental law.

Additionally, states should *increase transparency and participation* in contract and treaty negotiation and in dispute resolution. Developing countries should also make efforts to *cooperate* to a greater extent on investment issues to avoid the bidding wars that competition for investment can create. Finally, international organizations, research institutions, lawyers, NGOs and states should collaborate to create a *legal assistance centre* for developing countries.

While it could be argued that these recommendations represent a significant erosion of the institution of investment protection that has been built up over recent years and leaves investors with little security in developing countries, it must be recalled that investors have other means of protecting themselves (e.g., investment insurance). Furthermore, foreign investment has always been risky, and yet investors continue to engage in it for a reason; it is also very lucrative.

---

[69] 'What is the Bolivarian Alternative for Latin America and the Caribbean?', Venezuelan Bank of External Commerce, 5 February 2004, www.venezuelanalysis.com.

9.3.2.1   Omit access to investor-state arbitration

Absent the creation of an entirely new mechanism of investor-state dispute settlement, such as the investment court proposed by Van Harten, it would seem that the most sensible option for governments is to restrict access to investment arbitration. State-state dispute settlement can be maintained but investors should only have recourse to local remedies. Such a statement will undoubtedly be met with great consternation from the majority of writers in the investment arbitration field. However, if it is acceptable for Australia to refuse to have investor-state dispute resolution included in an agreement with the US, then it should be equally acceptable for any developing country to do so. In response, a supporter of investment protection could argue that the courts in Australia are equipped to deal fairly and justly with investor-state disputes, while the courts of many developing countries are not. Even if one accepts this claim, it does not justify circumventing domestic courts with a completely inadequate international system. If anything, it suggests that countries concerned about how their investors will be treated in foreign courts should, for example, invest in targeted aid to support legal education in developing countries.

9.3.2.2   Omit reference to the minimum standard/fair and equitable treatment

Reference to the international minimum standard and/or fair and equitable treatment should not be included in new IIAs because these standards are simply too broad and have been interpreted too expansively by tribunals. Providing an interpretation that equates the minimum standard/fair and equitable treatment with customary international law, as done by NAFTA Parties, may not eliminate this problem but only open the door to debate on what constitutes custom in this area. Given the widespread support for the idea that fair and equitable treatment is essentially equivalent to a requirement for good governance, the potential for future claimants to rely on this standard is significant.

9.3.2.3   Omit stabilization clauses

Foreign investment contracts, if they are to be employed by states, should not include stabilization clauses or be stabilized through enactment into law. Given the fact that in many developing countries environmental regulation of foreign investment is minimal to begin with, agreeing to general or specific commitments to stability of the environmental regulatory framework could lock a country into deteriorating environmental

conditions. If a developing country is determined to adopt stability commitments, then it should, at the very least, frame the clause or agreement
in such a way as to favour renegotiation rather than arbitration. Furthermore, if investors are really only concerned with the predictability of
legislation and not with the strictness of it, then they could conceivably
agree to stabilize their environmental commitments at a higher level (e.g.,
home country standards) from the beginning of the contract.

9.3.2.4   Add reference to principles of environmental law

When drafting IIAs and foreign investment contracts, governments should
ensure that it is explicitly stated that the purpose of these agreements is
to promote and protect investment *that contributes to sustainable development*. However, given the amorphous nature of this concept, governments
would be well advised to also incorporate in the text of investment agreements and contracts the most important and relevant principles of international environmental law. It is essential that the precautionary principle
be included to ensure that governments will not be punished for being
'first movers' on an issue when scientific evidence remains inconclusive.
Additionally, the adoption of the principle of common but differentiated
responsibilities would support the acceptance that developing countries,
particularly when they face extreme circumstances (e.g., debt, financial
crises), should be given greater leniency. This is not to say that poor countries should never have to compensate investors, but it does signal that
factors, such as the country's ability to pay, should be taken into consideration. The common but differentiated responsibilities principle, coupled
with the polluter pays principle, is essentially the modern-day equivalent of the appropriate compensation doctrine. However, given the broad
acceptance of these principles by the international community, there is
little justification not to include them in investment agreements. In fact, a
majority of the delegates who negotiated the draft MAI favoured explicit
mention of the polluter pays and precautionary principles in the preamble
of that agreement.[70]

9.3.2.5   Promote transparency

The way in which foreign investment contracts and IIAs are negotiated
must also be reformed. It is ironic that transparency (on the part of

---

[70] The Multilateral Agreement on Investment Draft Consolidated Text, DAFFE/MAI(98)7/
REV1, 22 April 1998: 8, www.oecd.org.

governments) is touted as a key ingredient of a friendly investment climate, and yet foreign investment contracts with investors are frequently confidential documents, and negotiations remain behind closed doors in most countries. While IIAs are public documents, that does not mean that negotiations are carried out transparently or with the participation of environmental ministries and agencies and lower levels of government. Transparency and participation in the negotiation of all foreign investment contracts and IIAs would decrease corruption and policy incoherence, lessening the chance that investor-state conflicts will arise.

In addition to promoting transparency in contract and treaty negotiations, the trend of increased transparency in arbitration should be encouraged and pushed further. All new contracts and IIAs should contain explicit clauses stipulating that proceedings will be open to the public and all documents and awards will be published. The UNCITRAL Rules should be revised along these lines and the ICSID Rules should also be revisited.[71]

9.3.2.6 Promote cooperation, rather than competition

The problem with recommending that developing countries not provide investors with access to arbitration and that they eliminate the fair and equitable treatment standard and stabilization clauses is, of course, that they do not have significant bargaining power in negotiations with other states or with investors. Even absent any proof of IIAs fostering greater flows of FDI, it is still the case that the conclusion of an IIA may be tied to other benefits for the host country, such as preferential trade access or economic aid. In such situations, it is understandable that developing countries will succumb to pressure to accept the terms offered in standard developed country models. The bilateral nature of the majority of IIAs exacerbates this problem. When developing countries cooperate, such as in the WTO context, they are often successful in defending their interests. However, as long as the prevailing ideological paradigm is that states must compete for foreign investment, developing countries will be trapped in a prisoner's dilemma.[72] In this regard, Beck's proposal that states pursue policies of cooperation, aiming to establish comparable conditions of production in different host countries and establishing 'host cartels' is

---

[71] In particular, the requirement in the ICSID Rules for agreement amongst the parties before a proceeding can be opened to the public should be eliminated.

[72] In a competitive environment, it is optimal for developing countries to collectively reject strong rules and norms of investment protection, but to agree to them on a bilateral basis. See Guzman 1998.

intriguing.[73] Beck argues that in addition to benefiting from an exchange of information, host countries will limit the risk of being played off against one another in a competition for FDI.[74]

Greater collaboration among developing countries has also been called for in the area of trade, where developing countries have been relatively successful in multilateral fora but not in coordinating their responses to an increasing number of bilateral trade agreements. Braithwaite suggests that a more organized and structured response, based on a visionary agenda that will attract support from within developed states (e.g., from NGOs), is the best, if not only, option for developing countries to resist the divide-and-conquer strategy of the US and Europe.[75]

Another way to achieve some degree of harmonization and to reduce competition among host states is through an international binding code of corporate conduct. However, given the apparent reluctance of developed countries to engage in negotiations for such a code, it would appear that developing countries have a greater chance of success if they focus on collaboration with other developing countries.

9.3.2.7   Create a legal assistance centre

All of the above recommendations relate generally to the future. It is clear that given the large number of existing disputes and agreements that will not expire for a decade or more, action is also needed to deal with the immediate situation. In this regard, this study echoes Gottwald's call for a legal assistance centre.[76] Wälde has also advocated a legal aid mechanism, suggesting the WTO Legal Advisory Centre as a model, and the IISD included a provision on a legal assistance centre in its Model Investment Agreement.[77] Such a centre could offer states access to relevant documents, training courses for both the negotiation of agreements and the settlement of disputes, specific legal advice on cases, and even representation in arbitration.[78]

Efforts to remedy issues of technical and financial capacity of developing countries have thus far been limited. In 2005, UNCTAD launched a pilot course with 'a view to equip especially developing country governments with the necessary capacity to manage investor-to-State disputes and to be able to mobilize the necessary expertise to assist in the proper conduct of such procedures'.[79] The ICSID Secretariat has also cooperated with

---

[73] Beck 2005: 202.   [74] *Ibid.*   [75] Braithwaite 2004: 313–14.
[76] Gottwald 2007.   [77] Wälde 2007: 67.   [78] Gottwald 2007: 269.
[79] Joubin-Bret 2005: 2.

UNCTAD and organizations such as the International Development Law Organization in training programmes for officials of developing countries.[80] The South Centre has recommended that the ICSID Secretariat should additionally consider the establishment of a fund for developing countries that could contribute to facility costs.[81] Finally, it is worth noting the work that the International Senior Lawyers Project has done in assisting governments in developing countries, such as Liberia, in contract renegotiations.[82]

It is argued here that a new centre, independent of UNCTAD or any arbitration supervisory body, should be established. Such a centre could be maintained by government contributions, or alternatively through a network of NGOs, law offices and academic institutions. Individuals already contribute significantly to fostering information exchange through websites devoted to publishing tribunal awards and decisions,[83] and the e-newsletter produced by Luke Eric Peterson (formerly, *Investment Treaty News* and now *Investment Arbitration Reporter*) has substantially increased public awareness about disputes.[84] Furthermore, many NGOs, particularly those involved in submitting *amicus curiae* briefs, have acquired substantial legal knowledge in the area. A new legal assistance centre should not reinvent the wheel; it should instead build on all of these commendable efforts.

---

[80] ICSID 2004: 14.   [81] South Centre 2005: 14.

[82] See 'Liberia Review of Concession Agreements', International Senior Lawyers Project website, www.islp.org/economic.html, accessed 17 December 2008.

[83] The NAFTA Claims website edited by Todd J. Grierson-Weiler, www.naftaclaims.com, and the Investment Treaty Arbitration website edited by Andrew Newcome, www.ita.uvic.ca, are worthy of particular note.

[84] *Investment Treaty News* is supported by the IISD and archives can be found on their website at www.iisd.org/investment/itn. Archives of *Investment Arbitration Reporter* are available at www.iareporter.com.

REFERENCES

Aaken, A. van 2008. 'Perils of Success? The Case of International Investment Protection', *European Business Organization Law Review*, 9: 1–27.

Abbott, F. 2000. 'NAFTA and the Legalization of World Politics: A Case Study', *International Organization*, 54(3): 519–47.

Abbott, K. and Snidal, D. 2000. 'Hard and Soft Law in International Governance', *International Organization*, 54(3): 421–56.

Addy, S. 1999. 'Ghana: Revival of the Mineral Sector', *Resources Policy*, 24(4): 229–39.

Akinsanya, A. 1980. *The Expropriation of Multinational Property in the Third World*. Praeger Publishers, New York.

Alexander, E. 2008. 'Taking Account of Reality: Adopting Contextual Standards for Developing Countries in International Investment Law', *Virginia Journal of International Law*, 48: 817–41.

Allee, T. and Huth, P. 2006. 'Legitimizing Dispute Settlement: International Legal Rulings as Domestic Political Cover', *American Political Science Review*, 100(2): 219–34.

Alvarez, G. and Park, W. 2003. 'The New Face of Investment Arbitration: NAFTA Chapter 11', *Yale Journal of International Law*, 28: 365–401.

Alvarez-Jiménez, A. 2006. 'The Methanex Final Award: An Analysis from the Perspectives of Environmental Regulatory Authorities and Foreign Investors', *Journal of International Arbitration*, 23(5): 427–34.

Amirfar, C. and Dreyer, E. 2007. 'Thirteen Years of NAFTA's Chapter 11: The Criticisms, the United States' Responses, and Lessons Learned', *New York International Law Review*, 20: 39–56.

Amnesty International UK 2003. *Human Rights on the Line: The Baku-Tbilisi-Ceyhan Pipeline Project*. Amnesty International UK, London.

Amnesty International UK 2005. *Contracting Out of Human Rights: The Chad-Cameroon Pipeline Project*. Amnesty International UK, London.

Anderson, S. and Grusky, S. 2007. *Challenging Corporate Investor Rule*. Institute for Policy Studies and Food and Water Watch, Washington, DC.

Araya, M. 2005. 'FDI and the Environment: What Empirical Evidence Does and Does Not Tell Us?', in Zarsky (ed.), *International Investment and Sustainable Development: Balancing Rights and Rewards*, Earthscan, London, pp. 46–73.

Awudi, G. 2002. 'The Role of Foreign Direct Investment (FDI) in the Mining Sector of Ghana and the Environment', Paper Presented at the Conference on Foreign Direct Investment and the Environment, Paris, OECD.

Ayine, D. and Werksman, J. 1999. 'Improving Investor Accountability', in Picciotto and Mayne (eds.), *Regulating International Business: Beyond Liberalization*, Macmillan Press Ltd, Basingstoke, Hampshire, pp. 126–41.

Ayine, D., Blanco, H., Cotula, L., Djire, M., Kotey, N., Khan, S., Reyes, B., Ward, H. and Yusuf, M. 2005. *Lifting the Lid on Foreign Investment Contracts: The Real Deal for Sustainable Development.* International Institute for Environment and Development, London.

Balasubramanyam, V. 1999. 'Foreign Direct Investment to Developing Countries', in Picciotto and Mayne (eds.), *Regulating International Business: Beyond Liberalization*, Macmillan Press Ltd, Basingstoke, Hampshire, pp. 29–46.

Barberis, D. 1998. *Negotiating Mining Agreements: Past, Present and Future Trends.* Kluwer Law International, The Hague.

Bastida, E. 2001. 'A Review of the Concept of Mineral Tenure: Issues and Challenges', *Journal of Energy and Natural Resources Law*, 19(1): 31–43.

Bastida, E. 2002. 'Managing Sustainable Development in Competitive Legal Frameworks for Mining: Argentina, Chile and Peru Experiences', *Centre for Energy, Petroleum, and Mineral Law and Policy Internet Journal*, 12, www.dundee.ac.uk/cepmlp/journal.

Baughen, S. 2006. 'Expropriation and Environmental Regulation: The Lessons of NAFTA Chapter Eleven', *Journal of Environmental Law*, 18: 207–28.

Beck, U. 2005. *Power in the Global Age.* Polity Press, Cambridge.

Been, V. 2002. 'NAFTA's Investment Protections and the Division of Authority for Land Use and Environmental Controls', *Pace Environmental Law Review*, 20: 19–61.

Been, V. and Beauvais, J. 2003. 'The Global Fifth Amendment? NAFTA's Investment Protections and the Misguided Quest for an International "Regulatory Takings" Doctrine', *New York University Law Review*, 78: 30–143.

Begic, T. 2005. *Applicable Law in International Investment Disputes*, Eleven International Publishing, Utrecht.

Behrens, P. 2007. 'Towards the Constitutionalization of International Investment Protection', *Archiv des Völkerrechts*, 45: 153–79.

Bekhechi, M. 2001. 'International Investment and Environmental Protection: Notes on the Environmental Conditions of Investments in the Oil and Mining Sectors', in The International Bureau of the Permanent Court of Arbitration (ed.), *International Investments and Protection of the Environment: The Role of Dispute Resolution Mechanisms*, PCA Peace Palace Papers Series, Kluwer Law International, The Hague, pp. 73–90.

Bennaim-Selvi, O. 2005. 'Third Parties in International Investment Arbitrations: A Trend in Motion', *Journal of World Investment and Trade*, 6(5): 773–807.

Bernardini, P. 1996. 'Development Agreements with Host Governments', in Pritchard (ed.), *Economic Development, Foreign Investment and the Law*, Kluwer Law International, The Hague, pp. 161–74.

Biermann, F. and Bauer, S. 2004. 'Assessing the Effectiveness of Intergovernmental Organisations in International Environmental Politics', *Global Environmental Change*, 14: 189–93.

Blackaby, N. 2004. 'Public Interest and Investment Treaty Arbitration', *Transnational Dispute Management*, 1(1), www.transnational-dispute-management.com.

Blades, B. 2006. 'The Exhausting Question of Local Remedies: Expropriation Under NAFTA Chapter 11', *Oregon Review of International Law*, 8: 31–131.

Braithwaite, J. 2004. 'Methods of Power for Development: Weapons of the Weak, Weapons of the Strong', *Michigan Journal of International Law*, 26(1): 298–330.

Brewer, T. and Young, S. 1998. *The Multilateral Investment System and Multinational Enterprises*. Oxford University Press.

Brewster, R. 2006. 'Rule-Based Dispute Resolution in International Trade Law', *Virginia Law Review*, 92: 251–88.

Brookens, B. 1978. 'Diplomatic Protection of Foreign Economic Interests: The Changing Structure of International Law in the New International Economic Order', *Journal of Interamerican Studies and World Affairs*, 20(1): 37–67.

Brooks, D., Fan, E. and Sumulong, L. 2004. 'Foreign Direct Investment: Recent Trends and the Policy Context', in Brooks and Hill (eds.), *Managing FDI in a Globalizing Economy: Asian Experiences*, Palgrave Macmillan, Basingstoke, Hampshire, pp. 1–27.

Brower, C. 2001a. 'Investor-State Disputes Under NAFTA: A Tale of Fear and Equilibrium', *Pepperdine Law Review*, 29: 43–85.

Brower, C. 2001b. 'Investor-State Disputes Under NAFTA: The Empire Strikes Back', *Columbia Journal of Transnational Law*, 40: 43–88.

Brower, C. 2002. 'Beware the Jabberwock: A Reply to Mr. Thomas', *Columbia Journal of Transnational Law*, 40: 465–87.

Brower, C. 2003. 'Structure, Legitimacy, and NAFTA's Investment Chapter', *Vanderbilt Journal of Transnational Law*, 36: 37–93.

Brower, C. 2004. 'International Decision: S.D. Myers, Inc. v. Canada', *American Journal of International Law*, 98: 339–48.

Brower, C., Brower, C. and Sharpe, J. 2003. 'The Coming Crisis in the Global Adjudication System', *Arbitration International*, 19(4): 415–40.

Brower, C. and Hellbeck, E. 2001. 'The Implications of National and International Environmental Obligations for Foreign Investment Protection Standards, Including Valuation: A Report from the Front Lines', in The International Bureau of the Permanent Court of Arbitration (ed.), *International Investments and Protection of the Environment: The Role of Dispute Resolution Mechanisms*, PCA Peace Palace Papers, Kluwer Law International, The Hague, pp. 19–28.

Brower, C. and Wong, J. 2005. 'General Valuation Principles: The Case of Santa Elena', in Weiler (ed.), *International Investment Law and Arbitration: Leading Cases from the ICSID, NAFTA, Bilateral Treaties and Customary International Law*, Cameron May, London, pp. 747–75.

Brunnermeier, S. and Levinson, A. 2004. 'Examining the Evidence on Environmental Regulations and Industry Location', *Journal of Environment and Development*, 13(1): 6–41.

Bruno, K. and Karliner, J. 2002. 'The UN's Global Compact, Corporate Accountability and the Johannesburg Earth Summit', *Development*, 45(3): 33–8.

Bubb, R. and Rose-Ackerman, S. 2007. 'BITs and Bargains: Strategic Aspects of Bilateral and Multilateral Regulation of Foreign Investment', *International Review of Law and Economics*, 27: 291–311.

Buckley, R. and Blyschak, P. 2007. 'Guarding the Open Door: Non-Party Participation before the International Centre for Settlement of Investment Disputes', *Banking & Finance Law Review*, 22: 353–76.

Buergenthal, T. 2006. 'The Proliferation of Disputes, Dispute Settlement Procedures and Respect for the Rule of Law', *Arbitration International*, 22(4): 495–9.

Byrne, K. 2000. 'Regulatory Expropriation and State Intent', *Canadian Yearbook of International Law*, 38: 89–120.

Cameron, P. 2006. *Stabilisation in Investment Contracts and Changes of Rules in Host Countries: Tools for Oil & Gas Investors*, Association of International Petroleum Negotiators, Houston, TX.

Caspary, G. and Berghaus, S. 2004. 'The Changing Nature of Foreign Direct Investment in Developing Countries: Evidence and Implications', *Journal of World Investment and Trade*, 5(4): 683–704.

Chalker, J. 2006. 'Making the Investment Provisions of the Energy Charter Treaty Sustainable Development Friendly', *International Environmental Agreements: Politics, Law and Economics*, 6(4): 435–58.

Cheng, T. 2005. 'Power, Authority and International Investment Law', *American University International Law Review*, 20(3): 465–520.

Cheng, T. 2007. 'Precedent and Control in Investment Treaty Arbitration', *Fordham International Law Journal*, 30: 1014–49.

Choi, W.-M. 2007. 'The Present and Future of the Investor-State Dispute Settlement Mechanism', *Journal of International Economic Law*, 10: 725–47.

Christmann, P. and Taylor, G. 2004. 'Environmental Self-Regulation in the Global Economy: The Role of Firm Capabilities', in Lundan (ed.), *Multinationals, Environment and Global Competition*, Elsevier JAI, London, pp. 119–46.

Chudnovsky, D. and López, A. 1999. 'TNCs and the Diffusion of Environmentally Friendly Technologies to Developing Countries'. *Occasional Paper* 9, UNCTAD, Geneva.

Chung, O. 2007. 'The Lopsided International Investment Law Regime and its Effect on the Future of Investor-State Arbitration', *Virginia Journal of International Law*, 47(4): 953–76.

CIEL 2003a. *Comments to the IFC Baku-Tblisi-Ceyhan Pipeline Project*. CIEL, Washington, DC.

CIEL 2003b. *International Law on Investment: The Minimum Standard of Treatment*. DC. CIEL, Geneva.

CIEL and IISD 2007. *Revising the UNCITRAL Arbitration Rules to Address State Arbitrations*. CIEL and IISD, Geneva.

Clapp, J. 1998. 'Foreign Direct Investment in Hazardous Industries in Developing Countries: Rethinking the Debate', *Environmental Politics*, 7(4): 92–113.

Clapp, J. 2002. 'What the Pollution Havens Debate Overlooks', *Global Environmental Politics*, 2(2): 11–19.

Clapp, J. 2005. 'The Privatization of Global Environmental Governance: ISO 14000 and the Developing World', in Levy and Newell (eds.), *The Business of Global Environmental Governance*, MIT Press, Cambridge, MA, pp. 223–48.

Clapp, J. and Dauvergne, P. 2005. *Paths to a Green World: The Political Economy of the Global Environment*. MIT Press, Cambridge, MA.

Clémençon, R. 2000. 'Foreign Direct Investment and Global Environmental Protection: Why Environmentalists Should Favour Multilateral Investment Rules', *Journal of World Investment*, 1(1): 199–223.

Coe, J. 2005. 'The State of Investor-State Arbitration: Some Reflections on Professor Brower's Plea for Sensible Principles', *American University International Law Review*, 20: 929–56.

Coe, J. 2006. 'Transparency in the Resolution of Investor-State Disputes: Adoption, Adaption, and NAFTA Leadership', *University of Kansas Law Review*, 54(5): 1339–85.

Coe, J. and Rubins, N. 2005. 'Regulatory Expropriation and the Tecmed Case: Context and Contributions', in Weiler (ed.), *International Investment Law and Arbitration: Leading Cases from the ICSID, NAFTA, Bilateral Treaties and Customary International Law*, Cameron May, London, pp. 597–667.

Cohn, T. 2004. *Global Political Economy: Theory and Practice*. Longman, New York.

Cole, M. 2004. 'Trade, the Pollution Haven Hypothesis and the Environmental Kuznets Curve: Examining the Linkages', *Ecological Economics*, 48: 71–81.

Cole, M., Elliott, R. and Fredriksson, P. 2006. 'Endogenous Pollution Havens: Does FDI Influence Environmental Regulations?', *Scandinavian Journal of Economics*, 108(1): 157–78.

Comeaux, P. and Kinsella, N. 1994. 'Reducing Political Risk in Developing Countries: Bilateral Investment Treaties, Stabilization Clauses, and MIGA and OPIC Investment Insurance', *New York Law School Journal of International and Comparative Law*, 15(1): 1–48.

Commission, J. 2007. 'Precedent in Investment Treaty Arbitration: A Citation Analysis of Developing Jurisprudence', *Journal of International Arbitration*, 24(2): 129–58.

Cook, J. 2007. 'The Evolution of Investment-State Dispute Resolution in NAFTA and CAFTA: Wild West to World Order', *Pepperdine Law Review*, 34: 1085–138.

Copeland, B. and Taylor, M. 2004. 'Trade, Growth, and the Environment', *Journal of Economic Literature*, 42: 7–71.

Cordonier Segger, M.-C. 2003. 'Sustainability and Corporate Accountability Regimes: Implementing the Johannesburg Summit Agenda', *RECIEL*, 12(3): 295–309.

Correa, C. and Kumar, N. 2003. *Protecting Foreign Investment: Implications of a WTO Regime and Policy Options*. Zed Books, London.

Cosbey, A., Mann, H., Peterson, L. and von Moltke, K. 2004. *Investment and Sustainable Development*. IISD, Winnipeg.

Cotula, L. 2008. 'Reconciling Regulatory Stability and Evolution of Environmental Standards in Investment Contracts: Toward a Rethink of Stabilization Clauses', *Journal of World Energy Law and Business*, 1(2): 158–79.

Crane, W. 1998. 'Corporations Swallowing Nations: The OECD and the Multilateral Agreement on Investment', *Colorado Journal of International Environmental Law and Policy*, 9: 429–61.

Cremades, B. and Cairns, D. 2004. 'Contract and Treaty Claims and Choice of Forum in Foreign Investment Disputes', in Horn (ed.), *Arbitrating Foreign Investment Disputes*, Kluwer Law International, The Hague, pp. 325–51.

Cutler, A. 2001. 'Globalization, the Rule of Law, and the Modern Law Merchant: Medieval or Late Capitalist Associations?', *Constellations*, 8(4): 480–502.

Cutler, A. 2003. *Private Power and Global Authority: Transnational Merchant Law in the Global Political Economy*. Cambridge University Press.

Cutler, A., Haufler, V. and Porter, T. 1999. 'Private Authority and International Affairs', in Cutler, Haufler and Porter (eds.), *Private Authority in International Affairs*, State University of New York Press, pp. 1–28.

Dasgupta, S., Laplante, B., Wang, H. and Wheeler, D. 2002. 'Confronting the Environmental Kuznets Curve', *Journal of Economic Perspectives*, 16(1): 147–68.

Dattu, R. 2000. 'A Journey from Havana to Paris: The Fifty-Year Quest for the Elusive Multilateral Agreement on Investment', *Fordham International Law Journal*, 24: 275–316.

Dauvergne, P. 2008. *The Shadows of Consumption: Consequences for the Global Environment*. MIT Press, Cambridge, MA.

de Pencier, J. 2000. 'Investment, Environment and Dispute Settlement: Arbitration Under NAFTA Chapter Eleven', *Hastings International and Comparative Law Review*, 23: 409–18.

Dean, J., Lovely, M. and Wang, H. 2005. 'Are Foreign Investors Attracted to Weak Environmental Regulations?: Evaluating the Evidence from China'. *Policy Research Working Paper*, World Bank, Washington, DC.

Dezalay, Y. and Garth, B. 1996. *Dealing in Virtue: International Commercial Arbitration and the Construction of a Transnational Legal Order*. University of Chicago Press.

Dhooge, L. 2001. 'The North American Free Trade Agreement and the Environment: Lessons of Metalclad Corporation v. United Mexican States', *Minnesota Journal of Global Trade*, 10: 209–89.

Doan, D. 1998. *The Mineral Industry of Costa Rica*. USGS Minerals Information, US Geological Survey.

Dodge, W. 2000. 'National Courts and International Arbitration: Exhaustion of Remedies and *Res Judicata* under Chapter Eleven of NAFTA', *Hastings International and Comparative Law Review*, 23(3–4): 357–83.

Dolzer, R. 2005. 'The Impact of International Investment Treaties on Domestic Administrative Law', *International Law and Politics*, 37: 953–72.

Dolzer, R. and Stevens, M. 1995. *Bilateral Investment Treaties*. Martinus Nijhoff, The Hague.

Doornbos, M. 2001. '"Good Governance": The Rise and Decline of a Policy Metaphor', *Journal of Development Studies*, 37(6): 93–108.

Downes, D. 1999. *Integrating Implementation of the Convention on Biological Diversity and the Rules of the World Trade Organization*. International Union for the Conservation of Nature, Geneva.

Duffield, J. 2007. 'What Are International Institutions?', *International Studies Review*, 9(1): 1–22.

Edsall, R. 2006. 'Indirect Expropriation Under NAFTA and DR-CAFTA: Potential Inconsistencies in the Treatment of State Public Welfare Regulations', *Boston University Law Review*, 86: 931–62.

Egli, G. 2007. 'Don't Get BIT: Addressing ICSID'S Inconsistent Application of Most Favored-Nation Clauses to Dispute Resolution Provisions', *Pepperdine Law Review*, 34: 1045–84.

Egonu, M. 2007. 'Investor-State Arbitration Under ICSID: A Case for Presumption Against Confidentiality?', *Journal of International Arbitration*, 24(5): 479–89.

Einhorn, J. 1974. *Expropriation Politics*. Lexington Books, London.

Ekwueme, K. 2006. 'A Nigerian Perspective on a Forward-Looking Multilateral Agreement on Investment', *Journal of World Investment and Trade*, 7(1): 165–96.

Encarnation, D. and Wells, L. 1985. 'Sovereignty en Garde: Negotiating with Foreign Investors', *International Organization*, 39(1): 47–78.

Endicott, M. 2007. 'Remedies in Investor-State Arbitration: Restitution, Specific Performance and Declaratory Awards', in Kahn and Wälde (eds.), *New Aspects of International Investment Law*, Martinus Nijhoff Publishers, Leiden, pp. 517–52.

European Commission 2001. *Promoting a European Framework for Corporate Social Responsibility*, European Commission, Luxembourg.

Falkner, R. 2003. 'Private Environmental Governance and International Relations: Exploring the Links', *Global Environmental Politics*, 3(2): 72–87.

FAO 2007. *State of the World's Forests 2007*. UN, Rome.

Faruque, A. 2006a. 'The Rationale and Instrumentalities for Stability in Long-Term State Contracts: The Context for Petroleum Contracts', *Journal of World Investment and Trade*, 7(1): 85–112.

Faruque, A. 2006b. 'Validity and Efficacy of Stabilisation Clauses: Legal Protection vs. Functional Value', *Journal of International Arbitration*, 23(4): 317–36.

Fortier, L. and Drymer, S. 2004. 'Indirect Expropriation in the Law of International Investment: I Know It When I See It, or Caveat Investor', *ICSID Review: Foreign Investment Law Journal*, 19(2): 293–327.

Foy, P. 2003. 'The Effectiveness of NAFTA's Chapter Eleven Investor-State Arbitration Procedures', *ICSID Review: Foreign Investment Law Journal*, 18(1): 44–108.

Franck, S. 2005. 'The Legitimacy Crisis in Investment Treaty Arbitration: Privatising Public International Law through Inconsistent Decisions', *Fordham Law Review*, 73: 1521–1623.

Franck, S. 2007. 'Foreign Direct Investment, Investment Treaty Arbitration, and the Rule of Law', *Pacific McGeorge Global Business & Development Law Journal*, 19: 337–73.

Freedman, J. 2003. 'Implications of the NAFTA Investment Chapter for Environmental Regulation', in Kiss, Shelton and Ishibashi (eds.), *Economic Globalization and Compliance with International Environmental Agreements*, Kluwer Law International, The Hague, pp. 89–104.

Gagné, G. and Morin, J. 2006. 'The Evolving American Policy on Investment Protection: Evidence from Recent FTAs and the 2004 Model BIT', *Journal of International Economic Law*, 9(2): 357–82.

Gaines, S. 2002. 'The Masked Ball of NAFTA Chapter 11: Foreign Investors, Local Environmentalists, Government Officials, and Disguised Motives', in Kirton and MacLaren (eds.), *Linking Trade, Environment, and Social Cohesion: NAFTA Experiences, Global Challenges*, Ashgate, Aldershot, Hampshire, pp. 103–29.

Gaines, S. 2006. 'International Decision: Methanex Corp. v. United States, Partial Award on Jurisdiction and Admissibility; Methanex Corp. v. United States, Final Award on Jurisdiction and Merits', *American Journal of International Law*, 100: 683–9.

Gallagher, K. and Birch, M. 2006. 'Do Investment Agreements Attract Investment?: Evidence from Latin America', *Journal of World Investment and Trade*, 7(6): 961–74.

Gallagher, K. and Zarsky, L. 2005. 'No Miracle Drug: Foreign Direct Investment and Sustainable Development", in Zarsky (ed.), *International Investment and*

Sustainable Development: Balancing Rights and Rewards, Earthscan, London, pp. 13–45.

Gallagher, K. and Zarsky, L. 2007. *The Enclave Economy: Foreign Investment and Sustainable Development in Mexico's Silicon Valley*. MIT Press, Cambridge, MA.

Gantz, D. 2001. 'Potential Conflicts Between Investor Rights and Environmental Regulation Under NAFTA's Chapter 11', *George Washington International Law Review*, 33(3/4): 651–752.

Gantz, D. 2004. 'The Evolution of FTA Investment Provisions: From NAFTA to the United States-Chile Free Trade Agreement', *American University International Law Review*, 19: 679–767.

Gantz, D. 2006. 'An Appellate Mechanism for Review of Arbitral Decisions in Investor-State Disputes: Prospects and Challenges', *Vanderbilt Journal of Transnational Law*, 39(1): 39–76.

Gao, Z. 1994. *International Petroleum Contracts: Current Trends and New Directions*. Martinus Nijhoff, London.

Garcia, C. 2004. 'All the Other Dirty Little Secrets: Investment Treaties, Latin America, and the Necessary Evil of Investor-State Arbitration', *Florida Journal of International Law*, 16: 301–69.

García-Bolivar, O. 2005. 'The Teleology of International Investment Law: The Role of Purpose in the Interpretation of International Investment Agreements', *Journal of World Investment and Trade*, 6(5): 751–72.

Ginsburg, T. 2005. 'International Substitutes for Domestic Institutions: Bilateral Investment Treaties and Governance', *International Review of Law and Economics*, 25: 107–23.

Global Witness 2006. *Heavy Mittal? A State Within a State: The Inequitable Mineral Development Agreement between the Government of Liberia and Mittal Steel Holdings NV*. Global Witness, London.

González de Cossío, F. 2002. 'The International Centre for the Settlement of Investment Disputes: The Mexican Experience', *Journal of International Arbitration*, 19(3): 227–44.

Gottwald, E. 2007. 'Leveling the Playing Field: Is it Time for a Legal Assistance Center for Developing Nations in Investment Treaty Arbitration?', *American University International Law Review*, 22: 237–75.

Graham, D. and Woods, N. 2006. 'Making Corporate Self-Regulation Effective in Developing Countries', *World Development*, 34(5): 868–83.

Gray, K. 2002. 'Foreign Direct Investment and Environmental Impacts: Is the Debate Over?', *RECIEL*, 11(3): 306–13.

Gross, S. 2003. 'Inordinate Chill: BITS, Non-NAFTA MITS, and Host-State Regulatory Freedom: An Indonesian Case Study', *Michigan Journal of International Law*, 24(3): 893–960.

Grossman, G. and Krueger, A. 1993. 'Environmental Impacts of a North American Free Trade Agreement', in Garber (ed.), *The US-Mexico Free Trade Agreement*, MIT Press, Cambridge, MA, pp. 13–56.

Grossman, G. and Krueger, A. 1995. 'Economic Growth and the Environment', *Quarterly Journal of Economics*, 110(2): 353–77.

Grossman, G. and Krueger, A. 1996. 'The Inverted-U: What Does it Mean?' *Environment and Development Economics*, 1(1): 119–22.

Gudofsky, J. 2000. 'Shedding Light on Article 1110 of the North American Free Trade Agreement (NAFTA) Concerning Expropriations: An Environmental Case Study', *Northwestern Journal of International Law and Business*, 21(1): 243–316.

Gulbrandsen, L. 2004. 'Overlapping Public and Private Governance: Can Forest Certification Fill the Gaps in the Global Forest Regime?', *Global Environmental Politics*, 4(2): 75–99.

Gutbrod, M. and Hindelang, S. 2006. 'Externalization of Effective Legal Protection against Indirect Expropriation', *Journal of World Investment and Trade*, 7(1): 59–83.

Guzman, A. 1998. 'Why LDCs Sign Treaties that Hurt Them: Explaining the Popularity of Bilateral Investment Treaties', *Virginia Journal of International Law*, 38: 639–88.

Hall, R. and Biersteker, T. 2002. 'The Emergence of Private Authority in the International System', in Hall and Biersteker (eds.), *The Emergence of Private Authority in Global Governance*, Cambridge University Press, pp. 3–22.

Hallward-Driemeier, M. 2003. *Do Bilateral Investment Treaties Attract FDI? Only a Bit . . . and they Could Bite*. World Bank, Washington, DC.

Hamilton, C. and Rochwerger, P. 2005. 'Trade and Investment: Foreign Direct Investment through Bilateral and Multilateral Treaties', *New York International Law Review*, 18: 1–59.

Hamilton, M. 2005. *Mining Environmental Policy: Comparing Indonesia and the USA*. Ashgate, Aldershot, Hampshire.

Hansen, M. 2002. 'Environmental Regulation of Transnational Corporations: Needs and Prospects', in Utting (ed.), *The Greening of Business in Developing Countries: Rhetoric, Reality and Prospects*, Zed Books, London, pp. 159–84.

Harris, T. 2007. 'The "Public Policy" Exception to Enforcement of International Arbitration Awards Under the New York Convention', *Journal of International Arbitration*, 24(1): 9–24.

Hasenclever, A., Mayer, P. and Rittberger, V. 1997. *Theories of International Regimes*. Cambridge University Press.

Hasic, H. 2005. 'Article 1110 of NAFTA: Investment Barriers to "Upward Harmonization" of Environmental Standards', *Southwestern Journal of Law and Trade in the Americas*, 12: 137–57.

Head, J. 2007. *Global Business Law: Principles and Practice of International Commerce and Investment*, 2nd edn. Carolina Academic Press, Durham, NC.

Henderson, D. 1999. *The MAI Affair: A Story and its Lessons*. Royal Institute of International Affairs, London.

Hill, H. 2006. 'NAFTA and Environmental Protection: The First 10 Years', *Journal of the Institute of Justice and International Studies*, 2006: 157–68.

Hodges, B. 2002. 'Where the Grass is Always Greener: Foreign Investor Actions Against Environmental Regulations Under NAFTA's Chapter 11 – S.D. Myers, Inc. v. Canada', *Georgetown International Environmental Law Review*, 14(2): 367–408.

Hoed, H. 1997. 'Legal Aspects of Contracts of Work', in Indonesian Mining Association (ed.), *Indonesian Mining: Into the New Millennium*, Jakarta, pp. 117–24.

Horn, N. 2004. 'Arbitration and the Protection of Foreign Investment: Concepts and Means', in Horn and Kroll (eds.), *Arbitrating Foreign Investment Disputes*, Kluwer Law International, The Hague, pp. 3–31.

Houde, M. and Yannaca-Small, K. 2004. *Relationships between International Investment Agreements*. OECD, Paris.

Hurrell, A. 2005. 'Power, Institutions, and the Production of Inequality', in Barnett and Duvall (eds.), *Power in Global Governance*, Cambridge University Press, pp. 33–58.

ICSID Secretariat 2004. *Possible Improvements of the Framework for ICSID Arbitration*. ICSID, Washington, DC.

IISD 2007. 'A Parliamentarian's Guide to International Investment Agreements and their Implications for Domestic Policy-Making', *IIA Insighter* 1, IISD, Winnipeg.

ILA International Law on Foreign Investment Committee 2006. *International Law on Foreign Investment: First Report of the International Law Association*. ILA, Toronto.

IMF 2007. *Guide on Resource Revenue Transparency*. IMF, Washington, DC.

Jacobs, K. and Paulson, M. 2008. 'The Convergence of Renewed Nationalization, Rising Commodities, and "Americanization" in International Arbitration and the Need for More Rigorous Legal and Procedural Defenses', *Texas International Law Journal*, 43: 359–400.

Jenkins, R. 2001. *Corporate Codes of Conduct: Self-Regulation in a Global Economy*. United Nations Research Institute for Social Development, Geneva.

Jenkins, R. 2002a. 'Environmental Regulation, International Competitiveness and the Location of Industry', in *Environmental Regulation in the New Global Economy: The Impact on Industry and Competitiveness*, Edward Elgar, Cheltenham, pp. 16–41.

Jenkins, R. 2002b. 'Environmental Regulation, Trade and Investment in a Global Economy', in *Environmental Regulation in the New Global Economy: The Impact on Industry and Competitiveness*, Edward Elgar, Cheltenham, pp. 293–314.

Jenkins, R. 2002c. 'Introduction', in *Environmental Regulation in the New Global Economy: The Impact on Industry and Competitiveness*, Edward Elgar, Cheltenham, pp. 3–15.

Jones, R. 2002. 'NAFTA Chapter 11 Investor-State Dispute Resolution: A Shield to Be Embraced or a Sword to Be Feared?', *Brigham Young University Law Review*, 2: 527–59.

Joubin-Bret, A. 2005. 'How Do Relevant International Organisations Contribute to Capacity Building? The Way Forward', *Making the Most of International Investment Agreements: A Common Agenda*, OECD, Paris.

Kahler, M. 2000. 'Conclusion: The Causes and Consequences of Legalization', *International Organization*, 54(3): 661–83.

Kantor, M. 2004. 'The New Draft Model U.S. BIT: Noteworthy Developments', *Journal of International Arbitration*, 21(4): 383–96.

Kelemen, R. 2004. 'Globalization, Federalism, and Regulation', in Vogel and Kagan (eds.), *Dynamics of Regulatory Change: How Globalization Affects National Regulatory Policies*, University of California Press, Berkeley, pp. 269–97.

Kentin, E. 2004. 'Sustainable Development in International Investment Dispute Settlement: The ICSID and NAFTA Experience', in Schrijver and Weiss (eds.), *International Law and Sustainable Development: Principles and Practice*, Martinus Nijhoff Publishers, Leiden, pp. 309–38.

Kentin, E. 2007. 'Economic Crisis and Investment Arbitration: The Argentine Cases', in *New Aspects of International Investment Law*, Martinus Nijhoff Publishers, Leiden, pp. 629–67.

Kerremans, B. 2004. 'What Went Wrong in Cancun: A Principal-Agent View on the EU's Rationale Towards the Doha Development Round', *European Foreign Affairs Review*, 9: 363–93.

Kimerling, J. 2006. 'Indigenous Peoples and the Oil Frontier in Amazonia: The Case of Ecuador, ChevronTexaco, and Aguinda v. Texaco', *New York University Journal of International Law and Politics*, 38: 413–664.

Kinnear, M. and Hansen, R. 2005. 'The Influence of NAFTA Chapter 11 in the BIT Landscape', *U.C. Davis Journal of International Law and Policy*, 12: 101–16.

Kirkman, C. 2002. 'Fair and Equitable Treatment: Methanex v. United States and the Narrowing Scope of NAFTA Article 1105', *Law and Policy in International Business*, 34: 343–92.

Klein, N. 2000. *No Logo: Taking Aim at the Brand Bullies*. Vintage, Toronto.

Knahr, C. 2007. 'Transparency, Third Party Participation and Access to Documents in International Investment Arbitration', *Arbitration International*, 23(2): 327–55.

Knull III, W. and Rubins, N. 2000. 'Betting the Farm on International Arbitration: Is it Time to Offer an Appeal Option?', *American Review of International Arbitration*, 11: 531–65.

Kolk, A. and van Tulder, R. 2004. 'Internationalization and Environmental Reporting: The Green Face of the World's Leading Multinationals', in Lundan (ed.), *Multinationals, Environment and Global Competition*, Elsevier JAI, London, pp. 95–118.

Kotey, N., Francois, J., Owusu, J., Yeboah, R., Amanor, K. and Antwi, L. 1998. *Falling Into Place: Policy that Works for Forests and People*. Institute for Environment and Development, London.

Kozul-Wright, R. and Rayment, P. 2007. *The Resistable Rise of Market Fundamentalism: Rethinking Development Policy in an Unbalanced World*. Zed Books, London.

Kratochwil, F. and Ruggie, J. 1986. 'International Organization: A State of the Art on an Art of the State', *International Organization*, 40(4): 753–75.

Kriebaum, U. 2007. 'Privatizing Human Rights: The Interface Between International Investment Protection and Human Rights', in Reinisch and Kriebaum (eds.), *The Law of International Relations: Liber Amicorum Hanspeter Neuhold*, Eleven International Publishing, Utrecht, pp. 165–89.

Kurtz, J. 2007. 'National Treatment, Foreign Investment and Regulatory Autonomy: The Search for Protectionism or Something More?', in Kahn and Wälde (eds.), *New Aspects of International Investment Law*, Martinus Nijhoff Publishers, Leiden, pp. 311–51.

Laird, I. 2001. 'NAFTA Chapter 11 Meets Chicken Little', *Chicago Journal of International Law*, 2: 223–9.

Larson, A. and Ribot, J. 2005. 'Democratic Decentralisation through a Natural Resource Lens: An Introduction', in Ribot and Larson (eds.), *Democratic Decentralisation through a Natural Resource Lens*, Routledge, London, pp. 1–25.

Lawrence, J. 2006. 'Chicken Little Revisited: NAFTA Regulatory Expropriations after Methanex', *Georgia Law Review*, 41: 261–309.

Leader, S. 2006. 'Human Rights, Risks, and New Strategies for Global Investment', *Journal of International Economic Law*, 9(3): 657–705.

Legum, B. 2003. 'Trends and Challenges in Investor-State Arbitration', *Arbitration International*, 19(2): 143–7.

Legum, B. 2006. 'Defining Investment and Investor: Who is Entitled to Claim?', *Arbitration International*, 22(4): 521–6.

Leon, B. and Terry, J. 2006. 'Special Considerations When a State is a Party to International Arbitration: Why Arbitrating Against a State is Different, 12 Key Reasons', *Dispute Resolution Journal*, 61: 69–77.

Levy, D. 1996. 'BOT and Public Procurement: A Conceptual Framework', *Indiana International & Comparative Law Review*, 95: 102–10.

Lilley, T. 2002. 'Keeping NAFTA "Green" for Investors and the Environment', *California Law Review*, 75: 727–61.

Lipson, C. 1985. *Standing Guard: Protecting Foreign Capital in the Nineteenth and Twentieth Centuries*. University of California Press, Berkeley.

Lock, I. 2006. 'Corporate Social Responsibility and Codes of Conduct: The Fox Guarding the Chicken Coop?', in Johnston, Gismondi and Goodman (eds.), *Nature's Revenge: Reclaiming Sustainability in an Age of Corporate Globalization*, Broadview Press, Plymouth, pp. 117–33.

Lomborg, B. 2001. *The Skeptical Environmentalist*. Cambridge University Press.

Loy, F. 2002. 'On a Collision Course? Two Potential Environmental Conflicts Between the U.S. and Canada', *Canada-United States Law Journal*, 28: 11–26.

Lundan, S. 2004. 'Multinationals, Environment and Global Competition: A Conceptual Framework', in Lundan (ed.), *Multinationals, Environment and Global Competition*, Elsevier JAI, London, pp. 1–22.

Luz, M. and Miller, C. 2002. 'Globalization and Canadian Federalism: Implications of the NAFTA's Investment Rules', *McGill Law Journal*, 47: 951–97.

Mabey, N. 1999. 'Defending the Legacy of Rio: The Civil Society Campaign Against the MAI', in Picciotto and Mayne (eds.), *Regulating International Business: Beyond Liberalization*, Macmillan Press, Basingstoke, Hampshire, pp. 60–81.

Mabey, N. and McNally, R. 1998. *Foreign Direct Investment and the Environment: From Pollution Havens to Sustainable Development*. World Wildlife Fund-UK, Godalming, Surrey.

MacArthur, D. 2003. 'NAFTA Chapter 11: On an Environmental Collision Course with the World Bank?', *Utah Law Review*, 2003(3): 913–47.

Madalena, I. 2003. 'Foreign Direct Investment and the Protection of the Environment: The Border between National Environmental Regulation and Expropriation', *European Environmental Law Review*, 12: 70–82.

Malanczuk, P. 2000. 'State-State and Investor-State Dispute Settlement in the OECD Draft Multilateral Investment Agreement', *Journal of International Economic Law*, 3(3): 417–39.

Maniruzzaman, A. 2007. 'National Laws Providing for Stability of International Investment Contracts: A Comparative Perspective', *Journal of World Investment and Trade*, 8(2): 233–41.

Maniruzzaman, A. 2008. 'The Pursuit of Stability in International Energy Investment Contracts: A Critical Appraisal of the Emerging Trends', *Journal of World Energy Law and Business*, 1(2): 121–57.

Mann, H. 2001. *Private Rights, Public Problems: A Guide to NAFTA's Controversial Chapter on Investor Rights*. IISD and World Wildlife Fund, Winnipeg.

Mann, H. 2005. *The Final Decision in Methanex v. United States: Some New Wine in Some New Bottles*. IISD, Winnipeg.

Mann, H. 2006. 'Is "Fair and Equitable" Fair, Equitable, Just, or Under Law?' *American Society of International Law Proceedings*, 100: 74–7.

Mann, H. and Araya, M. 2002. 'An Investment Regime for the Americas: Challenges and Opportunities for Environmental Sustainability', in Deere and Esty (eds.), *Greening the Americas: NAFTA's Lessons for Hemispheric Trade*, MIT Press, Cambridge, MA, pp. 163–80.

Mann, H. and Soloway, J. 2002. 'Untangling the Expropriation and Regulation Relationship: Is There a Way Forward?' Report to the Ad Hoc Expert Group on Investment Rules and the Department of Foreign Affairs and International Trade. Canadian Department of Foreign Affairs and International Trade, Ottawa.

Marshall, F. and Mann, H. 2006. *Revision of the UNCITRAL Arbitration Rules – Good Governance and the Rule of Law: Express Rules for Investor-State Arbitrations Required*. IISD, Winnipeg.

Martin, L. and Simmons, B. 1998. 'Theories and Empirical Studies of International Institutions', *International Organization*, 52(4): 729–57.

Mélanie, J., Marina, K., Hester, S., Berry, P., Bell, A., Schneider, K., Burke, P., Duong, L.H.A. and McCarty, A. 2005. 'Enhancing ASEAN Minerals Trade and Investment - Final Country Report Indonesia'. REPSF Project 04/009b, ASEAN Secretariat, Jakarta.

Minichiello, V., Aroni, R., Timewell, E. and Alexander, R. 1990. *In-Depth Interviewing: Researching People*. Longman Cheshire, Melbourne.

Miranda, N. 2007. 'Concession Agreements: From Private Contract to Public Policy', *Yale Law Journal*, 117: 510–49.

Mistelis, L. 2005. 'Confidentiality and Third Party Participation: UPS v. Canada and Methanex v. United States', *Arbitration International*, 21(2): 211–32.

Montembault, B. 2003. 'The Stabilisation of State Contracts Using the Example of Oil Contracts: A Return to the Gods of Olympia', *International Business Law Journal*, 6: 593–643.

Moran, T. and Pearson, C. 1990. 'Do TRIPs Trip Up Foreign Investment? An International Business Diplomacy Perspective', in Wallace (ed.), *Foreign Direct Investment in the 1990s: A New Climate in the Third World*, Martinus Nijhoff Publishers, Dordrecht, pp. 28–60.

Morgera, E. 2004. 'From Stockholm to Johannesburg: From Corporate Responsibility to Corporate Accountability for the Global Protection of the Environment?', *RECIEL*, 13(2): 214–22.

Mosoti, V. 2005. 'Bilateral Investment Treaties and the Possibility of a Multilateral Framework on Investment at the World Trade Organization: Are Poor Economies Caught In Between?', *Northwestern Journal of International Law and Business*, 26: 95–134.

Muchlinski, P. 1999. 'A Brief History of Business Regulation', in Picciotto and Mayne (eds.), *Regulating International Business: Beyond Liberalization*, Macmillan Press Ltd, Basingstoke, Hampshire, pp. 28–60.

Muchlinski, P. 2001. 'The Rise and Fall of the Multilateral Agreement on Investment: Lessons for the Regulation of International Business', in Fletcher, Loukas and Cremona (eds.), *Foundations and Perspectives of International Trade Law*, Sweet & Maxwell, London, pp. 114–34.

Murphy, D. 2004. 'The Business Dynamics of Global Regulatory Competition', in Vogel and Kagan (eds.), *Dynamics of Regulatory Change*, University of California Press, Berkeley, pp. 84–117.

Muse-Fisher, M. 2007. 'CAFTA-DR and the Iterative Process of Bilateral Investment Treaty Making: Towards a United States Takings Framework for Analyzing International Expropriation Claims', *Pacific McGeorge Global Business & Development Law Journal*, 19: 495–529.

Muttitt, G. 2007. *Hellfire Economics: Multinational Companies and the Contract Dispute over Kashagan, the World's Largest Undeveloped Oilfield*. Platform, London.

Nahman, A. and Antrobus, G. 2005a. 'The Environmental Kuznets Curve: A Literature Survey', *South African Journal of Economics*, 73(1): 105–20.

Nahman, A. and Antrobus, G. 2005b. 'Trade and the Environmental Kuznets Curve: Is Southern Africa a Pollution Haven?', *South African Journal of Economics*, 73(4): 803–14.

Neumayer, E. 2001a. *Greening Trade and Investment: Environmental Protection Without Protectionism*. Earthscan, London.

Neumayer, E. 2001b. 'Pollution Havens: An Analysis of Policy Options for Dealing With an Elusive Phenomenon', *Journal of Environment and Development*, 10(2): 147–77.

Neumayer, E. and Spess, L. 2005. 'Do Bilateral Investment Treaties Increase Foreign Direct Investment to Developing Countries?', *World Development*, 33(10): 1567–85.

Newcombe, A. 2007a. 'Sustainable Development and Investment Treaty Law', *Journal of World Investment and Trade*, 8(3): 355–407.

Newcombe, A. 2007b. 'The Boundaries of Regulatory Expropriation in International Law', in Kahn and Wälde (eds.), *New Aspects of International Investment Law*, Martinus Nijhoff Publishers, Leiden, pp. 391–449.

Newell, P. 2001. 'Managing Multinationals: The Governance of Investment for the Environment', *Journal of International Development*, 13: 907–19.

Newell, P. 2008. 'The Marketization of Global Environmental Governance: Manifestations and Implications', in Park, Conca and Finger (eds.), *The Crisis of Global Environmental Governance: Towards a New Political Economy of Sustainability*, Routledge, New York, pp. 77–95.

Ochs, A. 2005. 'Glamis Gold Ltd. – A Foreign United States Citizen?: NAFTA and its Potential Effect on Environmental Regulations and the Mining Law of 1872', *Colorado Journal of International Environmental Law and Policy*, 16: 495–526.

OECD 1997. *Foreign Direct Investment and the Environment: An Overview of the Literature*. DAFFE/MAI(97)33/REV1, OECD, Paris.

OECD 2004. *Most Favoured Nation Treatment in International Investment Law*. OECD, Paris.

Omalu, M. and Zamora, A. 1998. 'Key Issues in Mining Policy: A Brief Comparative Survey as a Background Study on the Reform of Mining Law', *Working Paper* CP9/98, Centre for Energy, Petroleum and Mineral Law and Policy, Dundee.

Oman, C. 2000. *Policy Competition for Foreign Direct Investment: A Study of Competition among Governments to Attract FDI*. OECD, Paris.

Ong, D. 2008. 'The Contribution of State-Multinational Corporation "Transnational" Investment Agreements to International Environmental Law', *Yearbook of International Environmental Law*, 17: 168–212.

Orellana, M. 2007. 'Science, Risk and Uncertainty: Public Health Measures and Investment Discipline', in Kahn and Wälde (eds.), *New Aspects of International Investment Law*, Martinus Nijhoff Publishers, Leiden, pp. 671–790.

Otto, J. 1999. 'Mineral Policy, Legislation and Regulation', *Mining, Environment and Development Series*. UNCTAD, Geneva.

Otto, J. and Cordes, J. 2002. *The Regulation of Mineral Enterprises: A Global Perspective on Economics, Law and Policy*. Rocky Mountain Mineral Law Foundation, Westminster, CO.

Paasivirta, E. 1989. 'Internationalization and Stabilization of Contracts Versus State Sovereignty', *British Yearbook of International Law*, 60: 315–50.

Parisi, M. 2005. 'Moving Toward Transparency? An Examination of Regulatory Takings in International Law', *Emory International Law Review*, 19: 383–426.

Paterson, M. 2000. *Understanding Global Environmental Politics*. Macmillan Press Ltd, Basingstoke, Hampshire.

Paterson, M., Humphreys, D. and Pettiford, L. 2003. 'Conceptualizing Global Environmental Governance: From Interstate Regimes to Counter-Hegemonic Struggles', *Global Environmental Politics*, 3(2): 1–9.

Pattberg, P. 2007. *Private Institutions and Global Governance: The New Politics of Environmental Sustainability*. Edward Elgar, Northampton, MA.

Paulsson, J. 1995. 'Arbitration Without Privity', *ICSID Review: Foreign Investment Law Journal*, 10: 232–7.

Paulsson, J. 2005. *Denial of Justice in International Law*. Cambridge University Press.

Paulsson, J. and Petrochilos, G. 2006. *Revision of the UNCITRAL Arbitration Rules*. Freshfields Bruckhaus Deringer, Washington, DC.

Perkins, R. 2003. 'Environmental Leapfrogging in Developing Countries: A Critical Assessment and Reconstruction', *Natural Resources Forum*, 27: 177–88.

Peter, W. 1995. *Arbitration and Renegotiation of International Investment Agreements*, 2nd edn. Kluwer Law International, Dordrecht.

Peterson, L. 2004a. 'All Roads Lead Out of Rome: Divergent Paths of Dispute Settlement in Bilateral Investment Treaties', in Zarsky (ed.), *International Investment for Sustainable Development: Balancing Rights and Rewards*, Earthscan, London, pp. 123–49.

Peterson, L. 2004b. *UK Bilateral Investment Treaty Programme and Sustainable Development*. Chatham House, London.

Phillips, N. 2005. 'State Debates in International Political Economy', in Phillips (ed.), *Globalizing International Political Economy*, Palgrave Macmillan, Basingstoke, Hampshire, pp. 82–115.

Porter, G. 1999. 'Trade Competition and Pollution Standards: "Race to the Bottom" or "Stuck at the Bottom"?', *Journal of Environment and Development*, 8(2): 133–51.

PricewaterhouseCoopers 2004. *Mine Indonesia 2004: Review of Trends in the Indonesian Mining Industry*. PricewaterhouseCoopers, Jakarta.

Pritchard, R. 2005. 'Safeguards for Foreign Investment in Mining', in Bastida, Wälde and Warden-Fernandez (eds.), *International and Comparative Mineral*

Law and Policy: Trends and Prospects, Kluwer Law International, The Hague, pp. 73–98.

Public Citizen and FOE 2001. *NAFTA Chapter 11 Investor-to-State Cases: Bankrupting Democracy: Lessons for Fast Track and the Free Trade Area of the Americas.* Public Citizen, Washington, DC.

Reed, L., Paulsson, J. and Blackaby, N. 2004. *Guide to ICSID Arbitration*, Kluwer Law International, The Hague.

Reisman, W. and Sloane, R. 2003. 'Indirect Expropriation and its Valuation in the BIT Generation', *British Yearbook of International Law*, 74: 115–50.

Reyes, A. 2006. 'Protecting the "Freedom of Transit Petroleum": Transnational Lawyers Making (Up) International Law in the Caspian', *Berkeley Journal of International Law*, 24: 842–80.

Robbins, J. 2006. 'The Emergence of Positive Obligations in Bilateral Investment Treaties', *University of Miami International and Comparative Law Review*, 13: 403–73.

Romano, C. 2002. 'International Justice and Developing Countries: A Qualitative Analysis', *The Law and Practice of International Courts and Tribunals*, 1: 539–611.

Rothman, D. 1998. 'Environmental Kuznets Curves – Real Progress or Passing the Buck? A Case for Consumption-Based Approaches', *Ecological Economics*, 25: 177–94.

Rubins, N. 2003. 'The Allocation of Costs and Attorney's Fees in Investor-State Arbitration', *ICSID Review: Foreign Investment Law Journal*, 18(1): 109–29.

Rubins, N. 2006. 'Opening the Investment Arbitration Process: At What Cost, for What Benefit?', *Transnational Dispute Management*, 3(3), www.transnational-dispute-management.com.

Ruggie, J. 2001. 'global_governance.net: The Global Compact as Learning Network', *Global Governance*, 7: 371–8.

Ryan, C. 2008. 'Meeting Expectations: Assessing the Long-Term Legitimacy and Stability of International Investment Law', *University of Pennsylvania Journal of International Law*, 29: 725–59.

Sabahi, B. 2007. 'The Calculation of Damages in International Investment Law', in Kahn and Wälde (eds.), *New Aspects of International Investment Law*, Martinus Nijhoff Publishers, Leiden, pp. 553–95.

Saggi, K. 2002. 'Trade, Foreign Direct Investment and International Technology Transfer: A Survey', *World Bank Research Observer*, 17(2): 191–235.

Salacuse, J. and Sullivan, N. 2005. 'Do BITs Really Work? An Evaluation of Bilateral Investment Treaties and their Grand Bargain', *Harvard International Law Journal*, 46: 67–129.

Salgado, V. 2006. 'The Case Against Adopting BIT Law in the FTAA Framework', *Wisconsin Law Review*, 2006: 1025–66.

Sayer, J. 2006. 'Do More Good, Do Less Harm: Development and the Private Sector', in Eade and Sayer (eds.), *Development and the Private Sector: Consuming Interests*, Kumarian Press, Bloomfield, CT, pp. 1–29.

Schill, S. 2007. 'International Investment Law and the Host-State's Power to Handle Economic Crises: Comment on the ICSID Decision in LG&E v. Argentina', *Journal of International Arbitration*, 24(3): 265–86.

Schneiderman, D. 2001. 'Investment Rules and the Rule of Law', *Constellations*, 8(4): 521–37.

Schneiderman, D. 2008. *Constitutionalizing Economic Globalization: Investment Rules and Democracy's Promise*. Cambridge University Press.

Schreuer, C. 2005. 'Investment Treaty Arbitration and Jurisdiction over Contract Claims: The Vivendi I Case Considered', in Weiler (ed.), *International Investment Law and Arbitration: Leading Cases from the ICSID, NAFTA, Bilateral Treaties and Customary International Law*, Cameron May, London, pp. 281–323.

Schrijver, N. 1997. *Sovereignty Over Natural Resources: Balancing Rights and Duties*. Cambridge University Press.

Schwebel, S. 2006. 'The United States 2004 Model Bilateral Investment Treaty: An Exercise in the Regressive Development of International Law', *Transnational Dispute Management*, 3(2), www.transnational-dispute-management.com.

Shalakany, A. 2006. 'Arbitration and the Third World: A Plea for Reassessing Bias Under the Specter of Neoliberalism', *Harvard International Law Journal*, 41: 419–68.

Shan, W. 2007. 'From "North-South Divide" to "Private-Public Debate": Revival of the Calvo Doctrine and the Changing Landscape in International Investment Law', *Northwestern Journal of International Law and Business*, 27(3): 631–64.

Shemberg, A. 2008. 'Stabilization Clauses and Human Rights', *A Research Project Conducted for IFC and the United Nations Special Representative to the Secretary General on Business and Human Rights*. Washington, DC.

Sikkel, M. 2001. 'How to Establish a Multilateral Framework for Investment?', in Niewenhuys and Brus (eds.), *Multilateral Regulation of Investment*, Kluwer Law International, The Hague, pp. 161–79.

Singh, R. 2004. 'The Impact of the Central American Free Trade Agreement on Investment Arbitrations: A Mouse that Roars?', *Journal of International Arbitration*, 21(4): 329–40.

Soloway, J. 2002. 'Environmental Expropriation under NAFTA Chapter 11: The Phantom Menace', in Kirton and MacLaren (eds.), *Linking Trade, Environment, and Social Cohesion: NAFTA Experiences, Global Challenges*, Ashgate, Aldershot, Hampshire, pp. 131–44.

Sornarajah, M. 1997. 'Power and Justice in Foreign Investment Arbitration', *Journal of International Arbitration*, 14(3): 103–40.

Sornarajah, M. 2000. *The Settlement of Foreign Investment Disputes*. Kluwer Law International, The Hague.

Sornarajah, M. 2002. 'A Developing Country Perspective of International Economic Law in the Context of Dispute Settlement', in Qureshi (ed.), *Perspectives in International Economic Law*, Kluwer Law International, The Hague, pp. 83–110.

Sornarajah, M. 2003. 'Economic Neo-Liberalism and the International Law on Foreign Investment', in Anghie, Chimni, Mickelson, and Okafor (eds.), *The Third World and International Order: Law, Politics, and Globalization*, Martinus Nijhoff Publishers, Leiden, pp. 173–90.

Sornarajah, M. 2004a. *The International Law on Foreign Investment*, 2nd edn, Cambridge University Press.

Sornarajah, M. 2004b. 'The New World Economic Order and Equity', in Dixit and Jayaraj (eds.), *Dynamics of International Law in the New Millennium*, Indian Society of International Law, New Delhi, pp. 209–35.

Sornarajah, M. 2006a. 'A Law for Need or a Law for Greed?: Restoring the Lost Law in the International Law of Foreign Investment', *International Environmental Agreements: Law, Politics and Economics*, 6(4): 329–57.

Sornarajah, M. 2006b. 'Power and Justice: Third World Resistance in International Law', *Singapore Year Book of International Law*, 10: 19–57.

South Centre 2005. *Developments on Discussions for the Improvement of the Framework for ICSID Arbitration and the Participation of Developing Countries*. South Centre, Geneva.

Spiermann, O. 2004. 'Individual Rights, State Interests and the Power to Waive ICSID Jurisdiction under Bilateral Investment Treaties', *Arbitration International*, 20(2): 179–211.

Stern, D. 2004. 'The Rise and Fall of the Environmental Kuznets Curve', *World Development*, 32(8): 1419–39.

Stiglitz, J. 2003. *Globalization and its Discontents*. W.W. Norton & Company, London.

Stiglitz, J. 2008. 'Regulating Multinational Corporations: Towards Principles of Cross-Border Legal Frameworks in a Globalized World: Balancing Rights with Responsibilities', *American University International Law Review*, 23: 451–558.

Stone Sweet, A. 1999. 'Judicialization and the Construction of Governance', *Comparative Political Studies*, 32(2): 147–84.

Strange, S. 1996. *The Retreat of the State: The Diffusion of Power in the World Economy*, Cambridge University Press.

Strohm, L. 2002. 'Pollution Havens and the Transfer of Environmental Risk', *Global Environmental Politics*, 2(2): 29–36.

Subedi, S. 1998. 'Foreign Investment and Sustainable Development', in Weiss, Denters and Waart (eds.), *International Economic Law with a Human Face*, Kluwer Law International, The Hague, pp. 413–28.

Subedi, S. 2008. *International Investment Law: Reconciling Policy and Principle*. Hart Publishing, Oxford.

Swan, A. 2000. 'Ethyl Corporation v. Canada, Award on Jurisdiction', *The American Journal of International Law*, 94(1): 159–66.

Tabb, W. 2004. *Economic Governance in the Age of Globalization*. Columbia University Press, New York.

Tetteh, F. 2004. 'Mining in the Forest Reserve', *Journal of Energy and Natural Resources Law*, 22(2): 241–2.

Tienhaara, K. 2006a. 'Mineral Investment and the Regulation of the Environment in Developing Countries: Lessons from Ghana', *International Environmental Agreements: Politics, Law and Economics*, 6(4): 371–94.

Tienhaara, K. 2006b. 'What You Don't Know Can Hurt You: Investor-State Disputes and the Environment', *Global Environmental Politics*, 6(4): 73–100.

Tienhaara, K. 2007. 'Third-Party Participation in Investment-Environment Disputes: Recent Developments', *RECIEL*, 16(2): 230–42.

Tienhaara, K. 2008. 'Unilateral Commitments to Investment Protection: Does the Promise of Stability Restrict Environmental Policy Development?' *Yearbook of International Environmental Law*, 17: 139–67.

Tobin, J. and Rose-Ackerman, S. 2005. 'Foreign Direct Investment and the Business Environment in Developing Countries: The Impact of Bilateral Investment Treaties'. *Working Paper*, Yale Center for Law, Economics, and Public Policy, New Haven.

Tobin, J. and Rose-Ackerman, S. 2006. 'When BITs Have Some Bite: The Political-Economic Environment for Bilateral Investment Treaties'. Yale Law School, New Haven, CT.

Tollefson, C. 2002. 'Metalclad v. United Mexican States Revisited: Judicial Oversight of NAFTA's Chapter Eleven Investor-State Claim Process', *Minnesota Journal of Global Trade*, 11: 183–213.

Trubek, D., Dezalay, Y. and Buchanan, R. 1994. 'Global Restructuring and the Law: Studies of the Internationalization of Legal Fields and the Creation of Transnational Arenas', *Case Western Reserve Law Review*, 44: 407–98.

Tuffuor, K. 1992. 'Statement on Mining and Degradation of Forest Reserves in Ghana', in Acquah (ed.) *Proceedings from the National Seminar on the Environmental Guidelines to Regulate Mining Activities in Ghana*, Ghana Minerals Commission, Accra.

Turk, J. 2005. 'Compensation for "Measures Tantamount to Expropriation" Under NAFTA: What it Means and Why it Matters', *International Law & Management Review*, 1: 41–78.

UNCITRAL 2008. *Report of the United Nations Commission on International Trade Law Forty-First Session (16 June–3 July 2008)*. A/63/17, United Nations, New York.

UNCTAD 1998. *Bilateral Investment Treaties in the Mid-1990s*. UNCTAD, Geneva.

UNCTAD 1999a. 'Fair and Equitable Treatment'. *Issues in International Investment Agreements*. UNCTAD/ITE/IIT/11(Vol. III), UNCTAD, Geneva.

UNCTAD 1999b. 'Lessons from the MAI'. *Issues in International Investment Agreements*. UNCTAD/ITE/IIT/Misc.22, UNCTAD, Geneva.

UNCTAD 1999c. 'National Treatment'. *Issues in International Investment Agreements*. UNCTAD/ITE/IIT/11 (Vol. IV), UNCTAD, Geneva.

UNCTAD 2000a. *International Investment Instruments: A Compendium, Volume V: Regional Integration, Bilateral and Non-governmental Instruments.* UNCTAD/DITE/2 (Vol.V), UNCTAD, Geneva.

UNCTAD 2000b. 'Taking of Property'. *Issues in International Investment Agreements.* UNCTAD/ITE/IIT/15, UNCTAD, Geneva.

UNCTAD 2003. *Foreign Direct Investment and Performance Requirements: New Evidence from Selected Countries.* UNCTAD/ITE/IIA/2003/7, UNCTAD, Geneva.

UNCTAD 2004a. 'Key Terms and Concepts in IIAs: A Glossary'. *Issues in International Investment Agreements,* UNCTAD/ITE/IIT/2004/2, UNCTAD, Geneva.

UNCTAD 2004b. 'State Contracts'. *Issues in International Investment Agreements.* UNCTAD/ITE/IIT/2004/11, UNCTAD, Geneva.

UNCTAD 2005a. *Economic Development in Africa: Rethinking the Role of Foreign Direct Investment.* UNCTAD/GDS/AFRICA/2005/1, UNCTAD, Geneva.

UNCTAD 2005b. *Investor-State Disputes and Policy Implications.* TD/B/COM.2/62, UNCTAD, Geneva.

UNCTAD 2005c. 'Transnational Corporations and the Internationalization of Research and Development'. *World Investment Report 2005.* UNCTAD/WIR/2005, United Nations, Geneva.

UNCTAD 2006a. *Investment Policy Review: Colombia.* UNCTAD/ITE/IPC/2005/11, UNCTAD, Geneva.

UNCTAD 2006b. 'The Entry into Force of Bilateral Investment Treaties (BITs)'. *IIA Monitor* No. 3, UNCTAD/WEB/ITE/IIA/2006/9, UNCTAD, Geneva.

UNCTAD 2007. *Bilateral Investment Treaties 1995–2006: Trends in Investment Rulemaking,* UNCTAD/ITE/IIA/2006/5, UNCTAD, Geneva.

UNCTAD 2008. 'Transnational Corporations and the Infrastructure Challenge'. *World Investment Report 2008,* UNCTAD/WIR/2008, UNCTAD, Geneva.

UNCTAD 2009a. 'Latest Developments in Investor-State Dispute Settlement', *IIA Monitor* No. 1, UNCTAD/WEB/DIAE/IA/2009/6/REV 1, UNCTAD, Geneva.

UNCTAD 2009b. 'Recent Developments in International Investment Agreements (2008–June 2009)', *IIA Monitor* No. 3, UNCTAD/WEB/DIAE/IA/2009/8, UNCTAD, Geneva.

UNCTAD and Japan Bank for International Cooperation 2006. *Blue Book on Best Practice in Investment Promotion and Facilitation: Ghana.* UNCTAD, Geneva.

UNCTC 1983. *Main Features and Trends in Petroleum and Mining Agreements: A Technical Paper.* UN, New York.

UNMIL 2006. *Human Rights in Liberia's Rubber Plantations: Tapping into the Future.* UN, Monrovia.

Utting, P. 2000. 'Business Responsibility for Sustainable Development'. *Occasional Paper* 2, United Nations Research Institute for Social Development, Geneva.

Utting, P. 2002. 'Towards Corporate Environmental Responsibility', in Utting (ed.), *The Greening of Business in Developing Countries: Rhetoric, Reality and Prospects,* Zed Books, London, pp. 1–13.

Utting, P. 2006. 'Corporate Responsibility and the Movement of Business', in Eade and Sayer (eds.), *Development and the Private Sector: Consuming Interests*, Kumarian Press, Bloomfield, CT, pp. 53–73.

Vagts, D. 1987. 'Foreign Investment Risk Reconsidered: The View from the 1980s', *ICSID Review: Foreign Investment Law Journal*, 2: 1–18.

Van Harten, G. 2007a. *Investment Treaty Arbitration and Public Law*. Oxford University Press.

Van Harten, G. 2007b. 'The Public-Private Distinction in the International Arbitration of Individual Claims Against the State', *International and Comparative Law Quarterly*, 56: 371–94.

VanDeveer, S. 2005. 'Effectiveness, Capacity Building and International Environmental Cooperation', in Dauvergne (ed.), *Handbook of Global Environmental Politics*, Edward Elgar, Cheltenham.

Vandevelde, K. 1998. 'Sustainable Liberalism and the International Investment Regime', *Michigan Journal of International Law*, 19: 373–99.

Velasco, P. 2000. *The Mineral Industries of Central America – Belize, Costa Rica, El Salvador, Guatemala, Honduras, Nicaragua, and Panama*. US Geological Survey, Reston, VA.

Verhoosel, G. 1998. 'Foreign Direct Investment and Legal Constraints on Domestic Environmental Policies: Striking a "Reasonable" Balance between Stability and Change', *Law and Policy in International Business*, 29: 451–79.

Vesel, S. 2007. 'Clearing a Path through a Tangled Jurisprudence: Most-Favoured-Nation Clauses and Dispute Settlement Provisions in Bilateral Investment Treaties', *Yale Journal of International Law*, 32: 125–89.

von Moltke, K. 2002. 'International Investment and Sustainability: Options for Regime Formation', in Gallagher and Werksman (eds.), *The Earthscan Reader on International Trade and Sustainable Development*, Earthscan, London, pp. 347–69.

Wagner, J. 1999. 'International Investment, Expropriation and Environmental Protection', *Golden Gate University Law Review*, 29: 465–538.

Wälde, T. 1998a. 'Law, Contract and Reputation in International Business: What Works?' *Centre for Energy, Petroleum, and Mineral Law and Policy Internet Journal*, 3, www.dundee.ac.uk/cepmlp/journal.

Wälde, T. 1998b. 'Sustainable Development and the 1994 Energy Charter Treaty: Between Pseudo-Action and the Management of Environmental Investment Risk', in Weiss, Denters and Waart (eds.), *International Economic Law with a Human Face*, Kluwer Law International, The Hague, pp. 223–70.

Wälde, T. 2001. 'International Disciplines on National Environmental Regulation: With Particular Focus on Multilateral Investment Treaties', in The International Bureau of the Permanent Court of Arbitration (ed.), *International Investments and Protection of the Environment: The Role of Dispute Resolution Mechanisms*, PCA Peace Palace Papers, Kluwer Law International, The Hague, pp. 29–71.

Wälde, T. 2004. 'Investment Arbitration as a Discipline for Good-Governance', in Weiler (ed.), *NAFTA Investment Law and Arbitration: Past Issues, Current Practice, Future Prospects*, Transnational Publishers Inc., Ardsley, NY, pp. 475–92.

Wälde, T. 2007. 'The Specific Nature of Investment Arbitration', in Kahn and Wälde (eds.), *New Aspects of International Investment Law*, Martinus Nijhoff Publishers, Leiden, pp. 43–120.

Wälde, T. and Kolo, A. 2001. 'Environmental Regulation, Investment Protection and "Regulatory Taking" in International Law', *International and Comparative Law Quarterly*, 50(4): 811–48.

Wälde, T. and N'Di, G. 1996. 'Stabilising International Investment Commitments: International Law Versus Contract Interpretation', *Texas International Law Journal*, 31: 215–67.

Wallace, J. 2005. 'Corporate Nationality, Investment Protection Agreements, and Challenges to Domestic Natural Resources Law: The Implications of Glamis Gold's NAFTA Chapter 11 Claim', *Georgetown International Environmental Law Review*, 17(2): 365–92.

Walter, A. 2001. 'NGOs, Business, and International Investment: The Multilateral Agreement on Investment, Seattle and Beyond', *Global Governance*, 7(1): 51–73.

Weiler, T. 2001. 'A First Look at the Interim Merits Award in S.D. Myers Inc. and Canada: It is Possible to Balance Legitimate Environmental Concerns with Investment Protection', *Hastings International and Comparative Law Review*, 24: 173–88.

Weiler, T. 2003. 'NAFTA Article 1105 and the Principles of International Economic Law', *Columbia Journal of Transnational Law*, 42: 35–85.

Weiler, T. 2004. 'Saving Oscar Chin: Non-Discrimination in International Investment Law', in Horn (ed.), *Arbitrating Foreign Investment Disputes*, Kluwer Law International, The Hague, pp. 159–92.

Weiler, T. 2005. 'Good Faith and Regulatory Transparency: The Story of Metalclad v. Mexico', in Weiler (ed.), *International Investment Law and Arbitration: Leading Cases from the ICSID, NAFTA, Bilateral Treaties and Customary International Law*, Cameron May, London, pp. 701–45.

Weintraub, J. 1997. 'The Theory and Politics of the Public/Private Distinction', in Weintraub and Kumar (eds.), *Public and Private in Thought and Practice: Perspectives on a Grand Dichotomy*, University of Chicago Press, pp. 1–42.

Weissbrodt, D. and Kruger, M. 2003. 'Norms on the Responsibilities of Transnational Corporations and Other Business Enterprises with Regard to Human Rights', *American Journal of International Law*, 97(4): 901–22.

Wells, L. and Ahmed, R. 2007. *Making Foreign Investment Safe: Property Rights and National Sovereignty*. Oxford University Press.

Werner, J. 2003 'Making Investment Arbitration More Certain: A Modest Proposal', *Journal of World Investment*, 4: 767–86.

Westcott, T. 2007. 'Recent Practice on Fair and Equitable Treatment', *Journal of World Investment and Trade*, 8(3): 409–30.

Wheeler, D. 2002. 'Beyond Pollution Havens', *Global Environmental Politics*, 2(2): 1–10.

World Commission on Environment and Development 1987. *Our Common Future*, Oxford University Press.

Xing, Y. and Kolstad, C. 2002. 'Do Lax Environmental Regulations Attract Foreign Investment?', *Environmental and Resource Economics*, 21: 1–22.

Yackee, J. 2006. 'Sacrificing Sovereignty: Bilateral Investment Treaties, International Arbitration, and the Quest for Capital'. *Research Paper* C06-15, USC Center in Law, Economics and Organization, Los Angeles.

Yackee, J. 2008a. 'Conceptual Difficulties in the Empirical Study of Bilateral Investment Treaties', *Brooklyn Journal of International Law*, 33: 405–62.

Yackee, J. 2008b. 'Do We Really Need BITs? Toward a Return to Contract in International Investment Law', *Asian Journal of WTO & International Health Law and Policy*, 3: 121–46.

Yannaca-Small, C. 2004. *Fair and Equitable Treatment Standard in International Investment Law*. OECD, Paris.

Yin, R. 2003. *Case Study Research: Design and Methods*. Sage Publications, London.

Young, O. 1994. *International Governance: Protecting the Environment in a Stateless Society*. Cornell University Press, Ithaca, NY.

Zarsky, L. 1997. 'Stuck in the Mud? Nation-States, Globalization and the Environment'. *Globalisation and Environment Study*. OECD, The Hague.

Zarsky, L. 2002. 'Global Reach: Human Rights and Environment in the Framework of Corporate Accountability', in Zarsky (ed.), *Human Rights and the Environment: Conflicts and Norms in a Globalizing World*, Earthscan, London, pp. 31–54.

INDEX

AAA, *see* American Arbitration Association

Abs-Shawcross Draft Convention on Investment Abroad, 47, 55

accountability
arbitrators, 118, 146, 268, 271, 283, 285
corporations, 28, 29, 56, 119
governments, 58, 114, 119, 120, 213, 271, 275–6

aid, 16, 45, 48, 213, 289, 291

air pollution, 2, 20, 24, 90, 151, 152, 153, 155, 189, 250

ALBA, *see* Alternativa Bolivariana para las Américas

Alcoa, 244

Alien Tort Claims Act, 36, 254

Alternativa Bolivariana para las Américas (ALBA), 287

American Arbitration Association (AAA), 254, 255, 256, 261

amicus curiae, 131–42, 145, 146, 147, 148, 201, 283, 293

annulment of arbitral awards, 128, 129, 158, 161–2, 166, 171, 279, 284

appeal of arbitral awards, 129, 162, 283–5, 286, 287

arbitrators
accountability, 118, 146, 268, 271, 283, 285
bias, 143–4
expertise, 112, 118, 206, 265
role, 56, 106, 267, 275, 277
selection process, 55, 122, 125–6, 268

Archer Daniels Midland, 195, 197

Argentina, 41, 51, 68, 136, 149, 150, 279, 280

Association of South-East Asian Nations (ASEAN), 65, 221

asymmetry
FDI flows, 15, 274
investment protection, 268–74

Australia, 36, 69, 83, 85, 220, 221, 231, 248, 282, 289

Baku-Tbilisi-Ceyhan (BTC) pipeline, 103, 110–11, 115, 118

banks, *see* Equator Principles; World Bank

bargaining power, *see* negotiations

Basel Convention on the Transboundary Movement of Hazardous Wastes, 179–80, 181, 184, 185

Bechtel, 282

best available technology, 18, 26–7

best international practices, 18, 27–37, 107

bilateral investment treaties (BITs)
arbitration clauses, 122
effect on FDI flows, 59–61
history, 53–4
models, 14, 63, 73, 74, 78, 83, 84, 86, 88, 89, 92, 93, 127, 134–5, 283, 291
number, 8, 54
renegotiation, 280, 281
South-South, 15, 54
termination, 54, 280, 281
unintended consequences, 62

biodiversity, 1, 2, 20, 24, 151, 163, 221, 229, 238, *see also* Convention on Biological Diversity

BITs, *see* bilateral investment treaties

Biwater, 136–40, 147
Bolivia, 46, 65, 74, 80, 136, 280, 282,
    287
BP, 101, 109, 110, 115
British Columbia, 168, 171, 199, 205
BTC pipeline, *see* Baku-Tbilisi-Ceyhan
    pipeline
Bush, George W., 248
Buyat Bay, 249–52, 258–60, 261,
    265

CAFTA-DR, *see* Central
    America-Dominican
    Republic-United States Free Trade
    Agreement
California, 1, 173, 188–203, 207, 209,
    210
Calvo doctrine, 40–2, 44, 281
Canada, *see also* British Columbia
    BITs, 66, 67, 68, 70, 81, 232, 236,
        237–8, 239, 243, 286
    EIAs, 85, 87–9, 94
    model, 74, 78, 83, 84, 88, 89,
        134–5, 283
    companies, 188, 191, 198, 199, 209,
        228, 231, 232, 234, 236, 248,
        266
    NAFTA, 14, 48, 132, 170, 196,
        282
    investor-state disputes, 1, 2, 52,
        133, 134, 151, 152–7, 178–88, 205,
        206, 208, 209, 210, 211, 212, 213,
        214, 215, 274
    threat of arbitration, 263
capital mobility, 9, 21
Central America-Dominican
    Republic-United States Free Trade
    Agreement (CAFTA-DR), 49, 50,
    67, 68, 83, 84, 85, 86, 87, 135, 151,
    243, 248, 284
CERDS, *see* Charter of Economic
    Rights and Duties of States
Charter of Economic Rights and Duties
    of States (CERDS), 44, 47
Chávez, Hugo, 280, 287
Chevron, 104, 252–8, 259, 260, 261, 265
Chile, 51, 68, 70, 83, 85, 87, 101, 102,
    158, 159, 236, 273, 284

Clinton, Bill, 62
Clinton, Hillary, 281
code of conduct, 27, 28, 29, 30, 56, 286,
    292
common but differentiated
    responsibilities, 215, 290
compensation, *see also* damages
    appropriate, 45, 79, 80, 128, 290
    future profits, 128, 169, 192, 215,
        239, 242, 248
    Hull formula, 42, 79, 128
    stabilization premium, 106
    valuation methods, 80, 128, 164–5,
        169, 202
concession agreements, 95, 107, 108,
    116
conditionality, 213
confidentiality
    arbitration, 121, 126–7, 129,
        136–40, 141, 142, 145–8, 275, 276,
        291
    foreign investment contracts, 97,
        114–16, 119–20, 228, 271, 276,
        290–1
contracts-of-work (COWs), 218–19,
    220, 221, 222, 226, 243, 244, 250,
    251, 261, 265
Convention on Biological Diversity, 90,
    220, 233
Convention to Combat Desertification,
    233
corporate social responsibility (CSR),
    28
Correa, Rafael, 254, 280
corruption, 24, 29, 33, 48, 70, 114, 115,
    129, 159, 161, 162, 208, 224, 249,
    255, 261, 273–4, 291
cost of arbitration, 60, 122, 128–9, 147,
    148–50, 154, 157, 159, 161, 162,
    166, 188, 189, 192, 198, 217, 259,
    265, 269, 274, 293
Costa Rica, 2, 3, 49, 67, 152, 162–6,
    215, 217, 236–43, 244, 245, 247,
    248, 261
courts, *see also* denial of justice; judges;
    judicial chill; local remedies
    enforcement of arbitral awards, 130,
        248

quality in developing countries, 48, 121, 265, 274, 289
review of arbitral awards, 129, 166, 171–2, 188, 205, 285
COWs, *see* contracts-of-work
CSR, *see* corporate social responsibility
customary international law, 39, 41, 47, 69, 70, 71, 73, 74, 78, 80, 124, 170, 172, 196, 203, 212–13, 289
Czech Republic, 65, 149, 150, 281

damages, 106, 127–8, 150, 154, 157, 159, 163, 165, 172, 174, 178, 182, 188, 192, 201, 213, 215, 238, 242, 248, 250, 259
Davis, Gray, 190, 191, 192, 195, 197
debt crisis, 27, 48
decentralization, 214, 272, 273
democracy, 3, 58, 114, 121, 142, 213, 214, 220, 222, 275–6
denial of benefits, 65
denial of justice, 70, 72, 81, 183, 252, 256–8, 259, 260, 265, 266, 274
developing countries
    bargaining power, 14, 16, 272, 291
    capacity, 9, 14, 16, 21, 27, 28, 37, 112, 113, 148–50, 210, 274, 283, 288, 292
    competition for FDI, 6, 22, 25, 60, 234, 278, 291–2
    environmental regulation, 19–25, 26, 27, 34, 273, 289
    position on a MAI, 51, 53
    UN General Assembly resolutions, 44–5, 47
discounted cash flow, 80
domestic courts, *see* courts
domestic investors, 26, 65, 69, 90, 119, 154, 269–70
Dow Chemical, 151, 211

Eastern Europe, 42, 281
ecological reserves, 157, 159, 160, 163, 205, 217, 218, 219, 220, 221, 222, 223, 224, 225, 227, 229, 230, 231, 232, 233, 234, 240, 243, 244, 245, 246, 247, 264

economic equilibrium clauses, *see* stabilization clauses
Ecuador, 3, 74, 125, 217, 252–8, 259, 260, 261, 265, 280–1
effectiveness, 39, 58, 59, 60, 61, 118, 270, 277
effects test, 76–7, 92, 176, 205, 206
EIAs, *see* environmental impact assessments
EKC, *see* Environmental Kuznets Curve
environmental impact assessments (EIAs), 31, 36, 64, 85–9, 90, 94, 111–12, 199, 236, 237, 238, 239, 241, 242, 283, 287
Environmental Kuznets Curve (EKC), 19–21
environmental liability, 3, 112–13, 169, 249–61, 264, 265, 274
Equator Principles, 35
ethanol, 154, 190, 191, 194, 195, 196, 197, 209
Ethyl, 52, 152–7, 208, 215
European Court of Human Rights, 76, 77
expectations, *see* legitimate expectations
expropriation
    compensation, 41, 42, 44, 45, 46, 69, 127, 164, 165, 169
    direct, 40, 41, 42, 43, 45, 74, 96, 105, 159, 162, 163, 164, 165, 170
    effects test, 76–7, 92, 176, 205, 206
    indirect, 74–5, 82
        creeping, 75
        regulatory, 52, 75–8, 92, 93, 106, 152, 153, 156, 165, 166, 168, 170, 171, 172, 174, 176–7, 178, 182, 184, 185, 187, 188, 192, 196, 197, 198, 200, 201, 202, 204, 205, 206, 207, 213, 221, 238
    legality, 78–80
    police powers, 75, 76, 77, 79, 156, 175, 176, 213, 221
    proportionality, 176, 205

extractive industries, 24, 95, 107, 115,
116, 247, *see also* mining;
petroleum industry

fair and equitable treatment, *see also*
minimum standard of treatment
ambiguity, 71, 91, 93, 289
customary international law, 71, 74,
212–13, 289
legitimate expectations, 72–3, 106,
175, 177, 203
NAFTA FTC Notes of Interpretation,
73, 187, 206, 212, 289
plain meaning, 71
transparency, 72, 168, 170, 171–2,
175, 177, 203, 205–6, 212, 213, 289
FDI, *see* foreign direct investment
Firestone, 108, 109, 111, 114
flags of convenience, 276
foreign direct investment (FDI)
competition, 6, 22, 25, 60, 234, 278,
291–2
definition, 4
economic development, 4, 5, 18, 19,
43, 47
global flows, 5–6, 7, 15, 43, 51, 274
effect of BITs, 59–61
sustainable development, 5, 17
technology transfer, 18, 26
foreign direct liability, 36–7, 112, 254,
265
arbitration clauses, 121, 122, 123,
124, 130, 228, 242, 243, 249, 251,
253, 263, 265
breach of contract, 1, 221, 265, 272
breach of treaty, 81–2, 125, 198
confidentiality, 97, 114–16, 119–20,
228, 271, 276, 290–1
definition, 7
duration, 117, 276
environmental issues, 107–13, 220,
241, 242, 243, 251, 290
internationalization, 46, 105
negotiation, 263
authoritarian governments, 114,
220, 222
corruption, 114, 115, 273

participation, 114, 228, 240, 262,
264, 271, 272, 276
renegotiation, 229, 288, 293
sanctity of contract, 105
stabilization, 57, 97–107, 110,
116–19, 198, 202, 219, 220, 221,
263, 269, 277, 289
types, 95–6
Forest Principles, 220
forests, 163, 217–34, 243, 244, 245,
246, 247, 248, 252, 254, 264,
265
fork in the road clauses, 125, 159,
160
forum shopping, 65
free trade agreements (FTAs), 8, 48, 83,
85, 86, 87, 135, 280, 282, 284, 289,
see also CAFTA-DR; FTAA;
NAFTA
Free Trade Area of the Americas
(FTAA), 49, 50, 84, 287
Friends of the Earth
Canada, 201
Ghana, 230, 231, 233
Indonesia (WALHI), 219, 251
United States, 201
FTAA, *see* Free Trade Area of the
Americas
FTAs, *see* free trade agreements
full protection and security, 69, 70,
71, 73, 166, 168, 170, 174, 175,
177

gasoline additives, *see* MMT; MTBE
GATT, *see* General Agreement on
Tariffs and Trade
General Agreement on Tariffs and
Trade (GATT), 44, 81, 131, 143,
154, *see also* WTO
Ghana, 3, 12, 103, 112, 217, 227–36,
243, 244, 245, 246, 247, 264
Glamis Gold, 134, 198–203, 206, 208,
213
Global Compact, 29–30
Global Reporting Initiative, 34–5
good governance, 2, 5, 72, 142, 212,
213, 271, 289

good petroleum industry practice,
107–8, 110
gunboat diplomacy, 43

Harken Energy, 240–3, 244, 245, 248,
261
Havana Charter, 43–4
hazardous waste, 1, 2, 151, 166–88, *see
also* Basel Convention
health, 22, 31, 32, 152, 153, 154, 155,
156, 157, 173, 175, 177, 179, 180,
181, 183, 188, 189, 190, 191, 193,
195, 197, 238, 241, 249, 251,
270
HGAs, *see* host government agreements
host government agreements (HGAs),
7, 103, 111, 115, 116, 118
Hull formula, 42, 79, 80, 128
human rights, 29, 30, 32–3, 37, 51,
76, 77, 118, 124, 142, 143, 173,
270

ICC, *see* International Chamber of
Commerce
ICSID, *see* International Centre for the
Settlement of Investment Disputes
IFC, *see* International Finance
Corporation
IISD, *see* International Institute for
Sustainable Development
IMF, *see* International Monetary Fund
Inco, 225
indigenous peoples, 32, 51, 90, 134,
199, 200, 240, 241, 270
Indonesia, 3, 12, 101, 114, 147, 217–27,
243, 244, 245, 246, 247, 248,
249–52, 258, 259, 260, 261,
265
industrial flight, 9, 22, 23, 24, 25, 262
International Centre for the Settlement
of Investment Disputes (ICSID)
Additional Facility, 122, 129, 166,
168, 174
annulment procedure, 129, 161, 284
arbitral rules, 121, 122, 129, 135–6,
137, 138, 141, 142, 158, 159, 163,
164, 228, 239, 242, 291
caseload, 122

Convention, 46, 122, 123, 124, 126,
127, 129, 130, 161, 168, 280
fees, 128, 293
Secretariat, 126, 128, 129, 137, 281,
293
International Chamber of Commerce
(ICC), 34, 40, 47, 55, 141
International Finance Corporation
(IFC), 35, 115
International Institute for Sustainable
Development (IISD)
amicus curiae briefs, 132, 134
Investment Treaty News, 293
model investment agreement, 286–7,
292
international institutions, 38, 58
international minimum standard of
treatment, *see* minimum standard
of treatment
International Monetary Fund (IMF),
48, 51, 114, 115, 280
International Organization for
Standardization (ISO), 33–4, 35,
55, 287
International Senior Lawyers Project,
293
investment climate, 6, 147, 168, 217,
225, 246, 251, 259, 260, 264, 274,
291
investment court, 121, 285–6, 289
investment insurance, 35–6, 60, 277,
288
Iran-United States Claims Tribunal, 76,
170
ISO 14000, *see* International
Organization for Standardization

joint-venture agreements, 96
judges, 126, 144, 206, 224, 244, 251,
255, 258, 260, 261, 276, 277, 285
judicial chill, 266, 270, 278

Karaha Bodas, 248

Latin America, 40, 41, 42, 74, 260, 279,
281, 287, *see also* Bolivia; Chile;
Ecuador; Peru; Venezuela
Layton, Jack, 282

legal assistance centre, 287, 292–3
legitimacy, 2, 34, 58, 78, 79, 131, 142, 145, 146, 165, 185, 197, 209–11, 267, 275
legitimate expectations, 72–3, 77, 78, 93, 106, 161, 175, 177, 202, 203, 211, 273
liability, see environmental liability; foreign direct liability
Liberia, 100, 108, 111, 114, 293
like circumstances, 66, 67, 68, 90, 154, 156, 169, 186, 188, 194, 195, 286
Lima, 1, 158, 159, 160
local courts, see courts; local remedies
local remedies, 68, 82, 124–5, 242, 243, 266, 270, 289
Lucchetti, 157–62, 208, 213

Maffezini, Emilio Agustín, 68–9
MAI, see multilateral agreement on investment
market-based environmental measures, 33, 118, 277
Metalclad, 147, 166–72, 204, 205, 206, 207, 211, 212, 213, 215
Methanex, 132–4, 140, 188–98, 202, 205, 206, 207, 208, 209, 210, 211, 212, 213
methanol, 191, 192, 193, 195, 209
methyl tertiary butyl ether (MTBE), 189–91, 193, 194, 195, 197, 210
methylcyclopentadienyl manganese tricarbonyl (MMT), 152–7, 208
Mexico, 2, 6, 15, 41, 42, 48, 49, 132, 133, 147, 152, 156, 157, 166–78, 184, 196, 204, 205, 212, 213, 215, 281
MIGA, see Multilateral Investment Guarantee Agency
minimum standard of treatment, 41, 42, 69–74, 166, 168, 170, 171, 178, 182, 183, 185, 186, 187, 188, 192, 196, 197, 200, 201, 204, 205, 206, 207, 212, 213, 289, see also denial of justice; fair and equitable treatment; full protection and security

mining, 9, 24, 29, 46, 99, 102, 110, 111, 112, 113, 114, 116, 119, 134, 151, 198–203, 208, 217–39, 243, 244, 246, 247, 249, 251, 259, 264, 281, see also extractive industries
Mittal Steel, 100, 114
MMT, see methylcyclopentadienyl manganese tricarbonyl
Morales, Evo, 280
most-favoured-nation treatment, 67–9, 71, 73, 90, 159, 166, 168, 174, 175, 269, 286
MTBE, see methyl tertiary butyl ether
multilateral agreement on investment (MAI)
    IISD model, 286–7
    OECD MAI, 7, 50–3, 55, 94, 290
    WTO, 7, 48, 53
multilateral environmental agreements, 117, 178, 213–15, 222, 264, see also Basel Convention; Convention on Biological Diversity; Forest Principles; Ramsar Convention on Wetlands
Multilateral Investment Guarantee Agency (MIGA), 35, 36
multilevel governance, 213–15, 272, 273
multinational corporations, see transnational corporations
municipalities, 1, 158, 159, 160, 166, 167, 168, 169, 171, 172, 173, 175, 176, 204, 214, 272

NAAEC, see North American Agreement on Environmental Cooperation
NAFTA, see North American Free Trade Agreement
national treatment, 65–7, 68, 71, 89, 153, 154, 155, 156, 166, 168, 174, 175, 178, 182, 185, 188, 194, 195, 198, 204, 206, 269
nationalization, 1, 41, 45, 76, 78, 99, 105
negotiations
    bargaining power, 14, 16, 114, 120, 242, 258, 269, 272, 291

capacity building, 292
participation, 52, 114, 228, 262, 264, 271, 272, 276, 291
transparency, 114, 291
Ness, Richard, 250, 251, 252
net book value, 80
New York Convention, 123, 129, 130
Newmont, 228, 231, 247, 249–52, 258, 259, 260, 261, 265, 281
non-governmental organizations (NGOs), 7, 9, 10, 11, 28, 29, 51–2, 89, 97, 110, 115, 120, 132, 134, 136, 138, 141, 142, 143, 145, 146, 147, 148, 167, 169, 182, 196, 208, 215, 219, 220, 221, 222, 223, 224, 227, 242, 243, 249, 258, 272, 279, 288, 292, 293
non-party participation, *see amicus curiae*
North American Agreement on Environmental Cooperation (NAAEC), 48, 170, 186
North American Free Trade Agreement (NAFTA)
  Chapter 11, 8, 48–9, 68, 70, 75, 81, 83, 84, 91, 93, 125
  investor-state disputes, 14, 15, 86, 133–4, 152–7, 166–72, 178–203, 265–6, 285
  unintended consequences, 61–2
  FTC
    guidelines on *amicus curiae*, 132–3, 134, 142
    Notes of Interpretation, 73, 187, 206, 212, 289
  renegotiation, 281–2

Obama, Barack, 281
OECD, *see* Organization for Economic Cooperation and Development
oil, *see* petroleum industry
OPIC, *see* Overseas Private Investment Corporation
Organization for Economic Cooperation and Development (OECD)
  countries, 22, 54, 59, 144

Draft Convention on the Protection of Foreign Property, 47
Guidelines on Multinational Enterprises, 30–1
Multilateral Agreement on Investment (MAI), 7, 50–3, 94, 290
Overseas Private Investment Corporation (OPIC), 36, 46, 227

Pacheco, Abel, 236–7, 242
Palacio, Alfredo, 280
parks, *see* ecological reserves
PCBs, *see* polychlorinated biphenyls
performance requirements, 63, 80–1, 90–1, 152, 153, 154, 156, 166, 168, 169, 178, 182, 183, 185, 187
permanent sovereignty over natural resources, 44–5, 46, 105
Peru, 2, 46, 88, 89, 101, 102, 135, 152, 157–62, 236
Petroecuador, 253, 254, 255, 256, 265
petroleum industry, 96, 100, 101, 107, 108, 109, 110, 114, 115, 116, 120, 236, 237, 239–42, 252–4, 258, 280
police powers, 75, 76, 77, 79, 156, 175, 176, 213, 221
policy space, 3, 92, 278
political cover, 263, 264, 276
political risk, 7, 9, 276, 288
polluter pays principle, 215, 290
pollution
  air, 2, 20, 151, 152, 153, 155, 189, 250
  EKC, 19–21
  halos, 26
  havens, 18, 21, 22–5, 26, 48, 83, 85, 93, 94, 102
  oil, 241, 242, 252, 253, 254, 265
  water, 2, 151, 188–91, 197, 228, 249, 250
polychlorinated biphenyls (PCBs), 178–82, 183, 185, 205, 209, 210, 211
portfolio investment, 4, 5, 40
pre-establishment, 63, 67, 68, 69, 90
precautionary principle, 29, 31, 32, 33, 210, 211, 242, 290

precedent, 71, 76, 127, 130–1, 207
principles of environmental law, *see* common but differentiated responsibilities; polluter pays principle; precautionary principle
private governance, 33, 55
production sharing agreements, 96, 101, 107, 109, 110
protected areas, *see* ecological reserves
protectionism, 11, 209–10

race to the bottom, 22, 23, 25
race to the top, 26
Ramsar Convention on Wetlands, 240, 242
regulatory chill, 3, 25, 262, 263, 264, 270, 278
regulatory takings, *see* expropriation
reputation, 10, 106, 148, 217, 245, 246, 247, 259, 260, 262, 274, 277
Rio Tinto, 29, 226

S.D. Myers, 178–88, 196, 205, 206, 209, 210, 211, 213, 214, 215
Santa Elena, 162–6, 206, 213, 214, 215
scientific evidence, 92, 154, 157, 190, 194, 195, 197, 210, 211, 277, 290, *see also* precautionary principle
South-South BITs, 15, 54
spaghetti bowl, 38, 279
stability agreements, 101, 102, 198, 234–6
stabilization clauses, 57, 97–107, 110, 117, 118, 220, 263, 269, 277, 289–90, 291
stuck at the bottom, 25
sustainable development, 3, 5, 9, 17, 18, 31, 32, 83, 87, 94, 138, 139, 215, 278, 283, 285, 286, 287, 290

Tanzania, 136–40
technology transfer, 26–7
Tecmed, 172–8, 205, 212, 213, 215
Texaco, *see* Chevron

transnational corporations (TNCs), 8, 28, 29, 30, 32, 35, 36, 37, 149, 270, 276, 279, 283
transparency
  arbitration, 2, 14, 87, 118, 121, 131–2, 133, 135, 136, 137, 138, 140, 142, 145–8, 261, 265, 271, 276, 285, 291
  fair and equitable treatment, 72, 168, 170–2, 175, 177, 203, 205–6, 212, 213, 271
  foreign investment contracts, 114–16, 119, 120, 228, 271, 273, 276, 290–1

umbrella clauses, 81–2
UNCITRAL, *see* United Nations Commission on International Trade Law
UNCTC, *see* United Nations Centre on Transnational Corporations
United Nations Centre on Transnational Corporations (UNCTC), 27–8
United Nations Commission on International Trade Law (UNCITRAL), 121, 123, 126, 127, 128, 129, 132, 134, 140–2, 152, 153, 156, 178, 184, 191, 198, 200, 219, 227, 228, 248, 257, 259, 291
United States, *see also* California
  BITs, 49, 60, 66, 67, 68, 70, 80, 81, 83, 227, 257, 258, 261, 280, 286
  EIAs, 85, 86, 94
    model, 73, 78, 83, 84, 86, 92, 127, 134, 135, 283
  companies, 152, 163, 166, 178, 180, 182, 194, 195, 209, 231, 232, 239, 248, 249, 252, 280
  domestic takings jurisprudence, 76, 77, 170
  economic sanctions, 45–6, 243
  EPA, 179, 180, 181, 182, 183, 184, 185, 190, 191, 197, 210, 211
  FTAs, 49, 83, 85, 135, 280, 282, 284, 289

United States (*cont.*)
   EIAs, 85, 86–7, 94
   NAFTA, 14, 48, 62, 170,
      281
   investor-state disputes, 2, 15,
      132–4, 151, 188–203, 205, 206–7,
      208, 209, 210, 211, 212, 213, 266,
      274, 285
   Trade Promotion Authority Act,
      86

Vannessa Ventures, 236–9, 243, 244,
   245, 248
Venezuela, 74, 280, 287

WALHI, *see* Friends of the Earth

water
   pollution, 2, 151, 188–91, 197, 228,
      249, 250
   privatization, 136, 282
West African Gas Pipeline, 103–4
World Bank, 16, 46, 48, 51, 59, 115,
   116, 130, 143, 227, 280, *see also*
   ICSID; IFC; MIGA
World Summit on Sustainable
   Development (WSSD), 5
World Trade Organization (WTO), 7,
   48, 51, 53, 63, 66, 81, 121, 154,
   185, 194, 268, 291, 292
WSSD, *see* World Summit on
   Sustainable Development
WTO, *see* World Trade Organization

TABLE OF CONTENTS
• MAKE INTRO FLOW BETTER - BETTER FOUNDATION - CHECK TRIPS
⮑ or FOOTNOTE

• CASE STUDY: ABSTRACT + CONCRETE → WTO RULES AND PRACTICES

DEVELOPED - DEVELOPING
WHY NOT ALL GOODS
PREVIOUS MULTILATERAL AGREEMENT TO GET EVERYONE IN SAME BOAT

CHANGE QUESTIONS TO SUBHEADINGS

SHORTEN: "A COLOSSAL MARKET FAILURE"

CRITIQUE RECOMMENDATIONS

CITATIONS
⮑ LECTURES
CHECK GRAPHS